Henry Jenkins

Convergence Culture

Where Old and New Media Collide

Updated and with a New Afterword

D0057445

New York University Press • *New York and London*

NEW YORK UNIVERSITY PRESS
New York and London
www.nyupress.org

First published in paperback in 2008.

Library of Congress Cataloging-in-Publication Data
Jenkins, Henry, 1958–
Convergence culture : where old and new media collide / Henry Jenkins.
p. cm.
Includes bibliographical references and index.
ISBN-13: 978-0-8147-4281-5 (cloth : alk. paper)
ISBN-10: 0-8147-4281-5 (cloth : alk. paper)
ISBN-13: 978-0-8147-4295-2 (pbk. : alk. paper)
ISBN-10: 0-8147-4295-5 (pbk. : alk. paper)
1. Mass media and culture—United States. 2. Popular culture—United States.
I. Title.
P94.65.U6J46 2006
302.230973—dc22   2006007358

New York University Press books are printed on acid-free paper, and their
binding materials are chosen for strength and durability. We strive to use
environmentally responsible suppliers and materials to the greatest
extent possible in publishing our books.

Manufactured in the United States of America

c 10
p 10 9 8 7 6 5 4 3 2

Praise for the Hardcover Edition

2007 *Choice* Outstanding Academic Title

"The standard convergence narrative of recent years presents media concentration as a threat both to the diversity of communication channels and to individuals' opportunities to engage in public discourse. A respected and well-established media scholar, Jenkins (MIT) here counters such pessimistic perspectives on the brave new media world with theoretical and evidentiary attestations to the growing power of individuals and grassroots groups to affect the larger media landscape."
—**Choice**

"Jenkins tries to bring clarity to cultural changes that are melting and morphing into new shapes on an hourly, daily, weekly, monthly basis. *Convergence Culture* provides a view that looks at the restless ocean and tracks the currents rather than just looking at the individual rocks on the beach." —**The McClatchy Newspapers**

"I thought I knew twenty-first-century pop media until I read Henry Jenkins. The fresh research and radical insights in *Convergence Culture* deserve a wide and thoughtful readership. Bring on the 'monolithic block of eyeballs!'"
—**Bruce Sterling**, author, blogger, visionary

"Henry Jenkins offers crucial insight into an unexpected and unforeseen future. Unlike most predictions about how New Media will shape the world in which we live, the reality is turning out far stranger and more interesting than we might have imagined. The social implications of this change could be staggering." —**Will Wright**, designer of SimCity and The Sims

"One of those rare works that is closer to an operating system than a traditional book: it's a platform that people will be building on for years to come. What's more, the book happens to be a briskly entertaining read—as startling, inventive, and witty as the culture it documents."
—**Steven Johnson**, author of the national best-seller
Everything Bad Is Good for You

"I simply could not put this book down! Henry Jenkins provides a fascinating account of how new media intersects old media and engages the imagination of fans in more and more powerful ways. Educators, media specialists, policy makers and parents will find *Convergence Culture* both lively and enlightening."
—**John Seely Brown**, former chief scientist,
Xerox Corp. and director of Xerox PARC

Contents

Acknowledgments   vii

Introduction: "Worship at the Altar of Convergence":
A New Paradigm for Understanding Media Change   1

1   Spoiling *Survivor*: The Anatomy of a Knowledge
Community   25

2   Buying into *American Idol*: How We Are Being Sold on
Reality Television   59

3   Searching for the Origami Unicorn: *The Matrix* and
Transmedia Storytelling   95

4   Quentin Tarantino's *Star Wars*? Grassroots Creativity
Meets the Media Industry   135

5   Why Heather Can Write: Media Literacy and the
Harry Potter Wars   175

6   Photoshop for Democracy: The New Relationship
between Politics and Popular Culture   217

Conclusion: Democratizing Television?
The Politics of Participation   251

Afterword: Reflections on Politics in the Age of YouTube   271

YouTubeOlogy   295
Notes   297
Glossary   319
Index   337
About the Author   353

Acknowledgments

Writing this book has been an epic journey, helped along by many hands. *Convergence Culture* is in many ways the culmination of the past eight years of my life, an outgrowth of my efforts to build up MIT's Comparative Media Studies Program as a center for conversations about media change (past, present, and future) and of my efforts to enlarge public dialogues about popular culture and contemporary life. A fuller account of how this book emerged from the concerns of *Textual Poachers: Television Fans and Participatory Culture* (New York: Routledge, 1991) and was shaped by my intellectual growth over the past decade can be found in the introduction to my anthology *Fans, Gamers, and Bloggers: Exploring Participatory Culture* (New York: New York University Press, 2006).

Given that history, it is perhaps appropriate that my first set of thanks goes to the students of the Comparative Media Studies Program. Each and every one of them has had an impact on my thinking, but I want especially to identify students whose work significantly influenced the content of this book: Ivan Askwith, R. J. Bain, Christian Baekkelund, Vanessa Bertozzi, Lisa Bidlingmeyer, Brett Camper, Anita Chan, Sam Ford, Cristobal Garcia, Robin Hauck, Colleen Kamen, Sean Leonard, Xiaochang Li, Zhan Li, Geoffrey Long, Susannah Mandel, Andrea McCarty, Karen Lori Schrier, Parmesh Shahani, Sangita Shresthova, David Spitz, Philip Tan, Ilya Vedrashko, Margaret Weigel, and Matthew Weise. You are what gets me up in the morning and keeps me working late into the night. In particular, I want to thank Aswin Punathambekar, who was the best possible research assistant on this project, not only digging up resources but challenging my assumptions, and continuing to remain dedicated to the project long after he had left MIT to begin his doctoral work at the University of Wisconsin–Madison.

I also want to thank the members of the Comparative Media Studies staff who supported these efforts in countless ways: R. J. Bain, Jason

Bentsman, Amanda Ford, Chris Pomiecko, Brian Theisen, and especially Susan Stapleton, whose cheerful disposition and calm resourcefulness always prevented impending disaster, and who supervised the proofing and fact checking of this project.

I also want to give a shout out to Philip S. Khoury, former Kenan Sahin Dean, School of Humanities, Arts, and Social Sciences at MIT, who has always been in my corner as we have struggled to make this program fly and who gave me time off to pursue this project. My research has also been supported through the three chairs the dean has provided me: the Ann Fetter Friedlaender chair, the John E. Burchard chair, and the Peter de Florez chair.

This book emerged from many, many conversations with Alex Chisholm on long drives, early morning waits at airports, and meetings with potential sponsors. While Alex was not always patient with my foolishness, he vetted and refined almost every concept in this book; he taught this humanist how to speak the language of business and, through this process, how to become a better analyst and critic of contemporary media trends. I am also deeply indebted to Christopher Weaver, who co-taught our "Popular Culture in the Age of Media Convergence" seminar with me on multiple occasions, bringing our students (and myself) into direct contact with leading figures in the media industry and sharing frontline experiences that complemented and complicated my theoretical perspectives. I would also like to single out Kurt Squire, my faithful squire and sometimes writing collaborator, who has helped me to appreciate what games can teach us about the current state of our culture. Finally, I should acknowledge all of those who participated in the joint Initiative Media/Comparative Media Studies research project on *American Idol* that forms the basis for chapter 3 of this book: in particular, Alex Chisholm, Stephanie Davenport, David Ernst, Stacey Lynn Koerner, Sangita Shresthova, and Brian Theisen.

I was blessed to be able to have the readers and editors of *Technology Review* as another sounding board for my ideas as they took shape. In particular, I want to thank the fine folks who have edited my "Digital Renaissance" column through the years: Herb Brody, Kevin Hogan, Brad King, and Rebecca Zacks. I also want to sing the praises of David Thorburn, Brad Seawell, and the MIT Communications Forum. For several decades, the Communications Forum has brought leading media figures to campus, providing the right context for exploring ideas about where our media is going and how it is impacting public life.

Early conceptualizations of this book passed before two literary agents, Elyse Cheney and Carol Mann, who hoped to make me into a commercial nonfiction writer. They were sufficiently frank and discouraging enough to send me running back to the world of the university press, but in the process, they taught me some new tricks that, I hope, have made this book much more readable. Maybe someday . . .

I am grateful for the many people who were willing to be interviewed for the book or who helped me to get in touch with key people I needed to interview: Sweeney Agonistes, Chris Albrecht, Mike Alessi, Marcia Allas, Danny Bilson, Kurt Busiek, ChillOne, Louise Craven, Mary Dana, Dennis Dauter, B. K. DeLong, David Ernst, Jonathon Fanton, Keith Ferrazzi, Claire Field, Chris Finan, Flourish, Carl Goodman, Denis Haack, Hugh Hancock, Bennett Haselton, J. Kristopher Huddy, Stacey Lynn Koerner, Raph Koster, David Kung, Mario Lanza, Garrett Laporto, Heather Lawver, Paul Levitz, John Love, Megan Morrison, Diane Nelson, Shawn Nelson, Dennis O'Neil, Chris Pike, David Raines, Rick Rowley, Eduardo Sanchez, Sande Scoredos, Warren Spector, Patrick Stein, Linda Stone, Heidi Tandy, Joe Trippi, Steve Wax, Nancy Willard, Will Wright, Neil Young, and Zsenya.

I also want to thank a host of friends and intellectual colleagues who offered me just-in-time advice and encouragement: Hal Abelson, Robert C. Allen, Todd Allen, Harvey Ardman, Reid Ashe, W. James Au, Rebecca Black, Andrew Blau, Gerry Bloustein, David Bordwell, danah boyd, Will Brooker, Amy Bruckman, David Buckingham, Scott Bukatman, John Campbell, Justine Cassell, Edward Castranova, Josh Cohen, Ian Condry, Ron Crane, Jon Cropper, Sharon Cumberland, Marc Davis, Thomas DeFrantz, Mark Dery, Mark Deuze, Kimberly DeVries, Julian Dibbell, Peter Donaldson, Tracy Fullerton, Simson L. Garfinkel, James Gee, Lisa Gitelman, Wendy Gordon, Nick Hahn, Mary Beth Haralovich, John Hartley, Heather Hendershott, Matt Hills, Mimi Ito, Mark Jancovich, Steven Johnson, Gerard Jones, Sara Gwenllian Jones, Louise Kennedy, Christina Klein, Eric Klopfer, Robert Kozinets, Ellen Kushner, Christopher Ireland, Jessica Irish, Kurt Lancaster, Brenda Laurel, Chap Lawson, Geoffrey Long, Peter Ludlow, Davis Maston, Frans Mayra, Scott McCloud, Grant McCracken, Jane McGonigal, Edward McNally, Tara McPherson, Robert Metcalfe, Jason Mittell, Janet Murray, Susan J. Napier, Angela Ndlianis, Annalee Newitz, Tasha Oren, Ciela Pearce, Steven Pinker, Warren Sack, Katie Salens, Nick Sammond, Kevin Sandler, Greg Shaw, Greg Smith, Janet Sonenberg, Constance Steinkuehler,

Mary Stuckey, David Surman, Steven J. Tepper, Doug Thomas, Clive Thompson, Sherry Turkle, Fred Turner, William Uricchio, Shenja van der Graaf, Jesse Walker, Jing Wang, Yuichi Washida, David Weinberger, Pam Wilson, Femke Wolting, Chris Wright, and Eric Zimmerman. I should note that the separation between this list and the previous one was relatively arbitrary since many in the first list are also friends and offered advice and encouragement.

And last but hardly least, I want to thank Henry Jenkins IV, who has always made intellectual contributions to my work but who was central to the development of chapter 2 of this book, helping to connect me with the leaders of the *Survivor* fan community; and Cynthia Jenkins, whose partnership in all matters, personal and professional, fannish and scholarly, is valued more than I can (or often do) say.

Parts of the introduction appeared as "The Cultural Logic of Media Convergence," *International Journal of Cultural Studies*, Spring 2004; "Convergence? I Diverge," *Technology Review*, June 2001; "Interactive Audiences," in Dan Harris (ed.), *The New Media Book* (London: British Film Institute, 2002); "Pop Cosmopolitanism: Mapping Cultural Flows in an Age of Media Convergence," in Marcelo M. Suarez-Orozco and Desiree Baolian Qin-Hilliard (eds.), *Globalization: Culture and Education in the New Millennium* (Berkeley: University of California Press, 2004); and "Welcome to Convergence Culture," *Receiver*, February 2005. The material in this chapter was presented at the New Media Conference, Nokea, the Humlab at Umea University, the New Orleans Media Experience, and the Humanities Center of the University of Pennsylvania.

Parts of chapter 1 appeared as "Convergence Is Reality," *Technology Review*, June 2003. This material has been presented at Georgia State University and Harvard University.

Parts of chapter 2 appeared as "War Games," *Technology Review*, November 2003; "Convergence Is Reality," *Technology Review*, June 2003; "Placement, People," *Technology Review*, September 2002; "Treating Viewers Like Criminals," *Technology Review*, July 2002; "TV Tomorrow," *Technology Review*, May 2001; "Affective Economics 101," *Flow*, September 20, 2004. Material from this chapter has been presented at Georgia State University, MIT, ESOMAR, and the Branded Entertainment Forum.

Parts of chapter 3 have appeared as "Chasing Bees without the Hive Mind," *Technology Review*, December 3, 2004; "Searching for the Origami Unicorn" (with Kurt Squire), *Computer Games Magazine*, December 2003; "Transmedia Storytelling," *Technology Review*, January 2003;

"Pop Cosmopolitanism: Mapping Cultural Flows in an Age of Media Convergence," in Marcelo M. Suarez-Orozco and Desiree Baolian Qin-Hilliard (eds.), *Globalization: Culture and Education in the New Millennium* (Berkeley: University of California Press, 2004). Material from this chapter has been presented at Northwestern, the University of Wisconsin, Georgia State University, MIT, Electronic Arts Creative Leaders Program, and IT University of Copenhagen.

Parts of chapter 4 have appeared in "Quentin Tarantino's Star Wars: Digital Cinema, Media Convergence, and Participatory Culture," in David Thorburn and Henry Jenkins (eds.), *Rethinking Media Change: The Aesthetics of Transition* (Cambridge, MA: MIT Press, 2003); "When Folk Culture Meets Mass Culture," in Christopher Hawthorne and Andras Szanto (eds.), *The New Gatekeepers: Emerging Challenges to Free Expression in the Arts* (New York: National Journalism Program, 2003); "Taking Media in Our Own Hands," *Technology Review,* November 2004; "When Piracy Becomes Promotion," *Technology Review,* August 2004; "The Director Next Door," *Technology Review,* March 2001. Material from this chapter has been presented at the Society for Cinema Studies Conference, the MIT Digital Cinema Conference, and the University of Tampiere.

Parts of chapter 5 have appeared in "Why Heather Can Write," *Technology Review,* February 2004; "The Christian Media Counterculture," *Technology Review,* March 2004 (reprinted in *National Religious Broadcasters,* October 2004); "When Folk Culture Meets Mass Culture," in Christopher Hawthorne and Andras Szanto (eds.), *The New Gatekeepers: Emerging Challenges to Free Expression in the Arts* (New York: National Journalism Program, 2003). Material has been presented at Console-ing Passions and The Witching Hour.

Parts of chapter 6 have appeared as "Playing Politics in Alphaville," *Technology Review,* May 2004; "Photoshop for Democracy," *Technology Review,* June 2004; "Enter the Cybercandidates," *Technology Review,* October 2003; "The Digital Revolution, the Informed Citizen and the Culture of Democracy" (with David Thorburn), in Henry Jenkins and David Thorburn (eds.), *Democracy and New Media* (Cambridge, MA: MIT Press, 2003); and "Challenging the Consensus," *Boston Review,* Summer 2001. Material was presented to gatherings of MIT alumni in Houston and San Francisco, the MIT Communications Forum, Nokea, and the Humlab at Umea University.

Introduction: "Worship at the Altar of Convergence"

A New Paradigm for Understanding Media Change

Worship at the Altar of Convergence
—slogan, the New Orleans Media Experience (2003)

The story circulated in the fall of 2001: Dino Ignacio, a Filipino-American high school student created a Photoshop collage of *Sesame Street*'s (1970) Bert interacting with terrorist leader Osama Bin Laden as part of a series of "Bert Is Evil" images he posted on his homepage (fig. I.1). Others depicted Bert as a Klansman, cavorting with Adolf Hitler, dressed as the Unabomber, or having sex with Pamela Anderson. It was all in good fun.

In the wake of September 11, a Bangladesh-based publisher scanned the Web for Bin Laden images to print on anti-American signs, posters, and T-shirts. *Sesame Street* is available in Pakistan in a localized format; the Arab world, thus, had no exposure to Bert and Ernie. The publisher may not have recognized Bert, but he must have thought the image was a good likeness of the al-Qaeda leader. The image ended up in a collage of similar images that was printed on thousands of posters and distributed across the Middle East.

CNN reporters recorded the unlikely sight of a mob of angry protestors marching through the streets chanting anti-American slogans and waving signs

Fig. I.1. Dino Ignacio's digital collage of *Sesame Street*'s Bert and Osama Bin Laden.

1

Fig.I.2. Ignacio's collage surprisingly appeared in CNN coverage of anti-American protests following September 11.

depicting Bert and Bin Laden (fig. I.2). Representatives from the Children's Television Workshop, creators of the *Sesame Street* series, spotted the CNN footage and threatened to take legal action: "We're outraged that our characters would be used in this unfortunate and distasteful manner. The people responsible for this should be ashamed of themselves. We are exploring all legal options to stop this abuse and any similar abuses in the future." It was not altogether clear who they planned to sic their intellectual property attorneys on—the young man who had initially appropriated their images, or the terrorist supporters who deployed them. Coming full circle, amused fans produced a number of new sites, linking various *Sesame Street* characters with terrorists.

From his bedroom, Ignacio sparked an international controversy. His images crisscrossed the world, sometimes on the backs of commercial media, sometimes via grassroots media. And, in the end, he inspired his own cult following. As the publicity grew, Ignacio became more concerned and ultimately decided to dismantle his site: "I feel this has gotten too close to reality. . . . "Bert Is Evil" and its following has always been contained and distanced from big media. This issue throws it out in the open."[1] Welcome to convergence culture, where old and new media collide, where grassroots and corporate media intersect, where the power of the media producer and the power of the media consumer interact in unpredictable ways.

This book is about the relationship between three concepts—media convergence, participatory culture, and collective intelligence.

By convergence, I mean the flow of content across multiple media platforms, the cooperation between multiple media industries, and the migratory behavior of media audiences who will go almost anywhere in search of the kinds of entertainment experiences they want. Convergence is a word that manages to describe technological, industrial, cultural, and social changes depending on who's speaking and what they think they are talking about. (In this book I will be mixing and matching terms across these various frames of reference. I have added a glossary at the end of the book to help guide readers.)

In the world of media convergence, every important story gets told, every brand gets sold, and every consumer gets courted across multiple media platforms. Think about the circuits that the Bert Is Evil images traveled—from *Sesame Street* through Photoshop to the World Wide Web, from Ignacio's bedroom to a print shop in Bangladesh, from the posters held by anti-American protestors that are captured by CNN and into the living rooms of people around the world. Some of its circulation depended on corporate strategies, such as the localization of *Sesame Street* or the global coverage of CNN. Some of its circulation depended on tactics of grassroots appropriation, whether in North America or in the Middle East.

This circulation of media content—across different media systems, competing media economies, and national borders—depends heavily on consumers' active participation. I will argue here against the idea that convergence should be understood primarily as a technological process bringing together multiple media functions within the same devices. Instead, convergence represents a cultural shift as consumers are encouraged to seek out new information and make connections among dispersed media content. This book is about the work—and play—spectators perform in the new media system.

The term *participatory culture* contrasts with older notions of passive media spectatorship. Rather than talking about media producers and consumers as occupying separate roles, we might now see them as participants who interact with each other according to a new set of rules that none of us fully understands. Not all participants are created equal. Corporations—and even individuals within corporate media—still exert greater power than any individual consumer or even the aggregate of consumers. And some consumers have greater abilities to participate in this emerging culture than others.

Convergence does not occur through media appliances, however sophisticated they may become. Convergence occurs within the brains of individual consumers and through their social interactions with others. Each of us constructs our own personal mythology from bits and fragments of information extracted from the media flow and transformed into resources through which we make sense of our everyday lives. Because there is more information on any given topic than anyone can store in their head, there is an added incentive for us to talk among ourselves about the media we consume. This conversation creates buzz that is increasingly valued by the media industry. Consumption has become a collective process—and that's what this book means by collective intelligence, a term coined by French cybertheorist Pierre Lévy. None of us can know everything; each of us knows something; and we can put the pieces together if we pool our resources and combine our skills. Collective intelligence can be seen as an alternative source of media power. We are learning how to use that power through our day-to-day interactions within convergence culture. Right now, we are mostly using this collective power through our recreational life, but soon we will be deploying those skills for more "serious" purposes. In this book, I explore how collective meaning-making within popular culture is starting to change the ways religion, education, law, politics, advertising, and even the military operate.

Convergence Talk

Another snapshot of convergence culture at work: In December 2004, a hotly anticipated Bollywood film, *Rok Sako To Rok Lo* (2004), was screened in its entirety to movie buffs in Delhi, Bangalore, Hyderabad, Mumbai, and other parts of India through EDGE-enabled mobile phones with live video streaming facility. This is believed to be the first time that a feature film had been fully accessible via mobile phones.[2] It remains to be seen how this kind of distribution fits into people's lives. Will it substitute for going to the movies or will people simply use it to sample movies they may want to see at other venues? Who knows?

Over the past several years, many of us have watched as cell phones have become increasingly central to the release strategies of commercial motion pictures around the world, as amateur and professional cell phone movies have competed for prizes in international film festivals, as mobile users have been able to listen in to major concerts, as Japanese novelists serialize their work via instant messenger, and as game players have used mobile devices to compete in augmented and alternate reality games. Some functions will take root; others will fail.

Call me old-fashioned. The other week I wanted to buy a cell phone

—you know, to make phone calls. I didn't want a video camera, a still camera, a Web access device, an MP3 player, or a game system. I also wasn't interested in something that could show me movie previews, would have customizable ring tones, or would allow me to read novels. I didn't want the electronic equivalent of a Swiss army knife. When the phone rings, I don't want to have to figure out which button to push. I just wanted a phone. The sales clerks sneered at me; they laughed at me behind my back. I was told by company after mobile company that they don't make single-function phones anymore. Nobody wants them. This was a powerful demonstration of how central mobiles have become to the process of media convergence.

You've probably been hearing a lot about convergence lately. You are going to be hearing even more.

The media industries are undergoing another paradigm shift. It happens from time to time. In the 1990s, rhetoric about a coming digital revolution contained an implicit and often explicit assumption that new media was going to push aside old media, that the Internet was going to displace broadcasting, and that all of this would enable consumers to more easily access media content that was personally meaningful to them. A best-seller in 1990, Nicholas Negroponte's *Being Digital*, drew a sharp contrast between "passive old media" and "interactive new media," predicting the collapse of broadcast networks in favor of an era of narrowcasting and niche media on demand: "What will happen to broadcast television over the next five years is so phenomenal that it's difficult to comprehend."[3] At one point, he suggests that no government regulation will be necessary to shatter the media conglomerates: "The monolithic empires of mass media are dissolving into an array of cottage industries. . . . Media barons of today will be grasping to hold onto their centralized empires tomorrow. . . . The combined forces of technology and human nature will ultimately take a stronger hand in plurality than any laws Congress can invent."[4] Sometimes, the new media companies spoke about convergence, but by this term, they seemed to mean that old media would be absorbed fully and completely into the orbit of the emerging technologies. George Gilder, another digital revolutionary, dismissed such claims: "The computer industry is converging with the television industry in the same sense that the automobile converged with the horse, the TV converged with the nickelodeon, the word-processing program converged with the typewriter, the CAD program converged with the drafting board, and digital desktop publishing converged with the linotype machine and the letterpress."[5] For Gilder, the computer had come not to transform mass culture but to destroy it.

The popping of the dot-com bubble threw cold water on this talk of a digital revolution. Now, convergence has reemerged as an important reference point as old and new media companies try to imagine the future of the entertainment industry. If the digital revolution paradigm presumed that new media would displace old media, the emerging convergence paradigm assumes that old and new media will interact in ever more complex ways. The digital revolution paradigm claimed that new media was going to change everything. After the dot-com crash, the tendency was to imagine that new media had changed nothing. As with so many things about the current media environment, the truth lay somewhere in between. More and more, industry leaders are returning to convergence as a way of making sense of a moment of disorienting change. Convergence is, in that sense, an old concept taking on new meanings.

There was lots of convergence talk to be heard at the New Orleans Media Experience in October 2003. The New Orleans Media Experience was organized by HSI Productions, Inc., a New York–based company that produces music videos and commercials. HSI has committed to spend $100 million over the next five years, to make New Orleans the mecca for media convergence that Slamdance has become for independent cinema. The New Orleans Media Experience is more than a film festival; it is also a showcase for game releases, a venue for commercials and music videos, an array of concerts and theatrical performances, and a three-day series of panels and discussions with industry leaders.

Inside the auditorium, massive posters featuring images of eyes, ears, mouths, and hands urged attendees to "worship at the Altar of Convergence," but it was far from clear what kind of deity they were genuflecting before. Was it a New Testament God who promised them salvation? An Old Testament God threatening destruction unless they followed His rules? A multifaced deity that spoke like an oracle and demanded blood sacrifices? Perhaps, in keeping with the location, convergence was a voodoo goddess who would give them the power to inflict pain on their competitors?

Like me, the participants had come to New Orleans hoping to glimpse tomorrow before it was too late. Many were nonbelievers who had been burned in the dot-com meltdown and were there to scoff at any new vision. Others were freshly minted from America's top business schools and there to find ways to make their first million. Still others were there because their bosses had sent them, hoping for enlightenment, but willing to settle for one good night in the French Quarter.

The mood was tempered by a sober realization of the dangers of moving too quickly, as embodied by the ghost-town campuses in the Bay Area and the office furniture being sold at bulk prices on eBay; and the dangers of moving too slowly, as represented by the recording industry's desperate flailing as it tries to close the door on file-sharing after the cows have already come stampeding out of the barn. The participants had come to New Orleans in search of the "just right"—the right investments, predictions, and business models. No longer expecting to surf the waves of change, they would be content with staying afloat. The old paradigms were breaking down faster than the new ones were emerging, producing panic among those most invested in the status quo and curiosity in those who saw change as opportunity.

Advertising guys in pinstriped shirts mingled with recording industry flacks with backward baseball caps, Hollywood agents in Hawaiian shirts, pointy-bearded technologists, and shaggy-haired gamers. The only thing they all knew how to do was to exchange business cards.

As represented on the panels at the New Orleans Media Experience, convergence was a "come as you are" party, and some of the participants were less ready for what was planned than others. It was also a swap meet where each of the entertainment industries traded problems and solutions, finding through the interplay among media what they can't achieve working in isolation. In every discussion, there emerged different models of convergence followed by the acknowledgment that none of them knew for sure what the outcomes were going to be. Then, everyone adjourned for a quick round of Red Bulls (a conference sponsor) as if funky high-energy drinks were going to blast them over all of those hurdles.

Political economists and business gurus make convergence sound so easy; they look at the charts that show the concentration of media ownership as if they ensure that all of the parts will work together to pursue maximum profits. But from the ground, many of the big media giants look like great big dysfunctional families, whose members aren't speaking with each other and pursue their own short-term agendas even at the expense of other divisions of the same companies. In New Orleans, however, the representatives for different industries seemed tentatively ready to lower their guard and speak openly about common visions.

This event was billed as a chance for the general public to learn first-hand about the coming changes in news and entertainment. In accepting an invitation to be on panels, in displaying a willingness to "go public" with their doubts and anxieties, perhaps industry leaders were acknowledging the importance of the role that ordinary consumers can play not just in accepting convergence, but actually in *driving* the process. If the media industry in recent years has seemed at war with its consumers, in that it is trying to force consumers back into old relationships and into obedience to well-established norms, companies hoped to use this New Orleans event to justify their decisions to consumers and stockholders alike.

Unfortunately, although this was not a closed-door event, it might as well have been. Those few members of the public who did show up were ill-informed. After an intense panel discussion about the challenges of broadening the uses of game consoles, the first member of the audience to raise his hand wanted to know when *Grand Theft Auto III* was coming out on the Xbox. You can scarcely blame consumers for not knowing how to speak this new language or even what questions to ask when so little previous effort has been made to educate them about convergence thinking.

At a panel on game consoles, the big tension was between Sony (a hardware company) and Microsoft (a software company); both had ambitious plans but fundamentally different business models and visions. All agreed that the core challenge was to expand the potential uses of this cheap and readily accessible technology so that it became *the* "black box," the "Trojan horse" that smuggled convergence culture right into people's living rooms. What was mom going to do with the console when her kids were at school? What would get a family to give a game console to grandpa for Christmas? They had the technology to bring about convergence, but they hadn't figured out why anyone would want it.

Another panel focused on the relationship between video games and traditional media. Increasingly, movie moguls saw games not simply as a means of stamping the franchise logo on some ancillary product but as a means of expanding the storytelling experience. These filmmakers had come of age as gamers and had their own ideas about the creative intersections between the media; they knew who the most creative designers were, and they worked the collaboration into their contract. They wanted to use games to explore ideas that couldn't fit within two-hour films.

Such collaborations meant taking everyone out of their "comfort zones," as one movieland agent explained. These relationships were difficult to sustain, since all parties worried about losing creative control, and since the time spans for development and distribution in the media were radically different. Should the game company try to align its timing to the often unpredictable production cycle of a movie with the hopes of hitting Wal-Mart the same weekend the film opens? Should the movie producers wait for the often equally unpredictable game development cycle to run its course, sitting out the clock while some competitor steals their thunder? Will the game get released weeks or months later, after the buzz of the movie has dried up or, worse yet, after the movie has bombed? Should the game become part of the publicity buildup toward a major release, even though that means starting development before the film project has been "green lighted" by a studio? Working with a television production company is even more nerve wracking, since the turnaround time is much shorter and the risk much higher that the series will never reach the air.

If the game industry folks had the smirking belief that they controlled the future, the record industry types were sweating bullets; their days were numbered unless they figured out how to turn around current trends (such as dwindling audiences, declining sales, and expanding piracy). The panel on "monetizing music" was one of the most heavily attended. Everyone tried to speak at once, yet none of them were sure their "answers" would work. Will the future revenue come from rights management, from billing people for the music they download, or from creating a fee the servers had to pay out to the record industry as a whole? And what about cell phone rings—which some felt represented an unexplored market for new music as well as a grassroots promotional channel? Perhaps the money will lie in the intersection between the various media with new artists promoted via music videos that are paid for by advertisers who want to use their sounds and images for branding, with new artists tracked via the Web, which allows the public to register its preferences in hours rather than weeks.

And so it went, in panel after panel. The New Orleans Media Experience pressed us into the future. Every path forward had roadblocks, most of which felt insurmountable, but somehow, they would either have to be routed around or broken down in the coming decade.

The messages were plain:

1. Convergence is coming and you had better be ready.
2. Convergence is harder than it sounds.
3. Everyone will survive if everyone works together. (Unfortunately, that was the one thing nobody knew how to do.)

The Prophet of Convergence

If *Wired* magazine declared Marshall McLuhan the patron saint of the digital revolution, we might well describe the late MIT political scientist Ithiel de Sola Pool as the prophet of media convergence. Pool's *Technologies of Freedom* (1983) was probably the first book to lay out the concept of convergence as a force of change within the media industries:

> A process called the "convergence of modes" is blurring the lines between media, even between point-to-point communications, such as the post, telephone and telegraph, and mass communications, such as the press, radio, and television. A single physical means—be it wires, cables or airwaves—may carry services that in the past were provided in separate ways. Conversely, a service that was provided in the past by any one medium—be it broadcasting, the press, or telephony—can now be provided in several different physical ways. So the one-to-one relationship that used to exist between a medium and its use is eroding.[6]

Some people today talk about divergence rather than convergence, but Pool understood that they were two sides of the same phenomenon.

"Once upon a time," Pool explained, "companies that published newspapers, magazines, and books did very little else; their involvement with other media was slight."[7] Each medium had its own distinctive functions and markets, and each was regulated under different regimes, depending on whether its character was centralized or decentralized, marked by scarcity or plenitude, dominated by news or entertainment, and owned by governmental or private interests. Pool felt that these differences were largely the product of political choices and preserved through habit rather than any essential characteristic of the various technologies. But he did see some communications technologies as supporting more diversity and a greater degree of participation than others: "Freedom is fostered when the means of communication are dispersed, decentralized, and easily available, as are printing presses or microcomputers. Central control is more likely when the means of communication are concentrated, monopolized, and scarce, as are great networks."[8]

Several forces, however, have begun breaking down the walls separating these different media. New media technologies enabled the same content to flow through many different channels and assume many different forms at the point of reception. Pool was describing what Nicholas Negroponte calls the transformation of "atoms into bytes" or digitization.[9] At the same time, new patterns of cross-media ownership that began in the mid-1980s, during what we can now see as the first phase of a longer process of media concentration, were making it more desirable for companies to distribute content across those various channels rather than within a single media platform. Digitization set the conditions for convergence; corporate conglomerates created its imperative.

Much writing about the so-called digital revolution presumed that the outcome of technological change was more or less inevitable. Pool, on the other hand, predicted a period of prolonged transition, during which the various media systems competed and collaborated, searching for the stability that would always elude them: "Convergence does not mean ultimate stability or unity. It operates as a constant force for unification but always in dynamic tension with change. . . . There is no immutable law of growing convergence; the process of change is more complicated than that."[10]

As Pool predicted, we are in an age of media transition, one marked by tactical decisions and unintended consequences, mixed signals and competing interests, and most of all, unclear directions and unpredictable outcomes.[11] Two decades later, I find myself reexamining some of the core questions Pool raised—about how we maintain the potential of participatory culture in the wake of growing media concentration, about whether the changes brought about by convergence open new opportunities for expression or expand the power of big media.

Pool was interested in the impact of convergence on political culture; I am more interested in its impact on popular culture, but as chapter 6 will suggest, the lines between the two have now blurred.

It is beyond my abilities to describe or fully document all of the changes that are occurring. My aim is more modest. I want to describe some of the ways that convergence thinking is reshaping American popular culture and, in particular, the ways it is impacting the relationship between media audiences, producers, and content. Although this chapter will outline the big picture (insofar as any of us can see it clearly yet), subsequent chapters will examine these changes through a series of case studies focused on specific media franchises and their audiences. My goal is to help ordinary people grasp how convergence is impacting the media they consume and, at the same time, to help industry leaders and policymakers understand consumer perspectives on these changes. Writing this book has been challenging because everything seems to be changing at once and there is no vantage point that takes me above the fray. Rather than trying to write from an objective vantage point, I describe in this book what this process looks like from various localized perspectives—advertising executives struggling to reach a changing market, creative artists discovering new ways to tell stories, educators tapping informal learning communities, activists deploying new resources to shape the political future, religious groups contesting the quality of their cultural environs, and, of course, various fan communities who are early adopters and creative users of emerging media.

I can't claim to be a neutral observer in any of this. For one thing, I am not simply a consumer of many of these media products; I am also an active fan. The world of media fandom has been a central theme of my work for almost two decades—an interest that emerges from my own participation within various fan communities as much as it does from my intellectual interests as a media scholar. During that time, I have watched fans move from the invisible margins of popular culture and into the center of current thinking about media production and consumption. For another, through my role as director of the MIT Comparative Media Studies Program, I have been an active participant in discussions among industry insiders and policymakers; I have consulted with some of the companies discussed in this book; my earlier writings on fan communities and participatory culture have been embraced by business schools and are starting to have some modest impact on the way media companies are relating to their consumers; many of the creative artists and media executives I interviewed are people I would consider friends. At a time when the roles between producers and consumers are shifting, my job allows me to move among different vantage points. I hope this book allows readers to benefit from my adventures into spaces where few humanists have gone before. Yet, readers should also keep in mind that my engagement with fans and producers alike necessarily colors what I say. My goal here is to document conflicting perspectives on media change rather than to critique them. I don't think we can meaningfully critique convergence until it is more fully understood; yet if the public doesn't get some insights into the discussions that are taking place, they will have little to no input into decisions that will dramatically change their relationship to media.

The Black Box Fallacy

Almost a decade ago, science fiction writer Bruce Sterling established what he calls the Dead Media Project. As his Web site (http://www .deadmedia.org) explains, "The centralized, dinosaurian one-to-many media that roared and trampled through the twentieth century are poorly adapted to the postmodern technological environment."[12] Anticipating that some of these "dinosaurs" were heading to the tar pits, he constructed a shrine to "the media that have died on the barbed wire of technological change." His collection is astounding, including relics like "the phenakistoscope, the telharmonium, the Edison wax cylinder, the stereopticon . . . various species of magic lantern."[13]

Yet, history teaches us that old media never die—and they don't even necessarily fade away. What dies are simply the tools we use to access media content—the 8-track, the Beta tape. These are what media scholars call *delivery technologies.* Most of what Sterling's project lists falls under this category. Delivery technologies become obsolete and get replaced; media, on the other hand, evolve. Recorded sound is the medium. CDs, MP3 files, and 8-track cassettes are delivery technologies.

To define media, let's turn to historian Lisa Gitelman, who offers a model of media that works on two levels: on the first, a medium is a technology that enables communication; on the second, a medium is a set of associated "protocols" or social and cultural practices that have grown up around that technology.[14] Delivery systems are simply and only technologies; media are also cultural systems. Delivery technologies come and go all the time, but media persist as layers within an ever more complicated information and entertainment stratum.

A medium's content may shift (as occurred when television displaced radio as a storytelling medium, freeing radio to become the primary showcase for rock and roll), its audience may change (as occurs when comics move from a mainstream medium in the 1950s to a niche medium today), and its social status may rise or fall (as occurs when theater moves from a popular form to an elite one), but once a medium establishes itself as satisfying some core human demand, it continues to function within the larger system of communication options. Once recorded sound becomes a possibility, we have continued to develop new and improved means of recording and playing back sound. Printed words did not kill spoken words. Cinema did not kill theater. Television did not kill radio.[15] Each old medium was forced to coexist with the emerging media. That's why convergence seems more plausible as a way of understanding the past several decades of media change than the old digital revolution paradigm was. Old media are not being displaced. Rather, their functions and status are shifted by the introduction of new technologies.

The implications of this distinction between media and delivery systems become clearer as Gitelman elaborates on what she means by "protocols." She writes: "Protocols express a huge variety of social, economic, and material relationships. So telephony includes the salutation 'Hello?' (for English speakers, at least) and includes the monthly billing cycle and includes the wires and cables that materially connect our phones. . . . Cinema includes everything from the sprocket holes that run along the sides of film to the widely shared sense of being able to wait and see 'films' at home on video. And protocols are far from static."[16] This book will have less to say about the technological dimensions of media change than about the shifts in the protocols by which we are producing and consuming media.

Much contemporary discourse about convergence starts and ends with what I call the Black Box Fallacy. Sooner or later, the argument goes, all media content is going to flow through a single black box into our living rooms (or, in the mobile scenario, through black boxes we carry around with us everywhere we go). If the folks at the New Orleans Media Experience could just figure out which black box will reign supreme, then everyone can make reasonable investments for the future. Part of what makes the black box concept a fallacy is that it reduces media change to technological change and strips aside the cultural levels we are considering here.

I don't know about you, but in my living room, I am seeing more and more black boxes. There are my VCR, my digital cable box, my DVD player, my digital recorder, my sound system, and my two game systems, not to mention a huge mound of videotapes, DVDs and CDs, game cartridges and controllers, sitting atop, laying alongside, toppling over the edge of my television system. (I would definitely qualify as an early adopter, but most American homes now have, or soon will have, their own pile of black boxes.) The perpetual tangle of cords that stands between me and my "home entertainment" center reflects the degree of incompatibility and dysfunction that exist between the various media technologies. And many of my MIT students are lugging around multiple black boxes—their laptops, their cells, their iPods, their Game Boys, their BlackBerrys, you name it.

As Cheskin Research explained in a 2002 report, "The old idea of convergence was that all devices would converge into one central device that did everything for you (à la the universal remote). What we are now seeing is the hardware diverging while the content converges. . . . Your email needs and expectations are different whether you're at home, work, school, commuting, the airport, etc., and these different devices are designed to suit your needs for accessing content depending on where you are—your situated context."[17] This pull toward more specialized media appliances coexists with a push toward more generic devices. We can see the proliferation of black boxes as symptomatic of a moment of convergence: because no one is sure what kinds of functions should be combined, we are forced to buy a range of specialized and incompatible appliances. On the other end of the spectrum, we may also be forced to deal with an escalation of functions within the same media appliance, functions that decrease the ability of that appliance to serve its original function, and so I can't get a cell phone that is just a phone.

Media convergence is more than simply a technological shift. Convergence alters the relationship between existing technologies, industries, markets, genres, and audiences. Convergence alters the logic by which media industries operate and by which media consumers process news and entertainment. Keep this in mind: convergence refers to a process, not an endpoint. There will be no single black box that controls the flow of media into our homes. Thanks to the proliferation of channels and the portability of new computing and telecommunications technologies, we are entering an era when media will be everywhere. Convergence isn't something that is going to happen one day when we have enough bandwidth or figure out the correct configuration of appliances. Ready or not, we are already living within a convergence culture.

Our cell phones are not simply telecommunications devices; they also allow us to play games, download information from the Internet, and take and send photographs or text messages. Increasingly they allow us to watch previews of new films, download installments of serialized novels, or attend concerts from remote locations. All of this is already happening in northern Europe and Asia. Any of these functions can also be performed using other media appliances. You can listen to the Dixie Chicks through your DVD player, your car radio, your Walkman, your iPod, a Web radio station, or a music cable channel.

Fueling this technological convergence is a shift in patterns of media ownership. Whereas old Hollywood focused on cinema, the new media conglomerates have controlling interests across the entire entertainment industry. Warner Bros. produces film, television, popular music, computer games, Web sites, toys, amusement park rides, books, newspapers, magazines, and comics.

In turn, media convergence impacts the way we consume media. A teenager doing homework may juggle four or five windows, scan the Web, listen to and download MP3 files, chat with friends, word-process a paper, and respond to e-mail, shifting rapidly among tasks. And fans of a popular television series may sample dialogue, summarize episodes, debate subtexts, create original fan fiction, record their own soundtracks, make their own movies—and distribute all of this worldwide via the Internet.

Convergence is taking place within the same appliances, within the same franchise, within the same company, within the brain of the consumer, and within the same fandom. Convergence involves both a change in the way media is produced and a change in the way media is consumed.

The Cultural Logic of Media Convergence

Another snapshot of the future: Anthropologist Mizuko Ito has documented the growing place of mobile communications among Japanese youth, describing young couples who remain in constant contact with each other throughout the day, thanks to their access to various mobile technologies.[18] They wake up together, work together, eat together, and go to bed together even though they live miles apart and may have face-to-face contact only a few times a month. We might call it telecocooning.

Convergence doesn't just involve commercially produced materials and services traveling along well-regulated and predictable circuits. It doesn't just involve the mobile companies getting together with the film companies to decide when and where we watch a newly released film. It also occurs when people take media in their own hands. Entertainment content isn't the only thing that flows across multiple media platforms. Our lives, relationships, memories, fantasies, desires also flow across media channels. Being a lover or a mommy or a teacher occurs on multiple platforms.[19] Sometimes we tuck our kids into bed at night and other times we Instant Message them from the other side of the globe.

And yet another snapshot: Intoxicated students at a local high school use their cell phones spontaneously to produce their own soft-core porn movie involving topless cheerleaders making out in the locker room. Within hours, the movie is circulating across the school, being downloaded by students and teachers alike and watched between classes on personal media devices.

When people take media into their own hands, the results can be wonderfully creative; they can also be bad news for all involved.

For the foreseeable future, convergence will be a kind of kludge—a jerry-rigged relationship among different media technologies—rather than a fully integrated system. Right now, the cultural shifts, the legal battles, and the economic consolidations that are fueling media convergence are preceding shifts in the technological infrastructure. How those various transitions unfold will determine the balance of power in the next media era.

The American media environment is now being shaped by two seemingly contradictory trends: on the one hand, new media technologies have lowered production and distribution costs, expanded the range of available delivery channels, and enabled consumers to archive, annotate, appropriate, and recirculate media content in powerful new ways. At the same time, there has been an alarming concentration of the ownership of mainstream commercial media, with a small handful of multinational media conglomerates dominating all sectors of the entertainment industry. No one seems capable of describing both sets of changes at the same time, let alone showing how they impact each other. Some fear that media is out of control, others that it is too controlled. Some see a world without gatekeepers, others a world where gatekeepers have unprecedented power. Again, the truth lies somewhere in between.

Another snapshot: People around the world are affixing stickers showing Yellow Arrows (http://global.yellowarrow.net) alongside public monuments and factories, beneath highway overpasses, onto lamp posts. The arrows provide numbers others can call to access recorded voice messages—personal annotations on our shared urban landscape. They use it to share a beautiful vista or criticize an irresponsible company. And increasingly, companies are co-opting the system to leave their own advertising pitches.

Convergence, as we can see, is both a top-down corporate-driven process and a bottom-up consumer-driven process. Corporate convergence coexists with grassroots convergence. Media companies are learning how to accelerate the flow of media content across delivery channels to expand revenue opportunities, broaden markets, and reinforce viewer commitments. Consumers are learning how to use these different media technologies to bring the flow of media more fully under their control and to interact with other consumers. The promises of this new media environment raise expectations of a freer flow of ideas and content. Inspired by those ideals, consumers are fighting for the right to participate more fully in their culture. Sometimes, corporate and grassroots convergence reinforce each other, creating closer, more rewarding relations between media producers and consumers. Sometimes, these two forces are at war, and those struggles will redefine the face of American popular culture.

Convergence requires media companies to rethink old assumptions about what it means to consume media, assumptions that shape both programming and marketing decisions. If old consumers were assumed to be passive, the new consumers are active. If old consumers were predictable and stayed where you told them to stay, then new consumers are migratory, showing a declining loyalty to networks or media. If old consumers were isolated individuals, the new consumers are more socially connected. If the work of media consumers was once silent and invisible, the new consumers are now noisy and public.

Media producers are responding to these newly empowered consumers in contradictory ways, sometimes encouraging change, sometimes resisting what they see as renegade behavior. And consumers, in turn, are perplexed by what they see as mixed signals about how much and what kinds of participation they can enjoy.

As they undergo this transition, the media companies are not behaving in a monolithic fashion; often, different divisions of the same company are pursuing radically different strategies, reflecting their uncertainty about how to proceed. On the one hand, convergence represents an expanded opportunity for media conglomerates, since content that succeeds in one sector can spread across other platforms. On the other, convergence represents a risk since most of these media fear a fragmentation or erosion of their markets. Each time they move a viewer from television to the Internet, say, there is a risk that the consumer may not return.

Industry insiders use the term "extension" to refer to their efforts to expand the potential markets by moving content across different delivery systems, "synergy" to refer to the economic opportunities represented by their ability to own and control all of those manifestations, and "franchise" to refer to their coordinated effort to brand and market fictional content under these new conditions. Extension, synergy, and franchising are pushing media industries to embrace convergence. For that reason, the case studies I selected for this book deal with some of the most successful franchises in recent media history. Some (*American Idol*, 2002, and *Survivor*, 2000) originate on television, some (*The Matrix*, 1999, *Star Wars*, 1977) on the big screen, some as books (*Harry Potter*, 1998), and some as games (*The Sims*, 2000), but each extends outward from its originating medium to influence many other sites of cultural production. Each of these franchises offers a different vantage point from which to understand how media convergence is reshaping the relationship between media producers and consumers.

Chapter 1, which focuses on *Survivor*, and chapter 2, which centers on *American Idol*, look at the phenomenon of reality television. Chapter 1 guides readers through the little-known world of *Survivor* spoilers—a group of active consumers who pool their knowledge to try to unearth the series's many secrets before they are revealed on the air. *Survivor* spoiling will be read here as a particularly vivid example of collective intelligence at work. Knowledge communities form around mutual intellectual interests; their members work together to forge new knowledge often in realms where no traditional expertise exists; the pursuit of and assessment of knowledge is at once communal and adversarial. Mapping how these knowledge communities work can help us better understand the social nature of contemporary media consumption. They can also give us insight into how knowledge becomes power in the age of media convergence.

On the other hand, chapter 2 examines *American Idol* from the perspective of the media industry, trying to understand how reality television is being shaped by what I call "affective economics." The decreasing value of the thirty-second commercial in an age of TiVos and VCRs is forcing Madison Avenue to rethink its interface with the consuming public. This new "affective economics" encourages companies to transform brands into what one industry insider calls "lovemarks" and to blur the line between entertainment content and brand messages. According to the logic of affective economics, the ideal consumer is active, emotionally engaged, and socially networked. Watching the advert or consuming the product is no longer enough; the company invites the audience inside the brand community. Yet, if such affiliations encourage more active consumption, these same communities can also become protectors of brand integrity and thus critics of the companies that seek to court their allegiance.

Strikingly, in both cases, relations between producers and consumers are breaking down as consumers seek to act upon the invitation to participate in the life of the franchises. In the case of *Survivor*, the spoiler community has become so good at the game that the producers fear they will be unable to protect the rights of other consumers to have a "first time" experience of the unfolding series. In the case of *American Idol*, fans fear that their participation is marginal and that producers still play too active a role in shaping the outcome of the competition. How much participation is too much? When does participation become interference? And conversely, when do producers exert too much power over the entertainment experience?

Chapter 3 examines *The Matrix* franchise as an example of what I am calling transmedia storytelling. Transmedia storytelling refers to a new aesthetic that has emerged in response to media convergence—one that places new demands on consumers and depends on the active participation of knowledge communities. Transmedia storytelling is the art of world making. To fully experience any fictional world, consumers must assume the role of hunters and gatherers, chasing down bits of the story across media channels, comparing notes with each other via online discussion groups, and collaborating to ensure that everyone who invests time and effort will come away with a richer entertainment experience. Some would argue that the Wachowski brothers, who wrote and directed the three *Matrix* films, have pushed transmedia storytelling farther than most audience members were prepared to go.

Chapters 4 and 5 take us deeper into the realm of participatory culture. Chapter 4 deals with *Star Wars* fan filmmakers and gamers, who are actively reshaping George Lucas's mythology to satisfy their own fantasies and desires. Fan cultures will be understood here as a revitalization of the old folk culture process in response to the content of mass culture. Chapter 5 deals with young *Harry Potter* fans who are writing their own stories about Hogwarts and its students. In both cases, these grassroots artists are finding themselves in conflict with commercial media producers who want to exert greater control over their intellectual property. We will see in chapter 4 that LucasArts has had to continually rethink its relations to *Star Wars* fans throughout the past several decades, trying to strike the right balance between encouraging the enthusiasm of their fans and protecting their investments in the series. Interestingly, as *Star Wars* moves across media channels, different expectations about participation emerge, with the producers of the *Star Wars Galaxies* game encouraging consumers to generate much of the content even as the producers of the *Star Wars* movies issue guidelines enabling and constraining fan participation.

Chapter 5 extends this focus on the politics of participation to consider two specific struggles over *Harry Potter*: the conflicting interests between *Harry Potter* fans and Warner Bros., the studio that acquired the film rights to J. K. Rowling's books, and the conflict between conservative Christian critics of the books and teachers who have seen them as a means of encouraging young readers. This chapter maps a range of responses to the withering of traditional gatekeepers and the expansion of fantasy into many different parts of our everyday lives. On the one hand, some conservative Christians are striking back against media convergence and globalization, reasserting traditional authority in the face of profound social and cultural change. On the other hand, some Christians embrace convergence through their own forms of media outreach, fostering a distinctive approach to media literacy education and encouraging the emergence of Christian-inflected fan cultures.

Throughout these five chapters, I will show how entrenched institutions are taking their models from grassroots fan communities, and reinventing themselves for an era of media convergence and collective intelligence—how the advertising industry has been forced to reconsider consumers' relations to brands, the military is using multiplayer games to rebuild communications between civilians and service members, the legal profession has struggled to understand what "fair use" means in an era when many more people are becoming authors, educators are reassessing the value of informal education, and at least some conservative Christians are making their peace with newer forms of popular culture. In each of these cases, powerful institutions are trying to build stronger connections with their constituencies and consumers are applying skills learned as fans and gamers to work, education, and politics.

Chapter 6 will turn from popular culture to public culture, applying my ideas about convergence to offer a perspective on the 2004 American presidential campaign, exploring what it might take to make democracy more participatory. Again and again, citizens were better served by popular culture than they were by news or political discourse; popular culture took on new responsibilities for educating the public about the stakes of this election and inspiring them to participate more fully in the process. In the wake of a divisive campaign, popular media may also model ways we can come together despite our differences. The 2004 elections represent an important transitional moment in the relationship between media and politics as citizens are being encouraged to do much of the dirty work of the campaign and the candidates and parties lost some control over the political process. Here again, all sides are assuming greater participation by citizens and consumers, yet they do not yet agree on the terms of that participation.

In my conclusion, I will return to my three key terms—convergence, collective intelligence, and participation. I want to explore some of the implications of the trends I will be discussing in this book for education, media reform, and democratic citizenship. I will be returning there to a core claim: that convergence culture represents a shift in the ways we think about our relations to media, that we are making that shift first through our relations with popular culture, but that the skills we acquire through play may have implications for how we learn, work, participate in the political process, and connect with other people around the world.

I will be focusing throughout this book on the competing and contradictory ideas about participation that are shaping this new media culture. Yet, I must acknowledge that not all consumers have access to the skills and resources needed to be full participants in the cultural practices I am describing. Increasingly, the digital divide is giving way to concern about the participation gap. Throughout the 1990s, the primary question was one of access. Today, most Americans have some limited access to the Internet, say, though for many, that access is through the public library or the local school. Yet many of the activities this book will describe depend on more extended access to those technologies, a greater familiarity with the new kinds of social interactions they enable, a fuller mastery over the conceptual skills that consumers have developed in response to media convergence. As long as the focus remains on access, reform remains focused on technologies; as soon as we begin to talk about participation, the emphasis shifts to cultural protocols and practices.

Most of the people depicted in this book are early adopters. In this country they are disproportionately white, male, middle class, and college educated. These are people who have the greatest access to new media technologies and have mastered the skills needed to fully participate in these new knowledge cultures. I don't assume that these cultural practices will remain the same as we broaden access and participation. In fact, expanding participation necessarily sparks further change. Yet, right now, our best window into convergence culture comes from looking at the experience of these early settlers and first inhabitants. These elite consumers exert a disproportionate influence on media culture in part because advertisers and media producers are so eager to attract and hold their attention. Where they go, the media industry is apt to follow; where the media industry goes, these consumers are apt to be found. Right now, both are chasing their own tails.

You are now entering convergence culture. It is not a surprise that we are not yet ready to cope with its complexities and contradictions. We need to find ways to negotiate the changes taking place. No one group can set the terms. No one group can control access and participation.

Don't expect the uncertainties surrounding convergence to be resolved anytime soon. We are entering an era of prolonged transition and transformation in the way media operates. Convergence describes the process by which we will sort through those options. There will be no magical black box that puts everything in order again. Media producers will find their way through their current problems only by renegotiating their relationship with their consumers. Audiences, empowered by these new technologies, occupying a space at the intersection between old and new media, are demanding the right to participate within the culture. Producers who fail to make their peace with this new participatory culture will face declining goodwill and diminished revenues. The resulting struggles and compromises will define the public culture of the future.

I

Spoiling *Survivor*

The Anatomy of a Knowledge Community

Survivor (2000)—the astonishingly popular CBS show that started the reality television trend—does not just pit sixteen strangers against one another. Around each carefully crafted episode emerges another contest —a giant cat and mouse game that is played between the producers and the audience. Every week, the eagerly anticipated results are fodder for water cooler discussions and get reported as news, even on rival networks. *Survivor* is television for the Internet age—designed to be discussed, dissected, debated, predicted, and critiqued.

The *Survivor* winner is one of television's most tightly guarded secrets. Executive producer Mark Burnett engages in disinformation campaigns trying to throw smoke in viewers' eyes. Enormous fines are written into the contracts for the cast and crew members if they get caught leaking the results. And so a fascination has grown up around the order of the "boots" (the sequence in which the contestants get rejected from the tribe), the "final four" (the last four contestants in the competition), and especially around the "sole survivor" (the final winner of the million-dollar cash prize).

The audience is one of the largest in broadcast television. In its first eight seasons, *Survivor* rarely dipped out of the top ten highest-rated shows. The most hard-core fans, a contingent known as the "spoilers," go to extraordinary lengths to ferret out the answers. They use satellite photographs to locate the base camp. They watch the taped episodes, frame by frame, looking for hidden information. They know *Survivor* inside out, and they are determined to figure it out—together—before the producers reveal what happened. They call this process "spoiling."

Mark Burnett acknowledges this contest between producer and fans is part of what creates *Survivor*'s mystique: "With so much of our show shrouded in secrecy until it's broadcast, it makes complete sense that many individuals consider it a challenge to try to gain information before it's officially revealed—sort of like a code they are determined to crack. While it's my job to keep our fans on their toes and stay one step ahead, it is fascinating to hear some of the lengths these individuals are willing to go."[1]

Into this intense competition entered ChillOne. Before his sudden fame within the fan realm, he claimed to be a lurker who has never previously posted to a discussion list. On vacation in Brazil for New Year's 2003, he said, he stumbled into a detailed account of who was going to get bumped from *Survivor: Amazon*, the series's sixth season. He posted this information on the Internet and lived through months of intense grilling by the spoiling community to defend his reputation. To some, ChillOne was a hero, the best spoiler of all time. For others, he was a villain, the guy who destroyed the game for everyone else.

As we have seen, the age of media convergence enables communal, rather than individualistic, modes of reception. Not every media consumer interacts within a virtual community yet; some simply discuss what they see with their friends, family members, and workmates. But few watch television in total silence and isolation. For most of us, television provides fodder for so-called water cooler conversations. And, for a growing number of people, the water cooler has gone digital. Online forums offer an opportunity for participants to share their knowledge and opinions. In this chapter I hope to bring readers inside the spoiling community to learn more about how it works and how it impacts the reception of a popular television series.

My focus here is on the process and ethics of shared problem-solving in an online community. I am less interested, ultimately, in who ChillOne is or whether his information was accurate than I am with how the community responded to, evaluated, debated, critiqued, and came to grips with the kinds of knowledge he brought to them. I am interested in how the community reacts to a shift in its normal ways of processing and evaluating knowledge. It is at moments of crisis, conflict, and controversy that communities are forced to articulate the principles that guide them.[2]

Spoiling as Collective Intelligence

On the Internet, Pierre Lévy argues, people harness their individual expertise toward shared goals and objectives: "No one knows everything, everyone knows something, all knowledge resides in humanity."[3] Collective intelligence refers to this ability of virtual communities to leverage the combined expertise of their members. What we cannot know or do on our own, we may now be able to do collectively. And this organization of audiences into what Lévy calls knowledge communities allows them to exert a greater aggregate power in their negotiations with media producers. The emergent knowledge culture will never fully escape the influence of commodity culture, any more than commodity culture can totally function outside the constraints of the nation-state. He suggests, however, that collective intelligence will gradually alter the ways commodity culture operates. Lévy sees industry panic over audience participation as shortsighted: "By preventing the knowledge culture from becoming autonomous, they deprive the circuits of commodity space . . . of an extraordinary source of energy."[4] The knowledge culture, he suggests, serves as the "invisible and intangible engine" for the circulation and exchange of commodities.

The new knowledge culture has arisen as our ties to older forms of social community are breaking down, our rooting in physical geography is diminished, our bonds to the extended and even the nuclear family are disintegrating, and our allegiances to nation-states are being redefined. New forms of community are emerging, however: these new communities are defined through voluntary, temporary, and tactical affiliations, reaffirmed through common intellectual enterprises and emotional investments. Members may shift from one group to another as their interests and needs change, and they may belong to more than one community at the same time. These communities, however, are held together through the mutual production and reciprocal exchange of knowledge. As Levy writes, such groups "make available to the collective intellect all of the pertinent knowledge available to it at a given moment." More importantly, they serve as sites for "collective discussion, negotiation, and development," and they prod the individual members to seek out new information for the common good: "Unanswered questions will create tension . . . indicating regions where invention and innovation are required."[5]

Lévy draws a distinction between shared knowledge, information that is believed to be true and held in common by the entire group, and collective intelligence, the sum total of information held individually by the members of the group that can be accessed in response to a specific question. He explains: "The knowledge of a thinking community is no longer a shared knowledge for it is now impossible for a single human being, or even a group of people, to master all knowledge, all skills. It is fundamentally collective knowledge, impossible to gather together into a single creature."[6] Only certain things are known by all —the things the community needs to sustain its existence and fulfill its goals. Everything else is known by individuals who are on call to share what they know when the occasion arises. But communities must closely scrutinize any information that is going to become part of their shared knowledge, since misinformation can lead to more and more misconceptions as any new insight is read against what the group believes to be core knowledge.

Survivor spoiling is collective intelligence in practice.

Each fan I spoke with had their own history of how they became a spoiler. Shawn was a history major who loved the process of investigation and the challenge of weighing different accounts of a past event. Wezzie was a part-time travel agent who became fascinated with the faraway locations and the exotic people represented on the series. As for ChillOne, who knows, but it would seem from the outside to have to do with the ability to make the world pay attention to him.

Survivor asks us to speculate about what happened. It practically demands our predictions. Media scholar Mary Beth Haralovich and mathematician Michael W. Trosset describe the role chance plays in shaping outcomes: "Narrative pleasure stems from the desire to know what will happen next, to have that gap opened and closed, again and again, until the resolution of the story. . . . In *Survivor*, unpredictability whets the desire to know what happens next, but how that gap will be closed is grounded in uncertainty due to chance. . . . In its invitation to prediction, *Survivor* is more like a horse race than fiction."[7] At the same time, for those viewers who are most aware of the production circumstances, there is also an "uncertainty due to ignorance," which is what galls these fans the most. Someone out there—Mark Burnett for one— knows something they don't. They want to know what can be known. And that's part of what makes spoiling *Survivor* such a compelling activity. The ability to expand your individual grasp by pooling knowledge with others intensifies the pleasures any viewer takes in trying to "expect the unexpected," as the program's ad campaign urges.

And, so, *Survivor*'s spoilers gather and process information. As they do so, they form a knowledge community. We are experimenting with new kinds of knowledge that emerge in cyberspace. Out of such play,

Pierre Lévy believes, new kinds of political power will emerge which will operate alongside and sometimes directly challenge the hegemony of the nation-state or the economic might of corporate capitalism. Lévy sees such knowledge communities as central to the task of restoring democratic citizenship. At his most optimistic, he sees the sharing of knowledge around the world as the best way of breaking down the divisions and suspicions that currently shape international relations. Lévy's claims are vast and mystifying; he speaks of his model of collective intelligence as an "achievable utopia," yet he recognizes that small local experiments will be where we learn how to live within knowledge communities. We are, he argues, in a period of "apprenticeship" through which we innovate and explore the structures that will support political and economic life in the future.

Imagine the kinds of information these fans could collect, if they sought to spoil the government rather than the networks. Later, we will look at the roles collective intelligence played in the 2004 presidential campaign, and we will see signs that players of alternate reality games are beginning to focus their energies toward solving civic and political problems. Having said that, I don't want to seem to endorse a very old idea that fandom is a waste of time because it redirects energies that could be spent toward "serious things" like politics into more trivial pursuits. Quite the opposite, I would argue that one reason more Americans do not participate in public debates is that our normal ways of thinking and talking about politics require us to buy into what we will discuss later in this chapter as the expert paradigm: to play the game, you have to become a policy wonk, or, more accurately, you have to let a policy wonk do your thinking for you. One reason why spoiling is a more compelling practice is because the way knowledge gets produced and evaluated is more democratic. Spoiling is empowering in the literal sense in that it helps participants to understand how they may deploy the new kinds of power that are emerging from participation within knowledge communities. For the moment, though, the spoilers are just having fun on a Friday night participating in an elaborate scavenger hunt involving thousands of participants who all interact in a global village. Play is one of the ways we learn, and during a period of reskilling and reorientation, such play may be much more important than it seems at first glance. On the other hand, play is also valuable on its own terms and for its own ends. At the end of the day, if spoiling wasn't fun, they wouldn't do it.

The word *spoiling* goes way back—or at least as far back as you can go—in the history of the Internet. Spoiling emerged from the mismatch between the temporalities and geographies of old and new media. For starters, people on the East Coast saw a series three hours earlier than people on the West Coast. Syndicated series played on different nights of the week in different markets. American series played in the United States six months or more before they broke in inter-national markets. As long as people in different locations weren't talking to each other, each got a first-time experience. But, once fans got online, these differences in time zones loomed large. Someone on the East Coast would go online and post everything about an episode, and someone in California would get annoyed because the episode was "spoiled." So, posters began putting the word "spoiler" in the subject line, so people could make up their own minds whether or not to read it.

Over time, though, the fan community turned spoiling into a game to find out what they could before the episodes even aired. Again, it is interesting to think about this in terms of temporality. Most viewers experience *Survivor* as something that unfolds week by week in real time. The show is edited to emphasize immediacy and spontaneity. The contestants don't appear publicly until after they are booted, and often they speak as if the events hadn't already happened. They can only speak concretely about things that have already been aired and seem at times to speculate about what is yet to come. Spoilers, on the other hand, work from the knowledge that the series has already been shot. As one fan explains, "The results were determined months ago and here we wait for the official results. And a few people out there who participated know the results and they are supposed to keep it under lock. Hahahahahaha!"

They are searching for signs of the aftermath, trying to find out which contestants lost the most weight (thus indicating that they spent more time surviving in the wilds) or which came back with full beards or bandaged hands; they seek leaks who are willing to give them some "small hints" about what took place, and then they pool their information, adding up all of the "small hints" into the "Big Picture." Ghandia Johnson (*Survivor: Thailand*) thought she was smarter than the fan boards; she would post what she thought were tantalizing tidbits no-body could figure out. It turned out that the community—at least as an aggregate—was a whole lot smarter than she was and could use her "hints" to put together much of what was going to happen on the series. More recently, a news crew interviewed a *Survivor* producer in front of a white board that outlined the challenges for the forthcoming season; the fans were able to do a "frame grab" of the image, blow it up, and decipher the entire outline, giving them a road map for what was to come.

On one level, the story of *Survivor: Amazon* was done before Chill-One arrived on the scene; his sources at the Ariau Amazon Hotel were already starting to forget what had happened. On another level, the story hadn't begun, since the cast hadn't been publicly announced, the show was still being edited, and the episodes wouldn't air for several more weeks when he made his first post at Survivor Sucks (http://p085.ezboard.com/bsurvivorsucks).

ChillOne knew he had some hot inside information and so he went where the hard-core fans hung out—Survivor Sucks, one of the oldest and most popular of the many discussion lists devoted to the series. The name bears some explanation, since clearly these people are dedicated fans who don't really think the show sucks. Initially, Survivor Sucks was a forum for "recaps," snarky summaries of the episodes. On the one hand, a recap is a useful tool for people who missed an episode. On the other hand, the recapping process was shaped by the desire to talk back to the television set, to make fun of formulas and signal your emotional distance from what's taking place on the screen. Somewhere along the way, the Sucksters discovered "spoiling," and the boards haven't been the same since. So, it was here—to these people who pretended to hate *Survivor* but were pretty much obsessed with it—that ChillOne brought his information.

Anticipating some reaction, he started his own thread, "ChillOne's Amazon Vacation Spoilers." Surely, even ChillOne never imagined that the full thread would run for more than three thousand posts and continue across the full season. ChillOne made his first post at 7:13:25 P.M. on January 9, 2003. By 7:16:40 P.M. he was already facing questions. It wasn't until 7:49:43 P.M. that someone implied that he might be connected to the show. A few minutes later, someone asked whether this might be a hoax.

It began innocently enough: "I have just returned from Brazil and a trip to the Amazon. . . . I will begin by saying that I do not have all the answers, or all the information about S6 [*Survivor 6*], but I have enough credible, spoiler type, information that I'd be open to sharing."[8]

Images from Space

We would learn later that ChillOne had gone on vacation with a bunch of friends to Rio to celebrate the New Year but had wanted to see more of the country. He made his way to the Amazon and then learned that the Ariau Amazon Towers had been the headquarters for the *Survivor* production staff, and as a fan of the series he wanted to see the locations firsthand. He wasn't a spoiler; he mostly asked questions of the hotel staff trying to figure out what might be meaningful sites on a *Survivor*-themed tour of the Amazon. Whereas most of the people who came there were eco-tourists who wanted to see nature untouched by human presence, he was a tele-tourist trying to visit a location made meaningful because it was transmitted by television.

His first post focused primarily around the shooting location: "First off, the map posted by Wezzie is very accurate. Let me start by filling in some of the gaps." This was a bold opening move, as "Wezzie" is one of the most respected members of the *Survivor* spoiling community. She and her partner, Dan Bollinger, have specialized in location spoiling. Offline, Wezzie is a substitute teacher, an arboretum docent, a travel agent, and a freelance writer. Dan is an industrial designer who runs a factory that makes refrigerator magnets. They live halfway across the country from each other, but they work as a team to try to identify and document the next *Survivor* location—what Mark Burnett calls "the seventeenth character"—and to learn as much as they can about the area. As a team, Wezzie and Dan have been able to pinpoint the series location with astonishing accuracy. The process may start with a throwaway comment from Mark Burnett or a tip from "somebody who knows somebody, who knows somebody, who works for CBS or a tourist company."[9] Wezzie and Dan have built up contacts

Flashback to *Twin Peaks*

My first introduction to the Internet, and to online fan communities, came in 1991 through alt.tv.twinpeaks.[1] Looking back, it is remarkable how much the discussion around the series was already starting to resemble one of Pierre Lévy's knowledge communities. The group emerged within just a few weeks after the first episode of David Lynch's quirky detective series aired and rapidly became one of the largest and most active discussion lists in the early Internet era, attracting by some estimates 25,000 readers (although a substantially smaller number of posters). The discussion group served many functions for its participants. Fans worked together to compile charts showing all of the series events or compilations of important bits of dialogue; they shared what they could find about the series in local

---

[1] For a fuller discussion of *Twin Peaks*' online fan community, see Henry Jenkins, "'Do You Enjoy Making the Rest of Us Feel Stupid?': alt.tv.twinpeaks, the Trickster Author, and Viewer Mastery," in *Fans, Gamers, and Bloggers: Exploring Participatory Culture* (New York: New York University Press, 2006).

with travel agencies, government officials, film bureaus, tourism directors, and resort operators. As Dan notes, "Word gets around the tourism industry very quickly about a large project that will be bringing in millions of American dollars."

From there, they start narrowing things down by looking at the demands of the production. Wezzie describes the process: "We look at latitude, climate, political stability, population density, road system, ports, accommodations, attractions, culture, predominant religion, and proximity to past *Survivor* locations." Dan notes, "In Africa I overlaid demographic maps of population, agricultural areas, national reserves, tourism destinations and even city lights seen from satellites at night. Sometimes knowing where *Survivor* can't be is important. That's how I found Shaba Reserve."

Wezzie is the people person: she works their network to pull together as much data as she can. Wezzie adds, "Then Dan works his magic!" Dan has developed contact with the Denver-based Space Imaging Company, owner of IKONOS, a high-resolution commercial remote-sensing satellite. Eager to show off what their satellite can do, IKONOS took snapshots of the location for *Survivor: Africa* that Dan had identified from 423 miles in space, and upon closer scrutiny, they could decipher specific buildings in the production compound, including the temporary production buildings, the tribal council site, and a row of Massai-style huts where the contestants would live, eat, and sleep. They take the snapshots from

papers; they used the Internet to locate tapes if they missed episodes; they traced through the complex grid of references to other films, television series, songs, novels, and other popular texts, matching wits with what they saw as a trickster author always trying to throw them off his trail. But, more than anything else, the list functioned as a space where people could pull together the clues and vet their speculations concerning the central narrative hook—who killed Laura Palmer? The pressure on the group mounted as the moment of dramatic revelation approached: "Break the code, solve the crime. We've only got four days left." In many ways, *Twin Peaks* was the perfect text for a computer-based community, combining the narrative complexity of a mystery with the complex character relationships of a soap opera and a serialized structure that left much unresolved and subject to debate from week to week.

The online community was fascinated to discover what it was like to work together, several thousand strong, in making sense of what they were watching, and they were all using recently acquired VCRs to go back through the tapes, again and again, looking for what they had missed. As one fan commented, "Video recording has made it possible to treat film like a manuscript, to be pored over and deciphered." Those on the periphery were astonished by the kinds of information they could compile and process, sometimes confusing the combined knowledge of the group with individual expertise: "Tell me! Tell me! How many times are people watching TP? Do you take notes on every subject as you are watching? Or, when a question comes up do you drag out each of the episodes, grab a yellow pad, some popcorn and start watching? Do you have a photographic memory? . . . Do you enjoy making the rest of us feel stupid?"

While most critics complained that *Twin Peaks* became so complicated that it was nearing incomprehensibility as the season continued, the fan community began to complain that the series was becoming too predictable. The community's ability to pool its collective resources was placing new demands on the series that no television production of the time would have been capable of satisfying. To keep themselves entertained, they were spinning out elaborate conspiracy theories and explanations that were more interesting, because they were more layered than would ever be aired. In the end, they felt betrayed because Lynch could not stay one step ahead of them. This should have been our first sign that there was going to be tension ahead between media producers and consumers. As one disappointed fan protested, "After so much build up, so much analysis, so much waiting and so many false clues, how can any answer totally satisfy the anticipation that has built up. If WKLP is firmly resolved on the 11/10 episode we will all be in for a huge let down. Even those who guessed right will only celebrate and gloat briefly and then be left empty inside." Television would have to become more sophisticated if it wanted to keep up with its most committed viewers.

space because the security-conscious Burnett negotiates a "no fly zone" policy over the location. Dan uses the Com Sat (Communications Satellite) images and sophisticated topographical maps to refine his understanding of the core locations. Meanwhile, Wezzie researches the ecosystem and culture. Everything she learns ends up on *Survivor* maps and becomes a resource for the fan community. And, after all of that, they still sometimes get it wrong. For example, they focused a lot of energy on a location in Mexico, only to learn that the new series was going to be filmed in the Pearl Islands near Panama. They weren't totally wrong, though —they had identified the location for a production company filming another reality television series.

The fan community has come to trust Wezzie and Dan to do an incredible amount of homework and ensure the accuracy of their posts. They also have a reputation as neutral observers who speak from above the fray. On the one hand, it was pretty cheeky for ChillOne to try to correct their map on his first post, a volley over the bow of the established spoiling community. On the other, it was smart, because the geographical information was the most easily confirmed. He posted some images with his very first message, and Wezzie and Dan were able to authenticate those images on the basis of weather conditions, tide level, and other geographical details. Over and over, people said they wouldn't have believed ChillOne if he hadn't been able to prove, beyond reasonable doubt, that he had actually been to the production location.

Over time, the Sucksters develop an intuition about whether alleged "intel" smells right or not. Shawn, a longtime spoiler, explained:

If it is a first time poster, it is normally written off as not very credible. You don't trust first time people. You have to wonder why NOW of all the times they could have posted. If the person has posted before and has been involved with the spoiling before, that would add credibility to their posts. . . . Nobody can know for sure the poster is lying until after the fact but once that person is found to be lying, they are never trusted again and they are pretty much blacklisted.

Many people felt that ChillOne knew the form and rhetoric of spoiling a little too well for a first-time poster, even one who had lurked for a while, and so they were convinced that the name, ChillOne, was a second identity—a "sock puppet"—for a longtime poster. Tell us who you really are, they begged, so we can check out your previous posts. ChillOne, however, never indulged such requests and continued to give bits of information. The community wasn't going to be satisfied with some tidbits about the location and a few photographs, though. They wanted the "good stuff," and they had every reason to think Chill-One was holding out on them. The issue was already on the table with the very first response to his original post: "Were there any Survivors that stayed at the hotel (i.e. loser lodge)? Were you able to get any leads on who might have been on the show?"

And then, at 7:55 P.M. on January 9, just a few minutes after his first post, ChillOne opens a can of worms:

As far as contestants . . . Yes, I do have information on this as well. What I can share is that you will find your first physically handicapped contestant on S6 . . . a woman who is hearing impaired (deaf). I will share more contestant information over the coming months. I will tell you that I do NOT know the entire "cast list." I do NOT know last names either. I only know the first names of about a handful of contestants and the basic descriptions of a few more.

From there, the next response from the Sucksters is predictable:

I don't want to cause you any burden or trouble, but why wait? Can you tell us.

Why are you holding out on the contestants' names and descriptions? Let's have 'em!

It would be fantastic to have the first names before the official release on Monday.

If you do not wish to release the names that you do know, then could you give us a hint to whether any of the speculated contestants we have are on the show?

Spoiling follows a logical sequence. The first phase is focused on identifying the location, because the impact of the production is felt first where the series was shot. The second phase is focused on identifying the contestants, since the second impact is felt on the local communities where these "average Americans" come from. The collective has its feelers out everywhere and responds to the slightest brush. As Shawn explained, "The locals can never keep their mouths shut." Milkshakey hears a rumor that a girls PE coach at his local high school might be on *Survivor* and starts pumping her current and former students for any information he can get. A small-town newspaper hints that some local might have been in the running for a million dollars. Sooner or later, it comes back to the Sucksters.

Sometimes, it takes a little effort. The Ellipsis Brain Trust tracked down the name of the person who designed the CBS *Survivor* Web site, hacked into their hotmail account, and found a single entry, a list of URLs that were to be acquired immediately, sixteen in all, each bearing the name of a man or woman. (There are sixteen contestants on each series of *Survivor.*) From there, the members of the EBT divided the listed names and began to investigate to see if they were real people. In most cases, there were many people who had that name, some deceased, some young and healthy, and the task was to find out as much about each of them as you could. In an age when all information sources are interconnected and when privacy is breaking down at an alarming rate, there is an immense amount that a team of several hundred people can dig out about a person, given enough time and determination. Armed with their hacked documents, the EBT successfully confirmed all sixteen contestants before CBS released a single name. Sometimes, though, the spoilers get the names wrong and spend lots of time collecting data on totally innocent people. And sometimes, people seeking attention leak their own names just so they can watch the community talk about them.

And even when the spoilers get it right, there is a thin, thin line here between investigating those who have chosen to insert themselves into the public spotlight and stalking them at their home or workplace. For example, one ambitious fan found out where CBS was running the initial interviews for *Survivor: Pearl Island,* booked time at the hotel before CBS did, and refused to move when they wanted to buy out the hotel for the weekend. She was able to take photographs of everyone interviewed, using a long-range telephoto lens, and her photographs were used to check any names that surfaced. The community spends a great deal of time debating exactly where you draw the line.

Sometimes, spoilers really hit the jackpot during this phase. Quartz-eye showed up at the used car lot where Brian (*Survivor: Thailand*) worked, pretending to want to buy a car, and took pictures of him standing next to the vehicle. Once the group compared her pictures with the official publicity shots, they could see that he had lost an enormous amount of weight, and it was then clear that he had been out there in the wilds for longer than most. Someone looked on the corporate Web site for Mike Skupin (*Survivor: The Australian Outback*) and found a picture of him standing with a business associate, his arm in a cast, and that led the group to detect early on that there was going to be an accident. Some local Photoshop experts remained unconvinced, diagramming various ways the image could have been doctored. As it turned out, Mike fell into a fire and had to be evacuated for medical attention.

With each season, Mark Burnett, CBS, and the production team have tightened security, further closed off leaks, anticipated hackers, and made it that much harder to play the game. For Season Six, the community had been working hard trying to get names and coming up largely empty-handed. They had a few confirmed names—Heidi, the gym teacher, most prominently—and some of the ones being currently proposed later turned out to be wrong. (The community places a high standard on confirming names. Only once has the community confirmed someone who did not appear in the show, and only rarely does the group discard the name of someone who turns out to be a real contestant. During this early stage, however, many names are proposed and investigated.) So, when ChillOne implied that he knew at least partial names or might be able to confirm some of the names that were already in circulation, the group went wild. Here was the breakthrough they had been waiting for, and it came only one day before the official announcement.

But ChillOne played with them, saying that he didn't want to post inaccurate information, that they would have to wait till later in the day when he could get home and double-check his notes. Later, some would find this timing suspicious, wondering if he had access to early copies of *TV Guide* or *USA Today* accounts that would be released in a matter of hours, or if he had a source at *The Early Show*, where the official announcement was going to be made. Maybe he was stalling for time.

"Gated [Knowledge] Communities"

"If you are eager to share information but are hesitant to spill it all out here, I suggest contacting someone privately," a poster suggests early in the process, nominating themselves for the task. The most sensitive personal information about the contestants doesn't get aired on Survivor Sucks, where it could be read by anyone with Internet access. Over the first five seasons, "brain trusts," which may be as small as twenty people or as large as a few hundred participants, had emerged as offshoots of the Survivor Sucks site. These "brain trusts" do much of their most hard-core investigation through password-protected sites. Think of these "brain trusts" as secret societies or private clubs, whose members are handpicked based on their skills and track records. Those who are left behind complain about the "brain drain," which locks the smartest and most articulate posters behind closed doors. The brain trusts, on the other hand, argue that this closed-door vetting process protects privacy and ensures a high degree of accuracy once they do post their findings.

One question Lévy never fully addresses is the scale on which these knowledge communities may operate. At his most utopian, he imagines the whole world operating as a single knowledge culture and imagines new modes of communication that would facilitate exchange and deliberation of knowledge on this scale. At other times, he seems to recognize the need for scalable communities, especially in the first phases of an emerging knowledge culture. He has a deep-seated distrust of hierarchy of all kinds, seeing de-

The Paradox of Reality Fiction

Spoiling is only one activity that engages *Survivor* fans. Like fans of many other series, *Survivor* fans also write and post original fiction about their favorite characters. One fan with the unlikely real name of Mario Lanza was inspired by talk about an all-star reunion series of *Survivor* to write three whole seasons' worth of imaginary episodes (*All Star: Greece, All Star: Alaska,* and *All Star: Hawaii*), featuring the fictional exploits of these real-world participants. Each installment may be between forty and

mocracy as the ideology that will best enable knowledge cultures to emerge. Lévy writes, "How will we be able to process enormous masses of data on interrelated problems within a changing environment? Most likely by making use of organizational structures that favor the genuine socialization of problem-solving rather than its resolution by separate entities that are in danger of becoming competitive, swollen, outdated and isolated from real life."[10] The brain trusts represent the return of hierarchy to the knowledge culture, the attempt to create an elite that has access to information not available to the group as a whole and that demands to be trusted as arbitrators of what it is appropriate to share with the collective.

Most spoilers argue that these brain trusts serve a useful purpose, but they can be paternalistic as hell. As one Suckster explained, "Everything we have is also theirs because we're open, everything they have most definitely is not ours because members of the gated communities may or may not feel like dropping in and sharing it. They have sources we do not, and they like to hoard information, which is what the private groups are all about." The trusts tend to dump data with no explanation about how they got it, essentially cutting the plebeians out of the process and constructing themselves as experts who are to be trusted at face value. Many of the brain trusts are rumored to have secret sources, often within the production company.

ChillOne posted everything he knew

seventy pages long. He unfolds these episodes week by week during the off-season. The stories follow the series's dramatic structure, yet they are even more focused on the character motivations and interactions. Lanza compares this process of getting to know the characters with police profiling: "I tried very hard to get into these people's heads, and I thought if I am going to play this game again, what am I going to change, how would I do this, what do I know about this person, how do I know them, how do they talk, how do they think."[1] While spoiling tries to anticipate how contestants will react to the incidents depicted in the series, the fan fiction takes this one step further, trying to imagine how they would respond confronting challenges and dilemmas that they never faced in real life.

So far, this may sound like the way any other fan fiction writers approach their task—get to know your characters, remain consistent with the aired material, and speculate based on what you know about people in the real world, except in this case, the characters are people who exist in the real world. Lanza's stories have, in fact, become very popular with the *Survivor* contestants themselves, who often write him letters telling him what he got right or where he misread some participant's personality. For example, he said that Gabriel Cade (a contestant on *Survivor: Marquesas*) was so flattered about being included in one of the all-star stories that he wanted to get more involved in the writing process: "He's really interested in how his character is going to come off, so he's told me all kinds of gossip about what these people are like, what they do, who likes who, and how they get along." As a writer of

[1] Personal interview with author, May 2003.

reality fiction, Lanza has been getting fan letters from his characters.

With *Survivor: Greece*, Lanza sought to tell the stories of those contestants who had been bumped early in the runs of their series. Because so little aired material dealt with these characters, he drew much more heavily on what he could learn by interviewing them and their teammates. After arbitrarily choosing Diane Ogden (*Africa*) and Gabriel Cade (*Marquesas*) as team leaders, he contacted them to see which players they would have selected to be on their teams. In some cases, he asked actual contestants to write their own "final words" as their fictionalized characters are voted out of the game. Chris Wright interviewed some of these players and found that they often felt Lanza's fiction more accurately reflected their real personalities and strategies than the television program itself because it was less reliant on stereotyping. Many of them felt a vicarious pleasure or psychological boost in watching their fictionalized characters overcome problems that had blocked them during the actual game.[2]

Lanza also wanted to preserve the show's fundamental element of chance: "I have talked to a lot of the survivors in real life over the phone or on e-mail, and this is one of the things they consistently bring up over and over. It doesn't matter what your plans are or how smart you are or how strong you are. So much of the game is based on luck. . . . I wanted that to work out the story somehow. As a writer, I didn't want to be able to cheat." So, as he started to write the challenges, he rolled dice to determine which team or player wins

[2] Chris Wright, "Poaching Reality: The Reality Fictions of Online *Survivor* Fans," unpublished seminar paper, Georgetown University, February 7, 2004.

in the most broadly accessible discussion list and let the vetting take place in public view. The brain trusts were working behind closed doors to see how far they could push his intel, but ChillOne himself wanted everything to remain out in the open. Some of the brain trusts sought to discredit ChillOne, urging Sucksters not to put their full faith in what he was saying, but they wouldn't say why. Some believed such warnings because the brain trusts had access to so much inside information; others suspected they were trying to discredit a rival.

But as of day 2, ChillOne wasn't revealing the contestants, and the group was watching the clock tick down before the names would be publicly announced. If that wasn't annoying enough, ChillOne closed his post with a bombshell: "Here is a little 'teaser' . . . the deaf girl is 22. I don't know her name but, she does make it to the Final 4." For the first time, ChillOne implied that he might even know who won the game.

By the end of day 2, ChillOne started to deliver the core of his intel and offer some hints about how he accessed it. ChillOne wanted to protect his sources, he said, so he wasn't going to disclose much. He spent time buying people drinks at the hotel bar and asking them questions, but not too many questions since he didn't want them to clamp down. At least some of the people he talked with spoke only Portuguese, so he had to rely on translators. In the following weeks, he was asked about the gestures they used and the tone of their voice, whether they had thick accents, and how comfortable the translator was with colloquial English. He did spell out a theory about how knowledge might have circulated back to the hotel, given that it wasn't the "loser lodge" as some had suspected, and that none of the contestants themselves ever went there: he implied that the information had come from the "boat guides" who ferried away the contestants once they were voted off the tribe. "Since there are only a small handful of 'boat guides' most of them working long hours driving the S6 crews in/out of the jungle, thus, enabling them to witness the filming. I'm sure that over the 3 months, they rapped among themselves and with the help of the English-speaking staff, figured out what was going on." ChillOne never actually said a boatman was his source. He let the spoilers draw their own conclusions, and in the weeks ahead, an enormous amount of speculation and mythology grew up around the boatman. ChillOne refused to confirm or deny any of the theories. He said he didn't want to cloud the water by engaging in speculation. Some think he was messing with their minds.

and then wrote the scene accordingly. A single roll of the dice could wipe out weeks of plotting, much as it did for the producers of the television series, and as a consequence, the stories are full of surprise twists and turns that capture something of the spirit of the series. One of his series ended with an all-female final four, something that never happened on the air. As he explains, "That's just the way the story happened to go."

Perhaps because of this close interaction with the contestants, Lanza has become a sharp critic of spoiling, which he says becomes too intrusive. As he explains, "People take it way too seriously. It's just a TV show." Only a few minutes later, however, he adds, "Get me talking about *Survivor* and I will talk forever." As they say, *Survivor* sucks.

"Here's what I know . . . it's not much," he said with classic understatement. He knew parts of everything—the first four boots, the final four, the location, the details of contestants and their behavior, some of the highlights of the series. He knew that for the first time the tribes would be organized by gender but that they would "merge much earlier . . . possibly after the first 3 or 4 contestants are gone." He knew the women would dominate the early challenges and that several of the first boots would be athletic young men who had fumbled in the competition. He knew that one of the contestants would strip down to gain an advantage. (It turns out that both Heidi and Jenna went skinny-dipping in return for chocolate and peanut butter during one of the immunity challenges.) He knew that a certain kind of local insect would be the gross food challenge. Some of what he knew, even some of what he was certain about—like the claim that the "deaf girl," Christy, was part of the final four—turned out to be dead wrong. Some of it turned out to be so vague that it could be massaged to seem right no matter what the outcome. But the general pattern of his knowledge held true. He got the order of the first four boots wrong, but in the end, his four were among the first five folks kicked out of their tribes. He misidentified one of the final four, but Christy did make the final five. The odds of getting all of that right without inside information are astronomical.

As for the outcome, he knew, or claimed to know, that it came down to a contest between a woman who was called "Jana" or something close to it and a man who was in his twenties, had a "strong build," and had a "tight haircut" that was combed to the side. The Oracle at Delphi spoke with greater clarity. First of all, the name "Jana" didn't perfectly match any of the contestants, and on a season where the women's names included Janet, Jenna, Jeanne, and Joanna, there was certainly room for confusion here. Matthew the globe-trotting restaurant de-signer might meet his description of the man, more or less: he certainly had a strong build and he did part his hair to the side, but he had longish hair going in and was apt to have even longer hair by the end, and he was a good deal older than twenty-six, so perhaps they were thinking about Alex the triathlon coach or Dave the rocket scientist. Before long, even the gawky nerd-boy Rob was starting to be put forward as someone who could have refined his muscle tone over a two-month stay in the rain forest. There was more than enough here to keep the community busy for the coming months, and for the most part there was enough that could support multiple theories and arguments.

Several people wanted to delegate tasks, rally the troops, and see what they all could put together before the season started. That is, they wanted to exploit the full resources of a knowledge community rather than put all of their trust in one previously unknown individual. One of the would-be leaders explained, "There is LOTS we need to know about them and could be compiling. Basically build a dossier on each of them. Pics from outside of *Survivor*, vidcaps, bios, descriptions (how friggin' TALL are these guys, exactly?). What hints have Jiffy [Jeff Probst], MB [Mark Burnett], and others made about them, what allusions to them exist? . . . Eventually, more clues are going to pop out at us. Pieces will fit together. The puzzle will start to make sense. A tremendous amount can be done in this way BEFORE the show airs." But ChillOne had refocused the spoiling community's efforts; everything was directed toward proving or disproving his theories—and nobody was searching in other directions. Over time, ChillOne's intel would spread outward to all of the other boards and discussion lists, until you couldn't turn around without running into an opinion about his veracity, whether you wanted to have contact with spoilers or not. You couldn't put forth an alternative theory without having someone dismiss you for going against what the group "already knew" from ChillOne.

Contested Information

Almost immediately, the skeptics on the listboard began to circle, because something about all of this didn't smell right, something here was too good to be true.

> Not that past history means *a lot* but how many times have we received legit contestant spoilers like this from somebody that just happened to be around where filming took place. I guess there's a first time for everything.

> It is, of course, still possible that ChillOne is MB and that he is establishing credibility by leaking good information a few days early only to slam us with a bad F4 prediction.

> MB is definitely the type of person that would have his lackeys make up fake spoilers and such during their lunch breaks.

They would continue in that manner for the rest of the season. Spoiling is an adversarial process—a contest between the fans and the producers, one group trying to get their hands on the knowledge the other is trying to protect. Spoiling is also adversarial in the same sense that a court of law is adversarial, committed to the belief that through a contest over information, some ultimate truth will emerge. The system works best when people are contesting every claim that gets made, taking nothing at face value. As one skeptic explained, "People with doubt should be welcomed, not scorned. It helps everyone in the long run. If I poke at holes that look thin, they either get firmed up (a win for you), or they become bigger holes (a win for me). Bigger holes could lead to other things. Either way, some resolution is forthcoming eventually." As participants struggle over the nature of the truth, things can get pretty nasty.

If enough contradicting evidence could be found to fully discredit ChillOne, the discussion list would be able to close off his thread and attention would be routed elsewhere. ChillOne wanted very much to keep his thread alive for the whole season; his rivals wanted to shut him down. There were the two camps in this struggle over ChillOne's claims. First, there were the absolutists, who believed that if any part of the ChillOne intel was false, it proved that he was lying: "If a person says four distinct things are going to happen and then the first one doesn't, that means he's wrong. Whether anything is right after that is irrelevant. . . . You can't 'partly' win. You either nail it or you don't. . . . [Otherwise], that person merely met the mathematical probability of being correct." And then there were the relativists, who argued that memory could be imprecise or that data could be corrupted: "Where do we get you people from? . . . People unable or unwilling to acknowledge any correctness in some elements, if there is incorrectness in any other elements." There was too much information here that came close to the facts for the whole thing to be fabricated.

Soon, the absolutists and the relativists were enmeshed in philosophical debates about the nature of truth. Think of such debates as exercises in popular epistemology. As we learn how to live within a knowledge culture, we can anticipate many such discussions centering as much on how we know and how we evaluate what we know as on the information itself. Ways of knowing may be as distinctive and personal as what kinds of knowledge we access, but as knowing becomes public, as knowing becomes part of the life of a community, those contradictions in approach must be worked over if not worked through.

At one point an exasperated ChillOne defender summed up the competing theories: "He was never in Brazil. He works for someone in the know. He's not quite right, he's working the perfect scam, he's one of us that got amazingly lucky." The poster continued, "To me, a spoiler as grand as this one opens the author to legitimate questions about his identity, his true sources of information, his true purpose, and so on. In other words, the author himself becomes a critical part of the spoiling information." Part of what gave ChillOne credibility was his willingness to log in day after day and face these questions, respond calmly and rationally, and maintain consistency about what he was saying. Others, however, noted strange shifts in his writing style, sometimes lucid and authoritative, other times vague, rambling, and incoherent, as if someone was ghostwriting some of his posts.

Early on, ChillOne's credibility took a licking. The "Asian American" (Daniel) wasn't the first one booted, as "Uncle Boatman" had predicted, and so everyone was ready to bury the theory until Daniel went the third week, pretty much according to the logic that ChillOne had outlined. And so it went, week by nail-biting week, with ChillOne's information proving to be more or less right, but each week something contradicted his claims. He gained some credibility by midseason when the news media picked up the story of a Las Vegas gambling operation that discontinued betting on the *Survivor* outcomes when it caught some CBS employees placing bets on what they suspected might be insider information. They had been gambling on Matthew and Jenna for the final two, and this seemed to prove ChillOne knew his stuff, until people realized that someone from CBS might have been monitoring the boards and had been betting that ChillOne was right. It had happened before when the spoiling community had trusted some consistently accurate predictions from a Boston newspaper as backing up their inside information on *Survivor: The Australian Outback* until it was clear that the reporter was just writing his column based on stuff he learned from the online discussions.

In the end, ChillOne got it right, assuming Jenna was "Jana" and the thirty-something shaggy-haired Matthew was the twenty-something man with the "close haircut." Maybe it would be more accurate to say that ChillOne's intel helped the spoilers get within striking distance of the right answer, even if many Sucksters trusted their guts over his inside dope: they couldn't believe that Jenna, the spoiled brat, could win out over the hardworking but mysterious Matthew. For a community like this one, which thrives on debates about the validity of information, a loose consensus is about all one can expect at the present time. Some things become common beliefs that everyone accepts, and on other matters, the group, gladly and gleefully, agrees to disagree.

The Evil Pecker and His Minions

We may never know for sure where ChillOne's information came from. From the start, the skeptics had two prevailing theories: that he was in some way linked to the production company, or that he was a hoaxer. Both of these theories were plausible, given their experiences over the previous seasons.

The spoilers had every reason to believe that Mark Burnett played an active role in shaping the flow of information around the series. They called him "Evil Pecker Mark," a play on EP (which also stands for "Executive Producer"). CBS had admitted that they, like many other production companies, monitored the discussion lists for information about the audience. Here's Chris Ender, CBS senior VP of communications: "In the first season, there was a ground swell of attention in there. We started monitoring the message boards to actually help guide us in what would resonate in our marketing. It's just the best marketing research you can get."[11] The fans had every reason to believe that someone from Burnett's office was listening to what they were saying —and some reason to believe that they were being lied to, at least some of the time, in a deliberate effort to shape the reception of the series. Here's host Jeff Probst describing his role in this process: "We have so many lies going, and we have so much misinformation that there is usually an out; there is usually a way to recover [from a slip]. I can tell you who the winner is right now and you wouldn't know whether to believe me or not."[12]

First-season fans started scrutinizing the opening credits for clues and spotted an image of nine contestants at what looked like a tribal council session.[13] They used that image to narrow down the boot order —though in some cases, questions remained, since it was possible one person was voting when the picture was taken and some of the people were in the shadows, leading to debates about who they really were. The picture turned out to be misleading, read out of context. No one was sure whether the producer meant to send them on a wild-goose chase. Later in the first season, the behind-the-scenes machinations of the show's producers made the national news in what became known as "Gervase X." Spoilers figured out the URL for the directory tree on the official CBS Web site and dug around behind the scenes, unearthing fifteen unlinked images showing all but one of the contestants, Gervase, Xed out. The fans were convinced that the African American coach was the only one who never got booted, up until the moment that Gervase got voted off the island. Both Mark Burnett and Ghen Maynard, the CBS executive in charge of reality programming, have publicly acknowledged that they planted that misleading clue. From then on, the rules of the game had changed. Shawn summarized the shift of attitude: "Before it was Mark Burnett that naïve unassuming producer/idiot letting all of his secrets flood out. Now it was Mark Burnett deceiver, Mark Burnett the Devil, Evil Pecker Mark. Now we knew he was trying to keep secrets and it was game on."[14]

Burnett had the last laugh in that first season. There was a really big clue in the opening credit: as the announcer is explaining that "only one will remain to win the title of sole survivor and one million dollars . . . in cash," he had shown, from the first episode forward, a shot of Richard Hatch, the actual winner, walking alone across a rope bridge with a big smile on his face. The spoilers had seen it and dismissed it, believing it couldn't be that simple—and after that, it wasn't.

From then on, the spoilers watched the episodes more closely, using their single frame advance to search for embedded clues, keeping track of the shots of animals that often functioned metaphorically to foreshadow the rising or falling fortunes of individuals or teams, looking at editing patterns to see which characters were being foregrounded and which hidden. Tapewatcher developed an intriguing theory about *Survivor: Africa* based on what he saw as biblical allusions surrounding the long-haired, bearded, and Jewish Ethan, who he believed was going to win out over his more transgressive competitors. Again and again, Ethan's image was coupled with a distinctive lens flair that looked a bit like the Star of David. "Follow the star," and you will find the winner, Tapewatcher predicted, and, strange as it seems, he was right. Tapewatcher presented his argument in page after page of richly detailed close textual analysis, accompanied in some cases by images grabbed off the video tape and in some cases by actual streaming footage.[15] Is it possible that the show's editors planted clues for viewers? This may not be as far-fetched as it sounds. Another reality series, *The Mole*, planted equally obscure clues that it assumed people armed with VCRs and the Internet would sort through. A good chunk of the final episode of each season was spent mapping them out for viewers "too dense" to spot them hidden in the background of shots or arranged in the first letters of the last names of the production crew on the closing credits.

As soon as the *Survivor* fans found an editing pattern that might help them foretell a winner, Burnett shifted his style for the next season. There were even rumors, never confirmed or denied, that once a guess circulated broadly, the production staff reedited subsequent episodes to strip out elements they knew the spoiler community was looking for. After all, the late episodes were still being cut as the early ones aired. Burnett liked to talk about *Survivor* as a psychological experiment to see how people would react under extreme circumstances. Was he also playing an experiment with his audience to watch how an information society would respond to misdirection?

By the sixth season, there was a growing sense that Burnett was losing interest in the spoilers, much as a segment of the audience was losing interest in the series. As one fan grumbled, "I want CBS to play the game. They are not playing the game." If ChillOne was telling the truth, then security on the *Survivor* production site was getting unforgivably sloppy. Or, more optimistically, the fans would have pulled off a coup for which the series might never recover. As one fan exclaimed, "Picture what a fine panic such a thing might cause!"

If ChillOne was lying, if ChillOne was a plant or, even better, if Burnett himself was going undercover on the boards, that would be the producer's biggest stunt ever. One Suckster explained: "CBS would never allow accidental information to come into the hand of a lay person. They are smart enough to hide it. Say what you will but there IS a direct connection between Chill and CBS." Others went further: "C1 may very well play the role of puppetmaster that guides us merrily along until the unexpected happens. Afterwards, there may be more planted spoilers, false leaks and doctored evidence unveiled to throw new curves into the mix. Ultimately, I'll be thrilled if MB and CBS have taken the reins in an effort to 'work' the spoiler community once again."

By the final weeks of the season, the rumors and theories had reached gargantuan proportions. One side was embracing a fantasy of the producers engaging in some form of cloak and dagger theatrics. The other side was embracing a fantasy of finally beating the "Evil Pecker" at his own game.

One of the most outrageous theories was that ChillOne was Rob, who had been an active poster on the boards before he was chosen as a contestant on the series. The fan community saw Rob as one of their own, sent in to enliven the sixth season, with his witty comments and dirty tricks. He seemed more interested in producing a fan-friendly drama than in winning the game. What if he had taken all of it a step farther and was manipulating the boards just as he was manipulating the other players? Rob certainly knew about the rumors and is said to have wanted to wear an "I am ChillOne" T-shirt at the *Survivor* reunion broadcast as a joke.

There is a long history of interaction between the fans and the *Survivor* contestants, many of whom became active participants on the boards, sometimes under their own name, sometimes under assumed names, once they were booted. Contestants read the fan boards to see how they were coming across on the air. Fans fired off e-mails to several former contestants as they sought to confirm the ChillOne posts, asking them questions about how the production process worked. Deena, one of the other *Survivor: Amazon* contestants, acknowledged, after the fact, that she had followed the ChillOne debates with great interest and threw her own wrench into the discussion: "Pretty good spoilers if you ask me, and it was a little disappointing because here I am under contract not to open my mouth and somebody already is. I think this board as a whole, would have liked this season much more if there had been no ChillOne. As to the mysterious boat driver . . . never saw anybody like the description given. Production members, those that have contact with us, are generally repeaters and those who have gained the supersecretpass."

Others were less romantic in their theories, continuing to suspect that they were dealing with a garden-variety hoax: "When will you learn? How many times has a mysterious new person shown up out of the blue to post spoilers? These 'super spoilers' are always huge fans of the show who know lots of info and have lots of insight about previous incarnations of the series, but they just never bothered to ever post on any message board until this amazing spoiler just fell into their lap." The most common reference point there was the "Uncle Cameraman" exploit a few seasons back. A young poster had claimed that his uncle was a cameraman and had started telling him things to watch for. He posted a list of the boot order and had the good fortune to get the first several right, including some rather unlikely twists of fate. He developed something of a following before his "uncle" was revealed to be a fabrication. "Uncle Cameraman" had become a running joke in the spoiling community, so ChillOne's source quickly got labeled "Uncle Boatman."

There had been lots of hoaxes—some of which had enough good information to make the bad data plausible, at least for a little while. Some posted hoaxes to get attention, some because they hated the spoilers and wanted them to waste their time, some to see if they could outsmart the spoilers. As one fan explained, "[Don't] assume that everyone comes to these boards for the same reason. Spoiling *Survivor* is a game. Spoiling the *Survivor* spoilers is a game. Planting fakes to see how long they go is a game. Spoiling certain elite spoiling groups is a game. . . . Many people come to play at this big wide open amusement park, and some of them could be playing with you."

The challenge was to construct a hoax that was plausible enough to get past the initial screening and occupy attention over a longer period of time. In the beginning, it was enough to claim to have a list of the names of the contestants and some explanation of how you got it. Soon, you had to produce names of real people who could be located using search engines, and those real people had to match the profile of the series. You had to weave into your list the names of some of the folks the spoilers had already outed so that it confirmed the group's consensus. After a while, people were producing fake photographs or; in some cases, photographs taken out of context. As one post explains, "It's like a chess game. Hoaxer makes the first move. If it's bad, it's checkmate very quickly. Others, like this thread, are a bit more challenging and take longer to play out."

If ChillOne was a hoax, he was a very good one. As one board member explained, "To concoct all this and create all the component pieces would be a lot of work and quite hard to do. Creating complicated lies and then sustaining them for weeks under interrogation is very hard. Keeping track of lies and inventing additional layers of lies to 'substantiate' the big lies is just a very difficult task."

As for ChillOne, after several weeks of such abuse, he threw up his hands: "My information is out there. Read into it as much as you like. Choose to believe what you like, choose to not believe what you like. Poke holes in that which you desire. Pat me on the back as you see fit. This is all fine by me. I heard what I heard." But he never really went away. By the next day, he was in there again, taking on all challengers, and he stuck it out to the bitter end.

Collective Intelligence and the Expert Paradigm

As more and more of his claims came true, the focus shifted away from discrediting ChillOne. The more accurate he was, the angrier it made some people. He hadn't "spoiled" the season; he "ruined" it. These were fundamental questions: Was spoiling a goal or a process? Was it an individual sport, in which contestants won bragging rights based on nailing information, or a collaborative sport, in which the team rejoiced in its collective victory? As one participant grumbled, "We have turned spoiling into a non-cooperative game. . . . 'Winning' means spoiling the whole season; hiding how you know about it and making others second guess you all season so you can humiliate them. ChillOne won. Everybody else lost."

From the start, sourcing — getting information from direct and often unidentified sources — had been a controversial practice. Snewser had an inside source, for example, which allowed him to post the results of the show a few hours before airtime; it was there if you wanted to read ahead, but it didn't get in the way of the group's deliberations until the last possible minute. Sourcing was a game only some could play; it depended on privileged access to information, and since the sources couldn't be revealed, sourced information was not subject to meaningful challenge and disconfirmation. Wezzie and Dan had made a specialization out of tracking down the locations. Not everyone has access to satellite data. Not everyone could play the game the way they did. But, ultimately, what they brought to the group was shared knowledge that could fuel a range of theories and speculation and that other group members could mine as they needed in the collaborative process of spoiling. By contrast, other forms of "spoiling" — making guesses based on weight loss or facial hair, reading the editing patterns of episodes, or interpreting

Monitoring Big Brother

Survivor is not the only reality television series whose fans and followers formed large-scale collaborative knowledge communities to unearth secrets, nor was it the only series where such efforts resulted in an antagonistic relationship between producers and consumers. Endemol, the Dutch production company that controls the worldwide *Big Brother* franchise, saw the Internet as an important dimension of its production and promotion strategy. The Web site for American *Big Brother* attracted 4.2 million visitors during its first season. Hard-core *Big Brother* fans paid to watch the action unfold in the household 24/7 throughout the entire run of the series with multiple webcams showing interactions in different rooms of the house. If the challenge of spoiling *Survivor* was a scarcity of officially released information, the challenge of *Big Brother* was that there was simply too much information for any given viewer to consume and process. The most hard-core consumers organized into shifts, agreeing to monitor and transcribe relevant conversations and posting them on discussion boards.

Fans regard the broadcast version as a family-friendly digest of the much racier and more provocative Web feed, and they are drawn toward talking about things they know were hidden from people who watch only the televised content. Season Three's resident sexpot, Chiara, naïvely tried to create a "secret code" that would allow her and the other "houseguests" to talk about personal matters without being exposed to the Internet voyeurs. Unfortunately, she worked out the code while being Webcast, generating much bemusement among the fan base, until the producers called her aside and explained the error in her logic. Subscribers complained, however, when the producers cut away at key moments—notably competitions, voting, and discussions central to the game play—so that they could hold content in reserve for the actual television series.

In the first season, the fans pushed further, seeking to alter the outcome of events in the house by breaking through the wall of silence that separated contestants from the outside world. A group calling itself the Media Jammers, which spun from discussions of the series on Salon.com, sought to get information into the *Big Brother* house by throwing messages contained in tennis balls into the yard, by shouting through megaphones, and by hiring airplanes to fly streaming messages over the production site. They wanted a mass walkout of all the contestants midseason to "raise awareness of the abuses the producers have committed against the contestants, the families, and the viewers of the show." The viewers could monitor the impact of their efforts on the "houseguests" as the producers called them (or the "hamsters" as the fans did) using the live Internet feed. They could coordinate their efforts via Internet chat groups and come up with real-time tactics even as they watched the producers trying to shield the show's participants from their messages.

Pam Wilson has offered a detailed account of what she calls "narrative

comments by Mark Burnett or Jeff Probst —enabled collective participation. Everyone could play, contribute their expertise, apply their puzzle-solving skills, and thus everyone felt like they had a stake in the outcome.

We might understand this dispute in terms of the distinction between Pierre Lévy's notion of collective intelligence and what Peter Walsh has described as "the expert paradigm."[16] Walsh argues that our traditional assumptions about expertise are breaking down or at least being transformed by the more open-ended processes of communication in cyberspace. The expert paradigm requires a bounded body of knowledge, which an individual can master. The types of questions that thrive in a collective intelligence, however, are open ended and profoundly interdisciplinary; they slip and slide across borders and draw on the combined knowledge of a more diverse community. As Lévy notes, "In a situation in flux, official languages and rigid structures do nothing more than blur or mask reality."[17]

This may be one reason why spoiling is so popular among college students; it allows them to exercise their growing competencies in a space where there are not yet prescribed experts and well-mapped disciplines. Shawn, for example, told me that he saw a strong connection between spoiling and the skills he was trying to cultivate as an undergraduate history major: "I like to dig. I like to look at primary source information. I like to find official manuscripts of an event.

I like to find out who were the people there, what did they see. I want to hear it from them. That's part of my love of spoiling. I like to dig to the bottom. I like it when people don't just say, 'here's who gets booted—here you go,' but elaborate a little bit about where they get their information."

Second, Walsh argues that the expert paradigm creates an "exterior" and "interior"; there are some people who know things and others who don't. A collective intelligence, on the other hand, assumes that each person has something to contribute, even if they will only be called upon on an ad hoc basis. Again, here's Shawn: "The people work together, put their heads together, in the absence of one person with inside info. . . . There are little tips which accumulate often during the week before the show. The group of spoilers have to figure out which ones are credible and which ones are wishful thinking or outright false." Someone might lurk for an extended period of time feeling like they have nothing significant to contribute, and then *Survivor* will locate in a part of the world where they have traveled extensively or a contestant may be identified in their local community, and suddenly they become central to the quest.

activism," the effort of these viewers to shape the televised events:

A window of opportunity emerged for only a brief period of time, allowing for the invasion of a slickly produced corporate television game show by amateur narrative terrorists whose weapons were clever words rather than bombs. The intervention could perhaps only have happened once, during a period of technological and programmatic flux, when the format was new, the formula was flexible, the unscripted narrative was emerging from the psyches of the not-yet-jaded improvisational players, the events were being closely followed around the clock by avid on-line viewers, and the Hollywood set was relatively unprotected.[1]

The effort was surprisingly effective, forcing the contestants to rethink their affiliation with the series, and the network to periodically shut down the live feed as it was trying to thwart a full-scale revolt.

[1] Pamela Wilson, "Jamming *Big Brother*: Webcasting, Audience Intervention, and Narrative Activism," in Susan Murray and Laurie Ouellette (eds.), *Reality TV: Remaking Television Culture* (New York: New York University Press, 2004), p. 323. See also Joan Giglione, "When Broadcast and Internet Audiences Collide: Internet Users as TV Advocacy Groups," paper presented at Media in Transition 3 Conference: Television, MIT, Cambridge, Mass., May 3, 2003.

Third, the expert paradigm, Walsh ar-gues, uses rules about how you access and process information, rules that are es-tablished through traditional disciplines. By contrast, the strength and weakness of a collective intelligence is that it is disorderly, undisciplined, and unruly. Just as knowledge gets called upon on an ad hoc basis, there are no fixed procedures for what you do with knowledge. Each participant applies their own rules, works the data through their own processes, some of which will be more convincing than others, but none of which are wrong at face value. Debates about the rules are part of the process.

Fourth, Walsh's experts are credentialized; they have gone through some kind of ritual that designates them as having mastered a particular domain, often having to do with formal education. While participants in a collective intelligence often feel the need to demonstrate or document how they know what they know, this is not based on a hierarchical system, and knowledge that comes from real-life experience rather than formal education may be, if anything, more highly valued here. ChillOne and the other "sources" were reinserting themselves into the process as "experts" (albeit experts by virtue of their experiences rather than any formal certification), and this threatened the more open-ended and democratic principles upon which a collective intelligence operates.

What holds a collective intelligence together is not the possession of knowledge, which is relatively static, but the social process of acquiring knowledge, which is dynamic and participatory, continually testing and reaffirming the group's social ties. Some said that having Chill-One tell them the final four before the season had really begun, before they had a chance to get to know these contestants and make their own predictions, was like having someone sneak into their house and unwrap all of their Christmas presents before they had a chance to shake and rattle them to try to guess what might be inside.

For many others, getting the information was all that mattered. As one explained, "I thought the name of the game was spoiling. . . . The fun is trying to find out how the boots go down by whatever means we can, isn't it?" Many claimed that it intensified their pleasure—being in the know about the secret—and watching the really silly guesses the uninformed were making on the official CBS Web site, where Jenna and Matthew were way down in the pack of likely winners. Others argued that this advanced information shifted the way they watched the series: "If C1 has successfully spoiled this installment of *Survivor*, the fun part is trying to figure out how the hell it will happen! It is the detective in us that not only wants to know what will happen, when it will happen, and how and why it happens." ChillOne, they argued, had given them a new game to play just as they had started to tire of the old one, and, as such, they predicted he would be a "shot of adrenaline" for the whole spoiler community, keeping the franchise fresh and new for another season or two.

The question was whether, within a knowledge community, one has the right to *not* know—or more precisely, whether each community member should be able to set the terms of how much they want to know and when they want to know it. Lévy speaks about knowledge communities in terms of their democratic operations; yet the ability for any member to dump information out there without regard to anyone else's preferences holds a deeply totalitarian dimension. Historically, spoiler warnings had been a device to allow people to determine whether or not they wanted to know every bit of available information. ChillOne and his allies argued that such warnings were not needed here, since the whole purpose of the group was spoiling, and yet, telling the answers cut off the game that many other group members wanted to play. In any case, this argument assumes that the information ChillOne unearthed would stay within the spoiling community.

Increasingly, spoiled information is finding its way into more and more public discussion forums, where it is picked up by mainstream news outlets. *New York Times*'s reporter Emily Nussbaum wrote about this phenomenon as "the End of the Surprise Ending," suggesting that this scurry to track down all available information and the accelerated circulation of that data across many different discussion lists was making it impossible for networks to keep secrets or for consumers to watch cult shows without knowing what is going to happen next. As she explains, "Shows are becoming more like books: If you want to know what happens later on, just peek at the last page. . . . It's an odd wish—for control of the story, for the chance to minimize your risk of disappointment. With spoilers in hand, a viewer can watch the show with distance, analyzing like a critic instead of being immersed like a newbie. . . . But the price for that privilege is that you never really get to watch a show for the first time."[18] ChillOne's critics would suggest that the problem extends beyond this: if you want to participate in the ongoing life of this community, you have to accept this knowledge whether you want it or not. Spoiling—at least within *Survivor* fandom —has now moved decisively from a game of puzzle-solving to one based on revelation of sourced information.

ChillOne stumbled onto his intel by accident; now the community was sending its own reporters. Since the *Survivor: Amazon* season, either ChillOne or someone else from the fan community had flown to the location while shooting was occurring and brought back a good deal of information about what took place. Two seasons later, a detailed list of all of the upcoming plot twists was dumped on Ain't It Cool News, a Web site with a traffic many, many times larger than Survivor Sucks. From there, it got picked up by *Entertainment Weekly* and a range of other mainstream publications. (This list turned out to be largely false, but who can say what will happen next time?) Suddenly, it was not just members of the spoiling community who had to decide whether they wanted to log on and read what someone like ChillOne had found by visiting the series location. Suddenly, every viewer and every reader of every publication ran the risk of learning more than they wanted to know.

As spoiling has moved more and more into the public eye, it has moved from a fun game that Mark Burnett occasionally liked to play with a small segment of his audience to a serious threat to the relationship he wanted to construct with the mass audience of his series. As Burnett told an interviewer, "It [spoiling] is what it is as long as it doesn't affect ratings. There may be 5000 people on the Internet but there are some 20 million viewers and they don't spend their time reading the Internet."[19] In and of itself, spoiling represents an extension of the pleasures built into the series. The producers want us to guess what is going to happen next, even if they never imagined teams of several thousand people working together to solve this puzzle. In the next chapter, we will see how the desire to build a community around such programs is part of a corporate strategy to ensure viewer engagement with brands and franchises. Yet, pushed to its logical extreme, spoiling becomes dangerous to those same interests, and they have begun using legal threats to try to shut it down. At the start of the eighth season, Jeff Probst told a reporter for the *Edmonton Sun*, "The Internet and the accessibility to information have made it very difficult to do shows like *Survivor*. And it wouldn't surprise me if ultimately it led to the demise of our show at some point. Sooner or later, you cannot combat people who betray you. We have a crew of 400 people, and everybody tells somebody something. I definitely believe that. Once you spread information like that and there's money to be made or fame to be had—'Hey, I know something you don't know, listen to this'—all we can do, honestly, is counter it with our own misinformation."[20] And the producers are not the only ones angered by such efforts to track down information at the source. Wezzie, who has herself participated in on-location scouting, wrote to me,

Soon (On Sept 16), the next *Survivor: Vanuatu* premieres. But, the boards feel different this time around. . . . They're D-E-A-D. I've kept a location-information thread going for the past few months with discussions about the environment and cultural traditions of Vanuatu and Dan put up some great maps, but that's about all that has been happening on the boards. The Internet fans are bored, angry and disinterested. As a result of Chill-One's (and Snewser of SurvivorNews) boot lists, *Survivor*'s most avid fans, the internet community, no longer seems interested in discussing the show. 'Spoiler free' boards and forums have sprung up but they are lightly visited. . . . Hopefully, interest will pick up once the show premieres. I wonder if CBS and SEG are happy that lethargy has set into the Internet community . . . or worried."[21]

Earlier, I described these emerging knowledge cultures as defined through voluntary, temporary, and tactical affiliations. Because they are voluntary, people do not remain in communities that no longer meet their emotional or intellectual needs. Because they are temporary, these communities form and disband with relative flexibility. Because they are tactical, they tend not to last beyond the tasks that set them in motion. Sometimes, such communities can redefine their purpose. Insofar as being a fan is a lifestyle, fans may shift between one series and another many times in the history of their affiliation. Yet, as a fan community disbands, its members may move in many different directions, seeking out new spaces to apply their skills and new openings for their speculations, and in the process those skills spread to new communities and get applied to new tasks. ChillOne's intervention no doubt shortened the life of the *Survivor* spoiling community, yet he merely sped up what was going to be an inevitable decline in interest. Once the game had been played through a few times, the members were going to seek out new avenues for their practice.

We can see such knowledge communities as central to the process of grassroots convergence. To be sure, as we will see in the next chapter, the producers wanted to direct traffic from the television show to the Web and other points of entry into the franchise. Those various points of contact became opportunities to promote both the series and its sponsors. Yet, fans also exploited convergence to create their own points of contact. They were looking for ways to prolong their pleasurable engagement with a favorite program, and they were drawn toward the collaborative production and evaluation of knowledge. This bottom-up process potentially generated greater interest in the series, amplifying these fans' investment in the aired material. But, insofar as it interfered with or reshaped the informational economy around a series, it also threatened the producer's ability to control public response.

What we need to keep in mind here and throughout the book is that the interests of producers and consumers are not the same. Sometimes they overlap. Sometimes they conflict. The communities that on one level are the producer's best allies on another level may be their worst enemies. In the next chapter, we will reverse perspectives—looking at the audiences of reality television from the vantage point of program producers and advertisers. In this way, we will come to understand how entertainment companies are reappraising the economic value of fan participation.

2

Buying into *American Idol*

How We Are Being Sold on Reality Television

Who would have predicted that reality television series, such as *Survivor* (2000) and *American Idol* (2002), would turn out to be the first killer application of media convergence—the big new thing that demonstrated the power that lies at the intersection between old and new media? Initial experiments with interactive television in the mid-1990s were largely written off as failures. Most people didn't want to stop watching television just to buy the clothes one of the *Friends* (1994) was wearing. Few were interested in trivia quizzes flashing up at the bottom of the screen during sportscasts or James Bond movies. Critics argued that most of us simply wanted to sit back and watch television rather than interact with it. The current success of reality television is forcing the media industry to rethink some of those assumptions. The shift is one from real-time interaction toward asynchronous participation.

Few can argue with *American Idol*'s success. By the final weeks of its second 2003 season, FOX Broadcasting Company was receiving more than 20 million telephone calls or text messages per episode casting verdicts on the *American Idol* contestants.[1] This made the phone companies happy because they have been trying to find a way to get Americans more excited about text messaging, which hasn't taken off in the United States the way it has in Asia and northern Europe. Of the 140 million mobile phones in the United States today, only 27 million are being used for text messaging.[2] AT&T Wireless reported that roughly a third of those who participated in *American Idol* through text messaging had never sent a text message before.[3] As an AT&T spokesman explained, "Our venture with FOX has done more to educate the public and get people texting than any marketing activity in this country to date."[4]

American Idol commanded two of the top five time slots throughout the important May 2003 sweeps period. More than 40 million people watched the final segment of the final episode of *American Idol*'s second season. By the third season, FOX devoted 13.5 hours to *American Idol* during the crucial May sweeps period, representing nearly one quarter of their total prime-time schedule for the month.[5]

This made advertisers happy. As MediaCom chief executive Jon Mandel explains, "We know when people are watching a show they care about, they tend to watch commercials more. Unfortunately, there aren't that many shows people care about."[6] *American Idol*, based on the successful British series *Pop Idol*, was sold to FOX through an aggressive campaign by the Creative Artists Agency, which saw the series as an ideal match for their client, Coca-Cola, and its 12–24-year-old target audience.[7] And what a match it has been. For those of you without a television or a teenage offspring, *American Idol* is a showcase of unknown singers—some good, some very bad—from around the country. Each week, the finalists perform and the audience votes out one contestant. In the end, the surviving performer gets a record contract and a promotion deal. *Forbes* ranked *American Idol* as the most profitable of all reality series, estimating that it had netted the network more than $260 million in profits by the end of its third season.[8]

All of this really made the networks happy. Reality television programs hold their own during the summer months, when network viewership is traditionally at its lowest ebb. And, as importantly, reality television has been a savior as broadcast networks try to resist cable television's attempts to siphon away their core audience. In 2002, for the first time, the cable networks' combined share outstripped that of the broadcast networks. No given cable channel has had the power and reach of a CBS, NBC, or ABC, but year by year broadcast networks become less central to their viewership. Overall, television audiences in summer decline 8–10 percent, but the major networks lost 30 percent of their market in the summer of 2002.[9] Cable networks like Showtime or HBO use the summer months to launch new episodes of their hot sitcoms (such as *Sex and the City*, 1998) and dramas (such as *Six Feet Under*, 2001), pitting them against broadcast network reruns. Viewers tend to remain with cable once the fall season starts. So, the broadcast networks are countering by offering more original programming in the summer, with the less-expensive reality television programs becoming their best weapon. When they are successful, reality series generate as much or more buzz than the cable shows they are competing against and thus slow viewership erosion. Even if a reality series doesn't make ratings history, as the first seasons of *Survivor* and *American Idol* did, its lower returns are almost always better than the network would get on a rerun. The trade-off is that reality programs have a shorter shelf life and limited life-after-syndication, though they can represent significant sales when sold directly to consumers on DVD.

And this makes the media conglomerates happier still, since *American Idol* was from the start not simply a television program but a trans-media franchise. The show's first-season winner, Kelly Clarkson, signed to RCA Records and had an immediate number 1 hit single on the Billboard Hot 100, "A Moment Like This." The song went on to become the top-selling U.S. single for 2002. Kelly's initial singles got played more than 80,000 times on radio stations in 2002. An *American Idol* book made the best-seller list,[10] and the *American Idol* contestants played to sold-out houses on their nationwide concert tour. Production began im-mediately on a feature-length movie, *From Justin to Kelly* (2003), though the film ultimately generated low box-office returns.

Not everyone, however, was enchanted with *American Idol*'s success. Speaking for many critics of reality television, Karla Peterson ranted in the *San Diego Union-Tribune*:

> *American Idol* was not a dumb summer fling, but a conniving multimedia monster. Shameless product placement. Bloodless nostalgia. Incestuous corporate hype. Like the show's Stepford divas—who dutifully parroted every shriek, quiver and growl from the Mariah Carey catalog—*American Idol* has absorbed the sins of our debauched culture and spit them out in a lump of reconstituted evil. And because we were so dazzled by its brazen lack of redeeming qualities, we stepped over the mess and happily followed it over the abyss.[11]

Peterson is correct that *American Idol* was shaped at every level by blatant commercial calculations. Yet, her moral outrage doesn't take us very far toward understanding its appeal to the networks, advertisers, or consumers.

To understand *American Idol*'s success, we need to better understand the changed context within which American broadcasting is operating and the changed model of consumer behavior shaping programming and marketing strategies. We need to know more about what I am calling "affective economics." By affective economics, I mean a new configuration of marketing theory, still somewhat on the fringes but gaining ground within the media industry, which seeks to understand the emotional underpinnings of consumer decision-making as a driving force behind viewing and purchasing decisions. In many ways, affective economics represents an attempt to catch up with work in cultural studies over the last several decades on fan communities and viewer commitments. There is a crucial difference, however: the cultural studies work sought to understand media consumption from the fan's point of view, articulating desires and fantasies that were ill-served by the current media system; the new marketing discourse seeks to mold those consumer desires to shape purchasing decisions. While they are increasingly interested in the qualities of audience experience, the media and brand companies still struggle with the economic side of affective economics—the need to quantify desire, to measure connections, and to commodify commitments—and perhaps most importantly of all, the need to transform all of the above into return on investment (ROI). These bottom-line pressures often deflect attempts to understand the complexity of audience behavior even when such knowledge is desperately needed by companies that want to survive in the coming decades. Rather than rethinking the terms of their analysis, they are struggling to fit these new insights into familiar economic categories. It is still a world where what can be counted is what counts most.

Arguably, fans of certain cult television shows may gain greater influence over programming decisions in an the age of affective economics. From time to time, networks reprioritize certain segments of their audience, and the result is a shift in program strategies to more fully reflect those tastes—a shift from rural to urban viewers changed television content in the 1960s, a renewed interest in minority viewers led to more Afrocentric sitcoms throughout the 1990s, and a shift toward an emphasis on loyal viewers has been changing what reaches the air in the early twenty-first century. Fans are seeing more shows reflecting their tastes and interests reaching the air; those shows are being designed to maximize elements that appeal to fans; and those shows that fans like are apt to remain on the air longer because they are more likely to get renewed in borderline cases. Here's the paradox: to be desired by the networks is to have your tastes commodified. On the one hand, to be commodified expands a group's cultural visibility. Those groups that have no recognized economic value get ignored. That said, commodification is also a form of exploitation. Those groups that are commodified find themselves targeted more aggressively by marketers and often feel they have lost control over their own culture, since it is mass produced and mass marketed. One cannot help but have conflicted feelings because one doesn't want to go unrepresented —but one doesn't want to be exploited, either.

For years, fan groups, seeking to rally support for endangered series, have argued that networks should be focused more on the quality of audience engagement with the series and less on the quantity of viewers. Increasingly, advertisers and networks are coming to more or less the same conclusion. Marketers seek to shape brand reputations, not through an individual transaction but through the sum total of interactions with the customer—an ongoing process that increasingly occurs across a range of different media "touch points." They don't simply want to get a consumer to make a single purchase, but rather to build a long-term relationship with a brand. New models of marketing seek to expand consumers' emotional, social, and intellectual investments, with the goal of shaping consumption patterns. In the past, media producers spoke of "impressions." Now, they are exploring the concept of audience "expressions," trying to understand how and why audiences re-act to the content. Marketing gurus argue that building a committed "brand community" may be the surest means of expanding consumer loyalty and that product placements will allow brands to tap some of the affective force of the affiliated entertainment properties. For this reason, shows such as *American Idol* are being watched closely by advertisers, marketing companies, television networks, and trade press reporters, all eager to understand how corporate convergence strategies may be reshaping the branding process. Early evidence suggests that the most valuable consumers are what the industry calls "loyals," or what we call fans. Loyals are more apt to watch series faithfully, more apt to pay attention to advertising, and more apt to buy products.

For the moment, I want readers to bracket their anxieties about consumerism and their fear of Madison Avenue. I do not intend this chapter to be in any simple sense an endorsement of or apology for the changes that are taking place. My own view is that this emerging discourse of affective economics has both positive and negative implications: allowing advertisers to tap the power of collective intelligence and direct it toward their own ends, but at the same time allowing consumers to form their own kind of collective bargaining structure that they can use to challenge corporate decisions. I will return to this issue of consumer power in the concluding chapter of this book. Even if you want to criticize the way American capitalism works, you need to recognize that the models of marketing depicted in classic accounts, such as Vance Packard's *Hidden Persuaders* (1957), no longer adequately describe the way the media industries are operating.[12] Even if you believe that fan and brand communities lack the clout to significantly alter corporate behavior, you still need to understand the way participation works within this new affective economy so that you can direct criticisms at the actual mechanisms by which Madison Avenue seeks to reshape our hearts and minds.

At industry gatherings around the country, corporate visionaries and brand gurus are promoting what I am calling affective economics as the solution to a perceived crisis in American broadcasting—a crisis brought about by shifts in media technology that are granting viewers much greater control over the flow of media into their homes. Affective economics sees active audiences as potentially valuable if they can be courted and won over by advertisers. In this chapter, we will be looking more closely at the ways that advertisers and networks think about their audiences in the age of media convergence and the ways those assumptions about branding, audience commitment, and social viewing are shaping series such as *American Idol*. *American Idol* offers up a fantasy of empowerment—"America" gets to "decide" upon the next Idol. This promise of participation helps build fan investments, but it may also lead to misunderstandings and disappointments as viewers feel that their votes have not been counted.

"Impress Me"

An advertisement created several years ago for Apple Box Productions, Inc., depicts the new youth consumer: his straggling dishwater-blond hair hangs down into his glaring eyes, his mouth is turned down into a challenging sneer, and his finger is posed over the remote (fig. 2.1). "You've got three seconds. Impress me," he says.[13] One false move and he will zap us. No longer a couch potato (if he ever was), he determines what, when, and how he watches media. He is itinerant—free of commitments to any particular series, going where his fancy takes him.

The word "impress" serves double duty here, depending if it is read from the consumer's point of view or the marketer's. It refers to the consumer's search for something so "impressive" that he pauses his

relentless search for novelty. It also refers to the "impression" that is the unit
of measurement historically deployed by
the networks in their conversations with
potential sponsors—the raw number of
"eyeballs" watching a television program
at a specific moment in time. What interests me here is the way the cultural
and economic, and the consumer and
corporate, meanings intersect. How does
the viewer's search for compelling content translate into exposure to sponsored
messages?

Much fuss was made a few years back
about the ineffectiveness of banner advertising on the Web because the "click
through" rate was so low. Relatively few
people who saw the banner were following its link and purchasing the product.
If television advertising had been judged
by that same standard, it would have
been found to be equally ineffective. The
impression is not a measurement of how

Fig. 2.1. The advertising industry
depicts its toughest challenge: the
young male consumer as channel
zapper.

many people buy the product or even comprehend the message; it is
purely a measurement of how many people have the set tuned to a particular channel. The impression is an even looser measurement when
applied to other media. For example, the impressions created by a billboard are measured in terms of the sheer number of cars that drive by
a particular intersection. According to marketing researcher Robert Kozinets, "It is not only that the impression is a clumsy way to track
media insights. . . . The impression is a symptom of the larger business
misunderstanding about what can be tracked, understood, and related
back to particular investments."[14] Advertisers, however, are increasingly demanding accountability from media outlets for the degree of
actual exposure they receive and for the quality of relationship this
creates with their consumers. They want to understand how effective
different media are about getting their messages before their potential
buyers.

Just as the clumsiness of audience measurements have been exposed,

the networks have also witnessed a breakdown in viewer loyalty—
the problem posed by our shaggy-haired young friend. First, there has
been a proliferation of media options—a move from three major networks to a cable environment with hundreds of more specialized channels and the introduction of alternative forms of home entertainment,
including the Internet, video, DVD, and computer and video games.
Initially, the amount of time people spent consuming media each day
expanded as the range of media options grew, but this expansion could
only go so far given what a large portion of time the average consumer
spent engaged with entertainment content outside of work, school,
or sleep. Confronted with seemingly infinite variety, the average consumer settled into a pattern of watching ten to fifteen different media
outlets. Broadcast programming still commands a higher degree of loyalty than cable programming, but the major broadcast networks are
attracting a smaller slice of the pie as audience fragmentation continues. In the 1960s, an advertiser could reach 80 percent of U.S. women
with a prime-time spot on the three networks. Today, it has been estimated that the same spot would have to run on one hundred TV channels to reach the same number of viewers.[15]

As advertisers grow anxious about whether network programming
can reach audiences, they are diversifying their advertising budgets
and looking to extend their brands across multiple distribution outlets
that they hope will allow them to target a diverse selection of smaller
niche markets. As Sumner Redstone, chairman of Viacom, told *Businessweek,* "What advertisers buy is platforms to get their brand promoted, and we've got four platforms for them. We're everywhere,
because in this day and age you have to be where advertisers need
to be."[16] A researcher for Forrester Research summarized the trends:
"Monolithic blocks of eyeballs are gone. In their place is a perpetually
shifting mosaic of audience microsegments that forces marketers to
play an endless game of audience hide-and-seek."[17]

Next-generation technologies—especially the digital videorecorder
(DVR)—are enabling more and more consumers to skip commercials.
Right now, 43 percent of VCR-using households are skipping adverts,
and many in the media industry are terrified of what's going to happen when technologies such as TiVo, which Nielsen Media Research
president Susan Whiting calls "the VCR on steroids," becomes more
widespread.[18] Current users of digital video recorders scan through

commercials about 59 percent of the time.[19] This doesn't mean that 59 percent of users skip commercials; it means that the average consumer watches about 41 percent of the aired advertisements. *Advertising Age* reporter Scott Donaton explains: "As advertisers lose the ability to invade the home, and consumers' minds, they will be forced to wait for an invitation. This means that they have to learn what kinds of advertising content customers will actually be willing to seek out and receive."[20]

Rishad Tobaccowala, president of the media-buying group Starcom MediaVest, sparked panic at a gathering of television executives in 2002 when he made what turned out to be the premature prediction that the thirty-second commercial would be dead by 2005. FOX Television chairman Sandy Grushow argued that the networks are nowhere near prepared for such a development: "Not only will everyone have to get drenched, but struck by lightning before significant progress is made."[21] As network executives search for their umbrellas, product placements are the most oft-discussed alternative, though no one really believes they can replace the $8 billion spent each year on commercials. For this transformation to occur, Lee Gabler, co-chairman and partner of Creative Artists Agency, argued, "The biggest hurdle we have to go over . . . is the integration of the networks, the studios, the ad agencies, the advertisers, the talent agencies, and anybody else that's involved in this space. We must be able to sit down collectively and cooperatively to come up with a solution. Right now, the ad agencies are frightened about anybody getting in their space, the networks are in denial, and the advertisers don't have a solution."[22]

In this context, the American viewing public is becoming harder and harder to impress. The television industry is increasingly focusing on understanding consumers who have a prolonged relationship and active engagement with media content, who show a willingness to track down that content across the cable spectrum and across a range of other media platforms. Such consumers, they believe, represent their best hope for the future. This next-generation audience research focuses attention on what consumers do with media content once it has passed across their eyeballs, seeing each subsequent interaction as valuable because it reinforces their relationship to the series and, potentially, its sponsors. Responding to that demand, Initiative Media, a company that advises many of the Fortune 500 companies about their adver-

tising placement, advocates an alternative approach to audience measurement they call "expression."[23] Expression charts attentiveness to
programming and advertising, time spent with the program, and the
degree of viewer loyalty and affinity to the program and its sponsors.
Their concept of expression emerged through collaboration with the
MIT Comparative Media Studies Program. Expression may start at the
level of the individual consumer, but by definition it situates consumption within a larger social and cultural context. Consumers not only
watch media; they also share media with one another, whether this
consists of wearing a T-shirt proclaiming their passion for a particular
product, posting a message on a discussion list recommending a product to a friend, or creating a parody of a commercial that circulates on
the Internet. Expression can be seen as an investment in the brand and
not simply an exposure to it.

Lovemarks and Emotional Capital

Delivering the keynote address at *Advertising Age*'s Madison + Vine
conference on February 5, 2003, Coca-Cola president Steven J. Heyer
outlined his vision for the future relations between the advertising
("Madison") and the entertainment industries ("Vine"). His speech
offers a glimpse into the thinking of one of *American Idol*'s primary
sponsors.[24] Heyer opened by identifying a range of problems that
"demand a new approach to connecting with audiences" and force a
rethinking of the old mass media paradigm: "The fragmentation and
proliferation of media, and the consolidation in media ownership—
soon to be followed by a wholesale unbundling. The erosion of mass
markets. The empowerment of consumers who now have an unrivaled
ability to edit and avoid advertising and to shift day parts. A consumer
trend toward mass customization and personalization." Confronting
profound shifts in consumer behavior, Heyer then outlined what he
saw as his "convergence" strategy—the greater collaboration between
content providers and sponsors to shape the total entertainment package. The focus, he argued, should be less on the content per se than
on the "why, where, and how" the various entertainment media are
brought together and the relationship that gets brokered with the consumer. As he explained, "Imagine if we used our collective tool kit to
create an ever-expanding variety of interactions for people that—over

time—built a relationship, an ongoing series of transactions, that is unique, differentiated and deeper" than any the entertainment industry has offered before.

Heyer's speech evokes the logic of brand extension, the idea that successful brands are built by exploiting multiple contacts between the brand and consumer. The strength of a connection is measured in terms of its emotional impact. The experience should not be contained within a single media platform, but should extend across as many media as possible. Brand extension builds on audience interest in particular content to bring them into contact again and again with an associated brand. Following this logic, Coca-Cola sees itself less as a soft drink bottler and more as an entertainment company that actively shapes as well as sponsors sporting events, concerts, movies, and television series. This intensification of feelings enables entertainment content—and brand messages—to break through the "clutter" and become memorable for consumers: "We will use a diverse array of entertainment assets to break into people's hearts and minds. In that order. . . . We're moving to ideas that elicit emotion and create connections. And this speeds the convergence of Madison + Vine. Because the ideas which have always sat at the heart of the stories you've told and the content you've sold . . . whether movies or music or television . . . are no longer just intellectual property, they're emotional capital."

Kevin Roberts, the CEO Worldwide of Saatchi & Saatchi, argues that the future of consumer relations lies with

Product Placement and *The Apprentice*

Mark Burnett, the executive producer of *Survivor* and *The Apprentice* (2004), has been on the cutting-edge of experiments in brand integration. After finding networks highly resistant to his initial *Survivor* proposal, the producer agreed to help offset the anticipated costs of the production by preselling sponsorship, convincing companies such as Reebok to pay $4 million apiece for product placements during the series.[1] His second series, *The Restaurant* (2003), was fully funded by product placements from Mitsubishi, American Express, and Coors Brewing Company.[2] With *The Apprentice*, Burnett charged up to $25 million per company for a significant product placement, and in the process the series became a test site for a range of different approaches of linking brands and series content.[3]

How many different ways is *The Apprentice* involved in branding?

1. *The Brand as Protagonist*: Program host Donald Trump casts himself and his corporate empire as the series protagonists. In the course of the

[1] Ted Nadger, "The End of TV 101: Reality Programs, Formats, and the New Business of Television," in Susan Murray and Laurie Ouellette (eds.), *Reality Television: Remaking Television Culture* (New York: New York University Press, 2004).

[2] Wade Paulsen, "NBC's *The Restaurant* Funded Solely by Product Placement," *Reality TV World*, July 18, 2003, http://www.realitytvworld.com/index/articles/stor.php?s=1429.

[3] Michael McCarthy, "Also Starring (Your Product Name Here)," *U.S.A. Today*, August 12, 2004.

series, we visit his many different companies, meet his staff (as well as his fiancée), visit his apartment, and learn about his business philosophy. The contestants are vying for a chance to help run one of his projects, which is presented as if it were the greatest opportunity any young business person might aspire toward.

2. *The Brand as Taskmaster*: In the second season (Fall 2004), contestants were asked to design and market test toys for Toys 'R' Us and Mattel, to develop new ice cream flavors for Ciao Bella, to redesign the bottle for a new Pepsi product, to sell a new M&M candy bar on the streets, and to market a new Vanilla Mint toothpaste for Procter & Gamble. Procter & Gamble spokesman Bryan McCleary commented, "Having an entire episode dedicated to selling the benefits of this new product was a very appealing story line—the viewer actually ends up rooting for the brand to succeed."[4]

3. *The Branding Process as Entertainment*: On the September 23, 2004, episode, contestants demonstrated ways of linking brands and entertainment (circus acrobats and clowns, the New York Mets) to create buzz for the new Crest product. Other storylines centered on their efforts to produce spots that would promote recruitment by the New York Police Department or to peddle household goods on the Home Shopping Network.

4. *The Brand as Helper*: Frequently, the contestants consult with a range of smaller companies (such as the Alliance Talent Agency) who aid them in their tasks in return for exposure.

[4] "Sponsors Buy into Reality TV," Product Placement News, *ITVX*, December 6, 2004, http://www.itvx.com/iPageCount,2,ppnews.asp.

"lovemarks" that are more powerful than traditional "brands" because they command the "love" as well as the "respect" of consumers: "The emotions are a serious opportunity to get in touch with consumers. And best of all, emotion is an unlimited resource. It's always there—waiting to be tapped with new ideas, new inspirations, and new experiences."[25] Arguing that only a small number of customers make purchase decisions based purely on rational criteria, Roberts urges marketers to develop multisensory (and multimedia) experiences that create more vivid impressions and to tap the power of stories to shape consumer identifications. For example, Coca-Cola's corporate Web site (http://www2.coca-cola.com/heritage/stories/index.html) includes a section where consumers can share their own personal stories about their relationship with the product, stories that get organized around themes such as "romance," "reminders of family," "childhood memories," "an affordable luxury," "times with friends," and a "memory of home." These themes merge core emotional relationships with core promotional themes, helping people not simply to integrate Coca-Cola into their memories of their lives, but also to frame those memories in terms of the marketing pitch.

American Idol wants its fans to feel the love or, more specifically, the "lovemarks." Audience participation is a way of getting *American Idol* viewers more deeply invested, shoring up their loyalty to the franchise and its sponsors. This investment begins with the turnout of millions of would-be contestants at auditions held in stadiums and convention hotels around the country. Many more people watch the series than try out; many more try out than make the air; many more make the air than become finalists. But, at every step along the way, the viewers are invited to imagine that "it could be me or someone I know." From there, the weekly votes increase the viewer's engagement, building a strong allegiance to the individual performers. By the time the records are released, many of the core consumers have already endorsed the performers, and fan clubs are already involved with grassroots marketing. For example, fans of Clay Aiken, the runnerup on Season Two, turned their disappointment into a campaign to ensure that his album, *Measure of a Man* (2003), outsold first-place finisher Ruben Studdard's *Soulful* (2003). Clay's album sold more than 200,000 more copies than Studdard's in its opening week on the charts—though one suspects that the record executives would have been happy whichever way the sales contest went.[26] Coca-Cola, in turn, brands key series elements: contestants wait in the "red room" before going on stage; judges sip from Coca-Cola cups; highlights get featured on the official program Web site surrounded by a Coca-Cola logo; soft drink promotions reward tickets to the finales; Coca-Cola sends *Idol* performers to NASCAR races and other sporting events that it sponsors; and Coca-Cola's sponsorship figures prominently at the *American Idol* finalist's national concert tour.[27]

5. **The Brand as Prize:** In many cases, Trump rewards contestants with access to himself and his "things" or to luxury meals and services (such as a caviar feast at Petrossian's or jewelry from Graff's).

6. **The Brand as Tie-in:** Following an episode in which the contestants designed ice cream, viewers at home were able to order samples of the flavors online to serve at their next *Apprentice* theme party. Similarly, although they had not planned on producing a tie-in with the series, Mattel was so excited with the results of their episode that they eventually marketed the Mighty Morpher toy car that was designed by the contestants. J. C. Penney distributed a catalog of Levi jeans that was designed by one of the teams during another challenge.

7. **The Brand as Community:** Through a tie-in between *The Apprentice* and Friendster, fans asserted their affiliation with specific contestants, and the producers collected real-time data about audience response.

8. **The Brand as Event:** Trump launched a sweepstakes competition with Yahoo! Hot Jobs, whose 25k award is designed to encourage new initiatives. A sign for the service was mounted on top of the cab that took the dejected contestants away, and in one comic interstitial, the colorful Raj appeared as a taxi driver.

9. **The Contestants as Brand:** The female contestants were showcased modeling lingerie as "The Women of *The Apprentice*" in *Maxim* magazine.

10. **The Brand as Judges:** As the second season neared its finale, Trump allowed a range of executives from other companies, including Unilever HPC, PepsiCo., Bear Stearns, and

the New England Patriots, to help him to winnow down the finalists.

These examples scarcely exhaust the roles brands play in the series (and don't include the various ways **NBC** is using the series to revise its own brand identity). The temptation among media-savvy people is to dismiss *The Apprentice* as nothing but one big product place-ment, but this would not adequately explain its popularity. *The Apprentice* is popular because it's a well-made show, and the brand tie-ins work because they are linked to its core emotional mechanics. We care about the brands because they become the focus of con-tests or because they shape our identifi-cations with the characters. But, as a general rule, the reality shows that have gotten the highest ratings have been those that have had the most original and compelling formats.

Heyer spoke of a shift "away from broadcast TV as the anchor medium" and toward "experience-based, access-driven marketing" as the ideal means of reach-ing the emerging generation of consum-ers. Cokemusic.com further aligns the soft drink company with people's enjoy-ment of popular music, allowing for a range of different participatory and in-teractive options. Members can pay for downloads of popular songs or redeem coupons that allow them to download songs for free. Members can create their own music mixes, share them with one another, and receive ratings from other site visitors. Ratings points reward "deci-bels" that can be redeemed to purchase virtual furnishing for their "pads," allow-ing further customization and a deeper sense of belonging in the world of Coca-Cola. "Performers" develop reputations and followings, which provide emotional incentives for them to spend even more time working on their "mixes." More casual site visitors can participate in a range of quizzes, games, and contests. Cokemusic.com has become the third most popular Web site among teens, registering more than 6 million users who spend an average of forty minutes per visit. As Carol Kruse, the director of interactive marketing for the com-pany, explains, "They're having fun, they're learning about music, they're building a sense of community . . . and it's all in a very safe and friendly Coke environment."[28]

Brand loyalty is the holy grail of affective economics because of what economists call the 80/20 rule: for most consumer products, 80 percent of purchases are made by 20 percent of their consumer base. Maintaining the allegiance of that 20 percent stabilizes the market and allows companies to adopt an array of other approaches to court those who would make the other 20 percent of purchases.[29] Corporations are turning toward active consumers because they must do so if they are going to survive; some have learned that such consumers can be allies, but many still fear and distrust them, seeking ways to harness this emerging power toward their own ends.

Something of this ambivalence can be seen in Roberts's description of what he calls "inspirational consumers" or others call "brand advocates": "They are the ones who promote and advocate for the brand. The ones . . . who suggest improvements and refinements, who create websites and spread the word. They are also the people who act as moral guardians for the brands they love. They make sure the wrongs are righted and hold the brand fast to its stated principles."[30] Roberts acknowledges that these "inspirational consumers," individually and collectively, place demands on corporations, citing the example of the outcry when Coca-Cola sought to replace its classic formula with "New Coke" and was forced within two months to back off from that decision. Roberts argues that companies need to listen closely when these inspirational consumers speak—especially when they criticize a company decision. A company that loses faith with its "inspirational consumers," he argues, will soon lose its core market: "When a consumer loves you enough to take action, any action, it is time to take notice. Immediately."[31] Roberts praises companies that actively court such fans through, to continue the Coca-Cola example, hosting events and conventions where their collectibles are appraised and showcased. The first fan club for Coca-Cola formed in 1974, a grassroots effort by a small group of enthusiasts. Today, fan clubs operate in twenty-eight different countries around the world and host a global network of local and national conventions that the company uses to bring together and address its most dedicated consumers.

Roberts's advice about courting "inspirational consumers" is echoed across a range of other business best-sellers, such as Marc Gobé's *Emotional Branding: The New Paradigm for Connecting Brands to People* (2001), Matthew W. Ragas's *The Power of Cult Branding: How 9 Magnetic Brands Turned Customers into Loyal Followers (and Yours Can, Too)* (2002), and John Hagel III and Arthur G. Armstrong's *Net.Gain: Expanding Markets through Virtual Communities* (1997).[32] They point toward a world where the most valued consumer may be the one who is most passionate, dedicated, and actively engaged. Far from marginal, fans are the central players in a courtship dance between consumers and marketers. As one noted industry guide explains, "Marketing in an interactive world is a collaborative process with the marketer helping the consumer to buy and the consumer helping the marketer to sell."[33] This search for "inspirational consumers" is starting to impact the way television audiences are appraised and the ways advertisers think about selling products.

Zappers, Casuals, and Loyals

Industry insiders often deploy the distinction among zappers, casuals, and loyals: this distinction manages to blur together how, why, and what consumers watch. Zappers are people who constantly flit across the dial—watching snippets of shows rather than sitting down for a prolonged engagement. Loyals actually watch fewer hours of television each week than the general population: they cherry pick those shows that best satisfy their interests; they give themselves over fully to them; they tape them and may watch them more than one time; they spend more of their social time talking about them; and they are more likely to pursue content across media channels. Loyals watch series; zappers watch television. Loyals form long-term commitments; zappers are like the folks at cocktail parties who are always looking over their shoulders to see if someone more interesting has just entered the room. Casuals fall somewhere in between; they watch a particular series when they think of it or have nothing better to do. They generally watch it from start to finish but are more apt to wander away if it starts to bore them. They may be more likely to conduct conversations or do other household activities over the show rather than give it their full attention.

No given viewer is exclusively a loyal, a casual, or a zapper; most watch television in different ways on different occasions. The most discriminating viewer will zap around the dial in a hotel room or at the end of a hard day. And sometimes zappers get hooked into a series and watch it every week. Nobody knows for sure yet whether the new media environment has produced more zappers, casuals, or loyals. For one thing, A. C. Nielsen's continued focus on entire pro-

America's Army

In 1997, the National Research Council, acting as an adviser to the U.S. Defense Department, issued its own vision for convergence culture, which they called "Modeling and Simulation: Linking Entertainment and Defense." Recognizing that the consumer electronic entertainment sector was outpacing defense research in developing simulation and artificial intelligence techniques, the defense department sought ways to collaborate with industry to develop games that could help them to recruit and train a next-generation fighting force: "The DOD is interested in this capacity for large scale training

gram blocks rather than more microscopic units of time means that they have no real way of measuring zapping or, indeed, the fluctuating loyalties of more casual viewers.

Throughout much of the 1990s, industry analysts overstressed the significance of the zappers. For example, Phillip Swann asserts in his book *TV.Com: How Television Is Shaping Our Future,* "Few viewers today can sit through an entire program without picking up the remote and checking out another channel. . . . Today's viewer needs constant gratification: if she's not entertained or intrigued for any stretch of time, she will flip the dial."[34] Swann thinks interactive television should and will be designed for zappers. In Swann's future, variety and magazine shows will almost entirely displace dramas, and the few remaining series will be shrunk to thirty minutes or less. According to Swann, "[There will be] fewer occasions where people sit down and watch a show from beginning to end without interruptions. People will start watching TV shows the way they read books: a little at a time. . . . The concept of 'appointment television'—arranging to be home at a precise time to watch a particular program—will soon be a thing of the past."[35] Refusing to bow out just yet, the networks want to hold on to appointment viewing by constructing new forms of programming that demand and reward immediate attention, and they want to build up viewer loyalty by intensifying the affective appeal of their programs.

Industry research now suggests that

exercises; the games industry is interested in networked games that would allow hundreds or thousands of players to participate."[1] Some have seen this report as representing a major first step toward the establishment of what is being called the military/entertainment complex. Yet, the report acknowledged many of the same challenges to collaboration we have identified elsewhere in convergence culture: "The entertainment industry and DOD are two different cultures, with different languages, different business models, and separate communities of constituents.... Success will rely on sustained commitment from both sides—and from a shared belief that the benefits of collaboration are worth the costs."[2]

Responding to this report, people in the U.S. military began to explore how games could be used to speak to younger Americans who were alienated or bored by traditional approaches to recruitment. The military also wanted to tap the communities that emerged around games as a means of rebuilding the social connections between military and civilians at a time when most military volunteers came from a relatively narrow sector of the population. Colonel E. Casey Wardynski, the man who originated the *America's Army* project, explains:

> Whereas in the past a young American could gain insights into military service by listening to the recollections or the

[1] Unless otherwise noted, my discussion of *America's Army* draws upon Zhan Li, "The Potential of America's Army: The Video Game as Civilian-Military Public Sphere," Master's thesis, Comparative Media Studies, MIT, Summer 2003.

[2] All quotes in this paragraph are taken from National Research Council, Committee on Modeling and Simulation, "Modeling and Simulation: Linking Entertainment and Defense," Washington, D.C., 1997, http://www.nap.edu/html/modeling/.

advice of an older brother, an uncle, a father, or perhaps a neighbor, today opportunities for such insights are relatively scarce. To the extent that information about military service shapes the career plans of young Americans today, these decisions are influenced by movies, magazines, books, and advertising. . . . Consequently, it is not surprising that young Americans with little or no contact with Soldiers are less likely to include Soldiering as a potential career. To counter this situation, the game's originator reasoned that the Army would reduce search costs by framing information about Soldiering within the entertaining and immersive context of a game. . . . A game would provide virtual experiences and insights into the development, organization, and employment of Soldiers in *America's Army*.[3]

The *America's Army* project has the ambitious vision of developing itself as a general popular culture brand for all kinds of media, hoping to extend outward to include comic books, television series, youth organizations, perhaps even feature films, though the game will continue to be the hub for this brand identity. When they launched the project, they made a decision to brand *America's Army* separately from the U.S. Army brand, allowing it to develop independently as an entertainment property. What they have produced are hard-core fans of *America's Army* who may or may not be supporters of the U.S. military. *America's Army* rapidly became one of the most popular games on the market. By August 2003, almost 2 million registered users had played

loyals are much more valuable than zappers. According to a study done by Initiative Media, the average network program was identified as a "favorite series" by only 6 percent of its viewers. But, in some cases, as many as 50 or 60 percent of viewers may rank a program as their favorites. Early evidence suggests that these loyals have a higher rate of brand recall (a key concern of advertisers) and are much less likely to be lured away from the networks toward competing cable content (a key concern of programmers). Loyals are twice as likely to pay attention to advertisements and two to three times more likely to remember product categories than more casual viewers. And they are between 5 to 20 percent more likely to recall specific sponsors—not huge numbers, perhaps, but big enough that they can give a competitive edge to advertisers who consistently target shows with a high degree of viewer loyalty. Historically, networks ignored those fan bases in making decisions about renewing series, seeing fans as unrepresentative of the general public; but advertisers are increasingly realizing that they may be better advised investing their dollars behind shows that have a high favorability than shows that have high ratings. As this research impacts programming decisions, the media industry is trying to generate content that will attract loyals, slow down zappers, and turn casuals into fans.

At first glance, *American Idol* looks like it was designed for zappers. Each episode breaks down into bite-size units of only a

[3] E. Casey Wardynski, "Informing Popular Culture: The America's Army Game Concept," in Margaret Davis (ed.), *America's Army PC Game: Vision and Realization* (San Francisco: Yerba Buena Art Center, 2004), pp. 6–8.

few minutes' duration as each of the competing performers sings and is judged. To some degree, reality series are built up of "attractions," short, highly emotionally charged units that can be watched in or out of sequence. But the series is designed to support and sustain multiple levels of engagement.

American Idol is designed to pull in every possible viewer and to give each a reason not to change the channel. Many elements loyals find repetitive ensure the program's continued accessibility to casuals—things like the recaps of the previous episodes, the recurring profiles of the contestants, the rereading of key quotes from the judges' assessments. Each of these segments reorients casuals to the contest's basic mechanics or provides the background that's needed to appreciate the dramatic conflicts in that night's episode. As they move into their final weeks and more casuals are drawn into the snowballing phenomenon, *American Idol* and many other reality shows may devote an entire episode to the season's highlights, designed to provide an easy entry point. Beyond this, each episode is constructed to allow a satisfactory entertainment experience. In *American Idol*, each Tuesday night episode includes performances by all of those contestants still in the competition. Each episode also includes a cliffhanger, so *American Idol* viewers are encouraged to tune in the following night to see how the voting went. These unresolved elements are intended to pull casuals toward a more committed relationship.

over 185 million ten-minute missions. In 2004, the marketing firm i to i Research surveyed high school and college students and found them overwhelmingly pro-military. Asked the source of their favorable impressions, 40 percent cited recent combat operations in Afghanistan and Iraq. Nearly as many—30 percent—cited their experiences playing *America's Army*.[4]

The U.S. Department of Defense wanted to use the game not simply to simulate military processes but also to inculcate values. Players are never to be rewarded for killing virtual American soldiers. Each player sees the members of his or her own team as American and the opposing team members as enemies. Fragging teammates would be grounds for immediate expulsion from the game. On the other hand, the game was designed to reward players with increases in rank and access to more advanced missions when they respect the military codes of conduct.

The game has attracted international interest—42 percent of visitors to the official *America's Army* Web site log in from outside the United States (though some of these are probably service personnel and their families stationed overseas). There are organized groups of players and brigades, representing a range of different nationalities, including some from parts of the world that have traditionally been regarded as enemies. The game's designers advocated successfully for the suspension of many military regulations restricting the expression of opposing ideas to create a robust forum—which they call a "Virtual Community of Interest in Soldiering." There, civilians and service men

[4] Wagner James Au, "John Kerry: The Video Game," *Salon*, April 13, 2004, http://www.salon.com/tech/feature/2004/04/13/battlefield_vietnam/.

and women could talk openly about the values of military service and even debate the merits of current military conflicts. The forum site initially offered links to a diverse array of alternative sources for information about the war, including the controversial Arabic news station Al Jazeera. A site design in 2004 seemed calculated, at least in part, to reduce the overtly political content, cutting back on news links and discussion forums that had become centers for debates about America's continued military presence in Iraq.

Seeking to deploy ambassadors of the same, military issues gold stars to any veteran or active soldier who joined the game, and these players enjoy such a high level of prestige in the community that some players try to pass themselves off as veterans just to grab a little of that respect. The veterans take great pleasure in exposing such hoaxes, drilling the players with questions that only someone who had served would know, and through this process, they assert the importance of real-world experience over game-play fantasies.

As the Iraqi war began, some players said they were playing the game and watching the news at the same time, trying to achieve through fantasy what they hoped would happen in reality. When several Americans were taken prisoner by the Iraqi army, many organized efforts staged hostage rescue scenarios that engaged in Hollywood-style fantasies of how one might get these men and women back safely. Some members of the veterans' clans shipped out to serve in the Middle East but remained in contact with the other players in their community, sending back home front-line perspectives on what was unfolding. As the death tolls mounted, some of the veterans and service-personnel groups gathered

As for loyals, perhaps the single most important factor separating reality from other kinds of nonfiction programming is serialization. Talent contests are a well-established genre in American broadcasting, going back at least as far as *Major Bowles' Original Amateur Hour* on radio in the 1930s. What *American Idol* added to the mix, however, was the unfolding of the competition across a season, rather than in the course of a single broadcast. Or to be more accurate, serialized talent competitions had already sprung up on cable networks, such as MTV and VH1, but FOX brought them over to the major networks and made them prime-time entertainment. In serializing the talent competition, *American Idol* is simply following a trend that runs across all contemporary television—a movement away from the self-contained episodes that dominated broadcasting for its first several decades in favor of longer and more complicated program arcs and more elaborate appeals to series history. Serialization rewards the competency and mastery of loyals. The reason loyals watch every episode isn't simply that they enjoy them; they need to have seen every episode to make sense of long-term developments.

Every reality series starts out with a cast larger than most audience members can grasp, and most of those characters will receive relatively limited airtime. As the winnowing process occurs, however, certain characters will emerge as audience favorites, and a good producer anticipates those interests and rewards them by providing those characters with

more airtime. Viewers move from thinking of the characters as generic types
toward thinking of the characters as particular individuals. Viewers get to know
the contestants, learn their personalities,
their motives for competing, their backgrounds, and, in some cases, other mem-
bers of their families. In *American Idol,* viewers watch them improve or
crash and burn. This may be why *American Idol* has become such a powerful marketing tool for launching the careers of young performers compared to earlier televised talent competition.

**together in the game world not to fight,
but to talk through their feelings of anx-
iety and loss. *America's Army,* thus, may
be more effective at providing a space
for civilians and service folk to discuss
the serious experience of real-life war
than providing a vehicle for propaganda.**

Talk among Yourselves!

There has historically been a tendency within industry discourse to
focus either on mass, undifferentiated audiences (of the kinds that get
measured by the ratings system) or on individual consumers. Marketing researchers now speak about "brand communities," trying to better
understand why some groups of consumers form intense bonds with
the product and, through the product, with fellow consumers. In one
study that helped to define the concept of "brand community," marketing professors Albert M. Muniz Jr. and Thomas C. O'Guinn concluded,
"Brand communities carry out important functions on behalf of the
brand, such as sharing information, perpetuating the history and culture of the brand, and providing assistance [to other users]. They provide social structure to the relationship between marketers and consumer. Communities exert pressure on members to remain loyal to the
collective and to the brand."[36] These brand ethnographers research specific groups of highly committed consumers (such as Harley-Davidson
riders, Apple Computer users, or Saturn drivers) or what they call
"brandfests," social events (either commercially sponsored or grassroots) that pull together large numbers of consumers.

As these brand communities move online, they are able to sustain
these social connections over long periods and thus to intensify the role
the community plays in their purchasing decisions; they expand the
number of potential consumers who interact with the community and
help to move casual consumers into a more intense engagement with
the product. Marketing professor Robert Kozinets sees these online

consumption communities, whether focused on a single product or a cluster of related products (coffee, wine, cigars), as places "where groups of consumers with similar interests actively seek and exchange information about prices, quality, manufacturers, retailers, company ethics, company history, product history, and other consumption-related characteristics."[37] In short, they are something like Pierre Lévy's knowledge communities applied to consumer decision making. Participation within such communities does not simply reaffirm their brand affiliation but also empowers these groups to assert their own demands on the company. As Kozinets explains, "Loyal consumers are creating their tastes together as a community. This is a revolutionary change. Online, consumers evaluate quality together. They negotiate consumption standards. Moderating product meanings, they brand and rebrand together. Individuals place great weight on the judgment of their fellow community of consumption members. . . . Collective responses temper individual reception of marketing communications. . . . Organizations of consumers can make successful demands on marketers that individual consumers cannot."[38]

Just as the social dynamic of these online communities reaffirms and/or redefines their individual members' brand loyalties, a similar social dynamic shapes the ways people consume media and products within their families or with friends. A team of researchers from MIT's Comparative Media Studies Program and Initiative Media joined forces to document audience response to the second season of *American Idol*.[39] The MIT team sent researchers into homes and dorm rooms to observe people watching television; we did one-on-one interviews with a range of different consumers; we did surveys through the official *American Idol* Web sites; and we monitored discussions within the fan community. The Initiative team ran large-scale surveys and focus groups and collected aggregate data from the official *Idol*-on-FOX home page. We wanted to better understand how people integrated the experience of watching *American Idol* into the rest of their social interactions.

The Initiative Media/MIT research team found that in almost every social space where *American Idol* was watched, viewers of different degrees of commitment were present.

In one family setting, for example, the two youngest children (girl, 9; boy, 7) were among the first into the family room for the start of *American Idol*; they generally watched the last few minutes of *Lizzie McGuire* (Disney, 2001) before turning the channel to FOX. As the program started, both routinely raised their voices to announce to those throughout the house that "it's starting!" As the opening segments began, they recalled last week's performances and made comments about what the judges are wearing or how their hair looks. By the end of the first segment, the mother had usually arrived and stood at the door. Typically, she would come and go for the first thirty minutes of the program, working in the kitchen or running up and down the stairs. Such distracted viewing is fairly common for women; even those fairly committed to the program must respond to competing demands on their attention in the early evening hours.[40] The father would typically enter the broadcast in progress, and the older daughter would only occasionally view the program, allowing other family members to bring her up to speed as needed. The son's attention would wander during the commercial break, and he would begin to zap around the dial, and they might miss the start of the next program segment unless the mother and daughter called him back to FOX on time. Finally, as the entire family was sitting in front of the television during *American Idol*'s recap in the last five minutes of the program, they would debate the contestant before the mother would call in the vote. The conversation never ended in disagreement, although in later weeks the young girl became more vocal about whom she expected to win, waffling between Ruben and Clay. The father took it all in and endorsed the family's choice based on the snippets of performance he saw in the recap.

Through family conversation, the loyals pulled the casuals into the fold and held on to the attention of the would-be zapper; they announced when the program was on and updated those who had missed segments. In the absence of such reinforcement, some of the family members probably would not return each week, yet even the most casual participants see watching the series as a family ritual. One of the effects of expanding audience participation is to give such families more different ways to engage with the content; discussing who to vote for becomes part of the viewing experience and provides an incentive for everyone to watch the recap if not the individual performances. Researchers have found that such shared rituals or mutual evaluations are central to the sense of affiliation members feel to the group, and it makes sense that similar rituals would be played out in individual households.[41] *American Idol* can become family entertainment because it lies at the intersection between youth and adult tastes, allowing everyone to show some expertise. Most of the contestants are in their teens or twenties. To broaden its focus, the show brings in aging pop stars as guest judges and coaches: Burt Bacharach, Billy Joel, and Olivia Newton-John appeal not to the kids who compete but to their parents' —or even their grandparents'—generation.

The researchers who observed college students watching *American Idol* in a dorm common area found similar patterns: different students had different investments in the various contestants and carried on debates from week to week about their relative merits. Catch phrases might be dropped ironically into the conversation. People who had missed some episodes could reenter the series with the help of their friends because they knew the rules of the competition and had some passing familiarity with the contestants. Some people wandered into the commons area with no prior plans of watching the series and got sucked in. The number of committed viewers grew week by week as the competition mounted and as watching the series became more central to the social life of the dorm community. Interestingly, the final episodes conflicted with final exams, so the group taped them, made a pact not to look at the results, and scheduled time to watch them together.

Across a range of studies, Initiative Media has found that different genres of entertainment provoke different degrees or kinds of social interactions. Drama viewers are the most likely to view alone, comedy viewers to view with family members, and reality viewers to view with friends. Demographically, 18–34-year-old viewers have the most varied habits, depending on program genre. Adults over 50 either view alone or with family, but rarely with friends, while 35–49-year-olds are most consistent, viewing all genres primarily with family members. People watching in groups pay more attention to the program content, are less likely to shift channels mid-broadcast, and are more likely to access program-related Web sites. Of course, as those viewers move onto the Web, some are choosing to discuss their interpretations and assessments of the programs via online fan communities. Social viewing, then, would ap-pear to be an important driver behind brand and content extension.

A survey of 13,280 *American Idol* viewers, conducted through the official FOX Web site, found that the majority of fans discovered the series on the basis of word-of-mouth and watched it regularly because other people they knew were also watching it. (On the zapper side of the equation, the same study found that significantly more viewers stumbled onto the series while channel surfing than tuned in consciously on the basis of prior awareness.) While historically men make the viewing decisions during the prime-time hours, only slightly more women (32 percent) than men (31 percent) said they started watching the show because other family members were watching it. Altogether, 78 percent of *American Idol* viewers surveyed said that they watched the show with family or friends, and 74 percent reported that they talked about the show with friends during the week between episodes.

Such conversations extended beyond the initial viewing group to friends, workmates, or more distanced relatives. As one respondent told us, "My mother lives in Africa, my aunt lives in Russia, but they are able to watch the show on the Armed Forces Network over the weekend. My other aunts, scattered about the country, will create tests and drop stupid hints that all come clear when they finally get to watch the show. It's a family viewing occurrence, which I don't usually have the opportunity to do." Even if they missed individual episodes, study participants made a conscious effort to keep up with developments to participate in casual conversations with peers and coworkers. Consequently, many more people know about *American Idol*, follow its development, and even get exposed to its marketing message than actually sit down and watch.

Phone companies, across the board, observed a marked increase in traffic on Tuesday nights following the broadcasts. In the third season's final week, Verizon reported an increase of 116 million calls, a 7 percent increase over a typical Tuesday, and SBC saw 100 million more calls, an 80 percent increase over a normal weeknight.[42] In all likelihood, this increase was not simply stimulated by the large number of people who were voting, but also indicates the number of people chatting about the program content.

How Gossip Fuels Convergence

One of the survey respondents captures the spirit of these conversations: "[Watching *American Idol*] helps me to relax because it gives me something to talk about with friends that doesn't affect our lives in any big way; therefore, it is an easy thing to discuss." Historically, gossip has been dismissed as "worthless and idle chatter," but over the past several decades, feminist scholars have begun to reappraise the place of gossip in women's community, and subsequent writers have extended it to talk about interactions within a much broader range of communities. Writing in 1980, Deborah Jones described gossip as "a way of talking between women in their roles as women, intimate in style, personal and domestic in topic and setting."[43] Gossip, she argued, allows women to talk about their common experiences, share expertise, and reinforce social norms. While the fluidity of gossip makes it difficult to study or document, Jones suggests that gossip is an important resource that women historically have used to connect their personal experiences within a larger sphere beyond their immediate domestic environment. The specific content of gossip is often less important than the social ties created through the exchange of secrets between participants —and for that reason, the social functions of gossip hold when dealing with television content. It isn't who you are talking *about* but who you are talking *with* that matters. Gossip builds common ground between participants, as those who exchange information assure one another of what they share. Gossip is finally a way of talking about yourself through critiquing the actions and values of others.

As cyberspace broadens the sphere of our social interactions, it becomes even more important to be able to talk about people we share in common via the media than people from our local community who will not be known by all of the participants in an online conversation. Into that space step the complex, often contradictory figures who appear on reality television. Reality television provides consumers with a steady stream of ethical dramas, as contestants are forced to make choices about whom to trust and what limits to set on their own behavior. Viewers can argue about whether Joe Millionaire picked the right woman or The Donald fired the right apprentice, whether it's OK to lie your way to success on *Survivor,* and whether Clay, Ruben, or Kimberley sang best on *American Idol.* In a focus group study of reality television viewers conducted by Initiative Media, 60.9 percent of the respondents said that the ethical conduct of the contestants was a central topic of their discussions around such series. By way of contrast, 67 percent discussed the outcomes, 35 percent discussed strategies, and 64 percent discussed personalities. Rather than being morally debasing, ethically dubious on-air conduct frequently encourages a public discussion of ethics and morality that reaffirms much more conservative values and assumptions. In a multicultural society, talking through differences in values becomes a mechanism by which different social groups can learn more about how they each see the world, so there is a real value in gossip that extends into virtual rather than face-to-face communities. The reality contestants put themselves forward to be judged by their audience; through their judgments, the audience members reaffirm their own shared values by expressing outrage over contestants' social transgressions, and they learn about their differences by sharing notes about how they respond to shared ethical dramas.

American Idol viewers debate whether the contest should be decided on the basis of "pure talent," or whether it is legitimate to draw on other factors, such as personality or appearance, which are often key to defining commercial success. Consider, for example, the self-righteous indignation expressed by one *American Idol* viewer who wrote to the CMS/Initiative Media research team convinced that we had a direct pipeline back to the producers. This message followed an episode where fan favorite and ultimate winner Ruben Studdard unexpectedly ranked near the bottom:

> Do you really think the American public believes for one second that Ruben could possibly be voted into the bottom? Ruben has never had one negative comment said about him nor has he ever not been excellent. He has never missed a tune. . . . It is very cruel to mislead these young people into trusting you are going to be honest and fair. This is a talent show isn't it? Hence the word TALENT SHOW. . . . So do the right thing and seriously look at who is counting those votes and maybe check to see if they actually know how to count. If you are rigging the show you will probably burn in hell for being so stupid. (A true and honest American).

What was striking to us about this comment, apart from its cynicism about the voting process, was its moral intensity, its firm belief that the outcome of a talent competition should be read in terms of questions of justice, honesty, and equity. Another respondent referenced her "responsibility" to monitor the results to see "whether America has chosen and voted fairly . . . whether or not America really votes based on real talents or just tits and asses."

Assessment is a two-part process: first, discussions about the performances, and then discussions about the outcomes. Among the most committed and socially linked members of a consumption community, these evaluative standards are arrived at collectively, just as the members of the family we described pooled their individual tastes to make a collective decision about who should win. Such a process tends to pull toward a consensus over time, and then, over a longer time, the consensus no longer seems to be something that was disputed or haggled over; it is the commonsense outcome. We can see this as part of the process through which collective intelligence generates shared knowledge. Some critics, such as Cass Sunstein, argue that this process of consensus formation tends to decrease the diversity of perspectives that any community member encounters; people tend to flock toward groups that share their existing biases, and over time they hear less and less disagreement about those core assumptions.[44] At the same time, this consensus-forming process increases the likelihood that these brand and fan communities will speak up when corporate interests cross the group's consensus. In the course of a season of *American Idol*, total consensus may not have been achieved, but most members of the online community saw Season Two as a contest between Clay and Ruben, making the buildup toward the season finale that much more powerful. The community expressed outrage, however, when voting went against the perceived consensus, as occurred one week when Ruben was almost bumped (the incident provoking the above response) or as occurred frequently throughout the third season.

Because the characters are real people whose lives continue beyond the series borders, viewers are left feeling like there is more and more they might know about them, which provides an incentive to track down additional information through multiple media channels. This search for the hidden "truth" of reality television is what motivated the spoiling described in chapter 2. The Initiative Media survey found that 45 percent of *American Idol*'s loyals went onto the Web in search of more information about the program, and it is generally agreed that reality television is one of the primary drivers of traffic to network Web sites.

These networks build upon synergies within the entertainment corporations to ensure that talk about their hit reality series continues throughout the week. The contestants are featured prominently on morning and late-night talk shows and on network-affiliated chatrooms. The results of at least the top-rated reality series are seen as news events that will be covered even by rival networks. In the case of *American Idol*, for example, *USA Today*, *Entertainment Weekly*, and AOL each conducted its own independent audience surveys designed to second-guess the likely results before they are aired on the network. Online gossip magazines, such as *The Smoking Gun*, have sought to tap public interest in the series, digging out old criminal records or divorce proceedings involving contestants. In some cases, reality series market access to exclusive content, which further expands the viewing experience. Given the pervasiveness and diversity of such publicity, any given fan is apt to know something his or her friends do not, thus creating an incentive to share knowledge. This publicity also has the effect of making some viewers more apt to want to watch the episodes as they are aired so they can avoid finding out the outcomes in a less dramatically compelling fashion. For other consumers, such coverage keeps their interest alive even if they are unable to watch some installments and makes it more likely they will tune in for the final episodes of a particular run.

Contesting the Vote

So far, we have focused our discussion on those factors that ensure viewer loyalty to *American Idol*, but as Heyer's speech suggests, sponsors are seeking to transfer viewer loyalty from entertainment properties onto their brands. The majority of the people our research team interviewed were acutely aware that *American Idol* was serving as a testing ground for branding strategies and were eager to offer their opinions about the experiments as they unfolded. Product placements and program-themed commercials became an acknowledged part of the *American Idol* phenomenon, something people, in some cases, tuned in to see—much as the Super Bowl has become as much a showcase for advertising as a sporting event. Coca-Cola spoofed the uncompromising honesty of judge Simon Cowell, depicting him as forced by a mobster to read an endorsement for Vanilla Coke; Ford created new musical segments each week featuring the program contestants; AT&T created a campaign that mimicked *Legally Blonde* (2001) and showed an airheaded teenager going around the country encouraging people to participate in the call-in voting process. Sponsors are not simply seeking the chance to advertise their products; they are seeking to brand the content so that the red of the *American Idol* set becomes inseparable from Coca-Cola's sponsorship of the series, so that the Ford spots featuring the contestants become part of the evidence fans mobilize in support of their favorite performers, and so that AT&T's text-messaging system becomes the preferred vehicle for voting.

Viewers are more accepting of product placements in reality programming than in any other genre (they are least comfortable with
product placements in drama, news, and children's programming).
Some are turned off by this hypercommercialism, but for others, recognizing marketplace interventions has become part of the "game": "I
find myself trying to pick out products placed in shows and get an a-ha
moment when I find one." Even those who claim not to watch commercials are drawn toward series-targeted spots: "You know what I
do in the commercial breaks? Refill my popcorn bowl. Go to the bathroom. Bake a cake. Sing a song. Dance a dance. I refuse to be made to
sit through that crap!!! However, I really like the Simon/Vanilla Coke
commercial." Even many of those who refused to watch the show because it was overcommercialized still accurately named its sponsors. In
some cases sponsors improved public perception of their brand, whereas others potentially damaged their standing. As one regular viewer
told our researchers, "Now I know for sure that AT&T Wireless and
Ford and Coca-Cola advertise with them, but it's to the point of being annoying and I want nothing to do with those particular brands
now." Others couldn't separate consumerism from their participation
in the series: "*Sigh* Yes, I purchased a sweatshirt from Old Navy
because Aiken wore it in the studio recording of 'God Bless the USA'
and I loathe Old Navy. Normally, I hate that kind of stuff." The early
evidence, however, suggests that as a general rule, the more invested
viewers became in *American Idol,* the more committed they became to
its sponsors.

Such a tight integration of advertising and content is not without its
risks, since the credibility of the sponsors became closely linked with
the credibility of the competition itself. Kozinets warns that participating in a consumption community heightens one's awareness of the consumption and marketing process and reaffirms feelings of resentment
if a company exploits that relationship. The collective voice speaks
louder and often more decisively than its individual members. Such
expressions reach the ear not only of the companies being challenged
but also of the mainstream media; consumer backlashes are increasingly being covered as "scandals," which puts further pressure on the
companies to respond. In some cases, Kozinets notes, the corporations,
angry over their loss of control, threaten or punish their most loyal consumers, undermining valuable relationships. Kevin Roberts argues that
companies need to see such scandals as opportunities to listen to and

learn from their most hard-core consumers, building up greater loyalty through their responsiveness rather than tearing it down through indifference or overreaction.

The down-to-the-wire contest between Clay Aiken and Ruben Studdard turned out to be almost as close as the 2000 presidential election, with the two finalists separated by a little more than a hundred thousand votes out of 24 million votes cast. The text-message votes all got through and were counted—several millions' worth—whereas millions of telephone callers faced endless busy signals. As one fan explained in our survey, "Hanging chads in Florida is nothing compared to this stupid voting procedure." Clay supporters were particularly vocal about the degree to which clogged phone lines made it impossible to get an accurate count, and some argued that the lines may have been ar-bitrarily restricted to ensure a close race. The *American Idol* producers had raised expectations about responsiveness to audience feedback and thus faced a backlash when they failed to meet those expectations. By the third season, inconsistencies in the voting made headlines in national newspapers, with the network forced to acknowledge that significant numbers of callers were not able to register their votes be-cause local phone lines were being flooded. The result was an uneven counting of votes from one region to another. For example, viewers in Hawaii, an area where there were relatively few people competing for access to the local connection, could have cast as much as a third of the total votes in the third season, an imbalance which some have argued accounted for the prolonged run of a Hawaiian contestant.[45] As the controversy intensified, the producers expanded voting hours and added more phone lines to try to lower public disappointment. An editorial in *Broadcasting & Cable* warned, "Viewer loyalty is hard to build and tough to maintain. . . . With AT&T one of the show's sponsors, FOX needs to go out of its way to avoid the appearance that it could be in cahoots with the phone company to drive as many calls as possible, whether or not they get through."[46] Despite such scrutiny, FOX has refused to release the actual vote counts, offering only partial information on a selective basis during the broadcasts. Many fans argue that such selective reporting makes it hard for them to put much faith in the reliability and impartiality of the process.

Complaints went beyond the voting mechanism to include concerns about how particular contestants were "pushed" by the judges and the producers, given higher prominence on the show and more supportive comments, or, in some cases, intentionally attacked to inspire audience backlash against the judging. Cynics saw the producers as more interested in generating controversial and compelling programming than in recognizing talent. Much as the spoilers sought to thwart Mark Burnett's efforts to keep the *Survivor* outcome a secret, the *American Idol* online community took pleasure in trying to read through the "mechanisms" by which the producers "engineer" the results. As one fan explained, "I like seeing Simon trying to figure out the power of saying evil things to create a backlash, and saying to a so-so performer that they are amazing."

For many, such efforts to shape public response were seen as an extension of the sponsor interference into program content. The performers, they argued, were becoming so "packaged" that they were no different from the other products being advertised. In some cases, the "Idols" became models who displayed new fashions, new makeup, and hair-styling products. Fans suggested this refashioning of their images was simply the first step in what would result in overprocessed versions of their performances when their albums were released.

This degree of anger suggests that product placements might be a double-edged sword—on the one hand, higher consumer awareness and, on the other, higher consumer scrutiny. Virtually every research participant had some criticism of the ways that commercialism tainted the series, complicating arguments which might see media-savvy marketers manipulating naïve and gullible consumers. Even loyals complained that the series was sometimes nothing more than a "merchandise machine."

These online communities gave "inspirational consumers" a place to talk about their resistance to these new forms of commercialism. In critiquing the results, fans often focused on the corporate interests they saw as shaping the outcome. Through this process, more economically conscious participants could educate others about the commercial structures shaping American broadcasting. In some cases, *American Idol* fans used the resources of these online communities to identify flaws in the voting system. This summary from one fan site suggests the sophistication with which they were collecting information:

> Most text messages go through—according to message board posts, websites maintained by the text messaging company, and through news arti-

cles. But viewers pay a small fee to send a vote in text—so paying for the vote does give you leverage. Yet last year when Ruben Studdard won, texters on an *American Idol* message board reported some of their messages didn't go through. Hours after the calls, people said their phone companies sent back text error messages from their phone carriers saying some messages failed. Up till that point, texters were reporting 100 percent completion.[47]

American Idol fans discussed voting strategies they felt would counter such distortions in the competition. Their efforts might be aimed at supporting the best singer, balancing out negative comments, or undermining "heavily marketed" contestants. The producers had, from day 1, sought to position the third season as a battle between three black "divas," and the judges had all but proclaimed Fantasia Barrino the likely winner. As the other two black "divas" went down and as Fantasia ranked near the bottom of the vote counts across several weeks, guest judge Elton John denounced America's voting patterns as "incredibly racist."[48] Such seemingly erratic voting patterns, however, make more sense if we see them in the context of a growing backlash among the most hard-core viewers to what they saw as open attempts to take away their right to choose the Idol.

This fan backlash continued to grow in subsequent seasons, giving rise to a group known as Vote for the Worst, which launched a Web campaign encouraging its followers to protect poor singers, most notably Sanjaya Malaka, in the 2007 season, from elimination. As the group explained its mission, "The show starts out every year encouraging us to point and laugh at all of the bad singers who audition. We want this hilariously bad entertainment to continue into the finals, so we choose the contestant that we feel provides the most entertaining train wreck performances and we start voting for them. . . . Vote for the Worst encourages you to have fun with *American Idol* and embrace its suckiness by voting for the less talented contestants. We rally behind one choice so that we can help make a difference and pool all of our votes toward one common goal. . . . Our aim isn't to win every single week, but to get a bad contestant as far as possible."[49] Some argue that the Vote for the Worst folks have their own aesthetic—they think it is more fun to see bad singing than to try to take the contest seriously—and their own politics —they don't want the producers and judges to tell them who they should vote for. Critics, on the other hand, describe the Vote for the Worst campaign as pure negation—an attempt to exploit the public's right to choose in order to inflict as much damage on mass media as possible.

The FOX Network initially dismissed the idea that Vote for the Worst might have any actual impact, arguing that the millions of votes cast would outweigh any group's efforts, but its influence was harder to dismiss when the cause got taken up by Howard Stern, the self-proclaimed "King of All Media," who used his satellite radio program to encourage listeners to vote to keep Sanjaya on the show.[50] In 1998, Stern had previously mobilized his regular listeners to get a comic sidekick, Hank the Angry Drunken Dwarf, selected as one of *People Magazine*'s most beautiful people in the world. Hank won over Leo DiCaprio, the pretty-boy actor who was then riding high off his *Titanic* appearance. The dwarf got a lot angrier and perhaps a little drunker when the magazine refused to feature him inside the magazine's print edition. Stern's involvement and the surprising longevity of the campy Sanjaya brought Vote for the Worst into the mainstream media, further amplifying public pushback over the *American Idol* voting process.

Sponsoring *American Idol* ensures that companies will get talked about, but it doesn't guarantee what the audience is going to say about them. Much of this chapter has looked at *American Idol* in terms of the behind-the-scenes calculations of media companies such as FOX, consumer brands such as Coca-Cola, and marketing researchers such as Initiative Media. Yet, we must also take seriously the backlash of Roberts's "inspirational consumers." Who wins *American Idol*, in the end, doesn't matter that much in the great scheme of things, but the debates about *Idol* voting are debates about the terms of audience participation in American media. At a time when networks and sponsors are joining forces to shape the emotional context through which we watch their shows, consumers are also scrutinizing the mechanisms of participation they are being offered. If the rhetoric of lovemarks emphasizes the audience's activities and investments as a central source of value in brands, then the consumption community may well hold the corporations accountable for what they do in the name of those brands and for their responsiveness (or lack thereof) to consumer demands. Such disputes have generated considerable "heat" around the series, drawing in many new viewers, but they have also alienated and disenfranchised many of the most dedicated ones.

Too much backlash can damage ratings or hurt sales of the products. The Initiative Media study found that AT&T, the company that had branded the voting mechanism, was damaged by the public backlash and that the other key sponsors—Coca-Cola and Ford—may have been hurt as well. No one would imagine that viewers might translate bad will toward one advertiser in a traditional segment of commercials to another advertiser. Yet, in a world where sponsors are more closely associated with the content, all of the hosting companies may be negatively affected by any negative perceptions that emerge around the series. It is through struggles that the relationship between media producers and consumers will get redefined in the coming decades.

Understanding when audience backlash hurts companies—or, for that matter, how far companies can go in shaping the nature of audience participation—is central to what I have been calling affective economics. If a program is going to become, in Heyer's terms, the "emotional capital" of its consumers, then we can expect consumers to make different investments in the program than the producers do, and we can expect the love behind the lovemarks to turn into hate when producers alter something that the brand community sees as fundamental to its experience. For the moment, the marketing industry still has a long way to go if it wants to understand the complexity of audiences' emotional investments in entertainment properties and brands. And audiences have a long way to go if they are going to exploit the points of entry that affective economics offers them for collective action and grassroots criticism of corporate conduct.

3

Searching for the Origami Unicorn

The Matrix *and Transmedia Storytelling*

In Peter Bagge's irreverent "Get It?," one of some twenty-five comic stories commissioned for *The Matrix* homepage, three buddies are exiting a theater where they have just seen the Wachowski brothers' opus for the first time (fig. 3.1). For two of them, *The Matrix* (1999) has been a transforming experience:

"Wow! That was Awesome!"
"*The Matrix* was the best movie I've seen in ages!"

The third is perplexed. From the looks on the faces of the prune-faced older couple walking in front of them, his confusion is not unique. "I didn't understand a word of it!"

"You mean you were sitting there scratching your head through the whole thing?"

Fig. 3.1. Peter Bagge suggests how perplexing some viewers found *The Matrix.*

When they retire to a local bar, one buddy persists in trying to explain *The Matrix*, patiently clarifying its concepts of manufactured reality, machine-controlled worlds, and "jacking in," while the other, being more pessimistic, grumbles, "I don't think you'll ever understand it." As their hapless pal walks away, the other two turn out to be cybernetic "agents," who concede that it's a good thing most humans don't get this movie, since "the fewer humanoids who comprehend what's really going on, the fewer we will have to destroy."[1]

Noted for his sharp social satire in *Hate* comics (1990–1998) and, more recently, *Reason* magazine, Bagge contrasts between those who "get" *The Matrix* and those who do not. Something about the film leaves some filmgoers feeling inadequate and others empowered. Bagge wrote this strip immediately after the release of the first *Matrix* movie. As we will see, things get only more complicated from there.

No film franchise has ever made such demands on its consumers. The original movie, *The Matrix*, took us into a world where the line between reality and illusion constantly blurred, and where the bodies of humans are stored as an energy source to fuel machines while their minds inhabit a world of digital hallucinations. Neo, the hacker protagonist-turned-messiah, gets pulled into the Zion resistance movement, working to overturn the "agents" who are shaping reality to serve their own ambiguous ends. The prerelease advertising for the first film tantalized consumers with the question, "What is the Matrix?" sending them to the Web in search of answers. Its sequel, *The Matrix Reloaded* (2003), opens without a recap and assumes we have almost complete mastery over its complex mythology and ever-expanding cast of secondary characters. It ends abruptly with a promise that all will make sense when we see the third installment, *The Matrix Revolutions* (2003). To truly appreciate what we are watching, we have to do our homework.

The filmmakers plant clues that won't make sense until we play the computer game. They draw on the back story revealed through a series of animated shorts, which need to be downloaded off the Web or watched off a separate DVD. Fans raced, dazed and confused, from the theaters to plug into Internet discussion lists, where every detail would be dissected and every possible interpretation debated.

When previous generations wondered whether they "got" a movie, it was usually a European art movie, an independent film, or perhaps an obscure late-night cult flick. But *The Matrix Reloaded* broke all box-office records for R-rated films, earning a mind-boggling $134 million in revenues in its first four days of release. The video game sold more than a million copies in its first week on the market. Before the movie was even released, 80 percent of the American filmgoing public identified *The Matrix Reloaded* as a "must see" title.[2]

The Matrix is entertainment for the age of media convergence, integrating multiple texts to create a narrative so large that it cannot be contained within a single medium. The Wachowski brothers played the transmedia game very well, putting out the original film first to stimulate interest, offering up a few Web comics to sustain the hard-core fan's hunger for more information, launching the anime in anticipation of the second film, releasing the computer game alongside it to surf the publicity, bringing the whole cycle to a conclusion with *The Matrix Revolutions*, and then turning the whole mythology over to the players of the massively multiplayer online game. Each step along the way built on what has come before, while offering new points of entry.

The Matrix is also entertainment for the era of collective intelligence. Pierre Lévy speculates about what kind of aesthetic works would respond to the demands of his knowledge cultures. First, he suggests that the "distinction between authors and readers, producers and spectators, creators and interpreters will blend" to form a "circuit" (not quite a matrix) of expression, with each participant working to "sustain the activity" of the others. The artwork will be what Lévy calls a "cultural attractor," drawing together and creating common ground between diverse communities; we might also describe it as a cultural activator, setting into motion its decipherment, speculation, and elaboration. The challenge, he says, is to create works with enough depth that they can justify such large-scale efforts: "Our primary goal should be to prevent closure from occurring too quickly."[3] *The Matrix* clearly functions as both a cultural attractor and a cultural activator. The most committed consumers track down data spread across multiple media, scanning each and every text for insights into the world. Keanu Reeves explained to *TV Guide* readers: "What audiences make of *Revolutions* will depend on the amount of energy they put into it. The script is full of cul-de-sacs and secret passageways."[4] Viewers get even more out of the experience if they compare notes and share resources than if they try to go it alone.

In this chapter, I am going to describe the *Matrix* phenomenon as transmedia storytelling. A transmedia story unfolds across multiple media platforms, with each new text making a distinctive and valuable contribution to the whole. In the ideal form of transmedia storytelling, each medium does what it does best—so that a story might be introduced in a film, expanded through television, novels, and comics; its world might be explored through game play or experienced as an amusement park attraction. Each franchise entry needs to be self-contained so you don't need to have seen the film to enjoy the game, and vice versa. Any given product is a point of entry into the franchise as a whole. Reading across the media sustains a depth of experience that motivates more consumption. Redundancy burns up fan interest and causes franchises to fail. Offering new levels of insight and experience refreshes the franchise and sustains consumer loyalty. The economic logic of a horizontally integrated entertainment industry—that is, one where a single company may have roots across all of the different media sectors—dictates the flow of content across media. Different media attract different market niches. Films and television probably have the most diverse audiences; comics and games the narrowest. A good transmedia franchise works to attract multiple constituencies by pitching the content somewhat differently in the different media. If there is, however, enough to sustain those different constituencies— and if each work offers fresh experiences—then you can count on a crossover market that will expand the potential gross.

Popular artists—working in the cracks of the media industry—have realized that they can surf this new economic imperative to produce more ambitious and challenging works. At the same time, these artists are building a more collaborative relationship with their consumers: working together, audience members can process more story information than previously imagined. To achieve their goals, these storytellers are developing a more collaborative model of authorship, co-creating content with artists with different visions and experiences at a time when few artists are equally at home in all media.

Okay, so the franchise is innovative, but is *The Matrix* any good? Many film critics trashed the later sequels because they were not sufficiently self-contained and thus bordered on incoherent. Many games critics trashed the games because they were too dependent on the film content and did not offer sufficiently new experiences to players. Many fans expressed disappointment because their own theories about the world of *The Matrix* were more rich and nuanced than anything they ever saw on the screen. I would argue, however, that we do not yet have very good aesthetic criteria for evaluating works that play them-selves out across multiple media. There have been far too few fully transmedia stories for media makers to act with any certainty about what would constitute the best uses of this new mode of storytelling, or for critics and consumers to know how to talk meaningfully about what works or doesn't work within such franchises. So let's agree for a moment that *The Matrix* was a flawed experiment, an interesting fail-ure, but that its flaws did not detract from the significance of what it tried to accomplish.

Relatively few, if any, franchises achieve the full aesthetic potential of transmedia storytelling—yet. Media makers are still finding their way and are more than willing to let someone else take the risks. Yet, at the heart of the entertainment industry, there are young and emerging lead-ers (such as Danny Bilson and Neil Young at Electronic Arts or Chris Pike at Sony Interactive) who are trying to push their companies to explore this new model for entertainment franchises. Some of them are still regrouping from their first bleeding-edge experiments in this space (Dawson's Desktop, 1998)—some of which had modest success (*The Blair Witch Project*, 1999), some of which they now see as spectac-ular failures (*Majestic*, 2001). Some of them are already having closed-door meetings to try to figure out the best way to ensure more produc-tive collaborations across media sectors. Some are working on hot new ideas masked by nondisclosure agreements. All of them were watching closely in 2003, which *Newsweek* had called "The Year of *The Matrix*," to see how audiences were going to respond to the Wachowski brothers' ambitious plans.[5] And, like Peter Bagge, they were looking at the faces of people as they exited the theaters, demanding to know if they "got" it.

What Is the Matrix?

Umberto Eco asks what, beyond being loved, transforms a film such as *Casablanca* (1942) into a cult artifact. First, he argues, the work must come to us as a "completely furnished world so that its fans can quote characters and episodes as if they were aspects of the private sectarian world."[6] Second, the work must be encyclopedic, containing a rich ar-ray of information that can be drilled, practiced, and mastered by de-voted consumers.

The film need not be well made, but it must provide resources consumers can use in constructing their own fantasies: "In order to transform a work into a cult object one must be able to break, dislocate, unhinge it so that one can remember only parts of it, irrespective of their original relationship to the whole."[7] And the cult film need not be coherent: the more different directions it pushes, the more different communities it can sustain, and the more different experiences it can provide, the better. We experience the cult movie, he suggests, not as having "one central idea but many," as "a disconnected series of images, of peaks, of visual icebergs."[8]

The cult film is made to be quoted, Eco contends, because it is made from quotes, archetypes, allusions, and references drawn from a range of previous works. Such material creates "a sort of intense emotion accompanied by the vague feeling of a déjà vu."[9] For Eco, *Casablanca* is the perfect cult movie because it is so unselfconscious in its borrowings: "Nobody would have been able to achieve such a cosmic result intentionally."[10] And for that reason, Eco is suspicious of cult movies by design. In the age of postmodernism, Eco suggests, no film can be experienced with fresh eyes; all are read against other movies. In such a world, "cult has become the normal way of enjoying movies."[11]

If *Casablanca* exemplifies the classical cult movie, one might see *The Matrix* as emblematic of the cult movie in convergence culture. Here's science fiction writer Bruce Sterling trying to explain its fascination:

> First and foremost, the film's got pop appeal elements. All kinds of elements: suicidal attacks by elite special forces, crashing helicopters, oodles of martial arts, a chaste yet passionate story of predestined love, bug-eyed monsters of the absolute first water, fetish clothes, captivity and torture and daring rescue, plus really weird, cool submarines. . . . There's Christian exegesis, a Redeemer myth, a death and rebirth, a hero in self-discovery, *The Odyssey*, Jean Baudrillard (lots of Baudrillard, the best part of the film), science fiction ontological riffs of the Philip K. Dick school, Nebuchadnezzar, the Buddha, Taoism, martial-arts mysticism, oracular prophecy, spoon-bending telekinesis, Houdini stage-show magic, Joseph Campbell, and Godelian mathematical metaphysics.[12]

And that's just in the first film!

The film's endless borrowings also spark audience response. Layers upon layers of references catalyze and sustain our epistemophilia; these gaps and excesses provide openings for the many different knowledge communities that spring up around these cult movies to display their expertise, dig deep into their libraries, and bring their minds to bear on a text that promises a bottomless pit of secrets. Some of the allusions— say, the recurring references to "through the looking glass," the White Rabbit, and the Red Queen, or the use of mythological names for the characters (Morpheus, Persephone, Trinity)—pop off the screen upon first viewing. Others—say, the fact that at one point, Neo pulls a copy of Baudrillard's *Simulacra and Simulation* (1981/1995) from his shelf— become clear only after you talk about the film with friends. Some— like the fact that Cypher, the traitor, is referred to at one point as "Mr. Reagan" and asks for an alternative life where he is an actor who gains political power—are clear only when you put together information from multiple sources. Still others—such as the license plates on the cars (such as DA203 or IS5416), which reference specific and context-appropriate Bible verses (Daniel 2:3 or Isaiah 54:16)—may require you to move through the film frame by frame on your DVD player.

The deeper you drill down, the more secrets emerge, all of which can seem at any moment to be *the key* to the film. For example, Neo's apartment number is 101, which is the room number of the torture chamber in George Orwell's *1984* (1949). Once you've picked up this number, then you discover that 101 is also the floor number for the Merovingians' nightclub and the number of the highway where the characters clash in *The Matrix Reloaded,* and from there, one can't help but believe that all of the other various numbers in the film may also carry hidden meanings or connect significant characters and locations together. The billboards in the backgrounds of shots contain cheat codes that can be used to unlock levels in the *Enter the Matrix* (2003) game.

The sheer abundance of allusions makes it nearly impossible for any given consumer to master the franchise totally. In this context, the Wachowski brothers have positioned themselves as oracles—hidden from view most of the time, surfacing only to offer cryptic comments, refusing direct answers, and speaking with a single voice. Here, for example, are some characteristic passages from one of their few online chat sessions:

Question: "There are quite a few hidden messages in the movie that I notice the more I watch it. Can you tell me about how many there are?"

Wachowski brothers: "There are more than you'll ever know."[13]

Question: "Have you ever been told that *The Matrix* has Gnostic overtones?"
Wachowski brothers: "Do you consider that to be a good thing?"

Question: "Do you appreciate people dissecting your movie? Do you find it a bit of an honor or does it annoy you a little, especially when the person may have it all wrong?"
Wachowski brothers: "There's not necessarily ever an 'all wrong.' Because it's about what a person gets out of the movie, what an individual gets out of the movie."

The Wachowskis were more than happy to take credit for whatever meanings the fans located, all the while implying there was more, much more, to be found if the community put its collective mind to work. They answered questions with questions, clues with clues. Each clue was mobilized, as quickly as it materialized, to support a range of different interpretations.

So what is *The Matrix*? As one fan demonstrates, the question can be answered in so many different ways:

- Is it a "love story"? (Keanu Reeves said that in an interview.)
- Is it a "titanic struggle between intuition and controlling intellect"? (Hugo Weaving = Agent Smith said that in an interview about *The Matrix Reloaded*.)
- Is it a story about religious salvation? (*The Matrix Reloaded* was banned in Egypt, because it is "too religious.")
- Is it a story about "Believing in something" or about "Not believing in something"?
- Is it a story about "artificial humanity" or "artificial spirituality"?
- Is it a story with elements from Christianity? Buddhism? Greek mythology? Gnosticism? Hinduism? Freemasonry? The secret society Priory of Zion (Prieure du Notre Dame du Sion) (and its connection to the use of chessboard imagery at the castle Rennes-le-Chateau)?
- Is Neo a reincarnated Buddha? Or a new Jesus Christ (Neo Anderson = new son of man)?
- Is it a science-fiction movie? A fantasy movie?
- Is it a story about secret societies keeping society under control?

- Is it a story about men's history or men's future?
- Is it just a visually enhanced futuristic Kung-Fu movie? A modern Japanime?[14]

Even with all of the film releases out on DVD, and thus subject to being scrutinized indefinitely, the most dedicated fans were still trying to figure out *The Matrix* and the more casual viewers, not accustomed to putting this kind of work into an action film, had concluded that the parts just didn't add up.

"Synergistic Storytelling"

The Matrix is a bit like *Casablanca* to the nth degree, with one important difference: *Casablanca* is a single movie; *The Matrix* is three movies and more. There is, for example, *The Animatrix* (2003), a ninety-minute program of short animated films, set in the world of *The Matrix* and created by some of the leading animators from Japan, South Korea, and the United States, including Peter Chung (*Aeon Flux*, 1995), Yoshiaki Kawajiri (*Wicked City*, 1987), Koji Morimoto (*Robot Carnival*, 1987), and Shinichiro Watanabe (*Cowboy Bebop*, 1998). *The Matrix* is also a series of comics from cult writers and artists, such as Bill Sienkiewicz (*Elektra: Assassin*, 1986–87), Neil Gaiman (*The Sandman*, 1989–96), Dave Gibbons (*Watchmen*, 1986–87), Paul Chadwick (*Concrete*, 1987–98), Peter Bagge (*Hate*, 1990–98), David Lapham (*Stray Bullets*, 1995–), and Geof Darrow (*Hard Boiled*, 1990–92). *The Matrix* is also two games—*Enter the Matrix*, produced by David Perry's Shiny Entertainment, and a massively multiplayer game set in the world of *The Matrix*, scripted in part by Paul Chadwick.

The Wachowskis wanted to wind the story of *The Matrix* across all of these media and have it all add up to one compelling whole. Producer Joel Silver describes a trip the filmmakers took to Japan to talk about creating an animated television series: "I remember on the plane ride back, Larry sat down with a yellow pad and kinda mapped out this scheme we would do where we would

The *Blair Witch* Phenomenon

The concept of transmedia storytelling first entered public dialogue in 1999 as audiences and critics tried to make sense of the phenomenal success of *The Blair Witch Project* (1999), a small-budget independent film that became a huge moneymaker. To think of *The Blair Witch Project* as a film was to miss the bigger picture. *The Blair Witch Project* had created a fan following on the Web more than a year before it hit any theaters. Many people learned about the

Burkittsville witch and the disappearance of the production crew that forms the central plot of the movie by going online and finding this curious Web site that seemed to be absolutely real in every detail. The site provided documentation of numerous witch sightings over the past centuries, most of which are not directly referenced in the film but form the backdrop for its action. A pseudodocumentary investigating the witch aired on the Sci Fi Channel, with little to set it apart from the many other documentaries about supernatural phenomena the network periodically airs. After the film's release, Oni Press released several comic books that it claimed were based on the accounts of another person who had met the witch while walking in the woods near Burkittsville. Even the soundtrack was presented as a tape found in the abandoned car.

All of these elements made the world of the film more convincing, enhancing the immediacy the Haxans, as the film's creative team called themselves, had achieved through their distinctive hand-held-video style and improvisational acting. Dan Myrick, one of the film's producers, spelled out what the group called their "prime directive": "We tried to create a fake legend, complete with multiple points of view, skeptics, and unexplainable mysteries. Nothing about the legend could be provable, and everything had to seem like it could have a logical explanation (which the reader would be led away from as quickly as possible.)"[1]

Ed Sanchez, another member of the team, explained: "Everything was based

have this movie, and these video games and these animated stories, and they would all interact together."[15] David Perry described the game as, in effect, another *Matrix* movie. The actors reportedly were uncertain which scenes were being filmed for the game and which for the movie.[16] The consumer who has played the game or watched the shorts will get a different experience of the movies than one who has simply had the theatrical film experience. The whole is worth more than the sum of the parts.

We may better understand how this new mode of transmedia storytelling operates by looking more closely at some of the interconnections between the various *Matrix* texts. For example, in the animated short *Final Flight of the Osiris* (2003), the protagonist, Jue, gives her life trying to get a message into the hands of the *Nebuchadnezzar* crew. The letter contains information about the machines boring their way down to Zion. In the final moments of the anime, Jue drops the letter into a mailbox. At the opening of *Enter the Matrix*, the player's first mission is to retrieve the letter from the post office and get it into the hands of our heroes. And the opening scenes of *The Matrix Reloaded* show the characters discussing the "last transmission of the *Osiris*." For people who see only the movie, the sources of the information remain unclear, but someone who has a transmedia experience will have played an active role in delivering the letter and may have traced its trajectory across three different media.

[1] FT Interviews, "The *Blair Witch* Producer-Director Dan Myrick and Production Designer Ben Rock," *Fortean Times*, November 1999, http://www.foretean times.com/articles/128_haxanint.shtml.

Similarly, the character of The Kid is introduced in another of the animated shorts, *The Kid's Story* (2003), about a high school student who discovers on his own the truth about the Matrix as Neo and his friends try to rescue him from the agents. In *The Matrix Reloaded*, they reencounter The Kid on the outskirts of Zion, where he begs to join their crew: "It's fate. I mean you're the reason I'm here, Neo," but Neo defers, saying, "I told you, kid, you found me, I didn't find you. . . . You saved yourself." The exchange is staged as if everybody in the audience would know what the two are talking about and feels more like a scene involving an already established character than their first on-screen introduction. The Kid's efforts to defend Zion become one of the core emotional hooks in the climactic battle in *Revolutions*.

In *The Matrix Reloaded*, Niobe appears unexpectedly in the freeway chase just in time to rescue Morpheus and Trinity, but for people who play the game, getting Niobe to the rendezvous point is a key mission. Again, near the end of *The Matrix Reloaded*, Niobe and her crew are dispatched to blow up the power plant, but apart from the sense that the plan must have worked to enable what we see on screen to unfold, the actual details of her operation is not represented, so that it can be played out in more depth in the game. We reencounter Niobe at the start of *The Matrix Revolutions* where she was left off at the climax of *Enter the Matrix*.

on this one decision to make everything as real as possible. . . . Let's continue with the prime directive—the idea that this is a Web site put up by people interested in the case, trying to bring justice or closure or promote an investigation into the mystery. We set up the timeline, added details to the backstory. . . . We started fabricating artifacts, paintings, carvings, old books, and I would scan them in."[2] Sanchez added a discussion board and saw the emergence of a community of fans who were fascinated with the *Blair Witch* mythology: "What we learned from *Blair Witch* is that if you give people enough stuff to explore, they will explore. Not everyone but some of them will. The people who do explore and take advantage of the whole world will forever be your fans, will give you an energy you can't buy through advertising. . . . It's this web of information that is laid out in a way that keeps people interested and keeps people working for it. If people have to work for something, they devote more time to it. And they give it more emotional value." Sanchez freely acknowledges that they had approached the site and the spin-offs as marketing, but they became an integral part of the experience: "It was the kind of marketing which I would have gotten into as a consumer. . . . We ended up exploiting the Web in ways that as far as movies were concerned, nobody had ever done before."

[2] Ed Sanchez, interview with author, June 2003. All quotations from Sanchez come from this interview.

By the standards of classical Hollywood storytelling, these gaps (such as the failure to introduce The Kid or to explain where Niobe came from) or ex-cesses (such as the reference to "the last transmission of the *Osiris*") confuse the spectator.[17] The old Hollywood system depended on re-dundancy to ensure that viewers could follow the plot at all times, even if they were distracted or went out to the lobby for a popcorn refill during a crucial scene. The new Hollywood demands that we keep our eyes on the road at all times, and that we do research before we arrive at the theater.

This is probably where *The Matrix* fell out of favor with the film critics, who were used to reviewing the film and not the surrounding apparatus. Few of them consumed the games or comics or animated shorts, and, as a consequence, few absorbed the essential information they contained. As Fiona Morrow from the *London Independent* explained, "You can call me old-fashioned—what matters to me is the film and only the film. I don't want to have to 'enhance' the cinematic experience by overloading on souped-up flimflam."[18] Those who realized there was relevant information in those other sources were suspicious of the economic motives behind what *Salon*'s Ivan Askwith called "synergistic storytelling": "Even if the new movies, game, and animated shorts live up to the high standards set by the first film, there's still an uneasy feeling that Warner Bros. is taking advantage of *The Matrix*'s cult following to cash in while it can." The *San Jose Mercury*'s Mike Antonucci saw it all as "smart marketing" more than "smart storytelling."[19]

So let's be clear: there are strong economic motives behind transmedia storytelling. Media convergence makes the flow of content across multiple media platforms inevitable. In the era of digital effects and high-resolution game graphics, the game world can now look almost exactly like the film world—because they are reusing many of the same digital assets. Everything about the structure of the modern entertainment industry was designed with this single idea in mind—the construction and enhancement of entertainment franchises. As we saw in the previous chapter, there is a strong interest in integrating entertainment and marketing, to create strong emotional attachments and use them to make additional sales. Mike Saksa, the senior vice president for marketing at Warner Bros., couldn't be more explicit on this point: "This [*The Matrix*] truly is Warner Bros.'s synergy. All divisions will benefit from the property. . . . We don't know what the upside is, we just know it's going to be very high."[20]

The enormous "upside" is not just economic, however. *The Matrix* franchise was shaped by a whole new vision of synergy. Franchising a popular film, comic book, or television series is nothing new. Witness the endless stream of plastic figurines available in McDonald's Happy Meals. Cross-promotion is everywhere. But much of it, like the Happy Meal toys, are pretty lame and easily forgotten. Current licensing arrangements ensure that most of these products are peripheral to what drew us to the original story in the first place. Under licensing, the central media company—most often the film producers—sells the rights to manufacture products using its assets to an often unaffiliated third party; the license limits what can be done with the characters or concepts to protect the original property. Soon, licensing will give way to what industry insiders are calling "co-creation." In co-creation, the companies collaborate from the beginning to create content they know plays well in each of their sectors, allowing each medium to generate new experiences for the consumer and expand points of entry into the franchise.

The current licensing system typically generates works that are redundant (allowing no new character background or plot development), watered down (asking the new media to slavishly duplicate experiences better achieved through the old), or riddled with sloppy contradictions (failing to respect the core consistency audiences expect within a franchise). These failures account for why sequels and franchises have a bad reputation. Franchise products are governed too much by economic logic and not enough by artistic vision. Hollywood acts as if it only has to provide more of the same, printing a *Star Trek* (1966) logo on so many widgets. In reality, audiences want the new work to offer new insights and new experiences. If media companies reward that demand, viewers will feel greater mastery and investment; deny it, and they stomp off in disgust.

In 2003, I attended a gathering of top creatives from Hollywood and the games industry, hosted by Electronic Arts; they were discussing how co-creation might work. Danny Bilson, the vice president of intellectual property development at Electronic Arts, organized the summit on what he calls "multiplatform entertainment."[21] As someone who has worked in film (*The Rocketeer*, 1991), television (*The Sentinel*, 1996; *Viper*, 1994), and comics (*The Flash*, 1990), as well as in games, Bilson understands the challenges of creating content in each medium and of coordinating between them. He wants to develop games that do not just move Hollywood brands into a new media space, but also contribute to a larger storytelling system. For this to work, he argues, the story needs to be conceived in transmedia terms from the start:

We create movies and games together, organically, from the ground up, with the same creative force driving them. Ideally that creative force involves movie writers and directors who are also gamers. In any art form, you have to like it to do well with it; in fact, you have to be a fan of it to do well at it. Take that talent and build multiplatform entertainment. The movie and game are designed together; the game deepens and expands the fiction but does not simply repeat material from the film. It should be organic to what made the film experience compelling.

Going forward, people are going to want to go deeper into stuff they care about rather than sampling a lot of stuff. If there's something I love, I want it to be bigger than just those two hours in the movie theater or a one-hour-a-week experience on TV. I want a deepening of the universe. . . . I want to participate in it. I've just been introduced to the world in the film and I want to get there, explore it. You need that connection to the world to make participation exciting.

Bilson wants to use his position as the man who supervises all creative properties for the world's leading game publisher to create multiplatform entertainment. His first step is the development of *GoldenEye: Rogue Agent* (2004), a James Bond game where one gets to play the part of classic Bond villains like Dr. No or Goldfinger, restaging confronting 007 within digital re-creations of the original movie sets. Everything in the game is consistent with what viewers know from the Bond movies, but the events are seen from an alternative moral perspective.

This level of integration and coordination is difficult to achieve even though the economic logic of the large media conglomerates encourages them to think in terms of synergies and franchises. So far, the most successful transmedia franchises have emerged when a single creator or creative unit maintains control. Hollywood might well study the ways that Lucasfilm has managed and cultivated its *Indiana Jones* (1981) and *Star Wars* (1977) franchises. When *Indiana Jones* went to television, for example, it exploited the medium's potential for extended storytelling and character development: *The Young Indiana Jones Chronicles* (1992) showed the character take shape against the backdrop of various historical events and exotic environments. When *Star Wars* moved into print, its novels expanded the timeline to show events not contained in the film trilogies, or recast the stories around secondary characters, as did the *Tales from the Mos Eisley Cantina* (1995) series, which fleshes out those curious-looking aliens in the background of the original movie.[22] When *Star Wars* went to games, those games didn't just enact film events; they showed what life would be like for a Jedi trainee or a bounty hunter. Increasingly, elements are dropped into the films to create openings that will be fully exploited only through other media.

While the technological infrastructure is ready, the economic prospects sweet, and the audience primed, the media industries haven't done a very good job of collaborating to produce compelling transmedia experiences. Even within the media conglomerates, units compete aggressively rather than collaborate. Many believe that much greater coordination across the media sectors is needed to produce transmedia content. Electronic Arts (EA) explored this model in developing its *Lord of the Rings* titles. EA designers worked on location with Peter Jackson's production unit in New Zealand. As Neil Young, the man in charge of the *Lord of the Rings* franchise for EA, explained,

> I wanted to adapt Peter's work for our medium in the same way that he has adapted Tolkien's work for his. Rather than being some derivative piece of merchandise along the same continuum with the poster, the pen, the mug, or the key chain, maybe we could turn that pyramid up the side of its head, leverage those pieces which have come before, and become the pinnacle of the property instead of the basement. Whether you are making the mug, whether you are making the key chain, or whether you are making the game, pretty much everyone has access to the same assets. For me, when I took over *Lord of the Rings*, that seemed untenable if you want to build something that captured Peter's unique vision, and Howard Shore's music, and the actors, and the look of this world, and . . . you needed much more direct access. Instead of working exclusively through the consumer products group, we built a partnership directly with the New Line Production company, 3 Foot 6 Productions, that functioned as a clearing house for the things we needed.[23]

This system allowed them to import thousands of "assets" from the film production into the game, ensuring an unprecedented degree of fidelity to the details of Tolkien's world. At the same time, working closely with Jackson and the other filmmakers gave Young greater latitude to explore other dimensions of that world that would not appear on screen.

David Perry has described his relationship with the Wachowski brothers in very similar terms: "The Wachowskis get games. They were standing on the set making sure we got what we needed to make this a quality game. They know what gamers are looking for. With the power they have in Hollywood, they were able to make sure we got everything we needed to make this game what it is."[24] Perry's team logged four months of motion-capture work with Jada Pinkett Smith, the ac-tress who played Niobe, and other members of the *Matrix* cast. All the movements and gestures were created by actual performers working on the set and were seen as extensions of their characterizations. The team used alpha-mapping to create a digital version of the actress's face and still preserve her own facial expressions. The game incorporat-ed many of the special effects that had made *The Matrix* so distinctive when the film was first released, allowing players to duplicate some of the stunts that Woo-ping Yuen (the noted Hong Kong fight choreographer) had created through his wire work or to move through "bul-let time," the film's eye-popping slow-motion technique.

Across the Mangaverse

Writing in the London newspaper *The Guardian*, Indian-born filmmaker Shekhar Kapur (*Elizabeth, Four Feathers*) noted that Hollywood's worldwide revenues were down 16 percent and local filmmakers were reaping the benefits.[1] He predicted that in a decade we will just as likely be talking about a world dominated by Asian media. Using a then current box-office success as his example, he wrote, "Ten years from now, *Spider-Man* will make $1 billion in its first week. But when *Spider-Man* takes off his mask, he'll probably be Chinese. And the city in which he operates will not be New York, it will be Shanghai. And yet it will be an international film, it will still be *Spider-Man*."

Major media companies, such as Bertelsmann Media Worldwide, Sony, or Vivendi Universal, contract talent worldwide, catering to the tastes of local markets rather than pursuing nationalistic interests; their economic structure encourages them not only to be the intermediaries between different Asian markets but also to bring Asian content into Western countries. Sony, Disney, Fox, and Warner Bros. have all opened companies to produce films in Chinese, German, Italian, Japanese, and

[1] Shekhar Kapur, "The Asians Are Coming," *The Guardian* (U.K.), August 23, 2002, accessed at http://www.shekharkapur.com/guardian.htm. For a useful discussion of trends linking Asian and American media production, see Christina Klein, "Martial Arts and the Globalization of US and Asian Film Industries," *Comparative American Studies* 2, no. 3 (September 2004): 360–384.

Collaborative Authorship

Media conglomeration provided a context for the Wachowski brothers' aesthetic experiment—they wanted to play with a new kind of storytelling and use Warner Bros.'s blockbuster promotion to open it to the largest possible public. If all they wanted was synergy, they could have hired hack collaborators who could crank out the games, comics, and cartoons. This has certainly occurred in other cases that have sought to imitate the *Matrix* model. More recent films, ranging from *Charlie's Angels* to *The Riddick Chronicles*, from *Star Wars* to *Spider-Man*, have developed cartoons, for example, which were intended to bridge between sequels or foreshadow plot developments. Of these, only the *Star Wars* shorts worked with a distinguished animator—in that case, Genndy Tartakovsky (*Samurai Jack*).[25] By contrast, the Wachowskis sought animators and comic-book writers who already had cult followings and were known for their distinctive visual styles and authorial voices. They worked with people they admired, not people they felt would follow orders. As Yoshiaki Kawajiri, the animator of *Program*, explained, "It was very attractive to me because the only limitation was that I had to play within the world of the *Matrix*; other than that I've been able to work with complete freedom."[26]

The Wachowski brothers, for example, saw co-creation as a vehicle for expanding their potential global market, bringing in collaborators whose very presence evoked distinct forms of popular culture from other parts of the world. Geof Darrow, who did the conceptual drawings for the ships and technology, trained under Moebius, the Eurocomics master noted for images that blur the line between the organic and the mechanical. The filmmakers hired the distinguished Hong Kong fight choreographer Woo-ping Yuen, who was noted for having helped to reinvent Jackie Chan's screen

other languages aimed both at their domestic markets and at global export. American television and film increasingly is remaking successful products from other markets, ranging from *Survivor* (2000) and *Big Brother* (2000), which are remakes of successful Dutch series, to *The Ring* (2002), a remake of a Japanese cult horror movie, or *Vanilla Sky* (2001), a remake of a Spanish science fiction film. Many of the cartoons shown on American television are made in Asia (increasingly in Korea), often with only limited supervision by Western companies. Many Western children today are more familiar with the characters of the Japanese *Pokémon* series than they are with those from the European fairy tales of the Brothers Grimm or Hans Christian Andersen.[2] With the rise of broadband communications, foreign media producers will distribute media content directly to American consumers without having to pass by U.S. gatekeepers or rely on multinational distributors.

The flow of Asian goods into the Western market has been shaped by two competing forces: the corporate convergence promoted by media industries, and the grassroots convergence

[2] For useful overviews of the Asian impact of American popular culture, see Anne Allison, *Millennial Monsters: Japanese Toys and the Global Imagination* (work in progress); Henry Jenkins, "Pop Cosmopolitanism: Mapping Cultural Flows in an Age of Media Convergence," in Marcelo M. Suarez-Orozco and Desiree B. Qin-Hilliard (eds.), *Globalization: Culture and Education in the New Millennium* (Berkeley: University of California Press, 2004); Joseph Tobin (ed.), *Pikachu's Global Adventure: The Rise and Fall of Pokémon* (Durham, N.C.: Duke University Press, 2004); Mizuko Ito, "Technologies of the Childhood Imagination: Yugioh, Media Mixes and Everyday Cultural Production," in Joe Karaganis and Natalie Jeremijenko (eds.), *Network/Netplay: Structures of Participation in Digital Culture* (Durham, N.C.: Duke University Press, 2005).

promoted by fan communities and immigrant populations. We will return to the role of grassroots convergence in the globalization process in chapter 4. For the moment, let's focus on corporate convergence. Three distinctive kinds of economic interests are at play in promoting these new cultural exchanges: national or regional producers who see the global circulation of their products not simply as expanding their revenue stream but also as a source of national pride; multinational conglomerates who no longer define their production or distribution decisions in national terms but seek to identify potentially valuable content and push it into as many markets as possible; and niche distributors who search for distinctive content as a means of attracting upscale consumers and differentiating themselves from stuff already on the market.

Kapur's image of a Chinese Spider-Man may not be too far fetched, after all. As comics and graphic novels have moved into chain bookstores, such as Barnes & Noble and Borders, the shelf space devoted to manga far outstrips the space devoted to American-produced content, reflecting a growing gap in sales figures as well. Seeking to reclaim the market they were losing to Asian competition, Marvel Comics experimented in 2002 with a new Mangaverse title, which reimagined and resituated their stable of superheroes within Japanese genre traditions: Spider-Man is a ninja, the members of the Avengers assemble into a massive robot, and the Hulk turns into a giant green monster.[3] Initially conceived as a one-shot novelty, the Mangaverse proved so successful that Marvel

persona, developing a distinctive female style for Michelle Yeoh, and bringing Asian-style fighting to global cinema via *Crouching Tiger, Hidden Dragon* (2000).[27] The films were shot in Australia, and the directors drew on local talent, such as Baz Luhrmann's longtime costume designer Kym Barrett. The cast was emphatically multiracial, making use of African American, Hispanic, South Asian, southern European, and aboriginal performers to create a Zion that is predominantly non-white.

Perhaps most importantly, the Wachowski brothers sought out Japanese and other Asian animators as collaborators on *The Animatrix*. They cite strong influences from manga (Japanese comics) and anime, with Morpheus's red leather chair a homage to *Akira* (1988) and Trinity's jumpsuit coming straight from *Ghost in the Shell* (1995). Arguably, their entire interest in transmedia storytelling can be traced back to this fascination with what anthropologist Mimi Ito has described as Japan's "media mix" culture. On the one hand, the media mix strategy disperses content across broadcast media, portable technologies such as game boys or cell phones, collectibles, and location-based entertainment centers from amusement parks to game arcades. On the other, these franchises depend on hypersociability, that is, they encourage various forms of participation and social interactions between consumers.[28] This media mix strategy has made its way to American shores through series like *Pokémon* (1998) and *Yu-Gi-Oh!* (1998), but operates

[3] Rene A. Guzman, "Manga Revises Marvel Heroes," *San Antonio Express-News*, January 23, 2002.

in even more sophisticated forms in more obscure Japanese franchises. In bringing in Japanese animators closely associated with this media mix strategy, the Wachowski brothers found collaborators who understood what they were trying to accomplish.

The Wachowski brothers didn't simply license or subcontract and hope for the best. The brothers personally wrote and directed content for the game, drafted scenarios for some of the animated shorts, and co-wrote a few of the comics. For fans, their personal engagement made these other *Matrix* texts a central part of the "canon." There was nothing fringe about these other media. The filmmakers risked alienating filmgoers by making these elements so central to the unfolding narrative. At the same time, few filmmakers have been so overtly fascinated with the process of collaborative authorship. The *Matrix* Web site provides detailed interviews with every major technical worker, educating fans about their specific contributions. The DVDs, shipped with hours of "the making of" documentaries, again focused on the full range of creative and technical work.

We can see collaborative authorship at work by looking more closely at the three comics stories created by Paul Chadwick, "Déjà Vu," "Let It All Fall Down," and "The Miller's Tale."[29] Chadwick's comics were ultimately so embraced by the Wachowski brothers that Chadwick was asked to help develop plots and dialogue for the online *Matrix* game. Chadwick might at first glance seem an odd choice

launched an entire new production line, Tsunami, which produced manga-style content for the American and global market, mostly working with Asian or Asian American artists.[4] Similarly, Disney's *Kingdom Hearts* (2002) emerged from collaboration with the Japanese game company SquareSoft, the creators of the successful *Final Fantasy* franchise. The game mixes more than one hundred characters from Disney's animated films with the more anime-style protagonists associated with previous SquareSoft titles.[5]

Japan is not the only Asian culture exerting a strong influence over American-made media. DC Comics created *Batman: Hong Kong* (2003), a hardcover prestige-edition graphic novel designed to introduce Western readers to the distinctive style of Chinese comic artist Tony Wong and the *manhua* tradition.[6] Marvel released a series of *Spider-Man: India* comics, timed to correspond with the release of *Spider-Man 2* in India and localized to South Asian tastes.[7] Peter Parker becomes Pavitr Prabhakar, and Green Goblin becomes Rakshasa, a traditional mythological demon. The graphics, which depict Spider-Man leaping over scooters in Mumbai streets and swinging past the Gateway of India, were drawn by Indian comic-book artist Jeevan J. Kang. Marvel calls it "transcreation," one step beyond translation. In creating these books, Marvel acknowledges that their superhero comics have done poorly outside of the

[4] "Tsunami Splash," *Wizard*, March 2003, p. 100.

[5] For more information, see http://www.kingdom hearts.com.

[6] Tony Wong, *Batman: Hong Kong* (New York: DC Comics, 2003); Wendy Siuyi Wong, *Hong Kong Comics: A History of Manhua* (New York: Princeton Architectural Press, 2002).

[7] Chidanand Rajghatta, "Spiderman Goes Desi," *Times of India*, June 17, 2004.

Anglo-American world, but there is some chance that the current films are creating an opening to tap that market. Even if the books bomb in India, however, they have generated a great deal of interest among Western comic fans.

We might describe *The Animatrix*, the Mangaverse, and *Spider-Man: India* in terms of corporate hybridity. Hybridity occurs when one cultural space—in this case, a national media industry—absorbs and transforms elements from another; a hybrid work thus exists betwixt and between two cultural traditions while providing a path that can be explored from both directions. Hybridity has often been discussed as a strategy of the dispossessed as they struggle to resist or reshape the flow of Western media into their culture—taking materials imposed from the outside but making them their own.[8] Here, hybridity can be seen as a corporate strategy, one that comes from a position of strength rather than vulnerability or marginality, one that seeks to control rather than contain transcultural consumption.

Christina Klein has examined the distinctly transnational status of *Crouching Tiger, Hidden Dragon*.[9] Its director, Ang Lee, was born in Taiwan but educated in the United States; this was the first film Lee had produced on Chinese soil. Its financing came from a mixture of Japanese and American-based media conglomerates. The film was produced and written by Lee's long-term collaborator,

to work on a major movie franchise. He is a cult comics creator best known for *Concrete* and for his strong commitment to environmentalist politics. Working on the very edges of the superhero genre, Chadwick uses Concrete, a massive stone husk that houses the mind of a former political speech writer, to ask questions about the current social and economic order. In *Think Like a Mountain* (1996), Concrete joins forces with the Earth First! movement that is spiking trees and waging war on the lumber industry to protect an old-growth forest.[30] Chadwick's political commitments are expressed not only through the stories but also through his visual style: he creates full-page spreads that integrate his protagonists into their environments, showing the small creatures that exist all around us, hidden from view but impacted by the choices we make.

Chadwick uses his contributions to the *Matrix* to extend the film's critique of the urban landscape and to foreground the ecological devastation that resulted from the war between the machines and the humans. In "The Miller's Tale," his protagonist, a member of the Zion underground, tries to reclaim the land so that he can harvest wheat and make bread. Risking his life, he travels across the blackened landscape in search of seeds with which he can plant new crops; he grinds the grain to make loaves to feed the resistance movement. Chadwick's miller is ultimately killed, but the comic ends with a beautiful full-page image of the plant life growing over the ruins

---

[8] For useful overviews on the literature about hybridity, see Jan Nederveen Pieterse, "Globalization as Hybridization," in Michael Featherstone (ed.), *Global Modernities* (New York: Sage, 1995); Nestor Garcia Canclini, *Consumers and Citizens: Globalization and Multicultural Conflicts* (Minneapolis: University of Minnesota Press, 2001).

[9] Christina Klein, "*Crouching Tiger, Hidden Dragon*: A Transnational Reading" (work in progress).

we recognize from their appearance in several of the *Matrix* movies. Of all of the comics' artists, Chadwick shows the greatest interest in Zion and its cultural rituals, helping us to understand the kinds of spirituality that emerge from an underground people.[31]

While he builds on elements found in the films, Chadwick finds his own emphasis within the material and explores points of intersection with his own work. The other animators and comic artists more or less do the same, further expanding the range of potential meanings and intertextual connections within the franchise.

The Art of World-Making

The Wachowski brothers built a playground where other artists could experiment and fans could explore. For this to work, the brothers had to envision the world of *The Matrix* with sufficient consistency that each installment is recognizably part of the whole and with enough flexibility that it can be rendered in all of these different styles of representation—from the photorealistic computer animation of *Final Flight of the Osiris* to the blocky graphics of the first *Matrix* Web game. Across those various manifestations of the franchise, there are dozens of recurring motifs, such as the falling green *kanji*, Morpheus's bald head and mirrorshade glasses, the insectlike ships, Neo's hand gestures, or Trinity's acrobatics.[32] No given work will reproduce every ele-

the American James Schamus. The cast included performers drawn from across the Chinese diaspora—Zhang Ziyi (Mainland China), Chan Chen (Taiwan), Chow Yun-Fat (Hong Kong), and Michelle Yeoh (Malaysia). Ang Lee describes *Crouching Tiger, Hidden Dragon* as a "combination platter," stressing its borrowings from multiple cultural traditions. James Schamus agrees: "We ended up making an eastern movie for western audiences and in some ways a more western movie for eastern audiences." These examples of corporate hybridity depend on consumers with the kinds of cultural competencies that could originate only in the context of global convergence, requiring not simply knowledge of Asian popular culture but an understanding of its similarities and differences with parallel traditions in the West.

While *The Animatrix* can be read, alongside *Spider-Man: India*, as an example of "transcreation," *The Matrix* feature films simply added various multinational and multicultural references largely invisible to Western consumers but designed to give people in many different parts of the world toeholds within the franchise. Some elements may move into the foreground or the background depending on the local competencies of media consumers. One of my graduate students, for example, shared with me this example: "Many friends in India told me about how discussions of the South Asian family in *Revolutions* ended up becoming discussions about labor migration to the U.S., the position of nonwhites in the high-tech software industry, outsourcing, etc." In Japan, where the tradition of "cosplay" (or costume play) is deeply rooted in fan cultures, and where fans of a particular show might all rally someplace like

Fig. 3.2. Japanese fans gather in Osaka to reenact scenes from *The Matrix Reloaded*.

Tokyo's Yoyogi Park on a Sunday afternoon, all dressed up and ready to play, there have been a series of *Matrix* reenactments (fig. 3.2). Hundreds of local fans arrive in costume and systematically stage key moments from the movies as a kind of participatory public spectacle.[10] These reenactments in effect localize the content by reading it through nationally specific fan practices.

That said, the political economy of media convergence does not map symmetrically around the world; audiences outside "developed" economies often have access only to the films and, in some cases, only to pirated copies that may have scenes missing. Even in more developed economies, because they tap different distribution circuits or because the rights may be acquired by different companies or simply because of different corporate goals and strategies, the parts may move separately and in different sequences—the games or comics following or preceding the films themselves. As information spreads from the film into other media, it creates

[10] Tobias C. Van Veen, "Matrix Multitudes in Japan: Reality Bleed or Corporate Performance?" *Hallucinations and Antics*, June 27, 2003, http://www.quadrantcrossing.org/blog/C1692035385/E1656161427/.

ment, but each must use enough that we recognize at a glance that these works belong to the same fictional realm. Consider one of the posters created for the *Matrix* Web page: an agent dressed in black is approaching a bullet-shattered phone booth, his gun in hand, while in the foreground the telephone dangles off its hook. Which of these elements is exclusive to *The Matrix*? Yet, anyone familiar with the franchise can construct the narrative sequence from which this image must have been taken.

More and more, storytelling has become the art of world building, as artists create compelling environments that cannot be fully explored or exhausted within a single work or even a single medium. The world is bigger than the film, bigger even than the franchise—since fan speculations and elaborations also expand the world in a variety of directions. As an experienced screenwriter told me, "When I first started, you would pitch a story because without a good story, you didn't really have a film. Later, once sequels started to take off, you pitched a character because a good character could support multiple stories. And now, you pitch a world because a world can support multiple characters and multiple stories across multiple media." Different franchises follow their own logic: some, such as the *X-Men* (2000) movies, develop the world in their first installment and then allow the sequels to unfold different stories set within that world; others, such as the *Alien* (1979) films or George Romero's *Living Dead* (1968) cycle, introduce new aspects of the world with each new installment, so that more energy gets put into mapping the world than inhabiting it.

inequalities of participation within the franchise. *The Matrix* may be a global cult phenomenon but it is experienced differently in each country around the world.

World-making follows its own market logic, at a time when filmmakers are as much in the business of creating licensed goods as they are in telling stories. Each truly interesting element can potentially yield its own product lines, as George Lucas discovered when he created more and more toys based on the secondary characters in his movies. One of them, Boba Fett, took on a life of its own, in part through children's play.[33] Boba Fett eventually became the protagonist of his own novels and games and played a much larger role in the later films. Adding too much information, however, carries its own risks: fans had long debated whether Boba Fett could actually be a woman underneath the helmet, since we never actually got to see the character's face or hear its voice. But as Lucas fleshed out the character, he also closed down those possibilities, preempting important lines of fan speculation even as he added information that might sustain new fantasies.

As the art of world-making becomes more advanced, art direction takes on a more central role in the conception of franchises. A director such as Tim Burton developed a reputation less as a storyteller (his films often are ramshackle constructions) than as a cultural geographer, cramming every shot with evocative details. The plot and the performances in *Planet of the Apes* (2001), for example, disappointed more or less everyone, yet every shot rewards close attention as details add to our un-derstanding of the society the apes have created; a hard-core fan studies how they dress, how they designed their buildings, what artifacts they use, how they move, what their music sounds like, and so forth. Such a work becomes more rewarding when we watch it on DVD, stopping and starting

Dawson's Desktop

Chris Pike was one of the media industry folks who was inspired by what the Haxans had created with *The Blair Witch Project*. Pike was part of a team working at Sony trying to explore new ways to exploit the Web in promoting television series. What they came up with was Dawson's Desktop, a Web site that modeled the computer files of *Dawson's Creek*'s (1998) title character, allowing visitors to read his e-mail to the other characters, sneak a peak at his journal, his course papers, his screenplay drafts, and, for the most intrusive visitor, even to dig around in his trash bin. The site was updated each day, filling in the gaps between the aired episodes. At its peak popularity, the site was drawing 25 million page views per week. As Pike explained,

> We considered our episodes to be a seven day arc starting one minute after the show ended. . . . Inevitably *Dawson's Creek* would end on a cliffhanger of some kind, we would expand on it,

tackle it, address some of the elements fans would be calling each other and discussing. We wanted to grab that energy right after the show and propel us through the rest of the week. At 9:01, an e-mail or an instant message would start to happen. It would take on the life of a real desktop. E-mail would come in at irregularly scheduled times. Through the middle of the week we would extend a long storyline which was being developed across the season or do some online exclusive arcs which would give us more credibility that as a teen, online, he would go to websites and have chat buddies who may or may not be represented on the weekly show but which will give the character a three dimensional feel. And then as we approached each episode, a day or two before, it was our time to enflame the viewership and start giving a few more clues as to what was about to happen. . . . We had to give all of the clues without giving away the actual events. Our job was to whet the appetites.

Part of what makes a site like Dawson's Desktop possible has been a shift in the ways narratives operate in American television. In the 1960s, most episodes of most prime-time shows were totally self-contained, introducing a temporary crisis in the life of their protagonists, but having to end more or less as they began. Anyone who grew up during that era knew that Gilligan and the other castaways were never going to get off the island no matter how vivid the promise of rescue seemed at the first commercial break. By the 1970s and 1980s, television producers such as Stephen Bochco (*Hill Street Blues*, 1981) were pushing for the chance to expand the narrative complexity of episodic television and facing some resistance from network executives who were not certain people would remember what had

to absorb the background. Some fans trace these tendencies back to *Blade Runner* (1982), where urbanologist Syd Mead was asked to construct the future metropolis on the recognizable foundations of existing Los Angeles. These visions could be fully appreciated only by reading through the coffee-table books that accompany the release of such films and provide commentary on costume design and art direction decisions.

New-media theorist Janet Murray has written of the "encyclopedic capacity" of digital media, which she thinks will lead to new narrative forms as audiences seek information beyond the limits of the individual story.[34] She compares this process of world-making in games or cinema to Faulkner, whose novels and short stories added together to flesh out the life and times of a fictional county in Mississippi. To make these worlds seem even more real, she argues, storytellers and readers begin to create "contextualizing devices —color-coded paths, time lines, family trees, maps, clocks, calendars, and so on."[35] Such devices "enable the viewer to grasp the dense psychological and cultural spaces [represented by modern stories] without becoming disoriented."[36] The animated films, the game, and the comics function in a similar way for *The Matrix*, adding information and fleshing out parts of the world so that the whole becomes more convincing and more comprehensible.

Mahiro Maeda's "The Second Renaissance" (2003), for example, is a richly detailed, rapid-paced chronicle that takes us from the present moment to the era of machine rule that opens the first *Matrix* movie. The animated short is framed as a documentary produced by a machine intelligence to explain the events leading to machines' triumph over the humans. "The Second Renaissance" provides the timeline for the *Matrix* universe, giving a context for events such as the trial of B116ER, the first machine to kill a human, the Million Machine March, and the "darkening of the skies" that are mentioned in other *Matrix* texts. As Maeda explains,

> In Part One, we see humans treat robots as objects, while in Part Two the relationship between human being and robot switches, as humans are studied by the machines. I enjoyed examining how the two sides changed. . . . I wanted to show the broadness of the society, and how the robots were such a part of the background of life that they were treated as mere objects by human beings. . . . In exploring the history of *The Matrix,* I wanted to show the audi-

To shape our response to the images of human authorities crushing the machines, Maeda tapped the image bank of twentieth-century civil unrest, showing the machines throwing themselves under the treads of tanks in a reference to Tiananmen Square or depicting bulldozers rolling over mass graves of crashed robots in a nod toward Auschwitz.

"The Second Renaissance" provides much of the historical background view-

happened in previous episodes. By the 1990s, many of these battles had been fought and won, helped perhaps by the presence of the VCR that allowed people to review favorite series and the Internet that could provide summaries for people who did miss key plot points. The push on series such as *Babylon 5* (1994) or *The X-Files* (1993) was toward season-long story arcs (and plot information that unfolded gradually across multiple seasons). Today, even many sitcoms depend heavily on audience familiarity with program history. And shows such as *24* (2001) assume an audience will be able to remember events that occurred weeks before on television but only a few hours earlier in the story.

As a television series, *Dawson's Creek* was not a radical departure from network norms, but what it did on the Web was more innovative. The device of the desktop allowed the producers to take viewers deeper inside the heads of the characters, to see other dimensions of their social interactions. Because they coordinated with the series writers, the Web team could provide back story for upcoming events. As Pike explained, "If Aunt Jenny is sending e-mail out of the blue, there's a reason, and you had better keep an eye on it, because in three or four or five episodes, when Aunt Jenny arrives, you are going to feel good because you already know this character was from the 60s and drinks too much. You know the complete back story so that when the character walks on screen, you know who they are and your relationship to the series has been enriched. We've done our job."

From the start, the Dawson's Desktop team collaborated with the program's active fans. Its producers said they were inspired to expand the story from reading all of the fan fiction that sprang up around the characters. They closely monitored the five hundred or so *Dawson's Creek* fan sites and created an advisory board of twenty-five creators who they felt had developed the best amateur content. As Andrew Schneider, a leader of the project, explained, "We're in touch with them all the time. We wanted to make sure the fans were getting what they wanted. They helped us design the interface and they told us what they liked and did not like."[1] As the site continued, the fans were encouraged to send their own e-mails to Dawson as if they were fellow Capeside High students, and he would respond to their fictional personas on the site. In that way, the producers integrated the creative energy of the fan community into developing new content, which, in turn, would sustain fan interest.

[1] Darren Crosdale, *Dawson's Creek: The Official Companion* (London: Ebury, 1999), pp. 145–147.

ers need as they watch Neo return to 01, the machine city, to plead with its inhabitants for assistance in overthrowing the agents. Without learning about the many times the machines had pursued diplomatic relations with the humans and been rejected, it is hard to understand why his approach yielded such transforming results. Similarly, the images showing the humans' efforts to block off the Earth from solar rays resurfaces when we see Neo's craft go above the cloud level and into the blue skies that humans have not seen for generations. "Second Renaissance" introduces many of the weapons deployed during the final assault on Zion, including the massive "mecha" suits the humans wear as they fight off the invaders.

At the same time, "The Second Renaissance" builds upon "Bits and Pieces of Information," one of the *Matrix* comics drawn by Geof Darrow from a script by the Wachowski brothers.[38] The comic introduced the pivotal figure of B116ER, the robot who kills his masters when he is about to be junked and whose trial first asserted the concept of machine rights within human culture. Much like "The Second Renaissance," "Bits and Pieces of Information" draws on the existing iconography of human-rights struggles, quoting directly from the Dred Scott decision and naming the robot after Bigger Thomas, the protagonist of Richard Wright's *Native Son* (1940). If the first feature film started with a simple opposition between man and machines, the Wachowski brothers used these intertexts to create a much more emotionally nuanced and morally complicated story. In the end, man and machines can still find common interests despite centuries of conflict and oppression.

Most film critics are taught to think in terms of very traditional story structures. More and more, they are talking about a collapse of storytelling. We should be suspicious of such claims, since it is hard to imagine that the public has actually lost interest in stories. Stories are basic to all human cultures, the primary means by which we structure, share, and make sense of our common experiences. Rather, we are seeing the emergence of new story structures, which create complexity by expanding the range of narrative possibility rather than pursuing a single path with a beginning, middle, and end. *Entertainment Weekly* proclaimed 1999, the year that *The Matrix, Fight Club, The Blair Witch Project, Being John Malkovich, Run Lola Run, Go, American Beauty,* and *The Sixth Sense* hit the market, as "the year that changed the movies." Filmgoers educated on nonlinear media like video games were expecting a different kind of entertainment experience.[39] If you look at such works by old criteria, these movies may seem more fragmented, but the fragments exist so that consumers can make the connections on their own time and in their own ways. Murray notes, for example, that such works are apt to attract three very different kinds of consumers: "the actively engaged real-time viewers who must find suspense and satisfaction in each single episode and the more reflective long-term audience who look for coherent patterns in the story as a whole . . . [and] the navigational viewer who takes pleasure in following the connections between different parts of the story and in discovering multiple arrangements of the same material."[40]

For all of its innovative and experimental qualities, transmedia storytelling is not entirely new. Take, for example, the story of Jesus as told in the Middle Ages. Unless you were literate, Jesus was not rooted in a book but was something you

From Appointment Television to Engagement Television

The transmedia model has been closely linked to larger shifts in the ways that the American television industry thinks about its consumers—away from an appointment-based model towards an engagement-based paradigm. Under the appointment model, sometimes described as "Must See TV" (a phrase from a 1980s advertising campaign for NBC's Thursday night lineup), the networks sought committed viewers who would arrange their lives to be home at a certain time to watch their favorite programs. New mechanisms since then allow consumers to access television content on their own schedules—video cassette recorders and later digital video recorders, digital downloads, video iPods, and boxed sets of DVDs. By 2007, the networks were basing programming decisions on a hybrid model which combined data about those watching as the program was broadcast with those watching at some later point (though the value of this "time-shifting" was measured in terms of its proximity to the scheduled air date). Revenues from these alternative platforms were increasing central to the funding of content production.

These shifts in the context of viewing have pushed both the television and advertising industries to seek alternative mechanisms for measuring audience engagement. One participant at a media industry gathering summarized the challenges of defining engagement: "We're talking to one agency who thinks that loyalty is an important factor, and they measure that by the number of people who have watched three out of four episodes. Another thinks it's persistence, and that's measured by numbers of minutes watched per show. And there's others who want to look at 'persuasiveness.' We actually did a literature review and there are 8 different words and phrases that people have used to get at this concept."[1]

On the creative side, a series of groundbreaking cult programs, including *Alias, Lost, 24, Battlestar Galactica, The Sopranos, The Shield, The Wire,* and *Heroes,* defined what engagement television looked like. As writers like Jason Mittell and Stephen Johnson have noted, these series were marked by narrative and formal complexity, often represented through ensemble casts, extended story arcs, and a constant intensification and deferral of narrative enigmas.[2] The reliance on ensemble casts and on the mixing of different entertainment genres means that these series provide multiple points of entry, supporting fans with different perspectives and interests. So, *Lost* balances puzzles (what's the status of the Island? what can we learn from deciphering the map?) with backstory (how did each of these characters get here? what issues do they face back home?) and narrative enigmas (what will happen next as the characters work through interpersonal alliances, struggle with the Others, and undergo a process of personal redemption and corruption?). Whereas complexity in the 1980s might have been defined in terms of the need to provide "quality drama" for a demographically elite consumer, today's "complex" programs typically offer genre entertainment hoping to draw in the younger males who were abandoning television

---

[1] See Ivan Askwith, "TV 2.0: Turning Television into an Engagement Medium," Master's thesis, Comparative Media Studies Program, MIT, Cambridge, MA, 2007.

[2] Jason Mittell, "Narrative Complexity in Contemporary American Television," *The Velvet Light Trap* 58, no. 1 (2006): 29–40; Stephen Johnson, *Everything Bad Is Good for You* (New York: Riverhead, 2006).

---

encountered at multiple levels in your culture. Each representation (a stained-glass window, a tapestry, a psalm, a sermon, a live performance) assumed that you already knew the character and his story from someplace else. More recently, writers such as J. R. R. Tolkien sought to create new fictions that self-consciously imitated the organization of folklore or mythology, creating an interlocking set of stories that together flesh out the world of Middle Earth. Following a similar logic, Maeda explicitly compares "The Second Renaissance" to Homeric epics: "I wanted to make this film as beautiful as a story from ancient Greek myth, and explore what it means to be human, as well as not human, and how the ideas are related to one another. In Greek myths there are moments where the best side of human nature is explored, and others where the protagonists are shown as very cruel. I wanted to bring the same atmosphere to these episodes."[41]

When the Greeks heard stories about Odysseus, they didn't need to be told who he was, where he came from, or what his mission was. Homer was able to create an oral epic by building on "bits and pieces of information" from preexisting myths, counting on a knowledgeable audience to ride over any potential points of confusion. This is why high school students today struggle with *The Odyssey,* because they don't have the same frame of reference as the original audience. Where a native listener might hear a description of a character's helmet and recognize him as the hero of a particular city-state and, from there, know something of his character and importance, the contemporary high school student runs into a brick wall, with some of the information that once made these characters seem so real buried in some arcane tome. Their parents may confront a similar barrier to fully engaging with the film franchises so valued by their children—walking into an *X-Men* movie with no background in comics might leave you confused about some of the minor characters who have much deeper significance to long-term comics readers. Often, characters in transmedia stories do not need to be introduced so much as reintroduced, because they are known from other sources. Just as Homer's audience identified with different characters depending on their city-state, today's children enter the movie with preexisting identifications because they have played with the action figures or game avatars.

The idea that contemporary Hollywood draws on ancient myth structures has become common wisdom among the current generation of filmmakers. Joseph Campbell, the author of *The Hero with a Thousand Faces* (1949), praised *Star Wars* for embodying what he has described as the "monomyth," a conceptual structure abstracted from a cross-cultural analysis of the world's great religions.[42] Today, many screenwriting guides speak about the "hero's journey," popularizing ideas from Campbell, and game designers have similarly been advised to sequence the tasks their protagonists must perform into a similar physical and spiritual

for games and other interactive entertainment. Once such fans were drawn into a program, they demanded more in-depth and intensive relationships with the content.

By 2006–2007, the networks were announcing transmedia strategies for all of their programs. NBC called it 360 entertainment; ABC, EnhancedTV. Among the more common strategies were the development of short additional scenes for consumption via mobile platforms (such as a series of "mobisodes" developed around secondary characters in *The Office*, or a highly compressed storyline for *24*), the deployment of alternative reality games by shows like *Lost* or *Torchwood*, spinoff books that were embedded in the fiction (such as *Lost's Bad Twin* or the *Guiding Light's Oakdale Confidential*), podcasts which offered fans a more intimate glimpse into the thinking processes of producers (including those centering around *Battlestar Galactica*), and social network site profiles allowing fans to express their affiliations with particular characters (such as those created around *Veronica Mars* or *Gossip Girl*).

For the superhero drama *Heroes*, a series of Web comics, released each week in coordination with the aired content, provided an ideal vehicle for providing backstory on the expanding cast of characters: "We had so many stories to tell and there was only so much room in the TV show—so we decided that we could tell these alternative stories in the comics. The stories could be deeper, broader and reveal more secrets about our characters. It was also a way to tell stories that would be otherwise unproduceable on our show."[3] Having learned from earlier

[3] Jeph Loeb, *The Heroes Interview, Heroes Volume One* (La Jolla, CA: Wildstorm, 2007), pp. 233–235.

experiments such as **Dawson's Desktop** or *The Animatrix*, the producers sought to respect and reward different modes of viewing: "We have to service the broadcast audience first and make sure they understand what the hell is going on, that they can tune into the broadcast episodes and get it. But we want to add value for the core fans who are interested in going deeper into the show. Often we are struggling with what do we reveal online, what do we reveal on the show. That's an interesting challenge that we have because we have the transmedia outlet to be able to expand our stories" (*Heroes* executive producer Jesse Alexander).[4]

In another experiment in transmedia storytelling, the producers of *CSI:NY* collaborated with Linden Lab, the creators of *Second Life*, a popular virtual world, and with Electric Sheep, an advertising company closely associated with strategies of transmedia branding. Viewers could enter a digital re-creation of the crime scene introduced in one episode and work through clues together before the solution to the mystery was announced on a subsequent episode. Electric Sheep's Damon Taylor outlined the multiple goals behind this highly publicized initiative:

> Potential new users who are fans of *CSI: NY* will care about this crossover because it will give them the opportunity to wrestle with *CSI* content in a way that has never been made available to them before.... In the meantime, we give new users who have never been in a virtual world a closed universe experience where they can come into *Second Life*, familiarize themselves with this world and what it means to be in a vir-

ordeal.[43] Audience familiarity with this basic plot structure allows script writers to skip over transitional or expository sequences, throwing us directly into the heart of the action.

Similarly, if protagonists and antagonists are broad archetypes rather than individualistic, novelistic, and rounded characters, they are immediately recognizable. We can see *The Matrix* as borrowing these archetypes both from popular entertainment genres (the hacker protagonist, the underground resistance movement, the mysterious men in black) as well as from mythological sources (Morpheus, Persephone, The Oracle). This reliance on stock characters is especially important in the case of games, where players frequently skip through the instruction books and past early cut scenes, allowing little time for exposition before grabbing the controller and trying to navigate the world. Film critics often compared the characters in the *Matrix* films to video game characters. Roger Ebert, for example, suggests that he measured his concern for Neo in *Revolutions* less in terms of affection for the character and "more like the score in a video game."[44] *Slate*'s David Edelstein suggests that a spectacular opening stunt by Trinity in *The Matrix Reloaded* "has the disposable feel of a video game. You can imagine the program resetting itself, and then all of those little zeros and ones reassembling to play again."[45] In both cases, the writers use the video game analogy to imply a disinterest in the characters, yet, for gamers, the experience is

---

4 Jesse Alexander, "NBC's *Heroes*: 'Appointment TV' to 'Engagement TV'?", MIT Communications Forum, November 15, 2007, http://web.mit.edu/comm-forum/forums/heroes.html.

one of immediacy: the character becomes a vehicle for their direct experience of the game world. By tapping video game iconography, the *Matrix* movies create a more intense, more immediate engagement for viewers who come into the theater knowing who these characters are and what they can do. As the film continues, we flesh out the stick figures, adding more back story and motivation, and we continue to search for additional insights across other media as we exit the theater.

When I suggest parallels between *The Odyssey* and the *Matrix*, I anticipate a certain degree of skepticism. I do not claim that these modern works have the same depth of incrusted meanings. These new "mythologies," if we can call them that, are emerging in the context of an increasingly fragmented and multicultural society. While the *Matrix* films have been the subject of several books linking them to core philosophical debates, and while many fans see these films as enacting religious myths, articulating spirituality is not their primary function, the perspective they take is not likely to be read literally by their audience, and their expressed beliefs are not necessarily central to our everyday lives. Homer wrote within a culture of relative consensus and stability, whereas the *Matrix* emerges from a time of rapid change and cultural diversity. Its goals are not so much to preserve cultural traditions as to put together the pieces of the culture in innovative ways. *The Matrix* is a work very much of the moment, speaking to contemporary anxieties about technology and bureaucracy, feeding on current notions of multiculturalism, and tapping recent models of resistance. The story may reference a range of different belief sys-

tual world, and play and interact with mystery game experiences that interest them. This crossover gives fans of *CSI: NY* a reason and an excuse to come into a virtual world and do something that is functional, exciting, interesting, and engaging.[5]

This close collaboration between program producers, brand gurus, and new media companies suggests rapid growth of industry interest in transmedia entertainment over just a few short years. By late 2007, these transmedia strategies had become so fully integrated into the way American network television operates that they became one of the focal points for an extended writers' strike. Network executives and production companies sought to define transmedia content as "promotional," whereas the creative workers argued that such content was now integral to the program's creative development (not to mention its own source of revenue). Advertisers demanded deals which extended their brand campaigns into this transmedia space. Writers were not being compensated for this content in the same way as they would be for broadcast material. All of this points back to the complex interweaving of creative and economic goals behind these new cross-platform strategies.

[5] Sam Ford, "Producing The *CSI:NY*/Second Life Crossover: An Interview with Electric Sheep's Taylor and Krueger," Confessions of an Aca-Fan, October 24, 2007, http://henryjenkins.org/2007/10/producing_ the_csinysecond_life .html

tems, such as the Judeo-Christian Messiah myth, to speak about these present-day concerns with some visionary force. At the same time, by evoking these earlier narratives, *The Matrix* invites us to read more deeply in the Western tradition and bring what we find there to bear on contemporary media.[46]

Consider, for example, this reading of the tribal celebration in *The Matrix Reloaded* through the lens of biblical interpretation:

> The feet [stamping] on the ground means that Zion is on Earth. Plain and simple. This parallels the Architect scene, and gets to the main thesis. We are cast out of the "perfection" of Heaven and living in the Real World. Symbolically, the Matrix is Heaven. Cypher makes this point in the first movie. The Real World is hard, dirty, and uncomfortable. The Matrix is, well, paradise. This point is made again in the first movie by Agent Smith, who calls the Matrix "the perfect human world" [paraphrased]. Recall that the Architect scene happens in utterly clean, utterly white perfection. The Biblical reference is clear enough. Neo, Trinity, Morpheus, and the rest of Zion have rejected God's Garden of Eden where all their needs are taken care of in favor of a hard, scrabbling existence where at least they have free will.[47]

So, even if you see classical myths as more valuable than their contemporary counterpart, works such as *The Matrix* draw consumers back to those older works, giving them new currency.

Film critic Roger Ebert ridicules this attempt to insert traditional myth into a pop science fiction/kung fu epic:

> These speeches provide not meaning, but the effect of meaning: it sure sounds like those guys are saying some profound things. This will not prevent fanboys from analyzing the philosophy of *The Matrix Reloaded* in endless web postings. Part of the fun is becoming an expert in the deep meaning of shallow pop mythology; there is something refreshingly ironic about becoming an authority on the transient extrusions of mass culture, and Morpheus (Laurence Fishburne) now joins Obi-Wan Kenobi as the Plato of our age.[48]

This criticism looks different if you accept that value arises here from the process of looking for meaning (and the elaboration of the story by the audience) and not purely from the intentionality of the Wachowski brothers. What the Wachowski brothers did was trigger a search for meaning; they did not determine where the audience would go to find their answers.

Additive Comprehension

If creators do not ultimately control what we take from their transmedia stories, this does not prevent them from trying to shape our interpretations. Neil Young talks about "additive comprehension." He cites the example of the director's cut of *Blade Runner,* where adding a small segment showing Deckard discovering an origami unicorn invited viewers to question whether Deckard might be a replicant: "That changes your whole perception of the film, your perception of the ending. . . . The challenge for us, especially with *The Lord of the Rings,* is how do we deliver the origami unicorn, how do we deliver that one piece of information that makes you look at the films differently." Young ex-plained how that moment inspired his team: "In the case of *The Lord of the Rings: Return of the King* the added comprehension is the fact that Gandalf is the architect of this plan and has been the architect of this plan for some time. . . . Our hope is that you would play the game and that would motivate you to watch the films with this new piece of knowledge which would shift your perception of what has happened in the previous films." Here, Young points toward a possibility suggested by the books but not directly referenced in the films themselves.

Like his colleague Danny Bilson, Young sees transmedia storytelling as the terrain he wants to explore with his future work. His first experiment, *Majestic,* created a transmedia experience from scratch with bits of information coming at the player

The Cloudmakers and the "Beast"

They called it the "Beast." The name started with the Puppetmasters, the Microsoft team hired to put together what was perhaps the world's most complex puzzle, but soon the name was also being used by the Cloudmakers, a self-selected team of more than five hundred players who were working together to solve it. The "Beast" was created to help promote the Steven Spielberg film *Artificial Intelligence: A.I.* (2001), but most people who lived through it would laugh in your face if you thought the film was in any sense more important or more interesting than the game it spawned.[1]

[1] Charles Herold, "Game Theory: Tracking an Elusive Film Game Online," *New York Times,* May 3, 2001; Keith Boswell, "Artificial Intelligence—Viral Marketing and the Web," *Marketleap Report,* April 16, 2001, http://www.marketleap.com/report/ml_report_05 .htm; Pamela Parker, "Who Killed Evan Chan? The Intelligence behind an AI Marketing Effort," *Ad Insight,* May 8, 2001, http://www.channelseven.com/adinsight/ commentary/2001comm/comm20010508.shtml; Christopher Saunders, "The All-Encompassing Media Experience," *Internet Advertising Report,* June 27, 2001, http://www.turoads.com/richmedia_news/2001rmn/ rmn20010627.shtml.

Here's how one of the game's Puppetmasters, Sean Stewart, described the initial concept:

Create an entire self-contained world on the web, say a thousand pages deep, and then tell a story through it, advancing the plot with weekly updates, concealing each new piece of narrative in such a way that it would take clever teamwork to dig it out. Create a vast array of assets —custom photos, movies, audio recordings, scripts, corporate blurbage, logos, graphic treatments, web sites, flash movies—and deploy them through a net of (untraceable) web sites, phone calls, fax systems, leaks, press releases, phony newspaper ads, and so on ad infinitum.[2]

The threshold (or what designers call "the rabbit hole") into this vast universe of interconnecting Web sites was the mystery surrounding the death of Evan Chan and the question of what Jeanine Salla, the "sentient machine therapist," knew about it. But Chan's death was simply the device that set the plot into motion. Before the game was over, the players would have explored the entire universe where Spielberg's film was set, and the authors would have drawn upon pretty much everything they had ever thought about.

From the start, the puzzles were too complex, the knowledge too esoteric, the universe too vast to be solved by any single player. As one player told CNN, "To date, puzzles have had us reading *Gödel, Escher and Bach*, translating from German and Japanese, even an obscure language called Kannada, decrypting Morse code and Enigma, and performing an unbelievable range of operations on sound and image files."[3]

[2] Sean Stewart, "The A.I. Web Game," http://www.seanstewart.org/beast/intro/.

[3] Daniel Sieberg, "Reality Blurs, Hype Builds with Web A.I. Game," http://www.cnn.com/SPECIALS/2001/coming.attractions/stories/aibuzz.html.

via faxes, cell-phone calls, e-mail, and Web sites. With *The Lord of the Rings* games, he worked within the constraints of a well-established world and a major movie franchise. Next, he is turning his attention toward creating new properties that can be built from the ground up as cross-media collaborations. His thinking races far ahead: "I want to understand the kinds of story comprehension which are unique to transmedia storytelling. I've got my world, I've got my arcs, some of those arcs can be expressed in the video game space, some of them can be expressed in the film space, the television space, the literary space, and you are getting to the true transmedia storytelling."

With *Enter the Matrix*, the "origami unicorn" takes several forms, most notably refocusing of the narrative around Niobe and Ghost. As the game's designer, David Perry, explains, every element of the game went toward helping us understand who these people are: "If you play as Ghost, who's a Zen Buddhist Apache assassin, you'll automatically ride shotgun in the driving levels, which allow you to fire out the window at agents hunting you down. Niobe is known in Zion as being one of the fastest, craziest drivers in the *Matrix* universe, so when you play the game as her, you'll get to drive through a complex *Matrix* world filled with real traffic and pedestrians, while a computer-controlled Ghost takes out the enemies."[49] Cut scenes (those moments in the game which are prerecorded and not subject to player intervention) give us more insight into the romantic triangle among Niobe, Morpheus, and Locke, which helps to explain, in part, Locke's hostility to Morpheus throughout the film. Having played through the game, you can read the longing and tension within their on-screen relationship. As for Ghost, he remains a background figure in the movie, having only a handful of spoken lines, but his screen appearances reward those who have made the effort to play the game. Some film critics complained about the degree to which Niobe's character displaces Morpheus from the center of *The Matrix Revolutions*, as if a minor character were upstaging a well-established protagonist. Yet, how we felt about Niobe would depend on whether we had played *Enter the Matrix*. Someone who had played the games would have spent, perhaps, a hundred hours controlling Niobe's character, compared to less than four hours watching Morpheus; struggling to keep the character alive and to complete the missions would have resulted in an intense bond that would not be experienced by viewers who saw her on screen only for a handful of scenes.

Perhaps the most spectacular example of "additive comprehension" occurred after the film trilogy had been completed. With little fanfare or warning, on May 26, 2005, Morpheus, Neo's mentor, was killed off in *The Matrix Online*, while trying to reclaim Neo's body that had been carried away by the machines at the end of *Revolutions*. As Chadwick explained, "They wanted to start with something significant and meaningful and shock-

To confront the "beast" required players to work together, seeking out friends, tapping Web communities, drawing in anyone you could find. Before long, smaller teams joined forces, until there was an army of scavengers and puzzle-solvers, putting in hours and hours a day trying to find their way to the bottom of the conspiracies.

Both the Puppetmasters and the Cloudmakers have conceded that this was a game everyone was making up as they went along. The team at Microsoft had no idea that the Beast would spark this level of fan commitment and interest, and the fans had no idea how far the producers would be willing to go in order to keep them engaged with the mystery. Tom, one of the Cloudmakers, explained, "As we got better and better at solving their puzzles, they had to come up with harder puzzles. They were responding to stuff we were saying or doing. When we cracked a puzzle too fast, they would change the type of puzzles. There was one point that we found things in their source code that they didn't intend to be there. And they had to write some story to cover this. They were writing just a little ahead of players."[4] Writing the game proved to be every bit as challenging. Stewart explained, "At our best—like the players—we were scary good and scary fast. . . . It was street theater and a con game and a pennant drive rolled into one."[5]

The Beast was a new form of immersive entertainment or encyclopedic storytelling, which was unfolding at the points of contact between authors and consumers. Jane McGonigal, who worked with some of the Puppet-

[4] Tom, interview with author, April 2003.
[5] Stewart, "The A.I. Web Game."

masters to develop the follow-up game ilovebees, calls the genre alternate reality gaming (ARG). She defines ARGs as "an interactive drama played out online and in real world spaces, taking place over several weeks or months, in which dozens, hundreds, thousands of players come together online, form collaborative social networks, and work together to solve a mystery or problem that would be absolutely impossible to solve alone."[6] True to the logic of affective economics, 4orty2wo Entertainment, the company that Stewart and others created to advance alternate reality games, explains that such activities generate product and brand awareness: "Our aim is to carve the client's world into today's cultural landscape, so that, like Middle Earth or Hogwarts, it becomes a priority destination for the American imagination. . . . We create communities passionately committed to spending not just their money but their imaginations in the worlds we represent."[7] That's what they must have told the funders.

For the most hard-core players, these games can be so much more. ARGs teach participants how to navigate complex information environments and how to pool their knowledge and work together in teams to solve problems. McGonigal argues that ARGs are generating "players who feel more capable, more confident, more expressive, more engaged and more connected in their everyday lives."[8] A well-designed ARG reshapes the way participants think about their real and

ing and this was it."[50] A major turning point in the franchise occurred not on screen for a mass audience but in game for a niche public. Even many of those playing the game would not have witnessed the death directly but would have learned about it through rumors from other players or from some other secondary source. Morpheus's death was then used to motivate a variety of player missions within the game world.

EA's Young worried that the Wachowski brothers may have narrowed their audience by making too many demands on them:

> The more layers you put on something, the smaller the market. You are requiring people to intentionally invest more time in what it is you are trying to tell them and that's one of the challenges of transmedia storytelling. . . . If we are going to take a world and express it through multiple media at the same time, you might need to express it sequentially. You may need to lead people into a deep love of the story. Maybe it starts with a game and then a film and then television. You are building a relationship with the world rather than trying to put it all out there at once.

Young may well be right. The Wachowski brothers were so uncompromising in their expectations that consumers would follow the franchise that much of the emotional payoff of *Revolutions* is accessible only to people who have played the game. The film's attempts to close down

[6] Jane McGonigal, "Alternate Reality Gaming," presentation to MacArthur Foundation, November 2004, http://avantgame.com/McGonigal%20ARG%20MacArthur%20Foundation%20Nov%202004.pdf.

[7] "Capabilities and Approach," http://www.4orty2wo.com.

[8] McGonigal, "Alternate Reality Gaming."

its plot holes disappointed many hardcore fans. Their interest in *The Matrix* peaked in the middle that tantalized them with possibilities. For the casual consumer, *The Matrix* asked too much. For the hard-core fan, it provided too little. Could any film have matched the fan community's escalating expectations and expanding interpretations and still have remained accessible to a mass audience? There has to be a breaking point beyond which franchises cannot be stretched, subplots can't be added, secondary characters can't be identified, and references can't be fully realized. We just don't know where it is yet.

Film critic Richard Corliss raised these concerns when he asked his readers, "Is Joe Popcorn supposed to carry a *Matrix* concordance in his head?"[51] The answer is no, but "Joe Popcorn" can pool his knowledge with other fans and build a collective concordance on the Internet.[52] Across a range of fan sites and discussion lists, the fans were gathering information, tracing allusions, charting chains of command, constructing timelines, assembling reference guides, transcribing dialogue, extending the story through their own fan fiction, and speculating like crazy about what it all meant. The depth and breadth of the *Matrix* universe made it impossible for any one consumer to "get it," but the emergence of knowledge cultures made it possible for the community as a whole to dig deeper into this bottomless text.

Such works also pose new expectations on critics—and this may be part of

virtual environments. As McGonigal explains, "the best pervasive games do make you more suspicious, more inquisitive, of your everyday surroundings. A good immersive game will show you game patterns in non-game places; those patterns reveal opportunities for interaction and intervention."[9] A well-designed ARG also changes the ways participants think about themselves, giving them a taste of what it is like to work together in massive teams, pooling their expertise toward a common cause. They develop an ethic based on sharing rather than hording knowledge; they learn how to decide what knowledge to trust and what to discard. Here's how one of the Cloudmakers, the largest and most influential team on the AI game, described their self-perception: "The 7500+ people in this group . . . we are all one. We have manifested this idea of an unbelievably intricate intelligence. We are one mind, one voice. . . . We have become a part of something greater than ourselves."[10]

For Barry Joseph, one of the Cloudmakers, the game didn't just immerse him in the *A.I.* world. Solving the game together changed what the film meant, offering up an alternative vision of the ways that people would be living and interacting in an era of new information technologies. Against the pessimism many found at the heart of the story, "the image of humans living in fear of technology's ubiquitous eye," they had their own experience of "cooperative behavior that takes advantage of the powers of a group mind." The game's

[9] Jane McGonigal, "A Real Little Game: The Performance of Belief in Pervasive Play," http://avantgame .com/MCGONIGAL%20A%20Reak%20Kuttke% 20Game%20DIGRA%202003.pdf.

[10] Jane McGonigal, "This Is Not a Game: Immersive Aesthetics and Collective Play," http://www.sean stewart.org/beast/mcgonigal/notagame/paper.pdf.

content taught them to fear the future; the game's play experience to embrace it.[11]

[11] Barry Joseph, "When the Medium Is the Message," May 25, 2001, http://cloudmakers.cloudmakers.org/editorials/bjoseph525.shtml.

what Corliss was reacting against. In writing this chapter, I have had to tap into the collective intelligence of the fan community. Many of the insights I've offered here emerged from my reading of fan critics and the conversations on discussion lists. While I possess some expertise of my own as a longtime science fiction and comics fan (knowing for example the ways that Paul Chadwick's previous work in comics connects to his participation in the *Matrix* franchise), this merely makes me one more member of this knowledge community—someone who knows some things but has to rely on others to access additional information. I may have analytic tools for examining a range of different media, but much of what I suggest here about the links between the game and the films, for example, emerged not from my own game playing but from the conversations about the game online. In the process of writing this chapter, then, I became a participant rather than an expert, and there is much about this franchise which I still do not know. In the future, my ideas may feed back into the conversation, but I also will need to tap the public discussion in search of fresh information and insights. Criticism may have once been a meeting of two minds—the critic and the author—but now there are multiple authors and multiple critics.

Inhabiting such a world turns out to be child's play—literally. Transmedia storytelling is perhaps at its most elaborate, so far, in children's media franchises like *Pokémon* or *Yu-Gi-Oh!* As education professors David Buckingham and Julian Sefton-Green explain, "*Pokémon* is something you do, not just something you read or watch or consume."[53] There are several hundred different *Pokémon*, each with multiple evolutionary forms and a complex set of rivalries and attachments. There is no one text where one can go to get the information about these various species; rather, the child assembles what they know about the *Pokémon* from various media with the result that each child knows something his or her friends do not and thus has a chance to share this expertise with others. Buckingham and Sefton-Green explain: "Children may watch the television cartoon, for example, as a way of gathering knowledge that they can later utilize in playing the computer game or in trading cards, and vice versa. . . . The texts of *Pokémon* are not designed merely to be consumed in the passive sense of the word. . . . In order to be part of the *Pokémon* culture, and to learn what you need to know, you must actively seek out new information and new products and, crucially, engage with others in doing so."[54]

We might see such play with the possibilities of *Pokémon* or *Yu-Gi-Oh!* as part of the process by which young children learn to inhabit the new kinds of social and cultural structures Lévy describes.[55] Children are being prepared to contribute to a more sophisticated knowledge culture. So far, our schools are from others is still classified as cheating. Yet, in our adult lives, we are depending more and more on others to provide information we cannot process ourselves. Our workplaces have become more collaborative; our political process has become more decentered; we are living more and more within knowledge cultures based on collective intelligence. Our schools are not teaching what it means to live and work in such knowledge communities, but popular culture may be doing so. In *The Internet Galaxy* (2001), cybertheorist Manuel Castells claims that while the public has shown limited interest in hypertexts, they have developed a hypertextual relationship to existing media content: "Our minds—not our machines—process culture. . . . If our minds have the material capability to access the whole realm of cultural expressions— select them, recombine them—we do have a hypertext: the hypertext is inside us."[56] Younger consumers have be-come informational hunters and gatherers, taking pleasure in tracking down character backgrounds and plot points and making connections between different texts within the same franchise. And so it is predictable that they are going to be expecting these same kinds of experiences from works that appeal to teens and young adults, resulting in something like *The Matrix*. Soon, we may be seeing these same hypertextual or transmedia principles applied to the quality dramas that appeal to more mature consumers—shows such as *The West Wing* (1999) or *The Sopranos* (1999), for example, would seem to lend themselves readily to such expectations, and soap operas have long depended on elaborate character relationships and serialized plotlines that could easily expand beyond television and into other media. One can certainly imagine mysteries that ask readers to search for clues across a range of different media or historical fictions that depend on the additive comprehension enabled by multiple texts to make the past come alive for their readers. This transmedia impulse is at the heart of what I am calling convergence culture. More experimental artists, such as Peter Greenaway or Matthew Barney, are already experimenting with how they might incorporate transmedia principles into their work.

One can also imagine that kids who grew up in this media-mix culture would produce new kinds of media as transmedia storytelling becomes more intuitive. *The Matrix* may be the next step in that process of cultural evolution—a bridge to a new kind of culture and a new kind of society. In a hunting culture, kids play with bows and arrows. In an information society, they play with information. Now some readers may be shaking their heads in total skepticism. Such approaches work best with younger consumers, they argue, be-cause they have more time on their hands. They demand way too much effort for "Joe Popcorn," for the harried mom or the working stiff who has just snuggled onto the couch after a hard day at the office. As we have seen, media conglomeration creates an economic incentive to move in this direction, but Hollywood can go only so far down that direction if audiences are not ready to shift their mode of consumption. Right now, many older consumers are left confused or uninvolved with such entertainments, though some are also learning to adapt. Not every story will go in this direction—though more and more stories are traveling across media and offering a depth of experience that would have been unanticipated in previous decades. The key point is that going in deep has to remain an option—something readers choose to do—and not the only way to derive pleasure from media franchises. A growing number of consumers may be choosing their popular culture because of the opportunities it offers them to explore complex worlds and compare notes with others. More and more consumers are enjoying participating in online knowledge cultures and discovering what it is like to expand one's comprehension by tapping the combined expertise of these grassroots communities. Yet, sometimes, we simply want to watch. And as long as that remains the case, many franchises may re-main big and dumb and noisy. But don't be too surprised if around the edges there are clues that something else is also going on or that the media companies will offer us the chance to buy into new kinds of experiences with those characters and those worlds.

4

Quentin Tarantino's *Star Wars?*

Grassroots Creativity Meets the Media Industry

Shooting in garages and basement rec rooms, rendering F/X on home computers, and ripping music from CDs and MP3 files, fans have created new versions of the *Star Wars* (1977) mythology. In the words of *Star Wars or Bust* director Jason Wishnow, "This is the future of cinema —*Star Wars* is the catalyst."[1]

The widespread circulation of *Star Wars*–related commodities has placed resources into the hands of a generation of emerging filmmakers in their teens or early twenties. They grew up dressing as Darth Vader for Halloween, sleeping on Princess Leia sheets, battling with plastic light sabers, and playing with Boba Fett action figures. *Star Wars* has become their "legend," and now they are determined to remake it on their own terms.

When AtomFilms launched an official *Star Wars* fan film contest in 2003, they received more than 250 submissions. Although the ardor has died down somewhat, the 2005 competition received more than 150 submissions.[2] And many more are springing up on the Web via unofficial sites such as TheForce.net, which would fall outside the rules for the official contest. Many of these films come complete with their own posters or advertising campaigns. Some Web sites provide updated information about amateur films still in production.

Fans have always been early adapters of new media technologies; their fascination with fictional universes often inspires new forms of cultural production, ranging from costumes to fanzines and, now, digital cinema. Fans are the most active segment of the media audience, one that refuses to simply accept what they are given, but rather insists on the right to become full participants.[3] None of this is new. What has shifted is the visibility of fan culture. The Web provides a powerful new distribution channel for amateur cultural production. Amateurs have been making home movies for decades; these movies are going public.

When Amazon introduced DVDs of *George Lucas in Love* (1999), perhaps the best known of the *Star Wars* parodies, it outsold the DVD of *Star Wars Episode I: The Phantom Menace* (1999) in its opening week.[4] Fan filmmakers, with some legitimacy, see their works as "calling cards" that may help them break into the commercial industry. In spring 1998, a two-page color spread in *Entertainment Weekly* profiled aspiring digital filmmaker Kevin Rubio, whose ten-minute, $1,200 film, *Troops* (1998), had attracted the interests of Hollywood insiders.[5] *Troops* spoofs *Star Wars* by offering a *Cops*-like profile of the stormtroopers who do the day-in, day-out work of policing Tatooine, settling domestic disputes, rounding up space hustlers, and trying to crush the Jedi Knights. As a result, the story reported, Rubio was fielding offers from several studios interested in financing his next project. Lucas admired the film so much that he gave Rubio a job writing for the *Star Wars* comic books. Rubio surfaced again in 2004 as a writer and producer for *Duel Masters* (2004), a little-known series on the Cartoon Network.

Fan digital film is to cinema what the punk DIY culture was to music. There, grassroots experimentation generated new sounds, new artists, new techniques, and new relations to consumers which have been pulled more and more into mainstream practice. Here, fan filmmakers are starting to make their way into the mainstream industry, and we are starting to see ideas—such as the use of game engines as animation tools—bubbling up from the amateurs and making their way into commercial media.

If, as some have argued, the emergence of modern mass media spelled the doom for the vital folk culture traditions that thrived in nineteenth-century America, the current moment of media change is reaffirming the right of everyday people to actively contribute to their culture. Like the older folk culture of quilting bees and barn dances, this new vernacular culture encourages broad participation, grassroots creativity, and a bartering or gift economy. This is what happens when consumers take media into their own hands. Of course, this may be altogether the wrong way to talk about it—since in a folk culture, there is no clear division between producers and consumers. Within convergence culture, everyone's a participant—although participants may have different degrees of status and influence.

It may be useful to draw a distinction between interactivity and participation, words that are often used interchangeably but which, in this book, assume rather different meanings.[6] Interactivity refers to the ways that new technologies have been designed to be more responsive to consumer feedback. One can imagine differing degrees of interactivity enabled by different communication technologies, ranging from television, which allows us only to change the channel, to video games that can allow consumers to act upon the represented world. Such relationships are of course not fixed: the introduction of TiVo can fundamentally reshape our interactions with television. The constraints on interactivity are technological. In almost every case, what you can do in an interactive environment is prestructured by the designer.

Participation, on the other hand, is shaped by the cultural and social protocols. So, for example, the amount of conversation possible in a movie theater is determined more by the tolerance of audiences in different subcultures or national contexts than by any innate property of cinema itself. Participation is more open-ended, less under the control of media producers and more under the control of media consumers.

Initially, the computer offered expanded opportunities for interacting with media content, and as long as it operated on that level, it was relatively easy for media companies to commodify and control what took place. Increasingly, though, the Web has become a site of consumer participation that includes many unauthorized and unanticipated ways of relating to media content. Though this new participatory culture has its roots in practices that have occurred just below the radar of the media industry throughout the twentieth century, the Web has pushed that hidden layer of cultural activity into the foreground, forcing the media industries to confront its implications for their commercial interests. Allowing consumers to interact with media under controlled circumstances is one thing; allowing them to participate in the production and distribution of cultural goods—on their own terms—is something else altogether.

Grant McCracken, the cultural anthropologist and industry consultant, suggests that in the future, media producers must accommodate consumer demands to participate or they will run the risk of losing the most active and passionate consumers to some other media interest that is more tolerant: "Corporations must decide whether they are, literally, in or out. Will they make themselves an island or will they enter the mix? Making themselves an island may have certain short-term financial benefits, but the long-term costs can be substantial."[7] As we have seen, the media industry is increasingly dependent on active and committed consumers to spread the word about valued properties in an overcrowded media marketplace, and in some cases they are seeking ways to channel the creative output of media fans to lower their production costs. At the same time, they are terrified of what happens if this consumer power gets out of control, as they claim occurred following the introduction of Napster and other file-sharing services. As fan productivity goes public, it can no longer be ignored by the media industries, but it cannot be fully contained or channeled by them, either.

One can trace two characteristic responses of media industries to this grassroots expression: starting with the legal battles over Napster, the media industries have increasingly adopted a scorched-earth policy toward their consumers, seeking to regulate and criminalize many forms of fan participation that once fell below their radar. Let's call them the prohibitionists. To date, the prohibitionist stance has been dominant within old media companies (film, television, the recording industry), though these groups are to varying degrees starting to reexamine some of these assumptions. So far, the prohibitionists get most of the press—with lawsuits directed against teens who download music or against fan Webmasters getting more and more coverage in the popular media. At the same time, on the fringes, new media companies (Internet, games, and to a lesser degree, the mobile phone companies) are experimenting with new approaches that see fans as important collaborators in the production of content and as grassroots intermediaries helping to promote the franchise. We will call them the collaborationists.

The *Star Wars* franchise has been pulled between these two extremes both over time (as it responds to shifting consumer tactics and technological resources) and across media (as its content straddles between old and new media). Within the *Star Wars* franchise, Hollywood has sought to shut down fan fiction, later to assert ownership over it, and finally to ignore its existence; they have promoted the works of fan video makers but also limited what kinds of movies they can make;

and they have sought to collaborate with gamers to shape a massively multiplayer game so that it better satisfies player fantasies.

Folk Culture, Mass Culture, Convergence Culture

At the risk of painting with broad strokes, the story of American arts in the nineteenth century might be told in terms of the mixing, matching, and merging of folk traditions taken from various indigenous and immigrant populations. Cultural production occurred mostly on the grassroots level; creative skills and artistic traditions were passed down mother to daughter, father to son. Stories and songs circulated broadly, well beyond their points of origin, with little or no expectation of economic compensation; many of the best ballads or folktales come to us today with no clear marks of individual authorship. While new commercialized forms of entertainment—the minstrel shows, the circuses, the showboats—emerged in the mid-to-late nineteenth century, these professional entertainments competed with thriving local traditions of barn dances, church sings, quilting bees, and campfire stories. There was no pure boundary between the emergent commercial culture and the residual folk culture: the commercial culture raided folk culture and folk culture raided commercial culture.

The story of American arts in the twentieth century might be told in terms of the displacement of folk culture by mass media. Initially, the emerging entertainment industry made its peace with folk practices, seeing the availability of grassroots singers and musicians as a potential talent pool, incorporating community sing-a-longs into film exhibition practices, and broadcasting amateur-hour talent competitions. The new industrialized arts required huge investments and thus demanded a mass audience. The commercial entertainment industry set standards of technical perfection and professional accomplishment few grassroots performers could match. The commercial industries developed powerful infrastructures that ensured that their messages reached everyone in America who wasn't living under a rock. Increasingly, the commercial culture generated the stories, images, and sounds that mattered most to the public.

Folk culture practices were pushed underground—people still composed and sang songs, amateur writers still scribbled verse, weekend painters still dabbled, people still told stories, and some local communities still held square dances. At the same time, grassroots fan communities emerged in response to mass media content. Some media scholars hold on to the useful distinction between mass culture (a category of production) and popular culture (a category of consumption), arguing that popular culture is what happens to the materials of mass culture when they get into the hands of consumers—when a song played on the radio becomes so associated with a particularly romantic evening that two young lovers decide to call it "our song," or when a fan becomes so fascinated with a particular television series that it inspires her to write original stories about its characters. In other words, popular culture is what happens as mass culture gets pulled back into folk culture. The culture industries never really had to confront the existence of this alternative cultural economy because, for the most part, it existed behind closed doors and its products circulated only among a small circle of friends and neighbors. Home movies never threatened Hollywood, as long as they remained in the home.

The story of American arts in the twenty-first century might be told in terms of the public reemergence of grassroots creativity as everyday people take advantage of new technologies that enable them to archive, annotate, appropriate, and recirculate media content. It probably started with the photocopier and desktop publishing; perhaps it started with the videocassette revolution, which gave the public access to movie-making tools and enabled every home to have its own film library. But this creative revolution has so far culminated with the Web. To create is much more fun and meaningful if you can share what you can create with others, and the Web, built for collaboration within the scientific community, provides an infrastructure for sharing the things average Americans are making in their rec rooms. Once you have a reliable system of distribution, folk culture production begins to flourish again overnight. Most of what the amateurs create is gosh-awful bad, yet a thriving culture needs spaces where people can do bad art, get feedback, and get better. After all, much of what circulates through mass media is also bad by almost any criteria, but the expectations of professional polish make it a less hospitable environment for newcomers to learn and grow. Some of what amateurs create will be surprisingly good, and some artists will be recruited into commercial entertainment or the art world. Much of it will be good enough to engage the interest of some modest public, to inspire someone else to create, to provide new content which, when polished through many hands, may turn into something more valuable down the line. That's the way the folk process works, and grassroots convergence represents the folk process accelerated and expanded for the digital age.

Given this history, it should be no surprise that much of what the public creates models itself after, exists in dialogue with, reacts to or against, and/or otherwise repurposes materials drawn from commercial culture. Grassroots convergence is embodied, for example, in the work of the game modders, who build on code and design tools created for commercial games as a foundation for amateur game production, or in digital filmmaking, which often directly samples material from commercial media, or adbusting, which borrows iconography from Madison Avenue to deliver an anticorporate or anticonsumerist message. Having buried the old folk culture, this commercial culture becomes the common culture. The older American folk culture was built on borrowings from various mother countries; the modern mass media builds upon borrowings from folk culture; the new convergence culture will be built on borrowings from various media conglomerates.

The Web has made visible the hidden compromises that enabled participatory culture and commercial culture to coexist throughout much of the twentieth century. Nobody minded, really, if you photocopied a few stories and circulated them within your fan club. Nobody minded, really, if you copied a few songs and shared the dub tape with a friend. Corporations might know, abstractly, that such transactions were occurring all around them, every day, but they didn't know, concretely, who was doing it. And even if they did, they weren't going to come bursting into people's homes at night. But, as those transactions came out from behind closed doors, they represented a visible, public threat to the absolute control the culture industries asserted over their intellectual property.

With the consolidation of power represented by the Digital Millennium Copyright Act of 1998, American intellectual property law has been rewritten to reflect the demands of mass media producers—away from providing economic incentives for individual artists and toward protecting the enormous economic investments media companies made in branded entertainment; away from a limited duration protection that allows ideas to enter general circulation while they still benefit the common good and toward the notion that copyright should last forever; away from the ideal of a cultural commons and toward the ideal of intellectual property. As Lawrence Lessig notes, the law has been rewritten so that "no one can do to the Disney Corporation what Walt Disney did to the Brothers Grimm."[8] One of the ways that the studios have propped up these expanded claims of copyright protection is through the issuing of cease-and-desist letters intended to intimidate amateur cultural creators into removing their works from the Web. Chapter 5 describes what happened when Warner Bros. studio sent out cease-and-desist letters to young *Harry Potter* (1998) fans. In such situations, the studios often assert much broader control than they could legally defend: someone who stands to lose their home or their kid's college funds by going head-to-head with studio attorneys is apt to fold. After three decades of such disputes, there is still no case law that would help determine to what degree fan fiction is protected under fair-use law.

Efforts to shut down fan communities run in the face of what we have learned so far about the new kinds of affective relationships advertisers and entertainment companies want to form with their consumers. Over the past several decades, corporations have sought to market branded content so that consumers become the bearers of their marketing messages. Marketers have turned our children into walking, talking billboards who wear logos on their T-shirts, sew patches on their backpacks, plaster stickers on their lockers, hang posters on their walls, but they must not, under penalty of law, post them on their home pages. Somehow, once consumers choose when and where to display those images, their active participation in the circulation of brands suddenly becomes a moral outrage and a threat to the industry's economic well-being.

Today's teens—the so-called Napster generation—aren't the only ones who are confused about where to draw the lines here; media companies are giving out profoundly mixed signals because they really can't decide what kind of relationships they want to have with this new kind of consumer. They want us to look at but *not* touch, buy but *not* use, media content. This contradiction is felt perhaps most acutely when it comes to cult media content. A cult media success depends on courting fan constituencies and niche markets; a mainstream success is seen by the media producers as depending on distancing themselves from them. The system depends on covert relationships between producers and consumers. The fans' labor in enhancing the value of an intellectual property can never be publicly recognized if the studio is going to maintain that the studio alone is the source of all value in that property. The Internet, though, has blown their cover, since those fan sites are now visible to anyone who knows how to Google.

Some industry insiders—for example, Chris Albrecht, who runs the official *Star Wars* film competition at AtomFilms, or Raph Koster, the former MUDder who has helped shape the *Star Wars Galaxies* (2002) game—come out of these grassroots communities and have a healthy respect for their value. They see fans as potentially revitalizing stagnant franchises and providing a low-cost means of generating new media content. Often, such people are locked into power struggles within their own companies with others who would prohibit grassroots creativity.

"Dude, We're Gonna Be Jedi!"

George Lucas in Love depicts the future media mastermind as a singularly clueless USC film student who can't quite come up with a good idea for his production assignment, despite the fact that he inhabits a realm rich with narrative possibilities. His stoner roommate emerges from behind the hood of his dressing gown and lectures Lucas on "this giant cosmic force, an energy field created by all living things." His sinister next-door-neighbor, an archrival, dresses all in black and breathes with an asthmatic wheeze as he proclaims, "My script is complete. Soon I will rule the entertainment universe." As Lucas races to class, he encounters a brash young friend who brags about his souped-up sports car and his furry-faced sidekick who growls when he hits his head on the hood while trying to do some basic repairs. His professor, a smallish man, babbles cryptic advice, but all of this adds up to little until Lucas meets and falls madly for a beautiful young woman with buns on both sides of her head. Alas, the romance leads to naught as he eventually discovers that she is his long-lost sister.

George Lucas in Love is, of course, a spoof of *Shakespeare in Love* (1998) and of *Star Wars* itself. It is also a tribute from one generation of USC film students to another. As co-creator Joseph Levy, a twenty-four-year-old recent graduate from Lucas's alma mater, explained, "Lucas is definitely the god of USC. . . . We shot our screening-room scene in the George Lucas Instructional Building. Lucas is incredibly supportive of student filmmakers and developing their careers and providing facilities for them to be caught up to technology."[9] Yet what makes this film so endearing is the way it pulls Lucas down to the same level as countless other amateur filmmakers, and, in so doing, helps to blur the line between the fantastical realm of space opera ("A long, long time ago in a galaxy far, far away") and the familiar realm of everyday life (the world of stoner roommates, snotty neighbors, and incomprehensible professors). Its protagonist is hapless in love, clueless at filmmaking, yet somehow he manages to pull it all together and produce one of the top-grossing motion pictures of all time. *George Lucas in Love* offers us a portrait of the artist as a young geek.

One might contrast this rather down-to-earth representation of Lucas —the auteur as amateur—with the way fan filmmaker Evan Mather's Web site (http://www.evanmather.com/) constructs the amateur as an emergent auteur.[10] Along one column of the site can be found a filmography, listing all of Mather's productions going back to high school, as well as a listing of the various newspapers, magazines, Web sites, television and radio stations that have covered his work—*La Republica*, *Le Monde*, the *New York Times*, *Wired*, *Entertainment Weekly*, CNN, NPR, and so forth. Another sidebar provides up-to-the-moment information about his works in progress. Elsewhere, you can see news of the various film festival screenings of his films and whatever awards they have won. More than nineteen digital films are featured with photographs, descriptions, and links for downloading them in multiple formats.

Another link allows you to call up a glossy full-color, professionally designed brochure documenting the making of *Les Pantless Menace* (1999), which includes close-ups of various props and settings, reproductions of stills, score sheets, and storyboards, and detailed explanations of how he was able to do the special effects, soundtrack, and editing for the film (fig. 4.1). We learn, for example, that some of the dialogue was taken directly from Commtech chips that were embedded within Hasbro *Star Wars* toys. A biography provides some background:

> Evan Mather spent much of his childhood running around south Louisiana with an eight-millimeter silent camera staging hitchhikings and assorted buggery. . . . As a landscape architect, Mr. Mather spends his days designing a variety of urban and park environments in the Seattle area. By night, Mr. Mather explores the realm of digital cinema and is the renowned creator of short films which fuse traditional hand drawn and stop motion animation techniques with the flexibility and realism of computer generated special effects.

Though his background and production techniques are fairly ordinary, the incredibly elaborate, self-conscious, and determinedly professional design of his Web site is anything but. His Web site illustrates what

Fig. 4.1. Fan filmmaker Evan Mather's *Les Pantless Menace* creates anarchic comedy through creative use of *Star Wars* action figures. (Reprinted with the permission of the artist.)

happens as this new amateur culture gets directed toward larger and larger publics.

TheForce.net's Fan Theater, for example, allows amateur directors to offer their own commentary. The creators of *When Senators Attack IV* (1999), for example, give "comprehensive scene-by-scene commentary" on their film: "Over the next 90 pages or so, you'll receive an insight into what we were thinking when we made a particular shot, what methods we used, explanations to some of the more puzzling scenes, and anything else that comes to mind."[11] Such materials mirror the tendency of recent DVD releases to include alternative scenes, cut footage, storyboards, and director's commentary. Many of the Web sites provide information about fan films under production, including preliminary footage, storyboards, and trailers for films that may never be completed. Almost all of the amateur filmmakers create posters and advertising images, taking advantage of Adobe PageMaker and Adobe Photoshop. In many cases, the fan filmmakers produce elaborate trailers. These materials facilitate amateur film culture. The making-of articles share technical advice; such information helps to improve the overall quality of work within the community. The trailers also respond to the specific challenges of the Web as a distribution channel: it can take minutes to download relatively long digital movies, and the shorter, lower resolution trailers (often distributed in a streaming video format) allow would-be viewers to sample the work.

All of this publicity surrounding the *Star Wars* parodies serves as a reminder of what is the most distinctive quality of these amateur films—the fact that they are so public. The idea that amateur filmmakers could develop such a global following runs counter to the historical marginalization of grassroots media production. In her book, *Reel Families: A*

Social History of Amateur Film (1995), film historian Patricia R. Zimmermann offers a compelling history of amateur filmmaking in the United States, examining the intersection between nonprofessional film production and the Hollywood entertainment system. While amateur filmmaking has existed since the advent of cinema, and while periodically critics have promoted it as a grassroots alternative to commercial production, the amateur film has remained, first and foremost, the "home movie" in several senses of the term: first, amateur films were exhibited primarily in private (and most often, domestic) spaces lacking any viable channel of public distribution; second, amateur films were most often documentaries of domestic and family life; and third, amateur films were perceived to be technically flawed and of marginal interest beyond the immediate family. Critics stressed the artlessness and spontaneity of amateur film in contrast with the technical polish and aesthetic sophistication of commercial films. Zimmermann concludes, "[Amateur film] was gradually squeezed into the nuclear family. Technical standards, aesthetic norms, socialization pressures and political goals derailed its cultural construction into a privatized, almost silly, hobby."[12] Writing in the early 1990s, Zimmermann saw little reason to believe that the camcorder and the VCR would significantly alter this situation. The medium's technical limitations made it difficult for amateurs to edit their films, and the only public means of exhibition were controlled by commercial media makers (as in programs such as *America's Funniest Home Videos*, 1990).

Digital filmmaking alters many of the conditions that led to the marginalization of previous amateur filmmaking efforts—the Web provides an exhibition outlet moving amateur filmmaking from private into public space; digital editing is far simpler than editing Super-8 or video and thus opens up a space for amateur artists to reshape their material more directly; the home PC has even enabled the amateur filmmaker to mimic the special effects associated with Hollywood blockbusters like *Star Wars*. Digital cinema is a new chapter in the complex history of interactions between amateur filmmakers and the commercial media. These films remain amateur, in the sense that they are made on low budgets, produced and distributed in noncommercial contexts, and generated by nonprofessional filmmakers (albeit often by people who want entry into the professional sphere). Yet, many of the other classic markers of amateur film production have disappeared. No longer home movies, these films are public movies—public in that, from the start, they are intended for audiences beyond the filmmaker's immediate circle of friends and acquaintances; public in their content, which involves the reworking of popular mythologies; and public in their dialogue with the commercial cinema.

Digital filmmakers tackled the challenge of making *Star Wars* movies for many different reasons. As *George Lucas in Love* co-creator Joseph Levy has explained, "Our only intention . . . was to do something that would get the agents and producers to put the tapes into their VCRs instead of throwing them away."[13] *Kid Wars* (2000) director Dana Smith is a fourteen-year-old who had recently acquired a camcorder and decided to stage scenes from *Star Wars* involving his younger brother and his friends, who armed themselves for battle with squirt guns and Nerf weapons. *The Jedi Who Loved Me* (2000) was shot by the members of a wedding party and intended as a tribute to the bride and groom, who were *Star Wars* fans. Some films—such as *Macbeth* (1998)—were school projects. Two high school students—Bienvenido Concepcion and Don Fitz-Roy—shot the film, which creatively blurred the lines between Lucas and Shakespeare, for their high school advanced-placement English class. They staged light-saber battles down the school hallway, though the principal was concerned about potential damage to lockers; the Millennium Falcon lifted off from the gym, though they had to composite it over the cheerleaders who were rehearsing the day they shot that particular sequence. Still other films emerged as collective projects for various *Star Wars* fan clubs. *Boba Fett: Bounty Trail* (2002), for example, was filmed for a competition hosted by a Melbourne, Australia, Lucasfilm convention. Each cast member made his or her own costumes, building on previous experience with science fiction masquerades and costume contests. Their personal motives for making such films are of secondary interest, however, once they are distributed on the Web. If such films are attracting worldwide interest, it is not because we all care whether Bienvenido Concepcion and Don Fitz-Roy got a good grade on their Shakespeare assignment. Rather, what motivated faraway viewers to watch such films is their shared investment in the *Star Wars* universe.

Amateur filmmakers are producing commercial- or near-commercial-quality content on minuscule budgets. They remain amateur in the sense that they do not earn their revenue through their work (much the way we might call Olympic athletes amateur), but they are duplicating special effects that had cost a small fortune to generate only a decade earlier. Amateur filmmakers can make pod racers skim along the surface of the ocean or land speeders scatter dust as they zoom across the desert. They can make laser beams shoot out of ships and explode things before our eyes. Several fans tried their hands at duplicating Jar-Jar's character animation and inserting him into their own movies with varying degrees of success. The light-saber battle, however, has become the gold standard of amateur filmmaking, with almost every filmmaker compelled to demonstrate his or her ability to achieve this particular effect. Many of the *Star Wars* shorts, in fact, consist of little more than light-saber battles staged in suburban dens and basements, in empty lots, in the hallways of local schools, inside shopping malls, or more exotically against the backdrop of medieval ruins (shot during vacations). Shane Faleux used an open-source approach to completing his forty-minute opus, *Star Wars: Revelations* (2005), one of the most acclaimed recent works in the movement (fig. 4.2). As Faleux explained, "*Revelations* was created to give artisans and craftsmen the chance to showcase their work, allow all those involved a chance to live the dream, and maybe—just maybe—open the eyes in the industry as to what can be done with a small budget, dedicated people, and undiscovered talent."[14] Hundreds of people around the world contributed to the project, including more than thirty different computer-graphics artists, ranging from folks within special effects companies to talented teenagers. When the film was released via the Web, more than a million people downloaded it.

As amateur filmmakers are quick to note, Lucas and Steven Spielberg both made Super-8 fiction films as teenagers and saw this experience as a major influence on their subsequent work. Although these films are not publicly available, some of them have been discussed in detail in various biographies and magazine profiles. These "movie brat" film-makers have been quick to embrace the potentials of digital filmmaking, not simply as a means of lowering production costs for their own films, but also as a training ground for new talent. Lucas, for example, told *Wired* magazine, "Some of the special effects that we redid for *Star Wars* were done on a Macintosh, on a laptop, in a couple of hours. . . . I could have very easily shot the Young Indy TV series on Hi-8. . . . So you can get a Hi-8 camera for a few thousand bucks, more for the software and the computer for less than $10,000 you have a movie studio. There's nothing to stop you from doing something provocative and significant in that medium."[15] Lucas's rhetoric about the potentials of digital filmmaking has captured the imagination of amateur filmmakers, and they are taking on the master on his own ground.

As Clay Kronke, a Texas A&M University undergraduate who made

Fig. 4.2. Publicity materials created for *Star Wars: Revelations*, a forty-minute opus made through the combined efforts of hundreds of fan filmmakers worldwide.

The New World (1999), explained, "This film has been a labor of love. A venture into a new medium. . . . I've always loved light sabers and the mythos of the Jedi and after getting my hands on some software that would allow me to actually become what I had once only admired at a distance, a vague idea soon started becoming a reality. . . . Dude, we're gonna be Jedi."[16] Kronke openly celebrates the fact that he made the film on a $26.79 budget with most of the props and costumes part of their pre-existing collections of *Star Wars* paraphernalia, that the biggest problem they faced on the set was that their plastic light sabers kept shattering, and that its sound effects included "the sound of a coat hanger against a metal flashlight, my microwave door, and myself falling on the floor several times."

The mass marketing of *Star Wars* inadvertently provided many of the resources needed to support these productions. *Star Wars* is, in many ways, the prime example of media convergence at work. Lucas's decision to defer salary for the first *Star Wars* film in favor of maintaining a share of ancillary profits has been widely cited as a turning point in the emergence of this new strategy of media production and distribution. Lucas made a ton of money, and Twentieth Century Fox Film Corporation learned a valuable lesson. Kenner's *Star Wars* action figures are thought to have been the key in reestablishing the value of media tie-in products in the toy industry, and John Williams's score helped to revitalize the market for soundtrack albums. The rich narrative universe of the *Star Wars* saga provided countless images, icons, and artifacts that could be reproduced in a wide variety of forms. Despite the lengthy gap between the release dates for *Return of the Jedi* (1983) and *The Phantom Menace* (1999), Lucasfilm continued to generate profits from its *Star Wars* franchise through the production of original novels and comic books, the distribution of video tapes and audio tapes, the continued marketing of *Star Wars* toys and merchandise, and the maintenance of an elaborate publicity apparatus, including a monthly glossy newsletter for *Star Wars* fans.

Many of these toys and trinkets were trivial when read in relation to the kinds of transmedia storytelling described in the previous chapter: they add little new information to the expanding franchise. Yet they took on deeper meanings as they became resources for children's play or for digital filmmaking. The amateur filmmakers often make use of commercially available costumes and props, sample music from the soundtrack album and sounds of *Star Wars* videos or computer games, and draw advice on special effects techniques from television documentaries and mass market magazines. For example, the makers of *Duel* described the sources for their soundtrack: "We sampled most of the light saber sounds from *The Empire Strikes Back* Special Edition laserdisc, and a few from *A New Hope. Jedi* was mostly useless to us, as the light saber battles in the film are always accompanied by music. The kicking sounds are really punch sounds from *Raiders of the Lost Ark*, and there's one sound—Hideous running across the sand—that we got from *Lawrence of Arabia*. Music, of course, comes from *The Phantom Menace* soundtrack."[17] The availability of these various ancillary products has encouraged these filmmakers, since childhood, to construct their own fantasies within the *Star Wars* universe. One fan critic explained: "Odds are if you were a kid in the seventies, you probably fought in schoolyards over who would play Han, lost a Wookiee action figure in your backyard and dreamed of firing that last shot on the Death Star. And probably your daydreams and conversations weren't about William Wallace, Robin Hood or Odysseus, but, instead, light saber battles, frozen men and forgotten fathers. In other words, we talked about our legend."[18] The action figures provided this generation with some of their earliest avatars, encouraging them to assume the role of a Jedi Knight or an intergalactic bounty hunter, enabling them to physically manipulate the characters to construct their own stories.

Not surprisingly, a significant number of filmmakers in their late teens and early twenties have turned toward those action figures as resources for their first production efforts. *Toy Wars* (2002) producers Aaron Halon and Jason VandenBerghe launched an ambitious plan to produce a shot-by-shot remake of *Star Wars: A New Hope* cast entirely with action figures. These action figure movies require constant resourcefulness on the part of the amateur filmmakers. Damon Wellner and Sebastian O'Brien, two self-proclaimed "action figure nerds" from Cambridge, Massachusetts, formed Probot Productions with the goal of "making toys as alive as they seemed in childhood." The Probot Web site (www.probotproductions.com) offers this explanation of their production process:

> The first thing you need to know about Probot Productions is that we're broke. We spend all our $$$ on toys. This leaves a very small budget for special effects, so we literally have to work with what we can find in the garbage. . . . For sets we used a breadbox, a ventilation tube from a dryer, cardboard boxes, a discarded piece from a vending machine, and milk crates. Large Styrofoam pieces from stereo component boxes work very well to create spaceship-like environments![19]

No digital filmmaker has pushed the aesthetics of action figure cinema as far as Evan Mather. Mather's films, such as *Godzilla versus Disco Lando, Kung Fu Kenobi's Big Adventure*, and *Quentin Tarantino's Star Wars*, represent a no-holds-barred romp through contemporary popular culture. The rock-'em sock-'em action of *Kung Fu Kenobi's Big Adventure* takes place against the backdrop of settings sampled from the film, drawn by hand, or built from LEGO blocks, with the eclectic and evocative soundtrack borrowed from Neil Diamond, *Mission Impossible* (1996), *Pee-Wee's Big Adventure* (1985), and *A Charlie Brown Christmas* (1965). Disco Lando puts the moves on everyone from Admiral Ackbar to Jabba's blue-skinned dancing girl, and all of his pick-up lines come from the soundtrack of *The Empire Strikes Back*. Mace Windu "gets medieval" on the Jedi Council, delivering Samuel L. Jackson's lines from *Pulp Fiction* (1994) before shooting up the place. The camera focuses on the baldhead of a dying Darth Vader as he gasps "rosebud." Apart from their anarchic humor and rapid-fire pace, Mather's films stand out because of their visual sophistication. Mather's own frenetic style has become increasingly distinguished across the body of his works, constantly experimenting with different forms of animation, flashing or masked images, and dynamic camera movements.

Yet, if the action figure filmmakers have developed an aesthetic based on their appropriation of materials from the mainstream media, then the mainstream media has been quick to imitate that aesthetic. Nickelodeon's short-lived *Action League Now!!!* (1994), for example, had a regular cast of characters consisting of mismatched dolls and mutilated action figures. In some cases, their faces had been melted or mangled through inappropriate play. One protagonist had no clothes. They came in various size scales, suggesting the collision of different narrative universes that characterizes children's action figure play. MTV's *Celebrity Deathmatch* (1998) created its action figures using claymation, staging World Wrestling Federation–style bouts between various celebrities, some likely (Monica Lewinsky against Hillary Clinton), some simply bizarre (the rock star formerly known as Prince against Prince Charles).

Or consider the case of the Cartoon Network's *Robot Chicken* (a stop-motion animation series) produced by Seth Green (formerly of *Buffy the Vampire Slayer* and *Austin Powers*) and Matthew Senreich: think of it as a sketch comedy series where all of the parts are played by action figures. The show spoofs popular culture, mixing and matching characters with the same reckless abandon as a kid playing on the floor with his favorite collectibles. In its rendition of MTV's *The Real World*, Superman, Aquaman, Batman, Wonder Woman, Cat Woman, the Hulk, and other superheroes share an apartment and deal with real life issues, such as struggles for access to the bathroom or conflicts about who is going to do household chores. Or, in its take on *American Idol*, the contestants are zombies of dead rock stars and the judges are breakfast cereal icons— Frankenberry (as Randy), Booberry (as Paula) and Count Chocula (as Simon).

The series originated as part of a regular feature in *Toy Fare*, a niche magazine which targets action figure collectors and model builders. Seth Green, a fan of the publication, asked the magazine's contributors to help him put together a special animated segment for Green's forthcoming appearance on *The Conan O'Brien Show*, which in turn led to an invitation to produce a series of Web toons for Sony's short-lived but highly influential Screenblast, which in turn led to an invitation to produce a television series as part of the Cartoon Network's Adult Swim lineup. We can thus trace step by step how this concept moves from the fan subculture across a range of sites noted for cult media content.[20] News coverage of the series stresses Seth Green's own status as a toy collector and often describes the challenges faced by the program's "toy wrangler," who goes onto eBay or searches retro shops for the specific toys needed to cast segments, blurring the line between amateur and commercial media making practices.[21]

The Web represents a site of experimentation and innovation, where amateurs test the waters, developing new practices, themes, and generating materials that may well attract cult followings on their own terms. The most commercially viable of those practices are then absorbed into the mainstream media, either directly through the hiring of new talent or the development of television, video, or big-screen works based on those materials, or indirectly, through a second-order imitation of the same aesthetic and thematic qualities. In return, the mainstream media materials may provide inspiration for subsequent amateur efforts, which push popular culture in new directions. In such a world, fan works can no longer be understood as simply derivative of mainstream materials but must be understood as themselves open to appropriation and reworking by the media industries.

"The 500-Pound Wookiee"

Fans take reassurance that Lucas and his cronies, at least sometimes, take a look at what fans have made and send them his blessing. In fact, part of the allure of participating in the official *Star Wars* fan cinema competition is the fact that Lucas personally selects the winner from finalists identified by AtomFilm's Chris Albrecht and vetted by staffers at LucasArts. There is no doubt that Lucas personally likes at least some form of fan creativity. As Albrecht explains, "Hats off to Lucas for recognizing that this is happening and giving the public a chance to participate in a universe they know and love. There's nothing else like this out there. No other producer has gone this far."[22] On other levels, the company—and perhaps Lucas himself—has wanted to control what fans produced and circulated. Jim Ward, vice president of marketing for Lucasfilm, told *New York Times* reporter Amy Harmon in 2002, "We've been very clear all along on where we draw the line. We love our fans. We want them to have fun. But if in fact somebody is using our characters to create a story

Pixelvision and Machinima

The hazy images of Kyle Cassidy's *Toy Soldiers* (1996) evoke faint childhood memories. This short film expresses the hopes and anxieties of a small boy as he awaits the next news from his father, who is serving in Vietnam. Adult concerns shape his everyday rituals and practices as he plays with his green plastic army guys in the backyard and reflects on the fate of those who have been run over by the lawnmower, as he watches the flickering television newscast with his mother, and as he awaits the next letter. *Toy Soldiers* has the intimacy of a home movie, even though it is re-created decades later from the director's own memories. Cassidy made the critically acclaimed film with his Pixelvision 2000 camera, which has a plastic case and plastic lens, runs on six AA batteries, and records its images on a regular audiocassette tape. The Pixelvision camera, marketed from 1987 to 1989 for $100 by Fisher-Price, is the cheapest self-contained camcorder ever made.

The Pixelvision camera has a fixed focus lens which, like a pinhole camera, theoretically has absolute focus from zero to infinity, but in practice does best when what is being filmed remains a few feet from the camera. The camera can shoot well in very low light settings, but almost everything has a shadowy and washed-out look. It was originally intended for children, but kids never really were wild about it because their movies didn't look anything like what they were seeing on television. The Pixelvision image has 2,000 black-and-white dots, making it far coarser than a standard TV image with its 200,000 pixels.

But the Pixelvision camera has found its way into the hearts and hands of a growing number of amateur and avant-garde filmmakers who like it for many of the reasons the device disappointed its target market. The Pixelvision's murky, grainy, and unstable image has become the marker of alternative media authenticity. Pixelvision enthusiasts love the "point and shoot" quality of the camera, which they say allows neophytes to start doing creative work right away. Budding artists can put their energies into communicating ideas rather than learning to control the technology. A once expensive toy has become an incredibly cheap tool.

The Pixelvision movement is the artistic equivalent of a cargo cult: a junked technology, abandoned by its manufacturer, found its way into unanticipated but highly dedicated hands, and we can now see two decades of elaboration as its worshippers have managed to turn its "bugs" into desirable features and have developed a new mode of expression around its unique properties. Pixelvision fans have created their own Web sites, spawned their own criticism, and developed their own film

unto itself, that's not in the spirit of what we think fandom is about. Fandom is about celebrating the story the way it is."[23] Lucas wants to be "celebrated" but not appropriated.

Lucas has opened up a space for fans to create and share what they create with others but only on his terms. The franchise has struggled with these issues from the 1970s to the present, desiring some zone of tolerance within which fans can operate while asserting some control over what happens to his story. In that history, there have been some periods when the company was highly tolerant and others when it was pretty aggressive about trying to close off all or some forms of fan fiction. At the same time, the different divisions of the same company have developed different approaches to dealing with fans: the games division has thought of fans in ways consistent with how other game companies think about fans (and is probably on the more permissive end of the spectrum), and the film division has tended to think like a motion picture company and has been a bit less comfortable with fan participation. I make this point not to say LucasArts is bad to fans—in many ways, the company seems more forward thinking and responsive to the fan community than most Hollywood companies—but to illustrate the ways the media industry is trying to figure out its response to fan creativity.

In the beginning, Lucasfilm actively encouraged fan fiction, establishing a no-fee licensing bureau in 1977 that would review material and offer advice about potential copyright infringement.[24] By the early 1980s, these arrangements broke down, allegedly because Lucas had stumbled onto some examples of fan erotica that shocked his sensibilities. By 1981, Lucasfilm was issuing warnings to fans who published zines containing sexually explicit stories, while implicitly giving permission to publish nonerotic stories about the characters as long as they were not sold for profit: "Since all of the *Star Wars* saga is PG-rated, any story those publishers print should also be PG. Lucasfilm does not produce any X-rated *Star Wars* episodes, so why should we be placed in a light where people think we do?"[25] Most fan erotica was pushed underground by this policy, though it continued to circulate informally. The issue resurfaced in the 1990s: fan fiction of every variety thrived on the "electronic frontier." One Web site, for example, provided regularly updated links to fan and fan fiction Web sites for more than 153 films, books, and television shows, ranging from *Airwolf* (1984) to *Zorro* (1975).[26] *Star Wars* zine editors poked their heads above ground, cautiously testing the waters. Jeanne Cole, a spokesman for Lucasfilm, explained, "What can you do? How can you control it? As we look at it, we appreciate the fans, and what would we do without them? If we anger them, what's the point?"[27]

Media scholar Will Brooker cites a 1996 corporate notice that explains: "Since the internet is growing so fast, we are in the process of developing guidelines for how we can enhance the ability of *Star Wars* fans to communicate with each other with-

festivals (such as **PXL THIS**), all in the face of total neglect, and at times open disdain, from Fisher-Price. As filmmaker Eric Sacks writes, "Pixelvision is an aberrant art form, underscored by the fact that since the cameras wear out quickly, and are no longer being manufactured, it holds within itself authorized obsolescence. Each time an artist uses a **PXL 2000**, the whole form edges closer to extinction."[1]

Many of the best Pixelvision movies reveal a fascination with the processes and artifacts of everyday life: the camera has spawned a genre of confessional films, with ghostly faces speaking directly into the camera with surprising frankness. Sadie Benning, the adolescent daughter of an established experimental filmmaker, went on to fame in the art world with her simple and direct shorts, filmed in her bedroom, about coming of age as a lesbian. At nineteen, Benning was the youngest person ever to win a Rockefeller grant.

Andrea McCarty, a graduate student in MIT's Comparative Media Studies Program, is studying the Pixelvision movement to better understand how grassroots creativity works. She told me, "Pixelvision's endurance and popularity prove that it was not a failed technology. . . . The fascination with Pixelvision belies its obsolescence—collectors are seeking the cameras, artists are creating with them, technology fans are modifying them and fans are watching the films at the **PXL THIS** festival."[2] The best Pixelvision films have been embraced by the art world, and the camera even has fans among commercial filmmakers. Director Michael

[1] Erik Saks, "Big Pixel Theory," http://www.thekitchen.org/MovieCatalog/Titles/BigPixelTheory.html.
[2] Andrea McCarty, personal correspondence, November 2004.

Almereyda has incorporated Pixelvision images into his big-screen releases, *Najia* (1994) and *Hamlet* (2000), to much critical praise.

This is what some had claimed would be the inevitable consequences of the digital revolution: the technology would put low-cost, easy-to-use tools for creative expression into the hands of average people. Lower the barriers of participation and provide new channels for publicity and distribution, and people will create remarkable things. Think of these subcultures as aesthetic petri dishes. Seed them and see what grows. In most, nothing really interesting will happen. We can pretty much count on Sturgeon's law holding for amateur cultural creation: 90 percent of everything is crap. But if you expand the number of people participating in the making of art, you may expand the amount of really interesting works that emerge. You can pretty much count on our creative impulses to overcome a lot of technical limitations and obstacles. Amateur artists do best when they operate within supportive communities, struggling with the same creative problems and building on one another's successes.

Let's consider a second powerful example of that process at work: Machinima. Its name a hybrid of machine and cinema, Machinima refers to 3-D digital animation created in real time using game engines. The Machinima movement started in 1993 when *Doom* was released with a program that supported the recording and playback of in-game actions. The idea was that people might want to watch their own game-play experiences as mini action movies. There is little evidence that this controversial first-person shooter generated school shooters, but there's plenty of evidence that it inspired a

out infringing on *Star Wars* copyrights and trademarks."[28] The early lawless days of the Internet were giving way to a period of heightened corporate scrutiny and expanding control. Even during what might be seen as a "honeymoon" period, some fans felt that Lucasfilm was acting like a "500-pound Wookiee," throwing its weight around and making threatening noises.[29]

Lucasfilm's perspective seemed relatively enlightened, even welcoming, when compared with how other media producers responded to their fans. In the late 1990s, Viacom experimented with a strong-arm approach to fan culture—starting in Australia. A representative of the corporation called together leaders of fan clubs from across the country and laid down new guidelines for their activities.[30] These guidelines prohibited the showing of series episodes at club meetings unless those episodes had previously been made commercially available in that market. (This policy has serious consequences for Australian fans because they often get series episodes a year or two after they air in the United States and the underground circulation and exhibition of video tapes had enabled them to participate actively in online discussions.) Similarly, Viacom cracked down on the publication and distribution of fanzines and prohibited the use of *Star Trek* (1966) trademarked names in convention publicity. Their explicitly stated goal was to push fans toward participation in a corporately controlled fan club.

In 2000, Lucasfilm offered *Star Wars*

fans free Web space (www.starwars.com) and unique content for their sites, but only under the condition that whatever they created would become the studio's intellectual property. As the official notice launching this new "Homestead" explained, "To encourage the on-going excitement, creativity, and interaction of our dedicated fans in the online *Star Wars* community, Lucas Online (http://www.lucasfilm.com/divisions/online/) is pleased to offer for the first time an official home for fans to celebrate their love of *Star Wars* on the World Wide Web."[31] Historically, fan fiction had proven to be a point of entry into commercial publication for at least some amateurs, who were able to sell their novels to the professional book series centering on the various franchises. If Lucasfilm Ltd. claimed to own such rights, they could publish them without compensation, and they could also remove them without permission or warning.

Elizabeth Durack was one of the more outspoken leaders of a campaign urging her fellow *Star Wars* fans not to participate in these new arrangements: "That's the genius of Lucasfilm's offering fans web space—it lets them both look amazingly generous *and* be even more controlling than before. . . . Lucasfilm doesn't hate fans, and they don't hate fan websites. They can indeed see how they benefit from the free publicity they represent—and who doesn't like being adored? This move underscores that as much as anything. But they're also scared, and that makes them hurt the people who love them."[32] Durack

generation of animators (amateur and professional).

Subsequent games offered ever more sophisticated tools that allowed players to create their own digital assets, or put their own "skins" over the characters and features of the game world. Soon, people were playing the games with an eye toward recording the actions they wanted for their movies and even redesigning the games to create the characters and settings they needed to stage their own stories. These game engines would allow artists to dramatically lower the costs and decrease the production time of digital animation. Picture complex animation with the spontaneity of improvisational performance!

Most Machinima films remain deeply rooted in gamer culture—*My Trip to Liberty City* is a travelogue of the world represented in *Grand Theft Auto 3* (2001); *Halo Boys* involves boy bands in the *Halo* (2001) universe; someone restaged classic moments from *Monty Python and the Holy Grail* (1975) using *Dark Ages of Camelot* (2001). But not all. Some people have taken up the technical challenge of reproducing classic action films—everything from *The Matrix* to the Omaha Beach sequence in *Saving Private Ryan* (1998). More political filmmakers have taken this farther, using game engines to comment on the war on terrorism or to restage the siege of the Branch Davidians at Waco. Hugh Hancock and Gordon McDonald's *Ozymandias* adopts a poem by Percy Shelley, and Fountainhead's *Anna* depicts the life story of a flower. As with Pixelvision, the Machinima movement has launched its own Web community, critics, training programs, and film festivals.

If Pixelvision has been embraced by the art world, Machinima's greatest impact so far has been on the commercial culture. The History Channel, for example, has launched a successful series, *Decisive Battles* (2004), which restages events such as the Battle of Marathon using Creative Assembly's *Rome: Total War* (2004) as its basic animation tool. MTV 2's *Video Mods* program features music videos by groups such as Black Eyed Peas and Fountains of Wayne that are produced using look-alike skins of the performers inserted in the world of games as diverse as *Tomb Raider*, *Leisure Suit Larry*, *The Sims 2*, and *SSX3*.

Pixelvision was largely abandoned by Fisher-Price. But Machinima—and game mods more generally—have been embraced by the games industry. Lionhead's release *The Movies* (2005) takes the Machinima movement a step further: the game allows you to run your own studio, produce your own movies using its characters and backlots, and then share them online with your friends.

argued that fan fiction does indeed pay respect to Lucas as the creator of *Star Wars*, yet the fans also wanted to hold on to their right to participate in the production and circulation of the Star *Wars* saga that had become so much a part of their lives: "It has been observed by many writers that *Star Wars* (based purposely on the recurring themes of mythology by creator George Lucas) and other popular media creations take the place in modern America that culture myths like those of the Greeks or Native Americans did for earlier peoples. Holding modern myths hostage by way of corporate legal wrangling seems somehow contrary to nature."

Today, relations between LucasArts and the fan fiction community have thawed somewhat. Though I haven't been able to find any official statement signaling a shift in policy, *Star Wars* fan fiction is all over the Web, including on several of the most visible and mainstream fan sites. The Webmasters of those sites say that they deal with the official production company all the time on a range of different matters, but they have never been asked to remove what once might have been read as infringing materials. Yet, what Lucas giveth, he can also taketh away. Many fan writers have told me that they remain nervous about how the "Powers That Be" are apt to respond to particularly controversial stories.

Lucas and his movie brat cronies clearly identified more closely with the young digital filmmakers who were making "calling card" movies to try to break into the film industry than they did with female fan writers sharing their erotic fantasies. By the end of the decade, however, Lucas's tolerance of fan filmmaking has given way to a similar strategy of incorporation and containment. In November 2000, Lucasfilm designated the commercial digital cinema site AtomFilms.com as the official host for *Star Wars* fan films. The site would provide a library of official sound effects and run periodic contests to recognize outstanding amateur accomplishment. In return, participating filmmakers would agree to certain constraints on content: "Films must parody the existing *Star Wars* universe, or be a documentary of the *Star Wars* fan experience. No 'fan fiction'—which attempts to expand on the *Star Wars* universe—will be accepted. Films must not make use of copyrighted *Star Wars* music or video, but may use action figures and the audio clips provided in the production kit section of this site. Films must not make unauthorized use of copyrighted property from any other film, song, or composition."[33] Here, we see the copyright regimes of mass culture being applied to the folk culture process.

A work like *Star Wars: Revelations* would be prohibited from entering the official *Star Wars* competition because it sets its own original dramatic story in the interstices between the third and fourth *Star Wars* films and thus constitutes "fan fiction." Albrecht, the man who oversees the competition, offered several explanations for the prohibition. For one thing, Lucas saw himself and his company as being at risk for being sued for plagiarism if he allowed himself to come into contact with fan-produced materials that mimicked the dramatic structure of the film franchise should anything in any official *Star Wars* material make use of similar characters or situations. For another, Albrecht suggested, there was a growing risk of consumer confusion about what constituted an official *Star Wars* product. Speaking about *Revelations,* Albrecht suggested, "Up until the moment the actors spoke, you wouldn't be able to tell whether that was a real *Star Wars* film or a fan creation because the special effects are so good. . . . As the tools get better, there is bound to be confusion in the marketplace." In any case, Lucasfilm would have had much less legal standing in shutting down parody, which enjoys broad protections under current case law, or documentaries about the phenomenon itself, which would fall clearly into the category of journalistic and critical commentary. Lucasfilm was, in effect, tolerating what it legally must accept in return for shutting down what it might otherwise be unable to control.

These rules are anything but gender neutral: though the gender lines are starting to blur in recent years, the overwhelming majority of fan parody is produced by men, while "fan fiction" is almost entirely produced by women. In the female fan community, fans have long produced "song videos" that are edited together from found footage drawn from film or television shows and set to pop music. These fan vids often function as a form of fan fiction to draw out aspects of the emotional lives of the characters or otherwise get inside their heads. They sometimes explore underdeveloped subtexts of the original film, offer original interpretations of the story, or suggest plotlines that go beyond the work itself. The emotional tone of these works could not be more different from the tone of the parodies featured in the official contests—films such as *Sith Apprentice,* where the Emperor takes some would-be stormtroopers back to the board room; *Anakin Dynamite,* where a young Jedi must confront "idiots" much like his counterpart in the cult success *Napoleon Dynamite* (2004); or *Intergalactic Idol* (2003), where audiences get to decide which contestant really has the force. By contrast, Diane Williams's *Come What May* (2001), a typical song-vid, uses images from *The Phantom Menace* to explore the relationship between Obi-Wan Kenobi and his mentor, Qui-Gon Jinn. The images show the passionate friendship between the two men and culminate in the repeated images of Obi-Wan cradling the crumbled body of his murdered comrade following his battle with Darth Maul. The images are accompanied by the song "Come What May," taken from the soundtrack of Baz Luhrmann's *Moulin Rouge!* (2001) and performed by Ewan McGregor, the actor who also plays the part of Obi-Wan Kenobi in *Phantom Menace.*

Whether AtomFilms would define such a work to be a parody would be a matter of interpretation: while playful at places, it lacks the broad comedy of most of the male-produced *Star Wars* movies, involves a much closer identification with the characters, and hints at aspects of their relationship that have not explicitly been represented on screen. *Come What May* would be read by most fans as falling within the slash subgenre, constructing erotic relations between same-sex characters, and would be read melodramatically rather than satirically. Of course, from a legal standpoint, *Come What May* may represent parody, which doesn't require that the work be comical but simply that it be appropriate and transform the original for the purposes of critical commentary. It would be hard to argue that a video that depicts Obi-Wan and Qui-Gon as lovers does not transform the original in

When Piracy Becomes Promotion

The global sales of Japanese animation and character goods, an astonishing 9 trillion yen (U.S. $80 billion) is ten times what it was a decade ago. Much of that growth has occurred in North America and western Europe. Japanese anime has won worldwide success in part because Japanese media companies were tolerant of the kinds of grassroots activities that American media companies seem so determined to shut down. Much of the risks of entering Western markets and many of the costs of experimentation and promotion were borne by dedicated consumers. Two decades ago, the American market was totally closed to these Japanese imports. Today, the sky is the limit, with many of the

a way that expands its potential meanings. Most likely, this and other female-produced song videos would be regarded as fan fiction; *Come What May* would also run afoul of AtomFilms' rules against appropriating content from the films or from other media properties.

These rules create a two-tier system: some works can be rendered more public because they conform to what the rights holder sees as an acceptable appropriation of their intellectual property, while others remain hidden from view (or at least distributed through less official channels). In this case, these works have been so cut off from public visibility that when I ask *Star Wars* digital filmmakers about the invisibility of these mostly female-produced works, most of them have no idea that women were even making *Star Wars* movies.

Anthropologist and marketing consultant Grant McCracken has expressed some skepticism about the parallels fans draw between their grassroots cultural production and traditional folk culture: "Ancient heroes did not belong to everyone, they did not serve everyone, they were not for everyone to do with what they would. These commons were never very common."[34] For the record, my claims here are altogether more particularized than the sweeping analogies to Greek myths that provoked McCracken's ire. He is almost certainly right that who could tell those stories, under what circumstances, and for what purposes reflected hierarchies operating within classical culture. My analogy, on the other hand, refers to a specific

most successful children's series, from *Pokémon* (1998) to *Yu-Gi-Oh!* (1998), coming directly from Japanese production houses. The shift occurred not through some concerted push by Japanese media companies, but rather in response to the pull of American fans who used every technology at their disposal to expand the community that knew and loved this content. Subsequent commercial efforts built on the infrastructure these fans developed over the intervening years. Grassroots convergence paved the way for new corporate convergence strategies.

Japanese animation was exported into the Western market as early as the 1960s, when *Astro Boy* (1963), *Speed Racer* (1967), and *Gigantor* (1965) made it into local syndication. By the late 1960s, however, reform efforts, such as Action for Children's Television, had used threats of boycott and federal regulation to rein in content they saw as inappropriate for American children. Japanese content targeted adults in its country of origin, often dealt with more mature themes, and was a particular target of the backlash. Discouraged Japanese distributors retreated from the American market, dumping their cartoons on Japanese-language cable channels in cities with large Asian populations.

With the rise of videotape recorders, American fans could dub shows off the Japanese-language channels and share them with their friends in other regions. Soon, fans were seeking contacts in Japan—both local youth and American GIs with access to newer series. Both Japan and the United States used the same NTSC format, easing the flow of content across national borders. American fan clubs emerged to support the archiving and circulation of Japanese animation. On college campuses, student organizations built extensive libraries of both legal and pirated materials and hosted screenings designed to educate the public about anime artists, styles, and genres. The MIT Anime Club, for example, hosts weekly screenings from a library of more than fifteen hundred films and videos. Since 1994, the club has provided a Web site designed to educate Americans about anime and anime fan culture. In most cases, the clubs would show content without translation. Much like listening to an opera on the radio, someone would stand up at the beginning and tell the plot, often drawing on what they remembered when they heard someone else recite the plot at another screening. Japanese distributors winked at these screenings. They didn't have permission from their mother companies to charge these fans or provide the material, but they wanted to see how much interest the shows attracted.

The late 1980s and early 1990s saw the emergence of "fansubbing," the amateur translation and subtitling of Japanese anime. Time synchronized VHS and S-VHS systems supported dubbing of the tapes so that they retained accurate alignment of text and image. As MIT Anime Club president Sean Leonard explains, "Fansubbing has been critical to the growth of anime fandom in the West. If it weren't for fans showing this stuff to others in the late 70s–early 90s, there would be no interest in intelligent, 'high-brow' Japanese animation like there is today." The high costs of the earliest machines meant that fansubbing would remain a collective effort: clubs pooled time and resources to ensure their favorite series reached a wider viewership. As costs lowered, fansubbing spread outward, with clubs using the Internet to coordinate their

moment in the emergence of American popular culture, when songs often circulated well beyond their points of origin, lost any acknowledgment of their original authorship, were repurposed and reused to serve a range of different interests, and were very much part of the texture of everyday life for a wide array of nonprofessional participants. This is how folk culture operated in an emergent democracy.

I don't want to turn back the clock to some mythic golden age. Rather, I want us to recognize the challenges posed by the coexistence of these two kinds of cultural logic. The kinds of production practices we are discussing here were a normal part of American life over this period. They are simply more visible now because of the shift in distribution channels for amateur cultural productions. If the corporate media couldn't crush this vernacular culture during the age when mass media power went largely unchallenged, it is hard to believe that legal threats are going to be an adequate response to a moment when new digital tools and new networks of distribution have expanded the power of ordinary people to participate in their culture. Having felt that power, fans and other subcultural groups are not going to return to docility and invisibility. They will go farther underground *if they have to* —they've been there before—but they aren't going to stop creating.

This is where McCracken's argument rejoins my own. McCracken argues that there is ultimately no schism between the public interest in expanding opportunities for grassroots creativity and the corporate interest in protecting its intellectual property: "Corporations will allow the public to participate in the construction and representation of its creations or they will, eventually, compromise the commercial value of their properties. The new consumer will help create value or they will refuse it. . . . Corporations have a right to keep copyright but they have an interest in releasing it. The economics of scarcity may dictate the first. The economics of plenitude dictate the second."[35] The expanding range of media options, what McCracken calls the "economics of plenitude," will push companies to open more space for grassroots participation and affiliation—starting perhaps with niche companies and fringe audiences, but eventually moving toward the commercial and cultural mainstream. McCracken argues that those companies that loosen their copyright control will attract the most active and committed consumers, and those who ruthlessly set limits will find themselves with a dwindling share of the media marketplace.[36] Of course, this model depends on fans and audience members acting collectively in their own interest against companies who may tempt them with entertainment that is otherwise tailored to their needs. The production companies are centralized and can act in a unified manner; fans are decentralized and have no ability to ensure conformity within their rights. And so far, the media companies have shown a remarkable willingness to antagonize

activities, divvying up what series to subtitle and tapping a broader community for would-be translators.

Beginning in the early 1990s, large-scale anime conventions brought artists and distributors from Japan, who were astonished to see a thriving culture surrounding content they had never actually marketed overseas. They went back home motivated to try to tap this interest commercially. Some key players in the Japanese animation industry had been among those who had aided and abetted American grassroots distribution a decade earlier.

The first niche companies to distribute anime on DVD and videotape emerged as fan clubs went pro, acquiring the distribution rights from reengaged Japanese media companies. The first material to be distributed already had an enthusiastic fan following. Interested in exposing their members to the full range of content available in Japan, the fan clubs often took risks that no commercial distributor would have confronted, testing the market for new genres, producers, and series with commercial companies following their path wherever they found popularity. The fansubbed videos often ran an advisory urging users to "cease distribution when licensed." The clubs were not trying to profit from anime distribution but rather to expand the market; they pulled back from circulating any title that had found a commercial distributor. In any case, the commercial copies were higher quality than their multigeneration dubs.

The first commercially available copies were often dubbed and reedited as part of an effort to expand their potential interest to casual consumers. Japanese cultural critic Koichi Iwabuchi used the term "de-odorizing" to refer to the ways that Japanese "soft goods" are stripped of signs of their national origins to open them for global circulation.[1] In this context, the grassroots fan community still plays an important role, educating American viewers to the cultural references and genre traditions defining these products through their Web sites and newsletters. The fan clubs continue to explore potential niche products that over time can emerge as mainstream successes.

Many U.S. media companies might have regarded all of this underground circulation as piracy and shut it down before it reached critical mass. The Japanese media companys' tolerance of these fan efforts is consistent with their similar treatment of fan communities in their local market. As Temple University School of Law professor Salil K. Mehra notes, the underground sale of fan-made manga, often highly derivative of the commercial product, occurs on a massive scale in Japan, with some comics markets attracting 150,000 visitors per day; such markets are held almost every week in some parts of the country.[2] Rarely taking legal action, the commercial producers sponsor such events, using them to publicize their releases, to recruit potential new talent, and to monitor shifts in audience tastes. In any case, they fear the wrath of their consumers if they take action against such a well-entrenched cultural practice, and the Japanese legal structure would provide for fairly small legal penalties if they did pursue infringers. More generally, as Yuichi Washida, a research director at Hakuhodo, Japan's

their consumers by taking legal actions against them in the face of all economic rationality. This is going to be an uphill fight under the best of circumstances. The most likely way for it to come about, however, may be to create some successes that demonstrate the economic value of engaging the participatory audience.

Design Your Own Galaxy

Adopting a collaborationist logic, the creators of massively multiplayer online role-playing games (MMORPGs) have already built a more open-ended and collaborative relationship with their consumer base. Game designers acknowledge that their craft has less to do with prestructured stories than with creating the preconditions for spontaneous community activities. Raph Koster, the man LucasArts placed in charge of developing *Star Wars Galaxies,* built his professional reputation as one of the prime architects of *Ultima Online* (1997). He was the author of an important statement of players' rights before he entered the games industry, and he has developed a strong design philosophy focused on empowering players to shape their own experiences and build their own communities. Asked to describe the nature of the MMORPG, Koster famously explained, "It's not just a game. It's a service, it's a world, it's a community."[37] Koster also refers to managing an online community, whether a noncommercial MUD or a commercial MMORPG, as an act of gov-

---

[1] Koichi Iwabuchi, *Recentering Globalization: Popular Culture and Japanese Transnationalism* (Durham, N.C.: Duke University Press, 2002), pp. 25–27.

[2] Salil K. Mehra, "Copyright and Comics in Japan: Does Law Explain Why All the Cartoons My Kid Watches Are Japanese Imports?" *Rutgers Law Review,* forthcoming, accessed at http://papers.ssrn.com/sol3/papers/cfm?abstract_id=347620.

ernance: "Just like it is not a good idea for a government to make radical legal changes without a period of public comment, it is often not wise for an operator of an online world to do the same."[38]

Players, he argues, must feel a sense of "ownership" over the imaginary world if they are going to put in the time and effort needed to make it come alive for themselves and for other players. Koster argues, "You can't possibly mandate a fictionally involving universe with thousands of other people. The best you can hope for is a world that is vibrant enough that people act in manners consistent with the fictional tenets."[39] For players to participate, they must feel that what they bring to the game makes a difference, not only in terms of their own experiences, but also the experiences of other players. Writing about the challenges of meeting community expectations on *Ultima Online*, Koster explains, "They want to shape their space, and leave a lasting mark. You must provide some means for them to do so."[40] Richard Bartle, another game designer and theorist, agrees: "Self expression is another way to promote immersion. By giving players free-form ways to communicate themselves, designers can draw them more deeply into the world—they feel more of a part of it."[41]

Koster is known as a strong advocate of the idea of giving players room to express themselves within the game world:

second largest advertising and marketing firm, has argued, Japanese corporations have sought to collaborate with fan clubs, subcultures, and other consumption communities, seeing them as important allies in developing compelling new content or broadening markets.[3] In courting such fans, the companies helped to construct a "moral economy" that aligned their interests in reaching a market with the American fans' desire to access more content.

Today, American companies are licensing content almost as rapidly as the Japanese are generating it. The gap between airing in Japan and in the North American market grows shorter, making it harder for fans to mount the large-scale efforts to familiarize themselves with and publicize this new content. Even many fan-started companies are adopting American corporate logic, shutting down unauthorized fan copies from the moment they acquire a license. The fans worry that these companies may be underestimating the value of the grassroots publicity and that such aggressive copyright patrolling will result in a less educated consumer base that may be less willing to experiment with unfamiliar content.[4]

[3] Yuichi Washida, "Collaborative Structures between Japanese High-Tech Manufacturers and Consumers," paper presented at MIT, Cambridge, Mass., January 2004.

[4] This account of the history of anime in North America was informed throughout by Sean Leonard, "Celebrating Two Decades of Unlawful Progress: Fan Distribution, Proselytization Commons, and the Explosive Growth of Japanese Animation," *UCLA Entertainment Law Review,* Spring 2005, pp. 191–265.

Making things of any sort does generally require training. It is rare in any medium that the naïf succeeds in making something really awesome or popular. By and large it is people who have taught themselves the craft and are making conscious choices. But I absolutely favor empowering people to engage in these acts of creation because not only does talent bubble up but also econ-omies of scale apply. If you get a large enough sample size, you will eventually create something good.

As Koster turned his attention to developing *Star Wars Galaxies,* he realized that he was working with a franchise known in all of its details by hard-core fans who had grown up playing these characters with action figures or in their backyard and who wanted to see those same fantasies rendered in the digital realm. In an open letter to the *Star Wars* fan community, Koster described what he hoped to bring to the project:

At the Mall of *The Sims*

Many games companies are releasing their design tools and game engines alongside their games. Such tools are available for amateur modders to try their hand at designing additional levels or worlds that can extend their game-play experiences. Some even developed elaborate tutorials designed to train amateurs in the use of these tools and may run contests to sponsor and recognize the modding community's accomplishments. Not every game player will take the time to develop original game content and share it with other players. But, as Bioware's Ray Muzyka explained, "If only one percent of a million user base makes content, then you have a lot of module designers. And that's enough to make a game self-sustaining for a long time."[1] To play the amateur games, you must buy the commercial game upon which they are based, which turns

[1] Ray Muzyka, "The Audience Takes Charge: Game Engines as Creative Tools," Entertainment in the Interactive Age conference, University of Southern California, January 29–30, 2001, accessed at http://www.annenberg.edu/interactive-age/assets/transcripts/atc.html.

Star Wars is a universe beloved by many. And I think many of you are like me. You want to be there. You want to feel what it is like. Even be-fore we think about skill trees and about Jedi advancement, before we consider the stats on a weapon or the distance to Mos Eisley and where you have to go to pick up power converters—you want to just *be* there. Inhale the sharp air off the desert. Watch a few Jawas haggle over a droid. Feel the sun beat down on a body that isn't your own, in a world that is strange to you. You don't want to know about the stage-craft in those first few moments. You want to feel like you are offered a pass-port to a universe of limitless possibil-ity. . . . My job is to try to capture that magic for you, so you have that experi-ence."[42]

Satisfying fan interests in the franchise proved challenging. Koster told me, "There's no denying it—the fans know

Star Wars better than the developers do. They live and breathe it. They know it in an intimate way. On the other hand, with something as large and broad as the *Star Wars* universe, there's ample scope for divergent opinions about things. These are the things that lead to religious wars among fans, and all of a sudden you have to take a side because you are going to be establishing how it works in this game."

To ensure that fans bought into his version of the *Star Wars* universe, Koster essentially treated the fan community as his client team, posting regular reports about many different elements of the game's design on the Web, creating an online forum where potential players could respond and make suggestions, ensuring that his staff regularly monitored the online discussion and posted back their own reactions to the community's recommendations. By comparison, the production of a *Star Wars* film is shrouded by secrecy. Koster compares what he did with the test screening or focus group process many Hollywood films endure, but the difference is that much of that testing goes on behind closed doors, among select groups of consumers, and is not open to the participation by anyone who wants to join the conversation. It is hard to imagine Lucas setting up a forum site to preview plot twists and character designs with his audience. If he had done so, he would never have included Jar Jar Binks or devoted so much screen time to the childhood and adolescence of Anakin Skywalker, decisions that alienated his

all of those enthusiastic modders into evangelists for the originating company.

Earlier in this chapter, I drew a distinction between interactivity (which emerged from the properties of media technologies) and participation (which emerged from the protocols and social practices around media). It might be productive to think about this distinction alongside a somewhat more famous one made by Lawrence Lessig between law and code. Law is social dicta: one is free to break the law, though one may suffer penalties if one does so. Code is technical data: the programming makes it impossible to violate its restrictions on use (even if those restrictions in practice exceed any reasonable legal demand). We might see modding as a special case where participatory culture seeks to reprogram the code so as to enable new kinds of interactions with the game. Yet, it is also a special case where the commercial producer continues to exert constraints on use even as the work gets appropriated by the grass-roots community. I can change the fundamental code of the game if I mod it, but at the same time, nobody can play my transformed version of the game unless they become a consumer of the original work.

Bioware and other games companies see the release of their mod tools as consumer research; they monitor the amateur mods to see what game features are popular and try to provide more professionally polished versions when they upgrade their franchises. In some cases, they buy the rights to amateur-produced games and market them directly to consumers or recruit the most gifted amateurs. *Counter-Strike* (2002), a mod on *Half-Life* (1998), is the most often cited example of a commercial success that emerged from the modding community, but a number of amateur mods have been included on the expansion packs **Bioware** has marketed around *Neverwinter Nights* (2002). **Other fan communities have historically functioned as training grounds for entry into the commercial media sector: most comic-book artists and science fiction writers, for example, got their start through fan publishing. Yet, the modding community may be unique in having amateur-produced works taken up directly by commercial companies for distribution. At the same time, the line between amateur and professional production is blurring as smaller start-up companies may build their games through the use of these same tools and subsequently license with the original company to enable their distribution.[2]**

Such practices lower the risks of innovation, allowing the amateurs to experiment with possible new directions and developments and the company to commodify those that hit pay dirt. At the same time, the modding process may prolong the shelf life of the product, with the modding community keeping alive the public interest in a property that is no longer necessarily state-of-the-art technologically. Such practices also increase consumer loyalty: the most hard-core fans are most apt to be drawn toward companies and products that support modding because they know that they can get free content that extends the life of the purchased games. In some cases, game companies are even cutting back on the material contained in the initial product they ship, counting on

core audience. Koster wanted *Star Wars* fans to feel that they had, in effect, designed their own galaxy.

Games scholars Kurt Squire and Constance Steinkuehler have studied the interactions between Koster and his fan community. Koster allowed fans to act as "content generators creating quests, missions, and social relationships that constitute the *Star Wars* world," but more importantly, fan feedback "set the tone" for the *Star Wars* culture:

> These players would establish community norms for civility and role playing, giving the designers an opportunity to effectively *create* the seeds of the *Star Wars Galaxies* world months before the game ever hit the shelves. . . . The game that the designers promised and the community expected was largely player-driven. The in-game economy would consist of items (e.g. clothing, armor, houses, weapons) created by players with its prices also set by players through auctions and player-run shops. Cities and towns would be designed by players, and cities' mayors and council leaders would devise missions and quests for other players. The Galactic Civil War (the struggle between rebels and imperials) would frame the game play, but players would create their own missions as they enacted the *Star Wars* saga. In short, the system was to be driven by *player interaction,* with the world being created less by designers and more by players themselves.[43]

2 David B. Nieborg, "Am I Mod or Not? An Analysis of First Person Shooter Modification Culture," presented at the Creative Gamers Conference, University of Tampiere, Tampiere, Finland, January 2005.

Players can adopt the identities of many different alien races, from Jawas to Wookiees, represented in the *Star Wars* universe, assume many different professional classes—from pod racers to bounty hunters—and play out many different individual and shared fantasies. What they cannot do is adopt the identity of any of the primary characters of the *Star Wars* movies, and they have to earn the status of Jedi Knight by completing a series of different in-game missions. Otherwise, the fiction of the game world would break down as thousands of Han Solos tried to avoid capture by thousands of Boba Fetts. For the world to feel coherent, players had to give up their childhood fantasies of being the star and instead become a bit player, interacting with countless other bit players, within a mutually constructed fantasy. What made it possible for such negotiations and collaborations to occur was the fact that they shared a common background in the already well-established *Star Wars* mythology. As Squire and Steinkuehler note, "Designers cannot require Jedis to behave consistently within the *Star Wars* universe, but they *can* design game structures (such as bounties) that elicit Jedi-like behavior (such as placing a high reward on capturing a Jedi which might produce covert action on the part of Jedis)."[44]

Coming full circle, a growing number of gamers are using the sets, props, and characters generated for the *Star Wars Galaxies* game as resources to produce

modders to expand the play experience. The analogy to Tom Sawyer whitewashing the fence lies close to the surface here: the games companies have been able to convince their consumers to generate a significant amount of free labor by treating game design as an extension of the game-play experience. At the same time, the modding community may come as close to an experimental or independent games movement as currently exists, with a large number of amateurs producing games that are only loosely affiliated with the commercial industry, at a time when the consolidation of control over games production falls more and more into the hands of a small number of major publishers who are risk-averse and driven toward blockbuster-scale profits.[3]

Mods represent the most extreme version of more widespread practices through which game players customize their characters, their environments, or their play experiences. Will Wright, the creator of *SimCity* (1989) and *The Sims* (2000), argues that the games industry maintains much lower walls between creators and consumers than most other sectors of the entertainment industry, in part because most of the people in the industry remember when people designed games out of their garages.[4]

With *The Sims*, Wright created the world's most spectacular dollhouse, convinced the public to pay to come

[3] Hector Postigo, "From Pong to Planet Quake: Post-Industrial Transitions from Leisure to Work," *Information, Communication & Society*, December 2003. Julian Kucklich, "Precarious Playbour: Modders and the Digital Games Industry," presented at the Creative Gamers Conference, University of Tampiere, Tampiere, Finland, January 2005.

[4] Unless otherwise noted, references to Will Wright reflect interview with author, June 2003.

inside and play, and encouraged them to modify it to their own specifications. Wright and his team tapped the preexisting fan base for his *SimCity* franchise, offering key Webmasters the right to participate in ongoing discussions around the game's design and development, giving them advanced access to mod tools they could use to design their own skins or produce their own furnishings, and allowed them to see Webcasts and download thousands of images as the game was being developed. By the time the first *Sims* game shipped, there were already more than fifty fan Web sites devoted to *The Sims*. Today, there are thousands. Wright estimates that in the end, more than 60 percent of the content for *The Sims* will have been developed by its fans. Fans are designing clothes, building houses, manufacturing furniture, programming behaviors, and writing their own stories, amply illustrated by screen shots from the games. He modestly notes, "We were probably responsible for the first million or so units sold, but it was the community which really brought it to the next level."

To distribute all of this content, fans have created a range of online sites. Perhaps the most elaborate and best known of these is "The Mall of *The Sims*." Visitors can browse at more than fifty different shops that offer everything from the most up-to-date electronics to vintage antiques, from medieval tapestries to clothes for hard-to-fit sizes—and skins that look like Britney Spears or Sarah Michelle Gellar or, for that matter, characters from *Star Wars*. The Mall has its own newspaper and television service. At present, the Mall boasts more than 10,000 subscribers. Wright notes that the success of the franchise just about led to the extinction of the fan

Fig. 4.3. Each character in this musical number from The Gypsies' *Christmas Crawl 1*, made using the *Star Wars Galaxies* game, is controlled by a separate player.

their own fan films. In some cases, they are using them to do their own dramatic reenactments of scenes from the movie or to create, gasp, their own "fan fiction." Perhaps the most intriguing new form of fan cinema to emerge from the game world are the so-called Cantina Crawls.[45] In the spirit of the cantina sequence in the original *Star Wars* feature film, the game created a class of characters whose function in the game world is to entertain the other players. They were given special moves that allow them to dance and writhe erotically if the players hit complex combinations of keys. Teams of more than three dozen dancers and musicians plan, rehearse, and execute elaborate synchronized musical numbers: for example, The Gypsies' *Christmas Crawl 1* featured such numbers as "Santa Claus Is Coming to Town" and "Have Yourself a Merry Little Christmas"; blue-skinned and tentacle-haired dance girls shake their bootie, lizard-like aliens in Santa caps play the sax, and guys with gills do boy-band moves while twinkly snow-flakes fall all around them (fig. 4.3). Imagine what *Star Wars* would have looked like if it had been directed by Lawrence Welk! Whatever aesthetic abuse is taking place here, one has to admire the technical accomplishment and social coordination that goes into producing these films. Once you put creative tools in the hands of everyday people, there's no telling what they are going to make with them—and that's a large part of the fun.

Xavier, one of the gamers involved in producing the Cantina Crawl videos, would turn the form against the production company, creating a series of videos protesting corporate decisions which he felt undermined his engagement with the game. Ultimately, Xavier produced a farewell video announcing the mass departure of many loyal fans. The fan-friendly policies Koster created had eroded over time, leading to increased player frustration and distrust. Some casual players felt the game was too dependent on player-generated content, while the more creative players felt that upgrades actually restricted their ability to express themselves and marginalized the Entertainer class from the overall experience. At the same time, the game failed to meet the company's own revenue expectations, especially in the face of competition from the enormously successful *World of Warcraft.*

In December 2005, the company announced plans to radically revamp the game's rules and content, a decision that resulted in massive defections without community because the most popular sites needed to pay massive bills for the bandwidths they consumed, until the company rewrote their terms of agreement so that the fans could charge modest fees to recover the costs of maintaining their distribution centers. Everything in the shops is produced by other players, and once you've paid your dues, you can download anything you want for free.

Perhaps most importantly, all of this bears the approval of Will Wright and Maxis, the company he works for. He didn't build the Mall; he doesn't police copyright infringers, nor does he assert ownership over what the fans had made. Wright just let it happen. As he explains,

> We see such benefit from interacting with our fans. They are not just people who buy our stuff. In a very real sense, they are people who helped to create our stuff.... We are competing with other properties for these creative individuals. All of these different games are competing for communities, which in the long run are what will drive our sales.... Whichever game attracts the best community will enjoy the most success. What you can do to make the game more successful is not to make the game better but to make the community better.

Here, Wright's image of game companies competing for the most creative consumers harks back to McCracken's prediction that the smart companies of the future would empower rather than constrain consumer participation, and those who did not build stronger relations with consumers would be unable to compete. As a result of Wright's enlightened perspective, *The Sims* has become perhaps the most successful game franchise of all time.

bringing in many new customers. A statement made by Nancy MacIntyre, the game's senior director, at LucasArts, to the *New York Times* illustrates the huge shift in thinking from Koster's original philosophy to this "retooled" franchise: "We really just needed to make the game a lot more accessible to a much broader player base. There was lots of reading, much too much, in the game. There was a lot of wandering around learning about different abilities. We really needed to give people the experience of being Han Solo or Luke Skywalker rather than being Uncle Owen, the moisture farmer. We wanted more instant gratification: kill, get treasure, repeat. We needed to give people more of an opportunity to be a part of what they have seen in the movies rather than something they had created themselves."[46]

Over a concise few sentences, MacIntyre had stressed the need to simplify the content, had indicated plans to recenter the game around central characters from the films rather than a more diverse range of protagonists, had dismissed the creative contributions of fans, and had suggested that *Star Wars Galaxies* would be returning to more conventional game mechanics. This "retooling" was the kind of shift in policy without player input that Koster had warned might prove fatal to these efforts. Thanks to the social networks that fans have constructed around the game, soon every gamer on the planet knew that MacIntyre had called her players idiots in the *New York Times*, and many of them departed for other virtual worlds which had more respect for their participation—helping, for example, to fuel the early growth of *Second Life*.

Where Do We Go from Here?

It is too soon to tell whether these experiments in consumer-generated content will have an influence on the mass media companies. In the end, it depends on how seriously, if at all, we should take their rhetoric about enfranchising and empowering consumers as a means of building strong brand loyalties. For the moment, the evidence is contradictory: for every franchise which has reached out to court its fan base, there are others who have fired out cease-and-desist letters. As we confront the intersection between corporate and grassroots modes of convergence, we shouldn't be surprised that neither producers nor consumers are certain what rules should govern their interactions, yet both sides seem determined to hold the other accountable for their choices. The difference is that the fan community must negotiate from a position of relative powerlessness and must rely solely on its collective moral authority, while the corporations, for the moment, act as if they had the force of law on their side.

Ultimately, the prohibitionist position is not going to be effective on anything other than the most local level unless the media companies can win back popular consent; whatever lines they draw are going to have to respect the growing public consensus about what constitutes fair use of media content and must allow the public to participate meaningfully in their own culture. To achieve this balance, the studios are going to have to accept (and actively promote) some basic distinctions: between commercial competition and amateur appropriation, between for-profit use and the barter economy of the Web, between creative repurposing and piracy.

Each of these concessions will be hard for the studios to swallow but necessary if they are going to exert sufficient moral authority to rein in the kinds of piracy that threaten their economic livelihood. On bad days, I don't believe the studios will voluntarily give up their stranglehold on intellectual property. What gives me some hope, however, is the degree to which a collaborationist approach is beginning to gain some toehold within the media industries. These experiments suggest that media producers can garner greater loyalty and more compliance to legitimate concerns if they court the allegiance of fans; the best way to do this turns out to be giving them some stake in the survival of the franchise, ensuring that the provided content more fully reflects their interests, creating a space where they can make their own creative contributions, and recognizing the best work that emerges. In a world of ever-expanding media options, there is going to be a struggle for viewers the likes of which corporate media has never seen before. Many of the smartest folks in the media industry know this: some are trembling, and others are scrambling to renegotiate their relationships with consumers. In the end, the media producers need fans just as much as fans need them.

5

Why Heather Can Write

Media Literacy and the Harry Potter *Wars*

So far, we have seen that corporate media increasingly recognizes the value, and the threat, posed by fan participation. Media producers and advertisers now speak about "emotional capital" or "lovemarks" to refer to the importance of audience investment and participation in media content. Storytellers now think about storytelling in terms of creating openings for consumer participation. At the same time, consumers are using new media technologies to engage with old media content, seeing the Internet as a vehicle for collective problem solving, public deliberation, and grassroots creativity. Indeed, we have suggested that it is the interplay—and tension—between the top-down force of corporate convergence and the bottom-up force of grassroots convergence that is driving many of the changes we are observing in the media landscape.

On all sides and at every level, the term *participation* has emerged as a governing concept, albeit one surrounded by conflicting expectations. Corporations imagine participation as something they can start and stop, channel and reroute, commodify and market. The prohibitionists are trying to shut down unauthorized participation; the collaborationists are trying to win grassroots creators over to their side. Consumers, on the other side, are asserting a right to participate in the culture, on their own terms, when and where they wish. This empowered consumer faces a series of struggles to preserve and broaden this perceived right to participate.

All of these tensions surfaced very visibly through two sets of conflicts surrounding J. K. Rowling's *Harry Potter* books, conflicts that fans collectively refer to as "the Potter wars." On the one hand, there was the struggle of teachers, librarians, book publishers, and civil liberty groups to stand up against efforts by the religious right to have the *Harry Potter* books removed from school libraries and banned from local bookstores. On the other, there were the efforts of Warner Bros. to rein in fan appropriations of the *Harry Potter* books on the grounds that they infringed on the studio's intellectual property. Both efforts threatened the right of children to participate within the imaginative world of *Harry Potter*—one posing a challenge to their right to read, the other a challenge to their right to write. From a purely legal standpoint, the first constitutes a form of censorship, the other a legitimate exercise of property rights. From the perspective of the consumer, on the other hand, the two start to blur since both place restrictions on our ability to fully engage with a fantasy that has taken on a central place in our culture.

The closer we look at these two conflicts, the more complex they seem. Contradictions, confusions, and multiple perspectives should be anticipated at a moment of transition when one media paradigm is dying and another is being born. None of us really knows how to live in this era of media convergence, collective intelligence, and participatory culture. These changes are producing anxieties and uncertainties, even panic, as people imagine a world without gatekeepers and live with the reality of expanding corporate media power. Our responses to these changes cannot be easily mapped in traditional ideological terms: there is not a unified right-wing or left-wing response to convergence culture. Within Christianity, there are some groups that embrace the potentials of the new participatory culture and others terrified by them. Within companies, as we have seen, there are sudden lurches between prohibitionist and collaborationist responses. Among media reformers, some forms of participation are valued more than others. Fans disagree among themselves on how much control J. K. Rowling or Warner Bros. should have over what consumers do with *Harry Potter*. It isn't as if any of us knows all of the answers yet.

All of the above suggests that the Potter wars are at heart a struggle over what rights we have to read and write about core cultural myths —that is, a struggle over literacy. Here, literacy is understood to include not simply what we can do with printed matter but also what we can do with media. Just as we would not traditionally assume that someone is literate if they can read but not write, we should not assume that someone possesses media literacy if they can consume but not express themselves. Historically, constraints on literacy come from attempts to control different segments of the population—some societies have embraced universal literacy, others have restricted literacy to specific social classes or along racial and gender lines. We may also see the current struggle over literacy as having the effect of determining who has the right to participate in our culture and on what terms. *Harry Potter* is a particularly rich focal point for studying our current constraints on literacy because the book itself deals so explicitly with issues of education (often lending its voice to children's rights over institutional constraints) and because the book has been so highly praised for inciting young people to develop their literacy skills.

Yet, the books have also been the focus of various attempts to constrain what kids read and write. My focus is on the *Harry Potter* wars as a struggle over competing notions of media literacy and how it should be taught: the informal pedagogy that emerged within the *Harry Potter* fan community, the attempts to tap kids' interests in the books in classrooms and libraries, the efforts of corporate media to teach us a lesson about the responsible treatment of their intellectual property, the anxieties about the secularization of education expressed by cultural conservatives, and the very different conception of pedagogy shared by Christian supporters of the *Harry Potter* novels within the "discernment movement." All sides want to claim a share in how we educate the young, since shaping childhood is often seen as a way of shaping the future direction of our culture.[1] By looking more closely at these various bids on education, we may map some of the conflicting expectations shaping con-

Fan Fiction in the Era of Web 2.0

You say "User-Generated Content."
We say "Fan Culture."
Let's call the whole thing off!

As this book has suggested, the media industry and its consumers alike now operate as if we were moving towards a more participatory culture, but they have not yet agreed upon the terms of our participation. Even companies that adopt a collaborationist logic have a lot to learn about creating and maintaining a meaningful and reciprocal relationship with their consumers.

Consider, for example, FanLib.com, a startup company founded by such established media players as *Titanic* producer Jon Landau, entertainment lawyer Jon Moonves, and former Yahoo CMO Anil Singh.[1] FanLib began by hosting officially sponsored fan fiction competitions around *The L Word* and *The Ghost Whisperer*. Soon, the company sought to become a general interest portal for all fan fiction, actively soliciting material from leading fan writers and ignoring rights holders. Chris Williams, the company's CEO, explained the company's business model: "The value proposition for fans is a free venue where they can pursue their passion by creating, showcasing, reading, reviewing, sharing, archiving, discovering stories, and by participating in fun events in a community with similar interests. . . . The value proposition for media companies and publishers is to connect, engage, and entertain fans of their media properties in a new online storytelling environment."[2]

[1] For more on the FanLib controversy, see Henry Jenkins, "Transforming Fan Culture into User-Generated Content: The Case of FanLib," Confessions of an Aca-Fan, May 22, 2007.

[2] Henry Jenkins, "Chris Williams Responds to Our Questions about FanLib," Confessions of an Aca-Fan, May 25, 2007.

Fans found reason to suspect the credibility of the company's commitment to defend the rights of fan fiction writers when fans stumbled onto an old business prospectus still posted on line which had been used to sell the initial fan fiction contests. Here, FanLib made a different set of promises to the commercial companies which controlled the rights over these characters: "Managed & Moderated to the Max."

- All the FanLib action takes place in a highly customized environment that you control.
- As with a coloring book, players must stay within the lines.
- Restrictive player's terms-of-service protects your rights and property.
- Moderated "scene missions" keep the story under your control.
- Full monitoring & management of submissions & Players.
- Automatic "profanity filter."
- Completed work is just 1st draft to be polished by the pros.

Each bullet signaled the death of the free and open space fans have carved out for their fiction writing activities in practice, if not in law, over the previous several decades.

FanLib had done its homework by the standards of the venture capitalist world: they had identified a potential market; they had developed a business plan; they had even identified potential contributors to the site; they had developed a board of directors. But they hadn't listened to, talked with, or respected the existing grassroots community that had grown up around the production and distribution of fan fiction. The company, for example, targeted the predominantly female fan writing community with an advertising campaign depicting amateur fan fiction as a 90-pound weakling and commercially hosted fan fiction as buff and muscular. The protesting fans were quick to note

vergence culture. In the process, I will consider what happens as the concept of participatory culture runs up against two of the most powerful forces shaping children's lives: education and religion.

Consider this a story of participation and its discontents.

Hogwarts and All

When she was thirteen, Heather Lawver read a book that she says changed her life: *Harry Potter and the Sorcerer's Stone.*[2] Inspired by reports that J. K. Rowling's novel was getting kids to read, she wanted to do her part to promote literacy. Less than a year later, she launched *The Daily Prophet* (http://www.dprophet.com), a Web-based "school newspaper" for the fictional Hogwarts. Today, the publication has a staff of 102 children from all over the world.

Lawver has been its managing editor, hiring columnists who covered their own "beats" on a weekly basis—everything from the latest quidditch matches to muggle cuisine. Heather personally edited each story, getting it ready for publication. She encourages her staff to closely compare their original submissions with the edited versions and consults with them on issues of style and grammar as needed. Heather initially paid for the site through her allowances until someone suggested opening a post office box where participants could send their contributions; she has since run it on a small budget, but at least she can draw on the allowances of her friends and contributors to keep it afloat during hard times.

Lawver, by the way, was home schooled and hadn't set foot in a classroom since first grade. Her family had been horrified by what they saw as racism and anti-intellectualism, which they encountered when she entered first grade in a rural Mississippi school district. She explained, "It was hard to combat prejudices when you are facing it every day. They just pulled me and one of my brothers out of school. And we never wanted to go back."

A girl who hadn't been in school since first grade was leading a worldwide staff of student writers with no adult supervision to publish a school newspaper for a school that existed only in their imaginations.

From the start, Lawver framed her project with explicit pedagogical goals that she used to help parents understand their children's participation. In an open letter to parents of her contributors, Lawver describes the site's goals:

The Daily Prophet is an organization dedicated to bringing the world of literature to life. . . . By creating an online "newspaper" with articles that lead the readers to believe this fanciful world of Harry Potter to be real, this opens the mind to exploring books, diving into the characters, and analyzing great literature. By developing the mental ability to analyze the written word at a young age, children will find

the total absence of women on the company's board of directors and the absence of any kind of fan advisory committee which might represent the interests of those who had been writing and publishing fan fiction for more than three decades.

The FanLib controversy should be understood against the backdrop of what industry insiders have been calling "web 2.0," a term popularized by business guru Tim O'Reilly to describe the revitalization of the digital economy fueled by companies such as photo-sharing site Flickr, social networking sites MySpace and Facebook, and video uploading sites such as YouTube and Veoh.[3] These web 2.0 enterprises built their business plans on the back of user-generated content. O'Reilly described such companies as constructing "an architecture of participation," which made them more responsive to consumers and enabled them to "harness collective intelligence," drawing much of their value from recirculating content generated by other users. Throughout 2005 and 2006, news magazines trumpeted these companies, with Business Week proclaiming "the Power of Us," Newsweek talking about "Putting the 'We' in the Web," and Time naming "You" (as in YouTube) its person of the year.[4]

Yet the controversy over FanLib was one of many signs that the informal and implicit social contract behind this talk of web 2.0 was starting to fray by 2007. Privacy advocates questioned how

[3] Tim O'Reilly, "What Is Web 2.0?: Design Patterns and Business Models for the Next Generation of Software," http://www.oreillynet.com/pub/a/oreilly/tim/news/2005/09/30/what-is-web-20.html

[4] "The Power of Us," Business Week, June 20 2006; "Putting the 'We' in the Web," Newsweek, April 3, 2006; Lev Grossman, "Time's Person of the Year: You," Time, December 13, 2006.

much personal data was being tapped by these commercial companies; social critics argued that users were often trapped into long-term relationships with these companies as a result of the efforts consumers invested in uploading their data and drawing their friends into these social networks. Some were calling for greater interoperability, which would allow people to easily transfer their data from one site to another. Tiziana Terranova has offered a cogent critique of web 2.0 as a form of "free labor": "Free labor is the moment where this knowledgeable consumption of culture is translated into productive activities that are pleasurably embraced and at the same time often shamelessly exploited."[5] A joke circulating on the Internet defined web 2.0: "You make all the content. They keep all the revenue."

FanLib embraced this web 2.0 model of "user-generated content," forgetting that it was interacting with an existing subcultural community rather than generating one from scratch around innovative tools or services. The industry tends to see these users in isolation—as individuals who want to express themselves, rather than as part of preexisting communities with their own norms and institutionalized practices. FanLib talked about fan fiction as a traditional practice, but its executives were more comfortable courting fans as free agents rather than dealing with them as members of a larger community.

For many fans, the noncommercial nature of fan culture is one of its most important characteristics. These stories are a labor of love; they operate in a gift economy and are given freely to other fans who share their passion for these

[5] Tiziana Terranova, "Free Labor: Producing Culture for the Digital Economy." *Electronic Book Review.* 2003, http://www.electronicbookreview.com/thread/technocapitalism/voluntary.

a love for reading unlike any other. By creating this faux world we are learning, creating, and enjoying ourselves in a friendly utopian society.[3]

Lawver is so good at mimicking teacherly language that one forgets that she has not yet reached adulthood. For example, she provides reassurances that the site will protect children's actual identities and that she will screen posts to ensure that none contain content inappropriate for younger participants.[4] Lawver was anxious to see her work recognized by teachers, librarians, and her fellow home schoolers. She developed detailed plans for how teachers can use her template to create localized version of a Hogwarts school newspaper as class projects. A number of teachers have taken up her offer.

Whether encountered inside or outside formal education, Lawver's project enabled kids to immerse themselves into the imaginary world of Hogwarts and to feel a very real sense of connection to an actual community of children around the world who were working together to produce *The Daily Prophet*. The school they were inventing together (building on the foundations of J. K. Rowling's novel) could not have been more different from the one she had escaped in Mississippi. Here, people of many different ethnic, racial, and national backgrounds (some real, some imagined) formed a community where individual differences were accepted and where learning was celebrated.

The point of entry into this imaginary school was the construction of a fictional identity, and subsequently these personas get woven into a series of "news stories" reporting on events at Hogwarts. For many kids, the profile is all they would write—having a self within the fiction was enough to satisfy the needs that brought them to the site. For others, it was the first step toward constructing a more elaborate fantasy about their life at Hogwarts. In their profiles, kids often combined mundane details of their everyday experiences with fantastical stories about their place within J. K. Rowling's world:

I recently transferred from Madame McKay's Academy of Magic in America to come to Hogwarts. Lived in southern California for most of my life, and my mother never told my father that she was a witch until my fifth birthday (he left shortly afterwards).

Orphaned at 5 when her parents died of cancer, this pure blood witch was sent to live with a family of wizards associated with the Ministry of Magic.

The image of the special child being raised in a mundane (in this case, muggle) family and discovering their identities as they enter school age is a classic theme of fantasy novels and fairy tales, yet here there are often references to divorce or cancer, real-world difficulties so many kids face. From the profiles themselves, we can't be sure whether

characters. Being free of the commercial constraints that surround the source texts, they gain new freedom to explore themes or experiment with structures and styles that could not be part of the "mainstream" versions of these worlds.[6] Others within fandom, however, were arguing that it was the failure of fans to capitalize on their own cultural production which left them vulnerable to outside commercial interests. The group's resistance to profit making, they argued, reflected longer gender divides which devalued women's creative contributions as "crafts."[7]

Whether making money off of fan fiction was right or wrong, few long-term fans wanted to see a startup moving into the space and profiting from their culture. Writing at the peak of the Fan-Lib controversy, one fan explained, "This is the reason I have been involved recently in arguments about whether our community should accept the monetization of fan fiction. Because I think it's coming whether we accept it or not, and I'd rather it was fan-creators getting the benefit of the $$$, not some cutthroat entrepreneur who doesn't care about our community except as a market niche."[8]

Far from being helpless, angry fans quickly and effectively rallied in opposition to FanLib, using their own channels of communication—especially LiveJournal—to inflict damage on the brand. They pooled their knowledge and

[6] Catherine Tossenberger, *Potterotics: Harry Potter Fanfiction on the Internet*, Dissertation, University of Florida 2007. Tossenberger derives her concept in part from a Live Journal post by Seperis, November 23, 2003, http://seperis.livejournal.com/108109.html.

[7] Abigail Derecho, *Illegitimate Media: Race, Gender, and Censorship in Digital Remix*, Dissertation, Comparative Literary Studies, Northwestern University, 2008.

[8] almostnever, Live Journal, May 14, 2007, http://almostnever.livejournal.com/572926.html?format=light.

deconstructed terms of service and promotional material, raising questions about the ways that web 2.0 companies related to their participants.

As the debate unfolded, a number of long-standing leaders in the fan community joined forces to form the Organization for Transformative Works as a means of protecting their traditional cultural practices and of bringing them into the twenty-first century:

> We envision a future in which all fannish works are recognized as legal and transformative, and accepted as legitimate creative activity. We are proactive and innovative in protecting and defending our work from commercial exploitation and legal challenge. We preserve our fannish economy, values, and way of life by protecting and nurturing our fellow fans, our work, our commentary, our history, and our identity, while providing the broadest possible access to fannish activity for all fans. We value our infinite diversity in infinite combinations. We value the unhindered cross-pollination and exchange of fannish ideas and cultures, while seeking to avoid the homogenization or centralization of fandom.[9]

Adopting models from the open source movement, fan coders and programmers are creating a new infrastructure for sharing fan fiction, fan vids, and other forms of fan cultural production; fans with legal background are constructing arguments they hope might deflect legal challenge; fans with business backgrounds are acquiring resources needed to sustain the effort; and fans with academic backgrounds are creating an online journal contextualizing the community's cultural practices and traditions.

[9] "Our Vision," Organization for Transformative Works, http://transformativeworks.org/.

these are problems they have confronted personally or are anxious possibilities they are exploring through their fantasies. Heather has suggested that many kids come to *The Daily Prophet* because their schools and families have failed them in some way; they use the new school community to work through their feelings about some traumatic event or to compensate for their estrangement from kids in their neighborhoods. Some children are drawn toward some of the fantasy races—elves, goblins, giants, and the like—while other kids have trouble imagining themselves to be anything other than muggle-born, even in their fantasy play. Children use stories to escape from or reaffirm aspects of their real lives.[5]

Rowling's richly detailed world allows many points of entry. Some kids imagine themselves as related to the characters—the primary ones like Harry Potter or Snape, of course, but also minor background figures—the inventors of the quidditch brooms, the authors of the textbooks, the heads of referenced agencies, classmates of Harry's mother and father, any affiliation that allows them to claim a special place for themselves in the story. In her book *Writing Superheroes* (1997), Anne Haas Dyson uses the metaphor of a "ticket to play" to describe how the roles provided by children's media properties get deployed by children in a classroom space to police who is allowed to participate and what roles they can assume.[6] Some children fit comfortably within the available roles;

others feel excluded and have to work harder to insert themselves into the fantasy. Dyson's focus has to do with divisions of gender and race, primarily, but given the global nature of *The Daily Prophet* community, nationality also was potentially at stake. Rowling's acknowledgment in subsequent books that Hogwarts interacted with schools around the world gave students from many countries a "ticket" into the fantasy: "Sirius was born in India to Ariel and Derek Koshen. Derek was working as a Ministry of Magic ambassador to the Indian Ministry. Sirius was raised in Bombay, and speaks Hindi fluently. While he was in Bombay he saved a stranded Hippogriff from becoming a jacket, cementing his long-lasting love of magical creatures. He at-tended Gahdal School of Witchcraft and Wizardry in Thailand." Here, it helps that the community is working hard to be inclusive and accepts fantasies that may not comfortably match the world described within the novels.

Despite their effectiveness at developing an alternative model for their community's future, fan protestors did not destroy FanLib's profitability. By late 2007, the company had attracted more than 10,000 contributors. Some of these contributors were "newbies" drawn into fandom by the company's promotional efforts, and others were estranged from the established fan community. Many understood fan fiction as an individualized rather than community based activity. Trying to build a "community" for fan fiction, FanLib had attracted many who had little investment in affiliating with other fans.[10]

[10] Xiaochang Li, "Fan, Inc.: Another Look at FanLib.com," *Convergence Culture Consortium Newsletter*, December 14, 2007.

One striking consequence of the value placed on education in the *Harry Potter* books is that almost all of the participants at *The Daily Prophet* imagine themselves to be gifted students. Kids who read recreationally are still a subset of the total school population, so it is very likely that many of these kids are teacher's pets in real life. Hermione represented a particularly potent role model for the studiously minded young girls who were key contributors to *The Daily Prophet*. Some feminist critics argue that she falls into traditional feminine stereotypes of dependency and nurturance.[7] This may be true, but this character provides some point of identification for female readers within a book otherwise so focused on young boys. Here's how one young writer framed her relationship to the character:

My name is Mandi Granger. I am 12 yrs old. I am also muggle born. Yes, I am related to Hermione Granger. I am Hermione's cousin. I am attending Hogwarts School for Witchcraft and Wizardry. This is my third year at Hogwarts. I am doing this article between all my studies. I guess I pick up my study habits from my cousin. I am in the Gryffindor house just like my cousin. I do know Harry Potter personally by my cousin. My cousin took him to my house before I went to Hogwarts. We mostly talk about Hogwarts and the Weasley's children.

Through children's fantasy play, Hermione takes on a much more active and central role than Rowling provided her. As Ellen Seiter notes in regard to girl-targeted series such as *Strawberry Shortcake* (1981), feminist parents sometimes sell their daughters short by underestimating their ability to extend beyond what is represented on the screen and by stigmatizing the already limited range of media content available to them.[8] Female readers are certainly free to identify across gender with a range of other characters—and one can see the claims of special family ties as one way of marking those identifications. Yet, at an age when gender roles are reinforced on all sides, transgressing gender roles through the fantasy may be harder than reconstructing the characters as vehicles for your own empowerment fantasies.

In some cases, the back stories for these characters are quite elaborate with detailed accounts of their wands, the animal familiars, their magical abilities, their favorite classes, their future plans, and the like. These fictional personas can contain the seeds of larger narratives, suggesting how the construction of an identity may fuel subsequent fan fiction:

> I'm the only sister of Harry Potter, and I am going to play for the Gryffindor quidditch team this year as a chaser. My best friend is Cho Chang, and I am dating Draco Malfoy (although Harry's not happy about that). One of my other good friends is Riley Ravenclaw, a co-writer. I have a few pets, a winged Thestral named Bostrio, a unicorn foal named Golden, and a snowy owl (like Hedwig) named Cassiddia. I was able to escape the Lord Voldemort attack on my family for the reason that I was holidaying with my Aunt Zeldy in Ireland at the time, though I mourn the loss of my mum and dad. I was mad about the awful things Ms. Skeeter wrote about my little brother, and I have sent her her own little package of undiluted bubotuber pus. HA!

As *The Daily Prophet* reporters develop their reports about life at Hogwarts, they draw each other's personas into their stories, trying to preserve what each child sees as its special place within this world. The result is a jointly produced fantasy—somewhere between a role-playing game and fan fiction. The intertwining of fantasies becomes a key element of bonding for these kids, who come to care about one another through interacting with these fictional personas.

What skills do children need to become full participants in convergence culture? Across this book, we have identified a number—the ability to pool knowledge with others in a collaborative enterprise (as in *Survivor* spoiling), the ability to share and compare value systems by evaluating ethical dramas (as occurs in the gossip surrounding reality television), the ability to make connections across scattered pieces of information (as occurs when we consume *The Matrix*, 1999, or *Pokémon*, 1998), the ability to express your interpretations and feelings toward popular fictions through your own folk culture (as occurs in *Star Wars* fan cinema), and the ability to circulate what you create via the Internet so that it can be shared with others (again as in fan cinema). The example of *The Daily Prophet* suggests yet another important cultural competency: role-playing both as a means of exploring a fictional realm and as a means of developing a richer understanding of yourself and the culture around you. These kids came to understand *Harry Potter* by occupying a space within Hogwarts; occupying such a space helped them to map more fully the rules of this fictional world and the roles that various characters played within it. Much as an actor builds up a character by combining things discovered through research with things learned through personal introspection, these kids were drawing on their own experiences to flesh out various aspects of Rowling's fiction. This is a kind of intellectual mastery that comes only through active participation. At the same time, role-playing was providing an inspiration for them to expand other kinds of literacy skills—those already valued within traditional education.

What's striking about this process, though, is that it takes place outside the classroom and beyond any direct adult control. Kids are teaching kids what they need to become full participants in convergence culture. More and more, educators are coming to value the learning that occurs in these informal and recreational spaces, especially as they confront the constraints imposed on learning via educational policies that seemingly value only what can be counted on a standardized test. If children are going to acquire the skills needed to be full participants in their culture, they may well learn these skills through involvement in activities such as editing the newspaper of an imaginary school or teaching one another skills needed to do well in massively multiplayer games or any number of others things that teachers and parents currently regard as trivial pursuits.

Rewriting School

University of Wisconsin–Madison School of Education professor James Paul Gee calls such informal learning cultures "affinity spaces," asking why people learn more, participate more actively, engage more deeply with popular culture than they do with the contents of their textbooks.[9] As one sixteen-year-old *Harry Potter* fan told me, "It is one thing to be discussing the theme of a short story you've never heard of before and couldn't care less about. It is another to be discussing the theme of your friend's 50,000-word opus about Harry and Hermione that they've spent three months writing."[10] Affinity spaces offer powerful opportunities for learning, Gee argues, because they are sustained by common endeavors that bridge across differences in age, class, race, gender, and educational level, because people can participate in various ways according to their skills and interests, because they depend on peer-to-peer teaching with each participant constantly motivated to acquire new knowledge or refine his or her existing skills, and because they allow each participant to feel like an expert while tapping the expertise of others. More and more literacy experts are recognizing that enacting, reciting, and appropriating elements from preexisting stories is a valuable and organic part of the process by which children develop cultural literacy.[11]

A decade ago, published fan fiction came mostly from women in their twenties, thirties, and beyond. Today, these older writers have been joined by a generation of new contributors who found fan fiction surfing the Internet and decided to see what they could produce. *Harry Potter* in particular has encouraged many young people to write and share their first stories. Zsenya, the thirty-three-year-old Webmistress of The Sugar Quill, a leading site for Harry Potter fan fiction, offered this comment:

> In many cases, the adults really try to watch out for the younger members (theoretically, everybody who registers for our forums must be at least 13). They're a little bit like den mothers. I think it's really actually an amazing way to communicate. . . . The absence of face-to-face equalizes

everyone a little bit, so it gives the younger members a chance to talk with adults without perhaps some of the intimidation they might normally feel in talking to adults. And in the other direction, I think it helps the adults remember what it was like to be at a certain age or in a certain place in life.[12]

These older fans often find themselves engaging more directly with people like Flourish. Flourish started reading *The X-Files* fan fiction when she was ten, wrote her first Harry Potter stories at twelve, and published her first online novel at fourteen.[13] She quickly became a mentor for other emerging fan writers, including many who were twice her age or more. Most people assumed she was probably a college student. Interacting online allowed her to keep her age to herself until she had become so central to the fandom that nobody cared that she was in middle school.

Educators like to talk about "scaffolding," the ways that a good pedagogical process works in a step-by-step fashion, encouraging kids to try out new skills that build on those they have already mastered, providing support for these new steps until the learner feels sufficient confidence to take them on their own. In the classroom, scaffolding is provided by the teacher. In a participatory culture, the entire community takes on some responsibility for helping newbies find their way. Many young authors began composing stories on their own as a spontaneous response to a popular culture. For these young writers, the next step was the discovery of fan fiction on the Internet, which provided alternative models for what it meant to be an author. At first, they might only read stories, but the fan community provides many incitements for readers to cross that last threshold into composing and submitting their own stories. And once a fan submits, the feedback he or she receives inspires further and improved writing.

What difference will it make, over time, if a growing percentage of young writers begin publishing and getting feedback on their work while they are still in high school? Will they develop their craft more quickly? Will they discover their voices at an earlier age? And what happens when these young writers compare notes, becoming critics, editors, and mentors? Will this help them develop a critical vocabulary for thinking about storytelling? Nobody is quite sure, but the potentials seem enormous. Authorship has an almost sacred aura in a world where there are limited opportunities to circulate your ideas to a larger public. As we expand access to mass distribution via the Web, our understanding of what it means to be an author—and what kinds of authority should be ascribed to authors—necessarily shifts. This shift could lead to a heightened awareness of intellectual property rights as more and more people feel a sense of ownership over the stories they create. Yet, it also can result in a demystification of the creative process, a growing recognition of the communal dimensions of expression, as writing takes on more aspects of traditional folk practice.

The fan community has gone to extraordinary lengths to provide informal instruction to newer writers. The largest *Harry Potter* archive, www.fictionalley.org, currently hosts more than 30,000 stories and book chapters, including hundreds of completed or partially completed novels. These stories are written by authors of all ages. More than two hundred people are on its unpaid staff, including forty mentors who welcome each new participant individually. At The Sugar Quill, www.sugarquill.net, every posted story undergoes beta reading (a peer-review process). Beta reading takes its name from beta testing in computer programming: fans seek out advice on the rough drafts of their nearly completed stories so that they can smooth out "bugs" and take them to the next level. As the editors explain, "We want this to be a place where fanfiction can be read and enjoyed, but where writers who want more than just raves can come for actual (gentle—think Lupin, not McGonagall) constructive criticism and technical editing. We've found this to be essential for our own stories, and would be pleased to help with the stories of others. Our hope is that this experience will give people the courage and confidence to branch out and start writing original stories."[14] (Lupin and McGonagall are two of the teachers Rowling depicts in the novels, Lupin a gentle pedagogue, McGonagall practicing a more tough-love approach.) New writers often go through multiple drafts and multiple beta readers before their stories are ready for posting. "The Beta Reader service has really helped me to get the adverbs out of my writing and get my prepositions in the right place and improve my sentence structure and refine the overall quality of my writing," explains Sweeney Agonistes, an entering college freshman with years of publishing behind her.[15]

Instructions for beta readers, posted at Writer's University (www.writersu.net), a site that helps instruct fan editors and writers, offers some insights into the pedagogical assumptions shaping this process:

A good beta reader:

- admits to the author what his or her own strengths and weaknesses are—i.e. "I'm great at beta reading for plot, but not spelling!" Anyone who offers to check someone else's spelling, grammar, and punctuation should probably be at least worthy of a solid B in English, and preferably an A.

- reads critically to analyze stylistic problems, consistency, plot holes, unclarity, smoothness of flow and action, diction (choice of words), realism and appropriateness of dialog, and so forth. Does it get bogged down in unnecessary description or back-story? Do the characters "sound" like they're supposed to? Is the plot logical and do the characters all have motives for the things they do?

- suggests rather than edits. In most cases a beta reader shouldn't rewrite or merely correct problems. Calling the author's attention to problems helps the author be aware of them and thereby improve.

- points out the things he or she likes about a story. Even if it was the worst story you ever read, say something positive! Say multiple somethings positive! See the potential in every story. . . .

- is tactful, even with things she considers major flaws—but honest as well.

- improves her skills. If you are serious about wanting to help authors, consider reading some of the writing resources linked at the bottom of the page, which will give you some great perspective on common mistakes fanfic writers make, in addition to basic tips about what makes for good writing.[16]

This description constructs a different relationship between mentors and learners than shapes much schoolroom writing instruction, starting with the opening stipulation that the editors acknowledge their own strengths and limitations, and continuing down through the focus on suggestion rather than instruction as a means of getting students to think through the implications of their own writing process.

As educational researcher Rebecca Black notes, the fan community can often be more tolerant of linguistic errors than traditional classroom teachers and more helpful in enabling the learner to identify what they are actually trying to say because reader and writer operate within the same frame of reference, sharing a deep emotional investment in the content being explored.[17] The fan community promotes a broader range of different literary forms—not simply fan fiction but various modes of commentary—than the exemplars available to students in the classroom, and often they showcase realistic next steps for the learner's development rather than showing only professional writing that is far removed from anything most students will be able to produce.

Beyond beta reading, The Sugar Quill provides a range of other references relevant to fan writers, some dealing with questions of grammar and style, some dealing with the specifics of the *Harry Potter* universe, but all designed to help would-be writers improve their stories and push themselves in new directions. The Sugar Quill's genre classifications provide models for different ways would-be writers might engage with Rowling's text: "Alternative Points of View," which reframe the events of the book through the eyes of a character other than Harry; "I Wonder Ifs," which explore "possibilities" that are hinted at but not developed within the novels; "Missing Moments," which fill in gaps between the plot events; and "Summer after Fifth Year," which extends beyond the current state of the novel, but does not enter into events Rowling will likely cover once she picks up her pen again. The Sugar Quill holds writers to a strict and literal interpretation, insisting that the information they include in their stories be consistent with what Rowling has revealed. As the editor explains,

> I don't write fanfic to "fix" things, I write it to explore corners that [the Harry Potter] canon didn't have the opportunity to peek into, or to speculate on what *might* have led up to something, or what *could* result from some other thing. A story that leaves these wonderful corners isn't a story that needs fixing, it's a story that invites exploration, like those pretty little tree-lined side streets that you never get a chance to go down when you're on a bus, heading for work along the main drag. That doesn't mean there's anything wrong with the bus, with the main drag, or with going to work —it just means there's more down there to take a look at.[18]

Many adults worry that these kids are "copying" preexisting media content rather than creating their own original works. Instead, one should think about their appropriations as a kind of apprenticeship. Historically, young artists learned from established masters, sometimes contributing to the older artists' works, often following their patterns, before they developed their own styles and techniques. Our modern expectations about original expression are a difficult burden for anyone at the start of a career. In this same way, these young artists learn what they can from the stories and images that are most familiar to them. Building their first efforts upon existing cultural materials allows them to focus their energies elsewhere, mastering their craft, perfecting their skills, and communicating their ideas. Like many of the other young writers, Sweeney said that Rowling's books provided her the scaffolding she needed to focus on other aspects of the writing process: "It's easier to develop a good sense of plot and characterization and other literary techniques if your reader already knows something of the world where the story takes place." Sweeney writes mostly about the Hogwarts teachers, trying to tell the novels' events from their perspectives and exploring their relationships when they are not in front of the class. As she explains,

> I figure J. K. Rowling is going to take care of the student portion of the world as Harry gets to it. The problem with world building is that there is so much backstory to play with. I like filling in holes. . . . See if you can figure out a plausible way that would fit into the established canon to explain why Snape left Voldemort and went to serve Dumbledore. There are so many explanations for that, but we don't know for sure yet, so when we find out, if we find out, there are going to be so many people reading for it, and if someone gets it right, they are going to go, yes, I nailed it.

Others noted that writing about someone else's fictional characters, rather than drawing directly on their own experience, gave them some critical distance to reflect on what they were trying to express. Sweeney described how getting inside the head of a character who was very different from herself helped her make sense of the people she saw around her in school who were coming from very different backgrounds and acting on very different values. She saw fan fiction, in that sense, as a useful resource for surviving high school. *Harry Potter* fan fiction yields countless narratives of youth empowerment as characters fight back against the injustices their writers encounter every day at school. Often, the younger writers show a fascination with getting inside the heads of the adult characters. Many of the best stories are told from teachers' perspectives or depict Harry's parents and mentors when they were school age. Some of the stories are sweetly romantic or bittersweet coming-of-age stories (where sexual consummation comes when two characters hold hands); others are charged with anger or budding sexual feelings, themes the authors say they would have been reluctant to discuss in a school assignment. When they discuss such stories, teen and adult fans talk openly about their life experiences, offering each other advice on more than just issues of plot or characterization.

Through online discussions of fan writing, the teen writers develop a vocabulary for talking about writing and learn strategies for rewriting and improving their own work. When they talk about the books themselves, they make comparisons with other literary works or draw connections with philosophical and theological traditions; they debate gender stereotyping in the female characters; they cite interviews with the writer or read critical analyses of the works; they use analytic concepts they probably wouldn't encounter until they reached the advanced undergraduate classroom.

Schools are still locked into a model of autonomous learning that contrasts sharply with the kinds of learning that are needed as students are entering the new knowledge cultures. Gee and other educators worry that students who are comfortable participating in and exchanging knowledge through affinity spaces are being deskilled as they enter the classroom:

> Learning becomes both a personal and unique trajectory through a complex space of opportunities (i.e., a person's own unique movement through various affinity spaces over time) and a social journey as one shares aspects of that trajectory with others (who may be very different from oneself and inhabit otherwise quite different spaces) for a shorter or longer time before moving on. What these young people see in school may pale by comparison. It may seem to lack the imagination that infuses the non-school aspects of their lives. At the very least, they may demand an argument for "Why school?"[19]

Gee's focus is on the support system that emerges around the individual learner, while Pierre Lévy's focus is on the ways that each learner contributes to the larger collective intelligence; but both are describing parts of the same experience—living in a world where knowledge is shared and where critical activity is ongoing and lifelong.

Not surprisingly, someone who has just published her first online novel and gotten dozens of letters of comment finds it disappointing to return to the classroom where her work is going to be read only by the teacher and feedback may be very limited. Some teens have confessed to smuggling drafts of stories to school in their textbooks and editing them during class; others sit around the lunch table talking plot and character issues with their classmates or try to work on the stories on the school computers until the librarians accuse them of wasting time. They can't wait for the school bell to ring so they can focus on their writing.

Lawver was not the only one to see the educational payoff from fan writing. A number of libraries have brought in imaginary lecturers on muggle life or run weekend-long classes modeled after those taught at the remarkable school. A group of Canadian publishers organized a writing summer camp for children, designed to help them perfect their craft. The publishers were responding to the many unsolicited manuscripts they had received from Potter fans.[20] One educational group organized Virtual Hogwarts, which offered courses on both academic subjects and the topics made famous from Rowling's books. Adult teachers from four continents developed the online materials for thirty different classes, and the effort drew more than three thousand students from seventy-five nations.

It is not clear that the successes of affinity spaces can be duplicated by simply incorporating similar activities into the classroom. Schools impose a fixed leadership hierarchy (including very different roles for adults and teens); it is unlikely that someone like Heather or Flourish would have had the same editorial opportunities they have found through fandom. Schools have less flexibility to support writers at very different stages of their development. Even the most progressive schools set limits on what students can write compared to the freedom they enjoy on their own. Certainly, teens may receive harsh critical responses to their more controversial stories when they publish them online, but the teens themselves are deciding what risks they want to take and facing the consequences of those decisions.

That said, we need to recognize that improving writing skills is a secondary benefit of participating in the fan fiction writing community. Talking about fan fiction in these terms makes the activity seem more valuable to teachers or parents who may be skeptical of the worthiness of these activities. And the kids certainly take the craft of writing seriously and are proud of their literacy accomplishments. At the same time, the writing is valuable because of the ways it expands their experience of the world of *Harry Potter* and because of the social connections it facilitates with other fans. These kids are passionate about writing because they are passionate about what they are writing about. To some degree, pulling such activities into the schools is apt to deaden them because school culture generates a different mindset than our recreational life.

Defense against Dark Arts

J. K. Rowling and Scholastic, her publisher, had initially signaled their support for fan writers, stressing that storytelling encouraged kids to expand their imaginations and empowered them to find their voices as writers. Through her London-based agent, the Christopher Little Literary Agency, Rowling had issued a statement in 2003 describing the author's long-standing policy of welcoming "the huge interest that her fans have in the series and the fact that it has led them to try their hand at writing."[21] When Warner Bros. bought the film rights in 2001, however, the stories entered a second and not so complimentary intellectual property regime.[22] The studio had a long-standing practice of seeking out Web sites whose domain names used copyrighted or trademarked phrases. Trademark law was set up to avoid "potential confusions" about who produces particular goods or content; Warner felt it had a legal obligation to police sites that emerged around their properties. The studio characterized this as a "sorting out" process in which each site was suspended until the studio could assess what the site was doing with the *Harry Potter* franchise. Diane Nelsen, senior vice president of Warner Bros. Family Entertainment, explained:

> When we dug down under some of these domain names, we could see clearly who was creating a screen behind which they were exploiting our property illegally. With fans you did not have to go far to see that they were just fans and they were expressing something vital about their relationship to this property. . . . You hate to penalize an authentic fan for the actions of an inauthentic fan, but we had enough instances of people who really were exploiting kids in the name of *Harry Potter*.

In many cases, the original site owner would be issued permission to continue to use the site under the original name, but Warner Bros. retained the right to shut it down if they found "inappropriate or offensive content."

The fans felt slapped in the face by what they saw as the studio's efforts to take control over their sites. Many of those caught up in these struggles were children and teens, who had been among the most active organizers of the *Harry Potter* fandom. Heather Lawver, the young editor of *The Daily Prophet*, formed the American-based organization, Defense Against the Dark Arts, when she learned that some fan friends had been threatened with legal action: "Warner was very clever about who they attacked. . . . They attacked a whole bunch of kids in Poland. How much of a risk is that? They went after the twelve- and fifteen-year-olds with the rinky-dink sites. They underestimated how interconnected our fandom was. They underestimated the fact that we knew those kids in Poland and we knew the rinky dink sites and we cared about them." Heather herself never received a cease-and-desist letter, but she made it her cause to defend friends who were under legal threats. In the United Kingdom, fifteen-year-old Claire Field emerged as the poster girl in the fans' struggle against Warner Bros. She and her parents had hired a solicitor after she received a cease-and-desist letter for her site, www.harrypotterguide.co.uk, and in the process, took the struggle to the British media. Her story was reported worldwide, and in each location other teen Webmasters who had been shut down by Warner's legal representatives also went public.[23] Lawver joined forces with Field's British supporters, helping to coordinate media outreach and activism against the studio.

Defense Against Dark Arts argued that fans had helped to turn a little-known children's book into an international best-seller and that the rights holders owed them some latitude to do their work. The petition ends with a "call to arms" against studios that fail to appreciate their supporters: "There are dark forces afoot, darker even than He-Who-Must-Not-Be-Named, because these dark forces are daring to take away something so basic, so human, that it's close to murder. They are taking away our freedom of speech, our freedom to express our thoughts, feelings, and ideas, and they are taking away the fun of a magical book."[24] Lawver, the passionate and articulate teen, debated a Warner Bros. spokesman on MSNBC's *Hardball with Chris Matthews* (1997). As Lawver explained, "We weren't disorganized little kids anymore. We had a public following, and we had a petition with 1,500 signatures in a matter of two weeks. They [Warner Bros.] finally had to negotiate with us."

As the controversy intensified, Diane Nelson, senior vice president of Warner Bros. Family Entertainment, publicly acknowledged that the studio's legal response had been "naïve" and "an act of miscommunication."[25] Nelson, now executive vice president for Global Brand Management, told me, "We didn't know what we had on our hands early on in dealing with *Harry Potter.* We did what we would normally do in the protection of our intellectual property. As soon as we realized we were causing consternation to children or their parents, we stopped it." Out of the conflict, the studio developed a more collaborative policy for engaging with *Harry Potter* fans, one similar to the ways that Lucas was seeking to collaborate with *Star Wars* fan filmmakers:

> Heather is obviously a very smart young woman and did an effective job drawing attention to the issue. . . . She brought to our attention fans who she felt had been victims of these letters. We called them. In one instance, there was a young man she was holding up as a poster child for what we were doing wrong. He was a young man out of London. He and two of his friends from school had started a Triwizard Tournament on the Internet. They were having contests through their sites. . . . Ultimately, what we did with them was the basis of what we did with subsequent fans. We deputized them. We ended up sponsoring their tournament and paying for their P.O. box for offline entries to this contest. . . . We were not at all opposed to his site or what he was doing on it or how he was expressing himself as a fan. In fact, we believed from day one that those sites were critical to the success of what we were doing, and the more of them the better. We ended up giving him official sanction and access to materials to include on the site so that we could keep him within the family and still protect *Harry Potter* materials appropriately.

Many *Potter* fans praised Warner for admitting its mistakes and fixing the problems in their relations with fans. Lawver remains unconvinced, seeing the outcome more as an attempt to score a public relations victory than any shift in their thinking. She has recently added a section to *The Daily Prophet* designed to provide resources for other fan communities that wish to defend themselves against studio restrictions on their expression and participation.[26]

Heather Lawver and her allies had launched their children's campaign against Warner Bros. under the assumption that such fan activism had a long history. She explained: "I figured with the history that *Star Wars* and *Star Trek* fan writers had, people would have done this before. I didn't think much of it. I thought we had precedence but apparently not." Other groups had tried, but not with nearly the same degree of success. After several decades of aggressive studio attention, there is literally no case law concerning fan fiction. The broad claims sometimes asserted by the studios have never been subjected to legal contestation. Studios threaten, fans back down, and none of the groups that would normally step forward to defend free expression rights consider it part of their agenda to defend amateur creators. Free-speech organizations, including the American Civil Liberties Union and the Electronic Frontier Foundation, joined Muggles for Harry Potter, a group created to support teachers who wanted to keep the *Harry Potter* books in the classroom, but failed to defend the fan fiction writers who asserted their rights to build their fantasies around Rowling's novel. The Stanford Center for Internet and Society posted a statement—explicitly supportive, implicitly condescending—about fan fiction on its Chilling Effects Web site (http://www.chillingeffects.org/fanfic). The statement in effect concedes most of the claims made by the studio attorneys.[27] Adopting a similar position, Electronic Frontier Foundation chairman of the board Brad Templeton writes, "Almost all 'fan fiction' is arguably a copyright violation. If you want to write a story about Jim Kirk and Mr. Spock, you need Paramount's permission, pure and simple."[28] Note how Templeton moves from legal hedge words like "arguably" in the first sentence to the moral certainty of "plain and simple" by the second. With friends like these, who needs enemies?

The fan community includes plenty of lawyers, some informed, some otherwise, who have been willing to step up where the public interest groups have failed, and to offer legal advice to fans about how to contest efforts to shut down their Web sites.[29] Fan activists, for example, support Writers University, a Web site that, among other services, provides periodic updates on how a range of different media franchises and individual authors have responded to fan fiction, identifying those who welcome and those who prohibit participation.[30] The site's goal is to allow fans to make an informed choice about the risks they face in pursuing their hobbies and interests. Legal scholars Rosemary J. Coombe and Andrew Herman note that fans have found posting their cease-

and-desist letters on the Web to be an effective tactic, one that forces media companies to publicly confront the consequences of their actions, and one that helps fans see the patterns of legal action that might otherwise be felt only by those Webmistresses directly involved.[31]

Nobody is sure whether fan fiction falls under current fair-use protections. Current copyright law simply doesn't have a category for dealing with amateur creative expression. Where there has been a "public interest" factored into the legal definition of fair use—such as the desire to protect the rights of libraries to circulate books or journalists to quote or academics to cite other researchers—it has been advanced in terms of legitimated classes of users and not a generalized public right to cultural participation. Our current notion of fair use is an artifact of an era when few people had access to the marketplace of ideas, and those who did fell into certain professional classes. It surely demands close reconsideration as we develop technologies that broaden who may produce and circulate cultural materials. Judges know what to do with people who have professional interests in the production and distribution of culture; they don't know what to do with amateurs, or people they deem to be amateurs.

Industry groups have tended to address copyright issues primarily through a piracy model, focusing on the threat of file sharing, rather than dealing with the complexities of fan fiction. Their official educational materials have been criticized for focusing on copyright protections to the exclusion of any reference to fair use. By implication, fans are seen simply as "pirates" who steal from the studios and give nothing in return. Studios often defend their actions against fans on the grounds that if they do not actively enforce their copyrights, they will be vulnerable to commercial competitors encroaching on their content.

The best legal solution to this quagmire may be to rewrite fair-use protections to legitimate grassroots, not-for-profit circulation of critical essays and stories that comment on the content of mass media. Companies certainly are entitled to protect their rights against encroachment from commercial competitors, yet under the current system, because other companies know how far they can push and are reluctant to sue each other, they often have greater latitude to appropriate and transform media content than amateurs, who do not know their rights and have little legal means to defend them even if they did. One paradoxical result is that works that are hostile to the original creators and thus can be read more explicitly as making critiques of the source material may have greater freedom from copyright enforcement than works that embrace the ideas behind the original work and simply seek to extend them in new directions. A story where Harry and the other students rise up to overthrow Dumbledore because of his paternalistic policies is apt to be recognized by a judge as political speech and parody, whereas a work that imagines Ron and Hermione going on a date may be so close to the original that its status as criticism is less clear and is apt to be read as infringement.

In the short run, change is more likely to occur by shifting the way studios think about fan communities than reshaping the law, and that's why the collaborative approaches we've seen across the past two chapters seem like important steps in redefining the space of amateur participation. Nelson said that the *Harry Potter* controversy was instrumental in starting conversations within the studio between business, public relations, creative, and legal department staffers, about what principles should govern their relations with their fans and supporters: "We are trying to balance the needs of other creative stakeholders, as well as the fans, as well as our own legal obligations, all within an arena which is new and changing, and there are not clear precedents about how things should be interpreted or how they would be acted upon if they ever reached the courts."

In the course of the interview, described fans as "core shareholders" in a particular property and the "life blood" of the franchise. The studio needed to find ways to respect the "creativity and energy" these fans brought behind a franchise, even as they needed to protect the franchise from encroachment from groups who wanted to profit for their efforts, to respond quickly to misinformation, or, in the case of material aimed at the youth market, to protect children from access to mature content. As far as fan fiction goes,

> We recognize that it is the highest compliment in terms of the fans inserting themselves into the property and wanting to express their love for it. We are very respectful of what that means. There is a degree to which fan fiction is acceptable to authors and there is a degree to which it moves into a place where it does not feel appropriate, respectful, or within the rights of fans. A lot has to do with how a fan wants to publish and whether they want to benefit commercially off of that fan fiction. If it is purely just an expression for others to read and experience and appreci-

ate, I think that is generally pretty tolerable by a studio rights holder and a creator. The more broadly the fan wants to see that fan fiction disseminated or trade upon it for revenue, promotion, or publicity, the less tolerant the studio or creator might be.

But, as Nelson acknowledged, the fan's "sense of ownership over a particular property" posed challenges for the studio:

> When we stray from the source material or what fans perceive as the true roots of a property, we are under their scrutiny. They can become either advocates for what we are doing or strong dissenters. They can shift the tide of how a property is introduced into the market place depending on whether they perceive us as having presented it carefully, respectfully, and accurately. . . . Fans may be trying to promote the property on the Internet in their terms, but they can sometimes compromise our responsibility to protect that intellectual property so as to keep it pure and to keep our legal rights intact.

There is still—and perhaps may always be—a huge gap between the studio's assumptions about what constitutes appropriate fan participation and the fans' own sense of moral "ownership" over the property. The studios are now, for the most part, treating cult properties as "lovemarks" and fans as "inspirational consumers" whose efforts help generate broader interests in their properties. Establishing the fans' loyalty often means lessening traditional controls that companies might exert over their intellectual properties and thus opening up a broader space for grassroots creative expression.

Muggles for *Harry Potter*

Studio attorneys were not the only group that posed a threat to children's rights to participate in the world of *Harry Potter*. The *Harry Potter* books have been at the center of more textbook and library controversies over the past several years than any other book. In 2002, they were the focus of more than five hundred "challenges" at schools and libraries around the United States.[32] In Lawrence, Kansas, for example, the Oskaloosa Public Library was forced to cancel plans for a special "Hogwarts class" for "aspiring young witches and wizards" because parents in the community thought the local librarian was trying to recruit children into demon worship. Paula Ware, the librarian who proposed the class, quickly backed down: "It's my busiest time of the year, and I don't want to enter into a confrontation. But if this had been about banning the books, I would have taken this to the Supreme Court."[33] In Alamogordo, New Mexico, the Christ Community Church burned more than thirty *Harry Potter* books, along with DVDs of Disney's *Snow White and the Seven Dwarfs* (1937), CDs by Eminem, and novels by Stephen King. Jack Brock, the pastor of the church, justified the book burning on the grounds that *Harry Potter*, a book he admitted he had not read, was "a masterpiece of satanic deception" and an instruction manual into the dark arts.[34] CNN quoted another minister, Reverend Lori Jo Scheppers, who suggested that children exposed to *Harry Potter* would "have a very good chance of becoming another Dylan Klebold and those guys in Columbine."[35]

So far, we have been focused on participation as a positive force in the lives of these kids—something that is motivating children to read, write, form communities, and master other kinds of content—not to mention, stand up for their rights. Yet, as we turn our attention to some of *Harry Potter*'s conservative critics, participation takes on altogether more sinister connotations. Evangelist Phil Arms, for example, describes *Harry Potter* and *Pokémon* (1998) as "fatal attractions" drawing children toward the realm of the occult: "Sooner or later, all who enter the world of *Harry Potter* must meet the true face behind the veil. And when they do, they discover what all those who toy with evil discover, and that is, that while they may have been just playing, the Devil always plays for keeps."[36] The moral reformers cite the example of kids dressing up like Harry Potter, putting a magic sorting cap on their heads in an imitation of the book's initiation ritual, or drawing lightning bolts on their foreheads to duplicate Harry's scar, as evidence that children are moving from reading the books into participating in occult activities. Tapping deep-seated anxieties about theatricality and role-playing, Arms and his allies worry that immersion into fictional worlds may amount to a form of "astral projection"[37] or that when we speak words of magic, the demon forces that we summon do not necessarily realize that we are only pretending. These conservative critics warn that the compelling experiences of popular culture can override real-world experiences until children are no longer able to distinguish between fact and fantasy. For some, this level of engagement is enough to leave the *Harry Potter* books suspect: "These books are read over and over by children in the same way the Bible should be read."[38]

More generally, these critics are concerned about the immersive and expansive nature of the imaginary worlds being constructed in contemporary media franchises. Another evangelist, Berit Kjos, compares the *Harry Potter* books with *Dungeons and Dragons* (1975) in that regard:

1. Both immerse their fans in a plausible, well-developed fantasy world, replete with an evolving history, a carefully mapped geography, and wizards that model the thrill-packed and power-filled way of the mythical shaman.
2. In this fantasy world, adults and children alike are led into imagined experiences that create memories, build new values, guide their thinking and mold their understanding of reality.[39]

Here, the conservative critics seem to be taking aim at the very concept of transmedia storytelling—seeing the idea of world-making as dangerous in itself insofar as it encourages us to invest more time mastering the details of a fictional environment and less time confronting the real world.

If these religious reformers are concerned about the immersive qualities of *Harry Potter*, they are equally concerned about its intertextuality. Kjos warns us:

The main product marketed through this movie is a belief system that clashes with everything God offers us for our peace and security. This pagan ideology comes complete with trading cards, computer and other wizardly games, clothes and decorations stamped with HP symbols, action figures and cuddly dolls and audio cassettes that could keep the child's minds focused on the occult all day and into night. But in God's eyes, such paraphernalia become little more than lures and doorways to deeper involvement with the occult.[40]

In particular, they argue that Rowling makes more than sixty specific references in the first four books to actual occult practices and personages from the history of alchemy and witchcraft. They identify some historical and literary allusions Rowling intended to be recognized by literate readers, such as her reference to Nicolas Flamel, the medieval alchemist who is credited with discovering the Sorcerer's Stone, or to Merlin and Morgana, from the Arthurian romances, as figures on the wizards' collectors' cards. But some fundamentalist critics read the lightning bolt on Harry's forehead as the "mark of the beast," or map Voldemort onto "the nameless one," an anti-Christian witch, both foretold in Revelations. They contend that children seeking additional information will be drawn toward pagan works that promise more knowledge and power. One Catholic writer explains: "When he has finished reading the *Potter* series, what will he turn to? There is a vast industry turning out sinister material for the young that will feed their growing appetites."[41] In fairness, librarians and educators tap many of these same intertextual references. For example, among the courses offered at Virtual Hogwarts are classes in fortunetelling, astrology, and alchemy, taught no doubt as historical beliefs and practices, but nevertheless deeply offensive to fundamentalists.

These moral reformers agree that the books are sparking literacy and learning, but they are anxious about what kids are being taught. Some activists see the books as a dilution of Christian influence on American culture in favor of a new global spiritualism. Kjos warns that "the *Harry Potter* books would not have been culturally acceptable half a century ago. Today's cultural climate—an 'open-mindedness' toward occult entertainment together with 'closed-mindedness' toward Biblical Christianity—was planned a century ago. It was outlined by the United Nations in the late 1940s and has been taught and nurtured through the developing global education system during the last six decades."[42] Whereas a generation ago these groups might have taken aim at secular humanism, they now see a new phase of globalization during which multinational companies and supranational organizations are actively erasing cultural differences. To reach a global market, these Christian critics argue, American capitalism must strip aside the last vestiges of the Judeo-Christian tradition, and to promote consumerism, it must erode away all resistance to temptation. Aspects of pagan and Eastern faiths are entering classrooms in a secularized form—the worship of the earth transformed into ecology, astral projection into visualization exercises—while Christianity remains locked outside by advocates of the separation of church and state. The *Harry Potter* books are, as a consequence, going to have very different effects than, say, *The Wizard of Oz* (1900), which was read by children within a deeply Christian culture. Instead, the fundamentalists warn, American children are susceptible to the pagan influences of these books because they are consumed alongside television shows like *Pokémon* (1998) or read in schools that already have a global and secular curriculum.

If some adults, like Paula Ware, were simply "too busy" to defend *Harry Potter* against these would-be censors, many teachers risked their jobs defending the books. Mary Dana, a middle school teacher in Zeeland, Michigan, was one of the educators who found herself caught up in these debates.[43] Dana had come to teaching as a second career after having spent more than a decade as an independent bookseller. She had weathered a range of previous controversies about books she had brought into this community. She drew a line in 2000 when the local superintendent decided that *Harry Potter* books should be outlawed from public readings, removed from the open shelves of the school library, barred from future purchase, and left accessible only to students who had written permission from their parents. Dana explains: "I don't like confrontations and I don't like to speak in public. I'm a pretty shy person actually. I had plenty of experience of First Amendment challenges when we owned our bookstore. I had been under attack before. It was a very ugly, difficult experience, but ultimately, when you think you just can't fight them, you still have to because they are wrong. . . . I wasn't going to let it drop." Like Lawver, Dana saw the potential of the *Harry Potter* books to excite kids about reading and learning; she felt that such books needed to be in the classroom.

Working with a local parent, Nancy Zennie, Dana organized opposition to the superintendent's decision, helping to frame and circulate petitions, organize rallies, and pull people to a school board meeting where the issue was going to be discussed. Trying to rally public support, Dana and Zennie helped to create an organization, Muggles for Harry Potter, which could tap national and international fan interest. They were joined by a group of eight organizations, representing booksellers, publishers, librarians, teachers, writers, civil libertarians, and consumers. "Muggles for Harry Potter is fighting for the right of students and teachers to use the best books that are available for children, even when some parents object," said Christopher Finan, president of the American Booksellers Foundation for Free Expression. "The Potter books are helping turn video-game players into readers. We can't allow censorship to interfere with that."[44] In the end, the school board removed many of the restrictions placed on the books, though the ban on reading them in the classroom remained.

Over the next nine months, over 18,000 people joined the Muggles campaign through its Web site, and the group has been credited with curbing the nationwide efforts of fundamentalists to get the books banned from schools.[45] The organization sought to teach young readers of the *Harry Potter* books about the importance of standing up for free expression. The organization, which later changed its name to kid-SPEAK! (www.kidspeakonline.org), created online forums where kids could share their views with one another about the Potter wars and other censorship issues. For example, Jaclyn, a seventh-grader, wrote this response to news that a fundamentalist minister had cut up copies of *Harry Potter* when the fire department refused to grant him a permit to have a book burning:

> Reverend Taylor, the host of Jesus Party should look closer before judging. Kids are reading these books and discovering there is more to life than going to school. What have they discovered exactly? Their imaginations. Does Reverend Doug Taylor realize what he is doing? Kids are fighting for their First Amendment rights but do they also have fight for their imaginations—the one thing that keeps one person different than the others? We stand back and watch him rip the books to shreds, almost symbolically, ripping up our imaginations. Children like the books because they want to live in that world, they want to see magic, not see some phony magician pull a rabbit out of his hat. They want to have a brave friend like Harry Potter and ride across the dark lake where the giant squid lurks to the grand castle of Hogwarts. Although they want to do all of these things, they know Hogwarts isn't real and Harry Potter does not exist.

One of the striking features of the discussions on kidSPEAK! is how often the kids are forced to recant their fantasies in order to defend their right to have them in the first place. Here's another example: "And another thing Anti-*Harry Potter* people it is FICTION get that entirely made up except like the setting (England) and the places (Kings Cross Station) etc. But I seriously doubt if you go to London you'll find The Leaky Cauldron or a Wizard. That's what fiction is—made up. So all you people against *Harry Potter.* Get over it."[46]

The fundamentalists claim that fantastical representations of violence or the occult shape children's beliefs and actions in the real world. Countering such claims, the books' defenders were forced to argue that fantasies do not really matter, when in fact, what we have said so far suggests that the immersive quality of the books is what makes them such a powerful catalyst for creative expression. Even the original name of the organization suggests uncertainty about what kind of relationship to the books' fantasy the adults wanted to foster. Dana explained: "The term refers to anyone who does not possess the magical powers. Anyone who is not a wizard by definition has to be a muggle. Of course, it was somewhat amusing because if people weren't willing to say they were muggles, then what were they saying, that they had witchcraft powers." On the one hand, the name does tap fannish knowledge: only those people familiar with Rowling's world would recognize the term. On the other hand, adopting a muggle identity aligned participants with the mundane world. Rowling is merciless in making fun of the closed-mindedness of the Dursleys, Harry's adopted family. The Dursleys are totally uncomfortable with his special abilities and have kept him literally closeted. The contrast between the group's embrace of muggleness and the fantastical identifications Lawver had enabled through *The Daily Prophet* could not be starker. The educators, librarians, and publishers saw the books as a means to an end—a way of getting kids excited about reading—whereas for the fans, reading and writing was the means to their end, having a more deeply engaged relationship with the world of Hogwarts.

By contrast, a subsequent activist group, the HP Alliance, aligned its politics with the fantasy realm constructed within the books, encouraging a generation of young people who learn to read and write from the *Harry Potter* books to also use J. K. Rowling's world as a platform for civic engagement. The *Harry Potter* series depicted its youth protagonists questioning adult authority, fighting evil, and standing up for their rights. The group reads the books' magical events as allegories for real-world issues:

> Genocide, poverty, AIDS, and global warming are ignored by our media and governments the way Voldemort's return is ignored by the Ministry and Daily Prophet.

> People are still discriminated against based on sexuality, race, class, religion, gender, ethnicity, and religion just as the Wizarding World continues to discriminate against Centaurs, Giants, House Elves, Half-Bloods, Muggle borns, Squibs, and Muggles.

Our governments continue to respond to terror by torturing prisoners (often without trial) just as Sirius Black was tortured by dementors with no trial.

A Muggle Mindset pervades over our culture—a mindset that values being "perfectly normal, thank you very much" over being interesting, original, loving, and creative.[47]

Unlike the Muggles for Harry Potter campaign, the HP Alliance distanced itself from the "Muggle mindset," which they defined as a refusal to embrace cultural diversity or challenge the status quo. Instead, the HP Alliance compared their efforts to Dumbledore's Army, an underground resistance group which Harry and his friends organized in the face of Dolores Umbridge's prohibitions against such gatherings (*Harry Potter and the Order of the Phoenix*).

While the Muggles campaign tapped existing civil liberties organizations to help spread its message, the HP Alliance sought allies from within the fan community. For example, in July 2007, the group worked with the Leaky Cauldron, one of the most popular Harry Potter news sites, to organize house parties around the country focused on increasing awareness of the Sudanese genocide. Participants listened to and discussed a podcast which featured real-world political experts—such as Joe Wilson, former U.S. ambassador; John Prendergast, senior adviser to the International Crisis Group; Dot Maver, executive director of the Peace Alliance; and John Passacantando, executive director of Greenpeace—alongside performances by Wizard rock groups such as Harry and the Potters.[48]

Wizard rock refers to a form of fan-generated music where artists often adopt identities and themes from Rowling's fictional universe; more than 200 such groups perform around the country, gaining visibility through cagey deployment of social networking and music sharing sites.[49] Wizard rock groups such as The Hermione Crookshanks Experience, The Whomping Willows, Draco and the Malfoys, DJ Luna Lovegood, and the Parselmouths, worked together to create and market a CD, *Wizards and Muggles Rock for Social Justice*, with proceeds going to support the HP Alliance's efforts.[50] The organization also tapped the talents of *Harry Potter* fan filmmakers to produce and distribute viral videos critical of Wal-Mart's policies toward its employees. The HP Alliance has created a new form of civic engagement which allows participants to reconcile their activist identities with the pleasurable fantasies that brought the fan community together in the first place.

The conservative Christians are simply the most visible of a broad range of groups, each citing its own ideological concerns, that are reacting to a shift in the media paradigm. Anti–*Harry Potter* Christians share many concerns with other reform groups linking worries about the persuasive power of advertising to concerns about the demonic nature of immersion, tapping anxieties about consumerism and multinational capitalism in their critiques of global spiritualism. In *Plenitude* (1998), Grant McCracken talks about the "withering of the witherers," that is, the breakdown of the power traditional groups exercise over cultural expression.[51] Corporate gatekeepers, educational authorities, and church leaders all represent different forces that historically held in check tendencies toward diversification and fragmentation. Over the past several decades, McCracken argues, these groups have lost their power to define cultural norms as the range of different media and communication channels have expanded. Ideas and practices that were once hidden from public view—say, the Wiccan beliefs that fundamentalist critics claim are shaping the *Harry Potter* books—are now entering the mainstream, and these groups are struggling to police the culture that comes into their own homes and communities.

If educational reformers such as James Gee hope to break the stranglehold formal education has on children's learning and to expand the opportunities for children to practice literacy outside the classroom, these voices are more cautious, trying to reassert traditional values and structures in a world they can no longer fully control. We see this impulse to restore the "witherers" when we look at battles to enforce ratings on video games or to ban the *Harry Potter* books from schools. Where some see a world more free from gatekeepers, they see a world where the floodgates have opened and no one can control the flow of "raw sewage" into their homes. Such groups want to assert a collective response to problems individual parents feel unable to confront on their own. Echoing concerns expressed by many secular parents, these fundamentalist critics contend that the pervasiveness of modern media makes it hard for parents to respond to its messages. As Michael O'Brien protests, "Our culture is continuously pushing us to let down our guard, to make quick judgments that feel easier because they reduce the tension of vigilance. The harassed pace and the high volume of consumption that modern culture seems to demand of us, makes genuine discernment more difficult."[52]

What Would Jesus Do with *Harry Potter*?

We would be wrong to assume that the Potter wars represented a struggle of conservative Christians against liberal educators and fans. If some simply want to reinscribe old authorities and build up the institutions being challenged by a more participatory culture, others want to help children learn to make judgments about media content. Many Christian groups defended the books, presenting the concept of "discernment" as an alternative to culture war discourse. Connie Neal, the author of *What's a Christian to Do with Harry Potter?*, framed the choices in terms of "building a wall" to protect children from outside influences or "fitting them with armor" so that they can bring their own values with them when they encounter popular culture. Neal notes that "restricting freedom can incite curiosity and rebellion, leading the one you're trying to protect to try to get past the protective barrier to see what he or she is missing. . . . Even if you could keep children separated from all potentially dangerous influences, you would also be keeping them from a situation in which they could develop the maturity to ward off such dangers for themselves."[53] Instead, Neal advocates giving children media literacy skills, teaching them to evaluate and interpret popular culture within a Christian framework.

The Christian Counterculture

Rather than rejecting popular culture outright, a growing number of Christians are producing and consuming their own popular media on the fringes of the mainstream entertainment industry. While many Christians have felt cut off from mass media, they have been quick to embrace new technologies—such as videotape, cable television, low-wattage radio stations, and the Internet—that allow them to route around established gatekeepers. The result has been the creation of media products that mirror the genre conventions of popular culture but express an alternative set of values. In *Shaking the World for Jesus* (2004), Heather Hendershot offers a complex picture of the kinds of popular culture being produced by and for evangelicals.[1] Frustrated by network television, cultural conservatives have created their own animated series and sitcoms distributed on video. They have produced their own science fiction, horror, mystery, and romance novels, all of which can be purchased online. And alarmed by contemporary video games, they have produced their own, such as *Victory at Hebron* (2003),

[1] Heather Hendershot, *Shaking the World for Jesus: Media and Conservative Evangelical Culture* (Chicago: University of Chicago Press, 2004).

where players battle Satan or rescue martyrs.

The emergence of new media technologies has allowed evangelicals some degree of autonomy from commercial media, allowing them to identify and enjoy media products that more closely align with their own worldviews. Technology has also lowered the costs of production and distribution, enabling what remains essentially a niche market to sustain a remarkably broad range of cultural products. Of course, as "niche markets" go, this one may be astonishingly large. According to a 2002 ABC News/Beliefnet poll, 83 percent of Americans consider themselves to be Christians, and Baptists (only one of the evangelical denominations) make up 15 percent of the nation.[2]

As commercial media producers have realized the size of this demographic, the walls between Christian and mainstream popular culture are breaking down. *VeggieTales* (1994) videos are finding their way into Wal-Mart, Focus on the Family's *Adventures in Odyssey* (1991) records get distributed as kids' meal prizes at Chick-fil-A, the *Left Behind* (1996) books become top sellers on Amazon.com, and Christian pop singer Amy Grant breaks into Top 40 radio. In the process, some of the more overtly religious markings get stripped away. Network television has begun to produce some shows, such as *Touched by an Angel* (1994), *7th Heaven* (1996), and *Joan of Arcadia* (2003), that deal with religious themes in a way designed to appeal to the "searchers" and the "saved" alike. Predictably, some evangelicals fear that Christianity has

[2] Gary Langer, "Poll: Most Americans Say They're Christian," *ABC News*, July 18, 2002, http://abcnews.go.com/sections/us/DailyNews/beliefnet_poll_-1-718.html.

One discernment group, Ransom Fellowship, defines discernment as "an ability, by God's grace, to creatively chart a godly path through the maze of choices and options that confront us, even when we're faced with situations and issues that aren't specifically mentioned in the Scriptures."[54] The discernment movement draws inspiration from a range of biblical passages that speak of people who maintained their faith even when living in an alien land. Christians, they argue, are living in "modern captivity," holding on to and transmitting their faith in an increasingly hostile context.

In "Pop Culture: Why Bother?" Denis Haack, the founder and director of the Ransom Fellowship, argues that engaging with, rather than hiding from, popular culture has important benefits. Discernment exercises can help Christians develop a greater understanding of their own value system, can provide insights into the worldview of "nonbelievers," and can offer an opportunity for meaningful exchange between Christians and non-Christians. According to Haack, "If we are to understand those who do not share our deepest convictions, we must gain some comprehension of what they believe, why they believe it, and how those beliefs work out in daily life."[55] Their site provides discussion questions and advice about how to foster media literacy within an explicitly religious context, finding ideas worth struggling with in mainstream works as diverse as *Bruce Almighty* (2003), *Cold Mountain* (2003), and *Lord of the Rings* (2001). The Oracle in *The Matrix*

(1999) is compared to a biblical prophet; viewers are invited to reflect on the role of prayer in the *Spider-Man* (2002) movies and on the kinds of "great responsibilities" Christians bear; and they are encouraged to show sympathy toward the spiritual quests undertaken by indigenous people in *Whale Rider* (2002) or by Bill Murray's character in *Lost in Translation* (2003). The site is very explicit that Christians are apt to disagree among themselves about what is or what is not valuable in such works, but that the process of talking through these differences focuses energy on spiritual matters and helps everyone involved to become more skillful in applying and defending their faith.

Whereas some cultural conservatives saw the immersiveness of contemporary popular culture as ensnaring young people in a dangerous realm of fantasies, some within the discernment movement have promoted the use of live-action role-playing and computer games as spaces for exploring and debating moral questions. The Christian Gamers Guild (whose monthly newsletter is known as *The Way, The Truth & The Dice*) emerged in the midst of strong attacks from some evangelical leaders on role-playing and computer games. As they turn their attention toward games, they take this concept of discernment one step further—arguing that individual game masters (the people who "run" live-action role-playing games) have the power to appropriate and transform these cultural materials according to their own beliefs. They are,

been commodified and that Jesus is becoming just another brand in the great big "marketplace of ideas."

It is in this context that we need to understand the staggering success of Mel Gibson's *The Passion of the Christ* (2004). The Christians knew how to get folks into the theater to support this film. For example, Gibson sought out the services of Faith Highway, a group that had previously produced public service messages that local churches could sponsor through local cable outlets to give their messages a more professional polish. Faith Highway urged churches to help raise money to support advertisements for the film and to link them back to their local messages. Many churches loaded up school buses full of worshippers to attend screenings and, with the release of the DVD, put together bulk orders to get the film into the hands of their congregations. Some church leaders have acknowledged backing this film in hopes that its commercial success would get Hollywood to pay attention to them. Faith Highway's CEO Dennis Dautel explained: "The leaders in the church are chomping at the bits to get media that is relevant to their message. Hollywood doesn't produce it. . . . The congregations went behind it because they wanted to see people turn out and see that movie. There was a strong desire in the Christian community for that movie to be a home run. This was our *Passion*."[3]

Passion's success with evangelical Christians has inspired other media producers to partner with faith-based groups. Consider, for example, the case of Walden Media, a company founded in 2001 by a Boston teacher, Michael Flaherty, and Cary Granat, former president of Dimension Pictures, to promote

---

[3] Dennis Dautel, personal interview, Fall 2004.

"entertainment that sparks the imagination and curiosity of kids and provides parents and teachers with materials to continue the learning process." Often distributing their films through the Disney Corporation, Walden produced *Holes* (2003), *Because of Winn-Dixie* (2005), *Charlotte's Web* (2006), and *Bridge to Terabithia* (2006). For the launch of *The Lion, the Witch, and the Wardrobe*, the first of a series of big screen adaptations of C. S. Lewis's *Narnia* books, Walden contracted with specialist evangelical marketing agency Outreach Inc., to develop a pamphlet of endorsements from church leaders and faith groups, a series of suggested Sunday school exercises, and an online collection of *Narnia*-themed sermons. While fantasy films have historically been a hard sell to conservative Christians, the *Narnia* franchise was endorsed by, among others, the Mission America Coalition, the National Association of Evangelicals, and the Billy Graham Center. James Dobson, of Focus the Family, even called off a long-standing boycott of the Disney Corporation to draw evangelicals into the theater to see *The Lion, the Witch and the Wardrobe*. Walden's choice of the Narnia books was no accident: Christian leaders often suggest C. S. Lewis's series as appropriate alternative to *Harry Potter* and *The Lord of the Rings*. While many of the mainstream televangelists and radiocasters such as Charles Colson and James Dobson made their peace with Rowling's universe, either endorsing it outright or urging parents to proceed with caution,[4] the anti-Potter voices most often came from new ministries that had staked a space for

to borrow the name of another group, Fans for Christ (FFC).

Groups like Fans for Christ and Anime Angels define themselves within the same kind of identity-politics language that sustains gay, lesbian, and bisexual or feminist Christian organizations. The FAQ for FFC explains:

We have been alone too long! There are many of us fans out there who feel *different* because we are what we are. Some call us freaks, weirdoes, geeks, nerds, whatever. FFC is here for all of you to talk with your brothers and sisters who are Christians and share your freakiness. . . . You are welcome here to be as freaky and geeky as you like. . . . FFC is here to help show that our fan lifestyle is perfectly acceptable to Jesus. We hope to help our FFC members be able to explain clearly to others that the Bible does not condemn what we do, that we know that fiction is fiction, and that God has made us different and it is wonderful.[56]

The site provides a list of "fan friendly" churches that respects members' lifestyle choices and values their unique perspectives on spiritual issues. In return, the members pledge to share their love of Christ with other fans, to hold their own gatherings to promote Christian fantasy and science fiction authors, and to write their own fan stories that address central religious concerns.

Many leaders of the discernment movement are less celebratory of the "geeky

[4] For a range of Christian response, see Neal, *What's a Christian to Do?* See also "Opinion Roundup: Positive about Potter," *Christianity Today*, http://www.christianitytoday.com/ct/1999/150/12.0.html.

and freaky" aspects of popular culture, but they do see the value in appropriating and rethinking works of popular culture. Many discernment advocates regard the *Harry Potter* books as the perfect opening for parents to talk with their children about the challenges of preserving their values in a secular society. Haack explains:

Truth is taught here, truth that is worth some reflection and discussion, and though it is taught in an imaginary world, it applies to reality as well. . . . The world in which Harry Potter lives is a world of moral order, where ideas and choices have consequences, where good and evil are clearly distinguished, where evil is both dehumanizing and destructive, and where death is distressingly real. . . . Even if what all the critics say were true, the defensiveness of their recommendations is frankly embarrassing. If the *Harry Potter* novels were introductions to the occult, the church should welcome the opportunity to read and discuss them. Neo-paganism is a growing reality in our post-Christian world, and our children need to be able to meet its challenge with a quiet confidence in the gospel. They need to know the difference between fantasy literature and the occult. And they need to see their elders acting righteously, not scandalously.[57]

Few discernment advocates go as far as Heather Lawver does in inviting children

themselves on the Internet. They used the debate to strike back at what they saw as a theological establishment. One such site, Trumpet Ministries, went so far as to denounce Colson and Dobson as "modern day Judas Iscariots" because of their refusal to join the campaign against the books.[5] Just as the fluidity of culture has allowed youth greater access to pagan beliefs than ever before, it also meant that small-scale ministries could exert worldwide influence by posting their sermons and critiques from the national hinterland. Similarly, smaller video production companies, such as Jeremiah Films, could produce DVD documentaries with titles such as *Harry Potter: Witchcraft Repackaged* (2001) and sell them to concerned parents via the Web or infomercials on late-night cable.

The evangelical community sought to identify some Christian fantasy writers as alternatives to *Harry Potter*. Following in the tradition of Lewis and Tolkien, G. P. Taylor, an Anglican vicar, used his fantasy novel, *Shadowmancer* (2004), to explore moral and theological questions. The book outpaced *Harry Potter* for fifteen weeks in the United Kingdom and held six straight weeks on the *New York Times* best-seller list in the summer of 2004. The book was heavily promoted through Christian media, including Pat Robertson's *The 700 Club* and James Dobson's Focus on the Family as "just the thing to counter Harry Potter's magic." *Shadowmancer* broke into Christian bookstores that normally did not carry fantasy books, and from there made it into secular bookstores that still don't carry large amounts of

[5] "Harry Potter? What Does God Have to Say?" http://www.lasttrumpetministries.org/tracts/tract7.html.

spiritual fiction. The film rights were quickly optioned by Fortitude Films, a group formed to support Mel Gibson's *The Passion of the Christ*, and there has been some speculation that Gibson may direct the film adaptation. For his part, Taylor has been explicit that he wrote the book to show children God's power and not as an alternative to the *Harry Potter* books, which he claims not to have read.[6]

[6] Dinitia Smith, "Harry Potter Inspires a Christian Alternative," *New York Times*, July 24, 2004, A15.

to adopt fantasy roles and play within the world of the story, but some do appropriate the books to speak to Christian values. Connie Neal asks Christian parents to consider what Jesus would do confronted with these stories:

> Jesus might read the *Harry Potter* stories and use them as starting points for parables. . . . Just as Jesus noticed and met others' physical needs, he might attend to the earthly needs revealed in the lives of those who identify with the characters in *Harry Potter*. He might get them talking about *Harry Potter* and listen to what they identify with most: neglect, poverty, discrimination, abuse, fears, dreams, the pressures to fit in, desires to accomplish something in life, or the stresses of school. Then he would show them how to deal with such real parts of their lives.[58]

Rather than ban content that does not fully fit within their worldview, the discernment movement teaches Christian children and parents how to read those books critically, how to ascribe new meanings to them, and how to use them as points of entry into alternative spiritual perspectives.

Rather than shut down the intertextuality that is so rampant in the era of transmedia storytelling, Neal, Haack, and the other discernment leaders are looking for ways to harness its power. They provide reading lists for parents who want to build on their children's interests in *Harry Potter* as a point of entry into Christian fantasy. Several discernment groups published study guides to accompany the *Harry Potter* books and films with "probing questions" designed to explore the moral choices the characters made coupled with Bible verses that suggest how the same decisions are confronted within the Christian tradition. They focus, for example, on the moment when Harry's mother sacrifices her life to protect him as representing a positive role model for Christian love, or they discuss the corrupt moral choices that led to the creation of the Sorcerer's Stone as an example of sin. If the anti–*Harry Potter* Christians want to protect children from any exposure to those dangerous books, the discernment movement focuses on the agency of consumers to appropriate and transform media content.

As we can see, the conflicts that gave rise to the Potter wars do not reduce themselves to evil censors and good defenders of civil liberties. The churn created by a convergence culture does not allow us to operate with this degree of moral certainty. All of those groups are struggling with the immersive nature and expansive quality of the new entertainment franchises. In the age of media convergence, consumer participation has emerged as the central conceptual problem: traditional gatekeepers seek to hold on to their control of cultural content, and other groups—fans, civil libertarians, and the Christian discernment movement—want to give consumers the skills they need to construct their own culture. For some, such as Heather Lawver or James Gee, role-playing and fan fiction writing are valuable because they allow kids to understand the books from the inside out; such activities involve a negotiation between self-expression and shared cultural materials, between introspection and collaborative fantasy building. Others, such as the Fans for Christ or the Christian gamers, embrace these activities because they allow players and writers to explore moral options, to test their values against fictional obstacles, and to work through in an imaginative way challenges that would have much higher stakes in their everyday lives. For still others, such as the conservative Christians who opposed the teaching of the books, role-playing and shared fantasies are dangerous because they distract youth from serious moral education and leave them susceptible to the appeals of pagan groups and occult practices. Yet, in some ways, groups such as Muggles for Harry Potter seemed to share their concern that fantasy may itself be dangerous for kids, especially if they are unable to discern what separates the imaginative realm from reality.

We can read this debate as a reaction against many of the properties of convergence culture we have seen so far—against the expansion of fictional realms across multiple media, against the desire to master the arcane details of those texts and turn them into resources for a more participatory culture. For some, the concern is with the specific content of those fantasies—whether they are consistent with a Christian worldview. For others, the concern is with the marketing of those fantasies to children—whether we want opportunities for participation to be commodified. Ironically, at the same time, corporations are anxious about this fantasy play because it operates outside their control.

Unlike many previous fights over children's culture, however, this is not a story of children as passive victims of adult attempts at regulation and restraint. They are active participants in these new media land-scapes, finding their own voice through their participation in fan communities, asserting their own rights even in the face of powerful entities, and sometimes sneaking behind their parents' back to do what feels right to them. At the same time, through their participation, these kids are mapping out new strategies for negotiating around and through globalization, intellectual property struggles, and media conglomeration. They are using the Internet to connect with children worldwide and, through that process, finding common interests and forging political alliances. Because the *Harry Potter* fandom involved both adults and children, it became a space where conversations could occur across generations. In talking about media pedagogies, then, we should no longer imagine this as a process where adults teach and children learn. Rather, we should see it as increasingly a space where children teach one another and where, if they would open their eyes, adults could learn a great deal.

6

Photoshop for Democracy

The New Relationship between Politics and Popular Culture

In the spring of 2004, a short video, edited together out of footage from newscasts and Donald Trump's hit TV show, *The Apprentice* (2004), was circulating across the Internet. Framed as a mock preview for *The Apprentice*, the narrator explains, "George W. Bush is assigned the task of being president. He drives the economy into the ground, uses lies to justify war, spends way over budget, and almost gets away with it until the Donald finds out." The video cuts to a boardroom, where Trump is demanding to know "who chose this stupid concept" and then firing Dubya. Trump's disapproving look is crosscut with Bush shaking his head in disbelief and then disappointment. Then came the announcer: "Unfortunately, 'The Donald' can't fire Bush for us. But we can do it ourselves. Join us at True Majority Action. We'll fire Bush together, and have some fun along the way."[1]

Who would have imagined that Donald Trump could emerge as a populist spokesman, or that sympathetic images of corporate control could fuel a movement to reclaim democracy? A curious mix of cynicism and optimism, the video made Democrats laugh at the current administration and then rally to transform it.

True Majority was founded by Ben Cohen (of Ben & Jerry's Ice Cream). Its goals were to increase voter participation in the 2004 election and to rally support behind a progressive agenda. According to its Web site (www.truemajority.org), the group has attracted more than 300,000 supporters, who receive regular alerts and participate in letter-writing campaigns.[2]

Interviewed a few weeks before the election, Garrett LoPorto, a senior creative consultant for True Majority, said that the core of viral marketing is getting the right idea into the right hands at the right time.[3]

This video generated a higher than average response rate, he argues, both because it expressed a widespread desire to end a failed administration and because *The Apprentice* provided a perfect metaphor to bring that decision closer to home: "We aren't here talking about this grand cause of appointing someone as the leader of the free world. We're just trying to get some guy who screwed up fired. It's that simple." True Majority's goal was to get these ideas into the broadest possible circulation. To do that, they sought to create images that are vivid, memorable, and evocative. And most important, the content had to be consistent with what people more or less already believed about the world. Locating people who share your beliefs is easy, LoPorto says, because we tend to seek out like-minded communities on the Web. Each person who passed along the video reaffirmed his or her commitment to those beliefs and also moved one step closer toward political action. A certain percentage of the recipients followed the link back to the True Majority site and expanded its core mailing list. Repeat this process enough times with enough people, he argued, and you can build a movement and start to "nudge" the prevailing structure of beliefs in your direction. At least that's the theory. The real challenge is to get those ideas back into mainstream media, where they will reach people who do not already share your commitments. As LoPorto acknowledged, "All we needed to do is to get NBC to sue us. If they would sue us over this, this thing would go global and everyone will know about it. That was our secondary hope. . . . NBC was too smart for that—they recognize it was a parody and didn't bite."

Hoping to make politics more playful, the True Majority home page offered visitors not only the "Trump Fires Bush" video, but also a game where you could spank Dubya's bare bottom, a video where "Ben the Ice Cream Man" reduces the federal budget to stacks of Oreo cookies and shows how shuffling just a few cookies can allow us to take care of a range of pressing problems, and other examples of what the group calls "serious fun."

In some senses, this whole book has been about "serious fun." The U.S. military develops a massively multiplayer game to facilitate better communications between service people and civilians. Companies such as Coca-Cola enter the entertainment industry to create a stronger emotional engagement with their brands. Educators embrace the informal pedagogy within fan communities as a model for developing literacy skills. First Amendment groups tap young people's interest in the

Harry Potter books. "Fan-friendly" churches use discussions of movies and television shows to help their congregations develop discernment skills. In each case, entrenched institutions are taking their models from grassroots fan communities, reinventing themselves for an era of media convergence and collective intelligence. So why not apply those same lessons to presidential politics? We may not overturn entrenched power (whether that of the political parties or their big money contributors) overnight: nobody involved in these popular-culture-inflected campaigns is talking about a revolution, digital or otherwise. What they are talking about is a shift in the public's role in the political process, bringing the realm of political discourse closer to the everyday life experiences of citizens; what they are talking about is changing the ways people think about community and power so that they are able to mobilize collective intelligence to transform governance; and what they are talking about is a shift from the individualized conception of the informed citizen toward the collaborative concept of a monitorial citizen.

This chapter shifts our focus from popular entertainment franchises and onto the selection of an American president. In conventional terms, these two processes are worlds apart—one is the stuff of consumption, the other the stuff of citizenship. Yet, with the 2004 election, we can see citizens starting to apply what they learned as consumers of popular culture toward more overt forms of political activism. Popular culture influenced the way that the campaigns courted their voters—but more importantly, it shaped how the public processed and acted upon political discourse.

I am focusing here less on changes in institutions or laws, which are the focus of traditional political science, but more on changes in communications systems and cultural norms, which need to be understood through tools that have originated in the study of media and popular culture. The current diversification of communication channels is politically important because it expands the range of voices that can be heard: though some voices command greater prominence than others, no one voice speaks with unquestioned authority. The new media operate with different principles than the broadcast media that dominated American politics for so long: access, participation, reciprocity, and peer-to-peer rather than one-to-many communication. Given such principles, we should anticipate that digital democracy will be decentralized, unevenly dispersed, profoundly contradictory, and slow to emerge. These forces are apt to emerge first in cultural forms—a changed sense of community, a greater sense of participation, less dependence on official expertise, and a greater trust in collaborative problem solving, all things we have seen throughout this book. Some of what this chapter discusses will look like old-style politics conducted in new ways—efforts to shape public opinion, register voters, mobilize supporters, and pump up the "negatives" of a rival candidate. Other things will look less familiar—elections conducted within massively multiplayer game worlds, parody news shows, Photoshopped images —yet these forms of popular culture also have political effects, representing hybrid spaces where we can lower the political stakes (and change the language of politics) enough so that we can master skills we need to be participants in the democratic process.

The 2004 campaign was a period of innovation and experimentation in the use of new media technologies and popular-culture-based strategies. On the one hand, the closeness of the election enflamed the passions of voters who tended to commit early and feel strongly about the candidate of their choice. On the other hand, the closeness made both campaigns desperate to mobilize their base, attract undecided voters, and register new participants—especially the young. Add to this a new generation of campaign organizers who had been monitoring developments in digital culture over the past decade and were ready to apply what they had learned. Howard Dean's campaign manager, Joe Trippi, posed the core questions in a much-discussed memo: "The tools, energy, leadership and the right candidate, are all in place to create the Perfect Storm of Presidential politics—where millions of Americans act together and organize their communities, their neighborhoods and their precincts. . . . How do these Americans find each other? How do they self-organize? How do they collaborate? How do they take action together?"[4] And this is where popular culture enters the picture.

"The Revolution Will Not Be Televised"

Working for an obscure insurgent candidate whom few pundits gave any real chance, Trippi sought to harness this emerging grassroots power. Dean raised more money online from small contributions than any other previous candidate, setting a model that John Kerry would subsequently follow to close the "money gap" with the Republicans.

His staff used blogging to create a more intimate, real-time relationship with his supporters. They deployed "smart mob"–style tactics, including an adept use of Meetup.com, to quickly launch rallies, drawing together thousands of people at a time when other candidates were still speaking to half-empty rooms. Dean didn't so much create the movement; his staff simply was willing to listen and learn.[5]

Trippi describes the Dean campaign's early successes as a "tipping point": this was where the politics of television gave way to the politics of the Internet. Like the dot-com executives before him, Trippi (and Dean) mistook their own sales pitch for a realistic model of how media change takes place. So far, the most active cybercandidates have been insurgents who have not been able to ride digital media into victory but who have been able to change the nature of the debate. It is significant that Trippi titles his memoir, *The Revolution Will Not Be Televised* (2005), after the Gil Scott Heron song. The slogan became self-fulfilling prophecy. If the Internet made Dean's candidacy, television unmade it.

In the 1960s, when Heron first performed the song, it was clear that a narrow pipeline controlled by major media companies was unlikely to transmit ideas that ran counter to dominant interests. The counterculture communicated primarily through grassroots media—underground newspapers, folk songs, posters, people's radio, and comics. The networks and newspapers filtered out messages they didn't want us to hear, and the exclusionary practices of these intermediaries fostered the demand for grassroots and participatory media channels. Trippi describes television as an inherently passive (and pacifying) technology: "While TV was a medium that rendered us dumb, disengaged, and disconnected, the Internet makes us smarter, more involved, and better informed."[6] Anyone who has read this far in the book knows enough to question both sets of claims.

If, circa 2004, we ask ourselves whether the revolution will be digitized, our answers look very different. The Web's low barriers to entry expand access to innovative or even revolutionary ideas at least among the growing segment of the population that has access to a computer. Those silenced by corporate media have been among the first to transform their computer into a printing press. This opportunity has benefited third parties, revolutionaries, reactionaries, and racists alike. It also sparks fear in the hearts of the old intermediaries and their allies. One person's diversity, no doubt, is another person's anarchy.

The subtitle of Trippi's book, *Democracy, the Internet, and the Over-*

throw of Everything, captures the revolutionary potential writers such as Hans Enzensberger saw in the development of technologies that would enable grassroots communication.[7] Trippi celebrates what he sees as the "empowerment age" when average citizens challenge the power of entrenched institutions: "If information is power, then this new technology—which is the first to evenly distribute information—is really distributing power. The power is shifting from institutions that have always been run top down, hording information at the top, telling us how to run our lives, to a new paradigm of power that is democratically distributed and shared by all of us."[8]

Now, consider a second slogan, which students in the streets of Chicago during the 1968 protests chanted at the network news trucks, "The whole world is watching." Whatever the difficulties, if the student protesters got their images and ideas broadcast via ABC, CBS, and NBC, they would reach a significant segment of the population. Is there any place on the Web where the whole world is watching?

As we have suggested throughout this book, contemporary media is being shaped by several contradictory and concurrent trends: at the same moment that cyberspace displaces some traditional information and cultural gatekeepers, there is also an unprecedented concentration of power within old media. A widening of the discursive environment coexists with a narrowing of the range of information being transmitted by the most readily available media channels.

The new political culture—just like the new popular culture—reflects the pull and tug of these two media systems: one broadcast and commercial, the other narrowcast and grassroots. New ideas and alternative perspectives are more likely to emerge in the digital environment, but the mainstream media will be monitoring those channels, looking for content to co-opt and circulate. Grassroots media channels depend on the shared frame of reference created by the traditional intermediaries; much of the most successful "viral" content of the Web (for example, the "Trump Fires Bush" video) critiques or spoofs mainstream media. Broadcasting provides the common culture, and the Web offers more localized channels for responding to that culture.

In parts of Trippi's book he recognizes the interplay between these two kinds of media power. For example, he writes of his astonishment at watching contributions come into the Web site in real time while doing a radio broadcast: "People were hearing me on the radio, going to their computers and donating to the campaign. The Internet was making it possible for people to register their feedback immediately. After that, we would chart the effect of newspaper, television, and radio stories and be able to predict accurately how much money would come in online after Dean appeared on *Hardball*, or after a story in *USA Today*, and we'd know which media to go to in the big fund-raising pushes."[9] This is not television politics or digital politics; this is the politics of convergence.

Elsewhere, Trippi dismisses convergence, which he associates with corporate control:

> At some point, of course, there will be convergence. One box. One screen. You'll check your e-mail and order your groceries and check your child's homework all on the same screen. That might be the most dangerous time for this burgeoning democratic movement—the moment when the corporations and advertisers will threaten to co-opt and erode the democratic online ethic. The future may well hinge on whether the box is dominated more by the old broadcast rules or by the populist power of the internet.[10]

Trippi falls prey to the Black Box Fallacy. I don't disagree with his core claim that the public needs to fight for its right to participate, for its emerging access to information, and for the corresponding power to shape democratic processes. I don't disagree that corporate consolidation poses a potential threat to that power. But, as this book has demonstrated, we are already living in a convergence culture. We are already learning how to live betwixt and between those multiple media systems. The key battles are being fought now. If we focus on the technology, the battle will be lost before we even begin to fight. We need to confront the social, cultural, and political protocols that surround the technology and define how it will get used.

It is a mistake to think about either kind of media power in isolation. Our evolving system of media convergence is full of checks and balances. *60 Minutes* (1983) aired a program that alleged to prove long-standing charges that George Bush had used his family influence to duck responsibilities during his Vietnam-era stint in the National Guard. Conservative bloggers instantly began to dissect those memos, conclusively demonstrating that they could not have been produced on the typewriters available to their alleged author at the time they were said to have been written. At first, CBS dismissed those bloggers as well-meaning but misguided amateurs—"a guy sitting in his living room in his pajamas writing"—who lacked the "multiple levels of checks and balances" that ensure the accuracy of television newscasts.[11] But, in the end, CBS was forced to apologize publicly for their initial misreporting of the story and fired several longtime producers and reporters.

Some writers saw that as a victory of new media over old. *Reason* magazine editor Jesse Walker saw it as evidence of the growing integration between the two:

> [Bloggers] were doing fresh reporting and fresh analysis of the story. So were ABC, the Associated Press, and *The Washington Post*. The professional media drew on the bloggers for ideas; the bloggers in turn linked to the professionals' reports. The old media and the new media weren't at loggerheads with each other—or to the extent that they were, they were also at loggerheads with themselves. They complemented each other. They were part of the same ecosystem. . . . The new outlets aren't displacing the old ones; they're transforming them. Slowly but noticeably, the old media are becoming faster, more transparent, more interactive—not because they want to be, but because they have to be. Competition is quickening the news cycle whether or not anyone wants to speed it up. Critics are examining how reporters do their jobs whether or not their prying eyes are welcome.[12]

The same would be true for presidential campaigns. Candidates may build their base on the Internet, but they need television to win elections. It's the difference between a push medium (where messages go out to the public whether they seek them or not) and a pull medium (which serves those with an active interest in seeking out information on   a particular topic). The Internet reaches the hard core, television the undecided. Dean developed his initial following via the Internet that brought him to visibility in broadcast and mass market media. He was able to raise large sums of money via the Internet that was eaten up by the need to fund television advertising. The tactics he used to fire up supporters on the Internet were cited out of context on television. His posts were reduced to sound bites. Once broadcast media drew blood —for example, in the notorious "I have a scream" speech—the Internet sharks circled and hacked him to bits. One Web site links to more than

Figs. 6.1 and 6.2. The cybercommunity turned on Howard Dean following his concession speech after the Iowa caucuses, resulting in many different Web parodies.

three hundred spoofs of Howard Dean's self-destructive "concession" speech following his upset in the Iowa caucuses, including images of him howling as he gropes Janet Jackson, shouting at a kitten, or simply exploding from too much pent-up passion (figs. 6.1 and 6.2). All of which suggests a moment of transition when the political role of the Internet is expanding without diminishing the power of broadcast media.

We might understand this transition by thinking a bit about the difference between "culture jamming," a political tactic that reflected the logic of the digital revolution, and blogging, which seems emblematic of convergence culture. In his 1993 essay "Culture Jamming: Hacking, Slashing and Sniping in the Empire of Signs," cultural critic Mark Dery documented emerging tactics of grassroots resistance ("media hacking, informational warfare, terror-art, and guerrilla semiotics") to an "ever more intrusive, instrumental technoculture whose operant mode is the manufacture of consent through the manipulation of symbols."[13] In Citizens Band Radio slang, the term "jamming" refers to efforts to "introduce noises into the signal as it passes from transmitter to receiver."

Dery's essay records an important juncture in the history of do-it-yourself media as activists learn to use new media to assert a counterperspective on mass media.

Perhaps, however, the concept of culture jamming has outlived its usefulness. The old rhetoric of opposition and co-optation assumed a world where consumers had little direct power to shape media content and faced enormous barriers to entry into the marketplace, whereas the new digital environment expands the scope and reach of consumer activities. Pierre Lévy describes a world where grassroots communication is not a momentary disruption of the corporate signal, but the routine way the new system operates: "Until now we have only reappropriated speech in the service of revolutionary movements, crises, cures, exceptional acts of creation. What would a normal, calm, established appropriation of speech be like?"[14]

Blogging might better describe the kinds of prolonged public conversations Lévy is describing. The term "blog" is short for Weblog, a new form of personal and subcultural grassroots expression involving summarizing and linking to other sites. In effect, blogging is a form of grassroots convergence. By pooling their information and tapping grassroots expertise, by debating evidence and scrutinizing all available information, and, perhaps most powerfully, by challenging one another's assumptions, the blogging community is "spoiling" the American government. We might draw an analogy between the fan community going on location to find more information about the *Survivor* boots and the blogging community pooling its money to send independent reporters to Baghdad or the party conventions in search of the kinds of information they feared would be filtered out by mainstream media.[15] Or consider the example of the photographs of dead Americans returning from Iraq in flag-draped coffins or the photographs of prisoner abuse at Abu Ghraib, both of which entered the mainstream media as digital photographs, shot and circulated outside official military channels. Donald Rumsfeld sounds a bit like Jeff Probst when he explains, "We're functioning with peacetime constraints, with legal requirements, in a wartime situation in the Information age, where people are running around with digital cameras and taking these unbelievable photographs and then passing them off, against the law, to the media, to our surprise."[16] (Or perhaps it is the other way around: *Survivor* often seems to be drawing on military tropes as it seeks to secure the area around its production, hardly a surprising development given

Mark Burnett's background as a British paratrooper.) In some cases, the bloggers, like the spoilers, are tracking down information about events that have already unfolded; but in many other cases, unlike the spoilers, they are attempting to shape future events, trying to use the information they have unearthed to intervene in the democratic process.

Just as brand communities become focal points for criticisms of companies that they feel have violated their trust, these online communities provide the means for their participants to express their distrust of the news media and their discontent with politics as usual. This impatience with traditional news channels was on display when bloggers decided to publish the exit polling data that networks drew upon for "calling" states for the candidates. Following complaints that premature release of exit polling information may have impacted past elections, the networks had chosen not to release those data. By late afternoon on Election Day, the exit polling data were widely available on the Internet, and the public was able to watch the news reports with a more critical eye. One blogger explained, "Our approach is: we post, you decide." Unfortunately, the exit polls were showing a Kerry sweep, whereas the actual vote counts pointed toward a more modest victory for Bush. The liberal bloggers—and through them the Kerry campaign—had their hopes raised and dashed because such information, normally rationed out by the networks, was more readily available than ever before. In the aftermath, professional journalists used the unreliability of these (professionally gathered) polling data to argue that nonprofessionals should not be in the business of reporting or interpreting the news.[17]

Since the grassroots power of blogging was new and largely untested, it is hardly surprising that Campaign 2004 saw as many misfires as it saw hits. Over the next four years, bloggers of all political persuasions will be refining their tools, expanding their reach, and sharpening their nails. Bloggers make no claims on objectivity; they are often unapologetically partisan; they deal often with rumors and innuendos; and as we will see, there is some evidence that blogs are mostly read by people who already agree with their authors' stated views. Blogging may on one level be facilitating the flow of ideas across the media landscape; on other levels, they are ensuring an ever more divisive political debate. Of course, as bloggers are quick to note, mainstream journalism itself is increasingly unreliable, being driven by ideological agendas rather than professional standards, burying stories that run counter to its economic interests, reducing a complex world to one big story at a time, and trivializing politics in its focus on power struggles and horse races. In such a context, the bloggers will be jousting with mainstream journalists story by story, sometimes getting it right, sometimes getting it wrong, but always forcing a segment of the public to question dominant representations. One can't count on either side to always provide the public with the truth, the whole truth, and nothing but the truth. Yet, the adversarial relationship between these two forces holds the opportunity to correct many mistakes.

As Campaign 2004 continued, the two major parties showed signs of developing a better understanding of how to work a message across those different media systems and how to draw the bloggers into their service. Consider, for example, John Kerry's announcement of his running mate. Kerry made the announcement first via e-mail to supporters who had registered through his Web site; the Kerry campaign used the announcement to expand its list of potential supporters for electronic mailings in the fall, and they used the buzz around the e-mail announcement to increase viewership of the televised announcement. The Republicans, however, were even more effective in using the Internet to respond to the announcement. Within a few minutes, they posted a series of talking points criticizing Edwards's nomination, including details of his legal career, his voting record in the Senate, and his comments on the campaign trail. Opposition research is nothing new, but usually such information is released piecemeal across the full duration of the campaign season rather than dumped in one package onto the Web. This was a preemptive strike designed to cut off mounting public support for Edwards. But, more than that, it was do-it-yourself spin.

Spin refers to campaign efforts to slant the news in its direction. Campaigns develop talking points that are repeated by every spokesman tied to the campaign. The talking points imply an interpretation on the events. Spin is in some ways a product of television culture. In the old days, it occurred without much fanfare, and much of the public didn't know that every interviewee was pushing a predesigned agenda. In more recent elections, the news media has focused enormous attention on the spin process—even as campaigns have more systematically coordinated their talking points. The public has been educated about the ways spin works. The process of crafting and spinning messages has become a central part of the drama on shows such as *The West Wing* (1999) or *Spin City* (1996). As spin is publicly acknowledged, the two campaigns dismiss each other's spin for what it is—an attempt to shape the meanings of events to their partisan advantages. Some hosts promise us a "no spin zone" (which, of course, is often the most partisan space of all).

In publishing their talking points about Edwards on the Web, the GOP was not so much trying to spin the story as to give the public a tool kit they could use to spin it themselves in their conversations with friends and neighbors. The talk-radio hosts used those resources extensively in their broadcasts, and their callers responded, reading from the same scripted message. And these same ideas found themselves into letters to the editor. Bloggers both linked to the site and also used it as a set of clues that could lead them to dig deeper into the candidate's past. Broadcast media reinforced these arguments, often providing sound files or images to support the raw information. While the Kerry campaign had hoped that Edwards would enthuse their efforts, the vice presidential candidate was damaged goods within hours of accepting Kerry's offer.

As the sudden visibility of blogging changed the dynamics of traditional news and public opinion, campaign finance reform helped to shift control from candidates and parties to independent action groups. A new loophole in the 2002 McCain-Feingold Act created an opening for independent political organizations—the so-called 501s (trade or business groups) and 527s (nonprofit advocacy groups)—to assert much greater autonomy and visibility in the election process.[18] These groups were prohibited by law from coordinating their activities with the campaigns. They also were prohibited from endorsing specific candidates, though not from criticizing candidates and their policies. They faced no caps on the amount of money they could raise, and their expenditures were not counted against the restrictions with which the campaigns had to comply. As a result, these groups became the attack dogs of the 2004 campaign. On the right, the Swift Boat Veterans for Truth and, on the left, Texans for Truth created headlines by buying commercial time in a limited number of markets, making provocative claims sure to engage the mainstream media, and then drawing traffic to their home pages. This mixture of different media systems made Campaign 2004 unusually complicated. In that sense, the political parties were no different than media producers or advertisers who wanted to tap the power of consumers' commitments to their properties, but remained uncertain how much freedom they should allow groups that might undermine their long-term communication strategies.

By the campaign's final weeks, both parties were adopting themes and mimicking tactics that had emerged from these independent organizations. For example, the official party Web sites released short, punchy, often sarcastic videos responding to the debates. Bush's site distributed a series of videos showing Kerry's "flip-flopping" explanations for his votes regarding the Iraq war, while Democrats used videos to catch Cheney in a series of "lies" and to show Bush's "desperation" during the first debate. These videos were produced overnight and posted the following morning. As with the "Trump Fires Bush" video, they were designed to be circulated virally by their supporters.

Fans, Consumers, Citizens

If we look more closely at the mechanisms by which Trippi and others sought to broaden popular participation within the campaign, we will see a number of ways that the campaigns were learning from fan culture. Meetup.com founder Scott Heiferman wanted a way to trade Beanie Baby stuffed toys with other collectors, and its power was first demonstrated when *The X-Files* (1993) fans used Meetup.com to organize an effort to keep their favorite series on the air. Heiferman told one interviewer, "We didn't design Meetup.com around politics or civics per se. We just knew that the *Lord of the Rings* nerds would want to meet up with each other, you know."[19] Dean's young supporters became known as "Deanie Babies," and Trippi describes the campaign's excitement as they surpassed other fan groups' registrations at Meetup.com.[20]

Moveon.org may have started with a more overtly political goal—trying to get lawmakers to "move on" from their obsessive focus on Bill Clinton's sex life and refocus on the needs of the country—yet they still often took lessons from popular culture. In the fall of 2003, for example, they launched a "Bush in 30 Seconds" contest, encouraging people around the country to use digital camcorders and produce their own commercial explaining why Bush should not be elected to a second term.[21] The submitted films were posted on the Web, where the community helped winnow them down, and then celebrity judges, most of them popular entertainers such as Jack Black, Margaret Cho, Al Franken, Janeane Garofalo, Moby, Eddie Vedder, and Gus Van Sant, made the final selection. This process closely paralleled Project Greenlight, a contest run by Matt Damon and Ben Affleck to help young filmmakers get a chance to produce and release independent movies. Many participants learned their skills making amateur fan movies or recording skateboard stunts and were now applying them for the first time to political activism. The selected spot would air during the Super Bowl, one of the most heavily watched events of the television season. Again, we can see the logic of convergence politics at play here: the effort to use grassroots media to mobilize and mainstream media to publicize. Yet, we can also see here the difference between grassroots media's openness to broad participation and the corporate control over broadcasting. CBS refused to air the spot because they found it "too controversial." Of course, compared with the baring of Janet Jackson's breast during the half-time show, the finished spot, which centered around the debts that were being passed on to the next generation by showing children working to pay off the deficit, would have seemed pretty mild. Historically, the networks have refused to sell airtime for issue-oriented advertisements to "special interest groups," seeing such spots as fundamentally different from the "normal" advertising sponsored by corporate America. Previously, the networks have used such policies to block the airing of anticonsumerist spots even as they promote the more general message that it is a good idea to buy as much stuff as possible. Of course, MoveOn.org almost certainly knew that their efforts to air their advertisement during the Super Bowl was doomed to fail and instead were seeking the inevitable news coverage that would surround the network's refusal to sell them airtime. The spot aired many times on the cable news networks as pundits on all sides discussed whether it should have been allowed to be shown on television.

One prehistory of groups like MoveOn.org and Meetup.com leads back to the alternative media movement, to people's radio, underground newspapers, activist zines, early Web activism, and the emergence of the "indy" media movement in the wake of the World Trade Organization protests in Seattle. Many bloggers explicitly define themselves in opposition to mainstream media and what they see as its corporately controlled content. A second prehistory, however, takes us through efforts of fans to connect online and to exert their combined influence to protect their favorite shows.

Activists, fans, and parodists of all stripes are using the popular graphics software package Photoshop to appropriate and manipulate images to make a political statement. Such images might be seen as the grassroots equivalent of political cartoons—the attempt to encapsulate topical concerns in a powerful image. John Kroll, one of Photoshop's co-creators, told *Salon* that the software program had democratized media in two ways: by allowing smaller groups to have professional-quality graphics at low cost, and by allowing the public to manipulate and recirculate powerful images to make political statements.[22]

These political uses of Photoshop were highly visible in the aftermath of the Florida recount, with both sides using images to ridicule the other's positions. Even more such images circulated in the wake of September 11, sometimes expressing violent fantasies about what would be done to Bin Laden and his supporters, sometimes expressing a sense of loss over what had happened to the country.[23] By Campaign 2004, Web sites such as FreakingNews.com and Fark.com were hosting daily contests to see which contributor might make the most effective use of Photoshop to spoof a particular event or candidate. JibJab, a team of professional animators, used a collage style modeled after the amateur Photoshop spoofs to create a series of parody videos, most notably "This Land," which enjoyed wide circulation in the final days of the campaign.

The use of images may be blunt, as when Bush's face is morphed into Hitler's or *Mad Magazine* icon Alfred E. Neuman, or when Kerry's face gets warped to look like Herman Munster. Some of the images can be much more sophisticated: when John Kerry claimed that he enjoyed the support of many foreign leaders, one satirist put together a mock

Fig. 6.3. Photoshop images spoofing the presidential campaign became part of the grassroots media war promoting and criticizing the candidates.

version of The Beatles's *Sergeant Pepper's Lonely Hearts Club Band* (1967) album cover with dozens of infamous dictators and terrorist leaders lining up behind the Democratic nominee (fig. 6.3). These Photoshop images often map themes from popular culture onto the political campaign: one collage depicts the Democratic candidates riding downhill inside a giant grocery cart borrowed from the poster for MTV's *Jackass* (2000) series.

It is easy to make fun of the concept of "Photoshop for democracy," especially given the persistence with which lowbrow and popular culture references are read over the more serious issues of the campaign. Some might well argue that circulating these images is a poor substitute for more traditional forms of political activism. I wouldn't totally disagree, especially in those situations where people are simply hitting the send key and thoughtlessly forwarding the images to everyone they know. Yet, I would also suggest that crystallizing one's political perspectives into a photomontage that is intended for broader circulation is no less an act of citizenship than writing a letter to the editor of a local newspaper that may or may not actually print it. For a growing number of young Americans, images (or more precisely the combination of words and images) may represent as important a set of rhetorical resources as texts. Passing such images to a friend is no more and no less a political act than handing them a campaign brochure or a bumper sticker. The tokens being exchanged are not that important in and of themselves, but they may become the focus for conversation and persuasion. What changes, however, is the degree to which amateurs are able to insert their images and thoughts into the political process—and in at least some cases, these images can circulate broadly and reach a large public.

Historically, critics have seen consumption as almost the polar opposite of citizenly participation. Lauren Berlant discusses consumption primarily in terms of privatization, blaming the shift toward a politics based on consumption for what she sees as the shrinking of the public sphere.[24] Today, consumption assumes a more public and collective dimension—no longer a matter of individual choices and preferences, consumption becomes a topic of public discussion and collective deliberation; shared interests often lead to shared knowledge, shared vision, and shared actions. A politics based on consumption *can* represent a dead end when consumerism substitutes for citizenship (the old cliché of voting with our dollars), but it *may* represent a powerful force when striking back economically at core institutions can directly impact their power and influence.[25] We are still learning to separate one from the other. For example, this issue was in play when conservative activists sought to boycott and progressive activists sought to purchase albums by the Dixie Chicks after the group's lead singer, Natalie Maines, made some off-handed negative comments about George Bush during a concert on the eve of the bombing of Baghdad.[26] What about when MoveOn.org rallied supporters to turn out for the opening weekend of *Fahrenheit 9/11* (2004), believing that the news media would take them more seriously if the film were seen to be a top box-office hit?

More and more, groups with ties to the entertainment community are using their visibility and influence to push young people toward greater participation in the political process. MTV, Nickelodeon, Norman Lear, Russell Simmons's Def Jam, and even World Wrestling Entertainment launched efforts to educate, register, and rally young voters. And these groups joined forces within what is being called the "20 Million Loud" campaign to mobilize around key public events—concerts, wrestling events, movie premieres, and the like—to get their message in front of as many young voters as possible. Although these groups were, for the most part, nonpartisan, seeking to recruit young voters regardless of their political beliefs, it was no secret that they emerged in response to the so-called culture wars, which had themselves sought to tap distaste over popular culture for political ends. According to the Center for Information and Research on Civic Learning and Engagement, the "20 Million Loud" campaign met its goals: almost 21 million people under the age of thirty voted in 2004—a 9.3 percent increase over 2000. In so-called battleground states, there was a 13 percent increase in youth participation over the previous election.[27]

Entertaining the Monitorial Citizen

In his famous essay, "The Work of Art in the Age of Mechanical Reproduction," Walter Benjamin argued that the ability to mass-produce and mass-circulate images would have a profoundly democratic impact.[28] His most famous claim was that mechanical reproduction erodes the "aura" surrounding works of high art and dethrones reigning cultural authorities. He also argued that a new form of popular expertise would emerge; people felt more authorized to offer judgment on sports teams or Hollywood movies than on artworks cloistered in museums. Does making politics into a kind of popular culture allow consumers to apply fan expertise to their civic responsibilities? Parody newscasts like *The Daily Show* (1996) may be teaching us to do just that.

In early 2004, the Pew Foundation released some telling statistics. In 2000, 39 percent of respondents regularly got campaign information from network newscasts. By 2004, that number had fallen to 23 percent. Over the same period, the percentage of people under the age of thirty who received much of their campaign information from comedy shows such as *Saturday Night Live* (1975) or *The Daily Show* had grown from 9 percent to 21 percent.[29] In this context, ABC's *This Week with George Stephanopoulos* added a segment showcasing highlights from the week's monologues by David Letterman, Jay Leno, and Jon Stewart.

As early as 1994, Jon Katz had argued in *Rolling Stone* that a growing percentage of young people felt that entertainment media, rather than traditional journalism, more fully reflected their perspectives on current events.[30] Katz claimed that young people gained much of their information about the world from music videos and rap songs, *Saturday Night Live* sketches and stand-up comedians, the plots of prime-time dramas and the gags on sitcoms. Katz saw this as a positive development, since the ideological perspectives of popular entertainment were less tightly policed than news, which he feared had fallen increasingly under a corporate stranglehold. Katz's argument was met with scorn by established journalists.

The Pew study, released on the eve of the 2004 campaign, added further fuel to the fire. Pew showed that young people were getting information from entertainment media instead of news media (although their questions only asked if entertainment media was one source of information, not the exclusive or even primary vehicle) and also demonstrated that people who got their information from such sources were on the whole less informed about the world—or at least less able to recall certain facts about the candidates—than consumers of traditional news. As others were quick to counter, recall is not at all the same thing as comprehension, and many of the items on Pew's survey, such as which candidate had been endorsed by Gore or which candidate had made a misstatement about the Confederate flag, illustrated the ways that news reports often trivialized the political process by focusing on horse-race polling, gaffes, and scandals.

The Daily Show, a nightly parody of news, quickly emerged as the focal point for this debate. Comedy Central offered more hours of coverage of the 2004 Democratic and Republican National Conventions than ABC, CBS, and NBC combined: the news media was walking away from historical responsibilities, and popular culture was taking its pedagogical potential more seriously. According to a study conducted by the Annenberg Public Policy Center at the University of Pennsylvania,

> People who watch *The Daily Show* are more interested in the presidential campaign, more educated, younger, and more liberal than the average American. . . . However, those factors do not explain the difference in levels of campaign knowledge between people who watch *The Daily Show* and people who do not. In fact, *Daily Show* viewers have higher campaign knowledge than national news viewers and newspaper readers— even when education, party identification, following politics, watching cable news, receiving campaign information online, age, and gender are taken into consideration.[31]

The controversy came to a head when *Daily Show* host Jon Stewart was invited onto CNN's news-discussion program, *Crossfire* (1982) and got into a heated argument with commentator and co-host Tucker Carlson. Carlson apparently wanted Stewart to tell jokes and promote his book, but Stewart refused to play that role: "I'm not going to be your monkey." Instead, Stewart charged the news program with corrupting the political process through partisan bickering: "You have a responsibility to the public discourse and you fail miserably. . . . You're helping the politicians and the corporations. . . . You're part of their strategies."[32] The circulation of this segment, legally and illegally, brought it to the attention of many more citizens than watched the actual newscast, representing perhaps the most visible illustration of a mounting public concern over the ways media concentration was distorting public access to important information.

   To understand why such controversies matter, we may need to rethink our assumptions about what it means to be an informed citizen. Michael Schudson traces shifting concepts of citizenship over the first two hundred plus years of the American republic. Our modern notion of the "informed citizen" emerged at the turn of the last century. Literacy rates were rising, the price of newspapers and other publications was coming down, and the right to vote was expanding to include many who had previously been disenfranchised. The notion of an informed citizen took shape in the context of an information revolution that made it conceivable that voters could follow the nuances of public policy debates. The notion of the informed citizen challenged more traditional notions of citizenship that deferred to the expertise of aristocrats or political parties.

At the end of the twentieth century, Schudson argues, explosions in information technology have flooded us with more data than we can possibly process. The promise of the digital revolution was complete mastery over the information flow: "Everyone can know everything! Each citizen will have the voting record of every politician at his or her fingertips! A whole world of political knowledge as close as one's computer and as fast as one's dial-up connection!"[33] In reality, Schudson argues, "The gap between readily available political information and the individual's capacity to monitor it grows ever larger."[34] No one citizen can be expected to know everything about even one core debate, let alone the range of issues that shape national politics. Instead, he argues, "Monitorial citizens tend to be defensive rather than pro-active. . . . The monitorial citizen engages in environmental surveillance more than information-gathering. Picture parents watching small children at the community pool. They are not gathering information; they are keeping an eye on the scene. They look inactive, but they are poised for action if action is required. The monitorial citizen is not an absentee citizen but watchful, even while he or she is doing something else."[35] Although monitorial citizens "are perhaps better informed than citizens of the past in that, somewhere in their heads, they have more bits of information," Schudson argues, "there is no assurance that they know at all what to do with what they know."[36]

One might see Schudson's monitorial citizen as a participant in the kind of knowledge culture Lévy described—knowledgeable in some areas, somewhat aware of others, operating in a context of mutual trust and shared resources. As we have seen in this book, many are learning how to share, deploy, trust, evaluate, contest, and act upon collective knowledge as part of their recreational lives. Applying those skills to a parody news show may be the next step toward fuller participation in democratic decision making—a way of mobilizing those skills that Benjamin suggested emerged spontaneously in our response to popular culture, but that are hard to cultivate in relation to news and politics. *The Daily Show* consistently focuses attention on issues badly covered through the mainstream media, ensuring that they register on the radar of many monitorial citizens. Given the nature of its genre, the show must pick its targets, but a growing number of viewers are talking about the targets the show identifies. Not every viewer will make the effort to learn more about the issues raised, but if the Annenberg statistics are accurate, more than one might expect do so.

The monitoring citizen needs to develop new critical skills in assessing information—a process that occurs both on an individual level within the home or the workplace, and on a more collaborative level through the work of various knowledge communities. The Daily Show's mix of spoof segments with interviews with actual public figures demands an active and alert viewer to shift through the distinctions between fact and fantasy. Such a program provides a good training ground for monitorial citizens.[37] John Hartley contends that news and entertainment have different "regimes of truth" that shape what information gets presented and how it is interpreted.[38] The conventions of news reassure us that it has provided all we need to know to make sense of the world and that it has presented this information in a "fair and balanced" manner. On the other hand, docudrama and parody programs invite audience skepticism because the balance between these competing regimes of truth are unstable and fluid. The Daily Show makes no pretense of offering an objective or total view of the world. As Stewart told Carlson during the Crossfire encounter, "You're on CNN. The show that leads into me is puppets making crank phone calls." Clips from other newscasts and interviews with newsmakers coexist with comic reenactments and parodies of common news practices. From the start, The Daily Show challenges viewers to look for signs of fabrication, and it consistently spoofs the conventions of traditional journalism and the corporate control of the media. Such shows pose questions rather than offering answers. In such spaces, news is something to be discovered through active hashing through of competing accounts rather than something to be digested from authoritative sources.

Playing Politics in Alphaville

In his book The Making of Citizens (2000), David Buckingham examines the factors that tend to discourage children and young people from consuming news.[39] Some of them we have already discussed—children find the language of politics unfamiliar and uninvolving compared to the immediacy offered by popular entertainment; news presents the world as hermetically sealed from their everyday lives. But he adds another: children and youth feel powerless in their everyday lives and, as a consequence, have difficulty imagining how they might exert power in a politically meaningful fashion. Children are not allowed to vote and are not defined as political subjects, so they do not think of themselves as being addressed by the news. If we want to get young people to vote, we have to start earlier, changing the process by which they are socialized into citizenship. If what Buckingham argues is true, then one way that popular culture can enable a more engaged citizenry is by allowing people to play with power on a microlevel, to exert control over imaginary worlds. Here again, popular culture may be preparing the way for a more meaningful public culture; in this case, the most compelling example comes from the world of video games. Let's consider what happened in Alphaville, one of the oldest and most densely populated towns in *The Sims Online,* a massively multiplayer version of the most successful game franchise of all time.

For democracy to function there needs to be a social contract between participants and a sense that their actions have consequence within the community. These things were at stake in Alphaville in 2004 just as they were in the offline world. In Alphaville, though, children had an active role to play, their voices mattered, and they were asked to think through complex ethical issues.

The game's creator, Will Wright, says he had no idea what would happen when he put *The Sims* online.[40] He knew players would become deeply invested in their characters and their communities. He could not have predicted that organized crime would run rampant, that community leaders would rally against con artists and prostitutes, or that the imaginary elections would devolve into mudslinging and manipulation. In an election to determine who would control the imaginary town's government, the incumbent, Mr. President (the avatar of Arthur Baynes, a twenty-one-year-old Delta Airlines ticket agent from Richmond, Virginia) was running against Ashley Richardson (the avatar of Laura McKnight, a middle-schooler from Palm Beach, Florida).

In spring 2004, as Howard Dean's campaign was starting to disintegrate, the Alphaville presidential elections attracted national and even international media attention. National Public Radio's *Talk of the Nation* hosted a debate between the candidates, complete with an array of pundits pontificating about cyberpolitics and virtual economies. (I was one of them.) The best coverage of the campaign came from the *Alphaville Herald,* the small-town newspaper serving the needs of the virtual community. The *Alphaville Herald* is run by Peter Ludlow, a professor of philosophy and linguistics at the University of Michigan. In the game realm, Ludlow goes by the moniker Urizenus.

Important issues were at stake here, both in the world of the game and the world beyond the game. Within the game, the candidates represented different perspectives on what would be best for their community; the choice of leaders would affect the way players experience the game world. Ashley Richardson wanted to set up information booths at the city limits to warn newcomers about some of the ways scammers might trick them out of their cash. It is significant that one of the leading candidates was five years too young to vote in the actual presidential elections and that participants in the online debates kept accusing one another of playing the "age card." Consider what it means to exercise power in a virtual world when you have so little control over what happens to you in your everyday life.

In another era, many of the youth involved in this online election would have been devoting their energies to student governments in their local high schools, representing a few hundred constituents. Alpha-ville has an estimated population of seven thousand, and its government employs more than 150 people (mostly in law enforcement). The student council members of the past might negotiate with the school principal over the theme for the school dance. The virtual town's leaders have to negotiate with Electronic Arts, the company that creates and markets *The Sims* franchise, to shape the policies that impact their community. On one level, some adults might still prefer engagement in student government elections because it represents action at the local level—actions that have real-world consequences. This is a classic critique of online communities—that they don't matter because they are not face-to-face. From another perspective, children have more opportunities to exert leadership and influence the actions of online worlds than they ever enjoyed in their high school governments. After all, it wasn't as if schools gave students much real power to change their everyday environments.

When the votes were counted, Mr. President had beaten Ashley, 469 to 411. Ashley cried foul play, contending that she knew of more than one hundred supporters who were not allowed to vote. Mr. President's defenders initially claimed that the undercounting resulted from a bug in the system that made it hard for America Online users to accept the cookies used on the election Web site. And in any case, they said, many of Ashley's supporters were not actually "citi-sims" of Alphaville. Mr. President argued that he had campaigned among hard-core participants in the game, while Ashley brought her offline friends and family members (many of whom are not subscribers) into the process. While the Alphaville constitution makes clear who is eligible to be a candidate, it doesn't specify who is permitted to vote. Nobody actually "lives" in Alphaville, of course, but many call the online community "home." Should one have to interact there for a specific period of time to earn the right to vote, or should voting be open to everybody, including those who have never before visited the community?

The situation blew up when the *Alphaville Herald* published what it claimed was a transcript of an Internet chat session between Mr. President and mobster J. C. Soprano (the avatar of a player who presumably lives a law-abiding life in the real world). The chat suggested that the election process may have been rigged from the very beginning, and that Mr. President may be the silent partner of the organized crime family that helped them fix the electronic voting apparatus. Mr. President had coded the program that determined the outcome. If this was play, then not everyone was playing by the same rules.

Writing under his real-world name in the *Alphaville Herald*, Ludlow raised the question, "What kinds of lessons were we teaching Ashley and other younger players about political life?" Yes, he wrote, *The Sims* online was a game, but "nothing is ever *just* a game. Games have consequences. Games also give us an opportunity to break out of the roles and actions that we might be forced into in real life. I decided to take advantage of that opportunity. I freed my game."[41]

Reading through the reader responses in the *Alphaville Herald*, it is clear that, for many, the stolen election forced them to ask some fundamental questions about the nature of democracy. The odd coincidence that many of those who tried and were unable to vote came from Palm Beach invited comparison to the dispute in Florida four years before. Ashley, a John Kerry supporter, evoked the specter of Bush-Cheney and the "stolen election" while she was called a "cry baby" and compared to Al Gore. As one participant exclaimed, "Where is the Alphaville Supreme Court when you really need them?"

Even in play, American democracy felt broken.

Before we write this all off as a "learning experience," we should ask some more fundamental questions about the ways that game worlds model ideal (or not so ideal) online democracies. Historically, the American courts have granted far greater freedom of speech in town squares than in shopping malls: the town square is a space intended for civic discourse, so there are broad but increasingly eroding guarantees protecting our right to assemble and debate public matters. Shopping malls are seen as private property, and their management is assumed to have the right to expel anyone who causes a disruption; there are few protections for dissent in such an environment. However much they represent themselves as civic experiments, massively multiplayer game worlds are, like the shopping malls, commercial spaces. We should be concerned about what happens to free speech in a corporate-controlled environment, where the profit motive can undo any decision made by the citizenry and where the company can pull the plug whenever sales figures warrant. For example, well before the election controversy, Ludlow, the editor of the *Alphaville Herald,* was temporarily expelled from *The Sims Online* (2002) because Electronic Arts was angered over his coverage of some of the issues confronting his online community—in particular an exposé he ran on child prostitution (teens selling cybersex for games credit). We would be outraged if we learned about a town government expelling the editor of the local newspaper: this would fundamentally shake our sense of how democracy operates. Yet, the expulsion of Ludlow from a commercial game generated only limited protest.

As we have seen throughout this book, people make passionate but often short-term investments in these online communities: they can always move elsewhere if the group reaches conclusions that run counter to their own beliefs or desires. As such, these games represent interesting and sometimes treacherous spaces to "play" with citizenship and democracy. Given all of these concerns, we might still think about an Alphaville-style democracy as a productive thought experiment, especially insofar as participants pulled back, talked about their different perspectives and experiences, and worked together to perfect the mechanisms governing their communities. It is through asking such questions that participants come to understand what values they invest in the concept of democracy and what steps they are prepared to take to protect it. It is through staging such debates that the Alphaville players found their voices as citizens and learned to flex their muscles as a community.

Ironically, while these events were unfolding in Alphaville, I was being asked by several major foundations to consult on civic-minded projects that sought to harness the power of games to encourage youth to think more deeply about social policy. My advice had centered on ways to encourage more reflection about what occurred within the game world and to connect things experienced through play to issues that affected participants in their everyday lives. Yet, all of these things were occurring spontaneously within a game designed purely for entertainment purposes. Participants were having heated debates about the events, and they were continuously drawing parallels to the actual presidential campaign. One might imagine that a broken election within a game might destroy any sense of empowerment in real-world politics, yet Ashley and her supporters consistently described the events as motivating them to go out and make a difference in their own communities, to become more engaged in local and national elections, and to think of a future when they might become candidates and play the political game on different terms. When something breaks in a knowledge culture, the impulse is to figure out how to fix it, because a knowledge culture empowers its members to identify problems and pose solutions. If we learn to do this through our play, perhaps we can learn to extend those experiences into actual political culture.

Jane McGonigal has found that the Cloudmakers, who had forged their community and tested their collective intelligence against "the Beast" (chapter 4), are now ready and eager to turn their attention toward larger social problems. There were active discussions in their online forums after September 11 about whether their puzzle-solving skills would be of use in tracking down the terrorists. As one explained, "We like to flout our 7000 members and our voracious appetite for difficult problems, but when the chips are down, can we really make a difference?"[42] After several days of debate, the group decided that unmasking a global terrorist network might be a problem of a different order of magnitude than solving fictional puzzles; but the issue resurfaced again when a sniper was terrorizing Washington, D.C., and this time the group did make a concerted effort to identify the culprit. As McGonigal explains, "This strategy drew on various methods developed by the Cloudmakers during the Beast, including combining technological resources to accomplish massive web analyses; interpreting character clues to track down more information; and employing all of the network available to them to interact with as many potential informants as possible."

Subsequently, another alternate reality group, Collective Detective, formed a think tank whose first task was to try to identify corruption and waste in U.S. federal government spending. One team member explained: "The perfect kind of case for Collective Detective. First phase is research into sources of information. Second phase is research within the sources. Third phase is analysis of research to see what kind of correlations we can draw. Fourth phase, secondary research to help tie together the connections we find. Sounds like fun to me. Can also actually make a difference in how the country is run." McGonigal is more skeptical that the groups are ready to tackle such large-scale problems, suggesting that their game-play experience has given them a "subjective" sense of empowerment that may exceed their actual resources and abilities. Yet, what interests me here is the connection the group is drawing between game play and civic engagement and also the ways this group, composed of people who share common cultural interests but not necessarily ideological perspectives, might work together to arrive at "rational" solutions to complex policy issues.

Vote Naked

An advertisement for the Webby Awards, given in recognition for outstanding contributions to digital culture, depicts a pair of feminine bare feet with what would seem to be a blurry bed in the background. Its slogan was "vote naked." Ever since I first saw that advertisement, I have been intrigued by what it might mean to "vote naked." The advertisement suggests that the computer now allows us to conduct the most public of actions within the privacy of our own home in whatever state of dress or undress we desire. More than that, the image and slogan invite us to imagine a time when we are as comfortable in our roles as citizens as we are within our own skins, when politics may be a familiar, everyday, and intimate aspect of our daily lives much the way popular culture is today. We watch television in our underwear; we dress up to vote.

We feel passionately about popular culture; we embrace its characters; we integrate its stories into our lives; we rework them and make them our own. We have seen throughout this book that consumers and fans are beginning to take pleasure in their newfound power to shape their media environment and that they are using elements borrowed from popular culture to broker conversations with people they have never met face-to-face. What would it take for us to respond to the political world in this same fashion? How do we break through the sense of distance and alienation many Americans feel toward the political process? How do we generate the same level of emotional energy challenging the current Powers That Be in Washington that fans routinely direct against the Powers That Be in Hollywood? When will we be able to participate within the democratic process with the same ease that we have come to participate in the imaginary realms constructed through popular culture?

In this chapter, I have suggested a range of different ways that activists mobilized popular culture to encourage voter awareness and participation in the 2004 presidential campaign. They adopted technologies and techniques pioneered by fan communities and used them to mobilize voters. They used concerts and performances as sites for voter registration. They used films as occasions for political discussions and public outreach. They created Photoshop parodies that encapsulated core debates. They built games where imaginary communities could learn to govern themselves. And yes, they allowed some of us for a short time to imagine a world where Bush was simply an apprentice who could be dismissed from power with a swat of The Donald's hand.

Many of the groups we have discussed above responded to the election results with profound disappointment. They had devoted so much effort to defeat Bush and felt that none of it had mattered in the end. More conservative activists felt that their efforts to get out the Christian vote and their criticisms of the Democratic nominee had proven to be decisive elements in Bush's victory. However we feel about the election results, we can argue a growing integration of politics into popular culture and everyday life helped to mobilize record levels of voter participation. Grassroots communities of all kinds—right as well as left—mobilized to promote their own agendas and get their members to the polls. Candidates and parties lost some degree of control over the political process, and networks seemed a bit less authoritative in defining the terms by which the public understood the campaign.

What happens next? Precisely because these efforts were linked so closely to a particular election, they treated political participation as a special event and not yet part of our everyday lives. The next step is to think of democratic citizenship as a lifestyle.

In *Collective Intelligence* (2000), Pierre Lévy proposes what he calls an "achievable utopia": he asks us to imagine what would happen when the sharing of knowledge and the exercise of grassroots power become normative. In Lévy's world, people from fundamentally different perspectives see a value in talking and listening to one another, and such deliberations form the basis for mutual respect and trust. A similar ideal underlies the work of the Center for Deliberative Democracy at Stanford University.[43] Interested in how to reconnect a notion of deliberation—the active "weighing" of evidence and argument—back to popular democracy, they have run a series of tests around the world of new processes whereby participants of diverse political backgrounds are brought together—online and sometimes face-to-face—over an extended period of time, given detailed briefing books on public policy issues as well as the chance to question one another and experts. Over time, they found dramatic shifts in the ways participants thought about the issues as they learned to listen to alternative viewpoints and factor diverse experiences and ideas into their thinking about the issues. For example, in one such session, support for foreign aid jumped from a 20 percent minority to a 53 percent majority in part because the group learned what a small percentage of the total federal budget went to such purposes; discussions on the Iraq war led a new consensus position that saw Iraq as a legitimate interest but one that was largely separate from the War on Terror and one that might best be combated through multinational rather than unilateral means.[44] They also found evidence that people who felt better informed on the issues were more likely to vote or otherwise participate in the political process. Theoretically, they argue, citizens have greater potential for deliberation than governmental bodies because they are not bound in any formal way to constituents or parties and thus are much freer to shift their views as they rethink issues. The challenge is to create a context where people of different backgrounds actually talk and listen to one another.

By the end of 2004, many were asking how we will be able to heal the rift that separates red America from blue America. As people integrate politics into their everyday lives, they find it harder to communicate within their families, their neighborhoods, their schools, their churches, and their workplaces. I was chilled during the election by the response of a friend to my suggestion that I had Republican friends. A look of horror crossed her face, and then she said, "I suppose Nazis had friends too, but I wouldn't want to associate with any myself." (And for the record, my friend lives in a red state!) As "attack politics" unfolds on a grassroots level, we either find ourselves at loggerheads with people around us, vilifying them for their political choices, or we find ourselves unwilling to share our political views for fear that expressing them may damage relationships we value. We vote naked not in the sense that we feel an intimate engagement with politics but in the sense that we feel raw, exposed, and vulnerable.

Having said that, despite apocalyptic claims to the contrary, we are not more polarized now than we have ever been in American history. Anyone who has read a good history textbook knows that America has faced a series of polarizing debates—struggles over the relative authority of the federal and local governments, debates over slavery and reconstruction, disagreements about the New Deal and the best response to the Great Depression, and the heated struggles surrounding the civil rights movement and the Vietnam War. In each instance, the polarization centered on important disagreements that had to be worked through, and we were better because activists forced us to confront and resolve those disagreements rather than pretending they didn't exist. In our current context, there are also important principles at stake surrounding the Iraq War or economic policies or cultural values that are making it hard for members of opposing parties to agree on core premises. Yet, the current polarization also means that we are unable to find unifying principles or to act upon points of consensus. To some degree, this polarization is opportunistic, shaped by insiders in both parties, who see the value of such disagreements for raising money and mobilizing voters.

Some are also arguing that such polarization is at least partially a product of a world in which it is possible to choose communications channels that perfectly match our own political beliefs and assumptions and as a consequence to develop a less rounded or nuanced picture of what other people believe. However narrow the range of ideas expressed by commercial or mainstream media, it did form the basis for what David Thorburn has called a "consensus culture," helping to map what most people believed and define a space of common culture that enabled further dialogue.[45] In the closing paragraphs of *Technologies without Boundaries*, written shortly before his death in 1984, Ithiel de Sola Pool warns of the potential dangers democracy might face from the emergence of communication niches:

We can expect that there will be a great growth in specialized intellectual subcultures. . . . If that happens, the complaints we would hear from social critics will be just the opposite from today's. . . . We are likely to hear complaints that the vast proliferation of specialized information serves only special interests, not the community. That they fractionate society, providing none of the common themes of interest and attention that makes a society cohere. The critics will mourn the weakening of the national popular culture that was shared by all within the community. We will be told that we are being deluged by undigested information on a vast un-edited electronic blackboard and that what a democratic society needs is shared organizing principles and consensus in concerns. Like the present criticism of mass society, these criticisms will be only partly true, but partly true they may be. A society in which it becomes easy for every small group to indulge its tastes will have more difficulty mobilizing unity.[46]

Much as Pool predicted, some writers in the wake of the 2004 elections argue that it is time to move out of the digital enclaves and learn to communicate across our differences.

Writing in the immediate aftermath of Kerry's election defeat, *Salon* technology columnist Andrew Leonard asked whether the blogosphere had become an "echo chamber":

For weeks, I've gotten up in the morning, made my coffee, and then armed myself for the day with arguments and anecdotes, spin and rhetoric often in large part derived from the thrust-and-parry of discourse in the lefty blogosphere. When I visited the right-wing blogosphere, it was like going to the zoo to look at exotic animals. . . . I dismissed it, secure in the armor provided by the communities of people who share my values. . . . What I find disturbing, however, is how easy the internet has made it not just to Google the fact that I need when I need it, but to get the mindset I want when I want it.[47]

Cass Sunstein, a law professor at the University of Chicago, has argued that Web communities fragmented the electorate and tended to exaggerate whatever consensus emerged in the group.[48] *Time* magazine adopted a similar argument when it described the growing divide between "Blue Truth" and "Red Truth": "Red Truth looks at Bush and sees a savior; Blue Truth sees a zealot who must be stopped. In both worlds there are no accidents, only conspiracies, and facts have value only to the extent that they support the Truth."[49] It is worth remembering that such divisions are not purely a product of the mediascape: increasingly people are choosing where to live based on desired lifestyles that include perceptions of the prevailing political norms of different communities. People, in other words, are choosing to live in red states and blue states, just as they are choosing to participate in red and blue communities as they move online.

As long as the overarching narrative of American political life is that of the culture war, our leaders will govern through a winner-take-all perspective. Every issue gets settled through bloody partisan warfare when, in fact, on any given issue there is a consensus that unites at least some segments of red and blue America. We agree on much; we trust each other little. In such a world, nobody can govern and nobody can compromise. There is literally no common ground.

What we have been describing as knowledge cultures depend on the quality and diversity of information people can access. The ability to learn by sharing insights or comparing notes with others is severely diminished when everyone else already shares the same beliefs and knowledge. The reason why Lévy was optimistic that the emergence of a knowledge-based culture would enhance democracy and global understanding was that it would model new protocols for interacting across our differences. Of course, those protocols do not emerge spontaneously as an inevitable consequence of technological change. They will emerge through experimentation and conscious effort. This is part of what constitutes the "apprenticeship" phase that Lévy envisioned. We are still learning what it is like to operate within a knowledge culture. We are still debating and resolving the core principles that will define our interactions with each other.

Sunstein's arguments assume that Web groups are primarily formed around ideological rather than cultural axes. Yet, few of us simply interact in political communities; most of us also join communities on the basis of our recreational interests. Many of us are fans of one or another form of popular culture. Popular culture allows us to entertain alternative framings in part because the stakes are lower, because our viewing commitments don't carry the same weight as our choices at the ballot box. Our willingness to step outside ideological enclaves may be greatest when we are talking about what kind of person Harry Potter is going to grow up to be or what kind of world will emerge as the machines and humans learn to work together in *The Matrix* (1999). That is, we may be able to talk across our differences if we find commonalities through our fantasies. This is in the end another reason why popular culture matters politically—because it doesn't seem to be about politics at all.

I don't mean to put forward popular culture or fan communities as a panacea for what ails American democracy. After all, as the country has become more polarized, so have our tastes in popular culture. Hollywood talent agent Peter Benedek offered the *New York Times* an analysis of the election results that centered around competing and contradictory taste cultures: "The majority of the American voting public is not comfortable with what's in the movies and on television. . . . Hollywood's obsessed with 18- to 34-year-olds and those people didn't come out and vote. My guess is that most people who watched *The Sopranos* voted for Kerry. Most people who saw *The Grudge* didn't vote."[50] And most people who watched *The Passion of the Christ* voted Republican. The strong identification of the Democratic Party with controversial performers and content may have mobilized as many cultural conservatives as it rallied youth voters. Yet, there does seem to be a much greater diversity of opinion on sites dealing with popular culture than on sites dealing directly with politics. If we want to bridge between red and blue America, we need to find that kind of common ground and expand upon it. We need to create a context where we listen and learn from one another. We need to deliberate together.

Conclusion

Democratizing Television? The Politics of Participation

In August 2005, former Democratic vice president Albert Gore helped to launch a new cable news network, Current. The network's stated goal was to encourage the active participation of young people as citizen journalists; viewers were intended not simply to consume Current's programming but also to participate in its production, selection, and distribution. As Gore explained at a press conference in late 2004, "We are about empowering this generation of young people in the 18-to-34 population to engage in a dialogue of democracy and to tell their stories of what's going on in their lives, in the dominant medium of our time. The Internet opened a floodgate for young people, whose passions are finally being heard, but TV hasn't followed suit. . . . Our aim is to give young people a voice, to democratize television."[1] The network estimates that as much as 25 percent of the content they air will come from their viewers. Amateur media producers will upload digital videos to a Web site; visitors to the site will be able to evaluate each submission, and those which receive the strongest support from viewers will make it onto the airwaves.

The idea of reader-moderated news content is not new. Slashdot was one of the first sites to experiment with user-moderation, gathering a wealth of information with a five-person paid staff, mostly part time, by empowering readers not only to submit their own stories but to work collectively to determine the relative value of each submission. Slashdot's focus is explicitly on technology and culture, and so it became a focal point for information about Internet privacy issues, the debates over mandatory filters in public libraries, the open-source movement, and so forth. Slashdot attracts an estimated 1.1 million unique users per month, and some 250,000 per day, constituting a user base as large as that of many of the nation's leading online general interest and technology-centered news sites.[2] Yet, this would be the first time that something like the Slashdot model was being applied to television.

Even before the network reached the air, Current's promise to "democratize television" became a focal point for debates about the politics of participation. Cara Mertes, the executive producer for the PBS documentary program *POV*, itself an icon of the struggle to get alternative perspectives on television, asked, "What are you talking about when you say 'democratizing the media'? Is it using media to further democratic ends, to create an environment conducive to the democratic process through unity, empathy and civil discourse? Or does it mean handing over the means of production, which is the logic of public access?"[3] Was Current going to be democratic in its content (focusing on the kinds of information that a democratic society needs to function), its effects (mobilizing young people to participate more fully in the democratic process), its values (fostering rational discourse and a stronger sense of social contract), or its process (expanding access to the means of media production and distribution)?

Others pushed further, arguing that market pressures, the demand to satisfy advertisers and placate stockholders, would ensure that no commercial network could possibly be as democratic on any of these levels as the Gore operation was promising. Any truly democratic form of broadcasting would necessarily arise outside corporate media and would likely see corporate America as its primary target for reform. Even if the network remained true to its goals, they argued, those most drawn to the alternative media perspective would be skeptical of any media channel shaped by traditional corporate gatekeepers. A growing number of Web services—such as participatoryculture.org and ourmedia.org—were making it easier for amateur media makers to gain visibility via the Web without having to turn over exclusive rights to their material to a network funded by some of the wealthiest men and women in the country. In a society where blogs—both text based and video enhanced—were thriving, why would anyone need to put their content on television?

Others expressed disappointment in the network's volunteeristic approach. Original plans to pay a large number of independent filmmakers to become roaming correspondents had given way to a plan to allow amateurs to submit material for consideration and then get paid upon acceptance. The first plan, critics argued, would have sustained an infrastructure to support alternative media production; the other would lead to little more than a glorified public access station.

The network defended itself as a work in progress—one that was doing what it could to democratize a medium while working under market conditions. A spokesman for the network observed, "For some people, the perfect is always the enemy of the good."[4] Current might not change everything about television, they pleaded, but it could make a difference. Gore held firm in his belief that enabling audience-generated content had the potential to diversify civic discourse: "I personally believe that when this medium is connected to the grassroots storytellers that are out there, it will have an impact on the kinds of things that are discussed and the way they are discussed."[5]

At about the same time, the British Broadcasting Company was embracing an even more radical vision of how consumers might relate to its content. The first signs of this new policy had come through a speech made by Ashley Highfield, director of BBC New Media & Technology, in October 2003, explaining how the widespread adoption of broadband and digital technologies will impact the ways his network serves its public:

> Future TV may be unrecognizable from today, defined not just by linear TV channels, packaged and scheduled by television executives, but instead will resemble more of a kaleidoscope, thousands of streams of content, some indistinguishable as actual channels. These streams will mix together broadcasters' content and programs, and our viewers' contributions. At the simplest level—audiences will want to organize and reorganize content the way they want it. They'll add comments to our programs, vote on them, and generally mess about with them. But at another level, audiences will want to create these streams of video themselves from scratch, with or without our help. At this end of the spectrum, the traditional "monologue broadcaster" to "grateful viewer" relationship will break down.[6]

By 2005, the BBC was digitizing large segments of its archive and making the streaming content available via the Web.[7] The BBC was also encouraging grassroots experimentation with ways to annotate and index these materials. Current's path led from the Web—where many could share what they created—into broadcast media, where many could consume what a few had created. The BBC efforts were moving in the other direction, opening up television content to the more participatory impulses shaping digital culture.

Both were in a sense promoting what this book has been calling convergence culture. Convergence does not depend on any specific delivery mechanism. Rather, convergence represents a paradigm shift—a move from medium-specific content toward content that flows across multiple media channels, toward the increased interdependence of communications systems, toward multiple ways of accessing media content, and toward ever more complex relations between top-down corporate media and bottom-up participatory culture. Despite the rhetoric about "democratizing television," this shift is being driven by economic calculations and not by some broad mission to empower the public. Media industries are embracing convergence for a number of reasons: because convergence-based strategies exploit the advantages of media conglomeration; because convergence creates multiple ways of selling content to consumers; because convergence cements consumer loyalty at a time when the fragmentation of the marketplace and the rise of file sharing threaten old ways of doing business. In some cases, convergence is being pushed by corporations as a way of shaping consumer behavior. In other cases, convergence is being pushed by consumers who are demanding that media companies be more responsive to their tastes and interests. Yet, whatever its motivations, convergence is changing the ways in which media industries operate and the ways average people think about their relation to media. We are in a critical moment of transition during which the old rules are open to change and companies may be forced to renegotiate their relationship to consumers. The question is whether the public is ready to push for greater participation or willing to settle for the same old relations to mass media.

Writing in 1991, W. Russell Neuman sought to examine the ways that consumer "habit" or what he called "the psychology of the mass audience, the semi-attentive, entertainment-oriented mind-set of day-to-day media behavior" would slow down the interactive potentials of emerging digital technologies.[8] In his model, the technology was ready at hand but the culture was not ready to embrace it: "The new developments in horizontal, user-controlled media that allow the user to amend, reformat, store, copy, forward to others, and comment on the flow of ideas do not rule out mass communications. Quite the contrary, they complement the traditional mass media."[9] The public will not rethink their relationship to media content overnight, and the media industries will not relinquish their stranglehold on culture without a fight.

Today, we are more apt to hear the opposite claim—that early adopters are racing ahead of technological developments. No sooner is a new technology—say, Google Maps—released to the public than diverse grassroots communities begin to tinker with it, expanding its functionality, hacking its code, and pushing it into a more participatory direction. Indeed, many industry leaders argue that the main reason that television cannot continue to operate in the same old ways is that the broadcasters are losing younger viewers, who expect greater influence over the media they consume. Speaking at MIT in April 2004, Betsy Frank, executive vice president for research and planning at MTV Networks, described these consumers as "media-actives" whom she characterized as "the group of people born since the mid-70s who've never known a world without cable television, the vcr, or the internet, who have never had to settle for forced choice or least objectionable program, who grew up with a 'what I want when I want it' view attitude towards media, and as a result, take a much more active role in their media choices."[10] Noting that "their fingerprints are on the remote," she said that the media industry was scrambling to make sense of and respond to sharp declines in television viewership among the highly valued 18–27 male demographic as they defected from television toward more interactive and participatory media channels.

This book has sought to document a moment of transition during which at least some segments of the public have learned what it means to live within a convergence culture. Betsy Frank and other industry thinkers still tend to emphasize changes that are occurring within individuals, whereas this book's argument is that the greatest changes are occurring within consumption communities. The biggest change may be the shift from individualized and personalized media consumption toward consumption as a networked practice.

Personalized media was one of the ideals of the digital revolution in the early 1990s: digital media was going to "liberate" us from the "tyranny" of mass media, allowing us to consume only content we found personally meaningful. Conservative ideologue turned digital theorist George Gilder argues that the intrinsic properties of the computer pushed toward ever more decentralization and personalization. Compared to the one-size-fits-all diet of the broadcast networks, the coming media age would be a "feast of niches and specialties."[11] An era of customized and interactive content, he argues, would appeal to our highest ambitions and not our lowest, as we enter "a new age of individualism."[12] Consider Gilder's ideal of "first choice media" as yet another model for how we might democratize television.

By contrast, this book has argued that convergence encourages participation and collective intelligence, a view nicely summed up by the *New York Times*'s Marshall Sella: "With the aid of the Internet, the loftiest dream for television is being realized: an odd brand of interactivity. Television began as a one-way street winding from producers to consumers, but that street is now becoming two-way. A man with one machine (a TV) is doomed to isolation, but a man with two machines (TV and a computer) can belong to a community."[13] Each of the case studies shows what happens when people who have access to multiple machines consume—and produce—media together, when they pool their insights and information, mobilize to promote common interests, and function as grassroots intermediaries ensuring that important messages and interesting content circulate more broadly. Rather than talking about personal media, perhaps we should be talking about communal media—media that become part of our lives as members of communities, whether experienced face-to-face at the most local level or over the Net.

Throughout the book, I have shown that convergence culture is enabling new forms of participation and collaboration. For Lévy, the power to participate within knowledge communities exists alongside the power that the nation-state exerts over its citizens and that corporations within commodity capitalism exert over its workers and consumers. For Lévy, at his most utopian, this emerging power to participate serves as a strong corrective to those traditional sources of power, though they will also seek ways to turn it toward their own ends. We are just learning how to exercise that power—individually and collectively—and we are still fighting to define the terms under which we will be allowed to participate. Many fear this power; others embrace it. There are no guarantees that we will use our new power any more responsibly than nation-states or corporations have exercised theirs. We are trying to hammer out the ethical codes and social contracts that will determine how we will relate to one another just as we are trying to determine how this power will insert itself into the entertainment system or into the political process. Part of what we must do is figure out how—and why—groups with different backgrounds, agendas, perspectives, and knowledge can listen to one another and work together toward the common good. We have a lot to learn.

Right now, we are learning how to apply these new participatory skills through our relation to commercial entertainment—or, more precisely, right now some groups of early adopters are testing the waters and mapping out directions where many more of us are apt to follow. These skills are being applied to popular culture first for two reasons: on the one hand, because the stakes are so low; and on the other, because playing with popular culture is a lot more fun than playing with more serious matters. Yet, as we saw in looking at Campaign 2004, what we learn through spoiling *Survivor* or remaking *Star Wars* may quickly get applied to political activism or education or the workplace.

In the late 1980s and early 1990s, cultural scholars, myself included, depicted media fandom as an important test site for ideas about active consumption and grassroots creativity. We were drawn toward the idea of "fan culture" as operating in the shadows of, in response to, as well as an alternative to commercial culture. Fan culture was defined through the appropriation and transformation of materials borrowed from mass culture; it was the application of folk culture practices to mass culture content.[14] Across the past decade, the Web has brought these consumers from the margins of the media industry into the spotlight; research into fandom has been embraced by important thinkers in the legal and business communities. What might once have been seen as "rogue readers" are now Kevin Roberts's "inspirational consumers." Participation is understood as part of the normal ways that media operate, while the current debates center around the terms of our participation. Just as studying fan culture helped us to understand the innovations that occur on the fringes of the media industry, we may also want to look at the structures of fan communities as showing us new ways of thinking about citizenship and collaboration. The political effects of these fan communities come not simply through the production and circulation of new ideas (the critical reading of favorite texts) but also through access to new social structures (collective intelligence) and new models of cultural production (participatory culture).

Have I gone too far? Am I granting too much power here to these consumption communities? Perhaps. But keep in mind that I am not really trying to predict the future. I want to avoid the kind of grand claims about the withering away of mass media institutions that make the rhetoric of the digital revolution seem silly a decade later. Rather, I am trying to point toward the democratic potentials found in some contemporary cultural trends. There is nothing inevitable about the outcome. Everything is up for grabs. Pierre Lévy described his ideal of collective intelligence as a "realizable utopia," and so it is. I think of myself as a critical utopian. As a utopian, I want to identify possibilities within our culture that might lead toward a better, more just society. My experiences as a fan have changed how I think about media politics, helping me to look for and promote unrealized potentials rather than reject out of hand anything that doesn't rise to my standards. Fandom, after all, is born of a balance between fascination and frustration: if media content didn't fascinate us, there would be no desire to engage with it; but if it didn't frustrate us on some level, there would be no drive to rewrite or remake it. Today, I hear a great deal of frustration about the state of our media culture, yet surprisingly few people talk about how we might rewrite it.

But pointing to those opportunities for change is not enough in and of itself. One must also identify the various barriers that block the realization of those possibilities and look for ways to route around them. Having a sense of what a more ideal society looks like gives one a yardstick for determining what we must do to achieve our goals. Here, this book has offered specific case studies of groups who are already achieving some of the promises of collective intelligence or of a more participatory culture. I do not mean for us to read these groups as typical of the average consumer (if such a thing exists in an era of niche media and fragmented culture). Rather, we should read these case studies as demonstrations of what it is possible to do in the context of convergence culture.

This approach differs dramatically from what I call critical pessimism. Critical pessimists, such as media critics Mark Crispin Miller, Noam Chomsky, and Robert McChesney, focus primarily on the obstacles to achieving a more democratic society. In the process, they often exaggerate the power of big media in order to frighten readers into taking action. I don't disagree with their concern about media concentration, but the way they frame the debate is self-defeating insofar as it disempowers consumers even as it seeks to mobilize them. Far too much media reform rhetoric rests on melodramatic discourse about victimization and vulnerability, seduction and manipulation, "propaganda machines" and "weapons of mass deception." Again and again, this version of the media reform movement has ignored the complexity of the public's relationship to popular culture and sided with those opposed to a more diverse and participatory culture. The politics of critical utopianism is founded on a notion of empowerment; the politics of critical pessimism on a politics of victimization. One focuses on what we are doing with media, and the other on what media is doing to us. As with previous revolutions, the media reform movement is gaining momentum at a time when people are starting to feel more empowered, not when they are at their weakest.

Media concentration is a very real problem that potentially stifles many of the developments I have been describing across this book. Concentration is bad because it stifles competition and places media industries above the demands of their consumers. Concentration is bad because it lowers diversity—important in terms of popular culture, essential in terms of news. Concentration is bad because it lowers the incentives for companies to negotiate with their consumers and raises the barriers to their participation. Big concentrated media can ignore their audience (at least up to a point); smaller niche media must accommodate us.

That said, the fight over media concentration is only one struggle that should concern media reformers. The potentials of a more participatory media culture are also worth fighting for. Right now, convergence culture is throwing media into flux, expanding the opportunities for grassroots groups to speak back to the mass media. Put all of our efforts into battling the conglomerates and this window of opportunity will have passed. That is why it is so important to fight against the corporate copyright regime, to argue against censorship and moral panic that would pathologize these emerging forms of participation, to publicize the best practices of these online communities, to expand access and participation to groups that are otherwise being left behind, and to promote forms of media literacy education that help all children to develop the skills needed to become full participants in their culture.

If early readers are any indication, the most controversial claim in this book may be my operating assumption that increasing participation in popular culture is a good thing. Too many critical pessimists are still locked into the old politics of culture jamming. Resistance becomes an end in and of itself rather than a tool to ensure cultural diversity and corporate responsibility. The debate keeps getting framed as if the only true alternative were to opt out of media altogether and live in the woods, eating acorns and lizards and reading only books published on recycled paper by small alternative presses. But what would it mean to tap media power for our own purposes? Is ideological and aesthetic purity really more valuable than transforming our culture?

A politics of participation starts from the assumption that we may have greater collective bargaining power if we form consumption communities. Consider the example of the Sequential Tarts. Started in 1997, www.sequentialtart.com serves as an advocacy group for female consumers frustrated by their historical neglect or patronizing treatment by the comics industry. Marcia Allas, the current editor of Sequential Tart, explained: "In the early days we wanted to change the apparent perception of the female reader of comics. . . . We wanted to show what we already knew—that the female audience for comics, while probably smaller than the male audience, is both diverse and has a collectively large disposable income."[15] In her study of Sequential Tart, scholar and sometime contributor Kimberly M. De Vries argues that the group self-consciously rejects the negative stereotypes about female comics readers constructed by men in and around the comics industry but also the well-meaning but equally constraining stereotypes constructed by the first generation of feminist critics of comics.[16] The Sequential Tarts defend the pleasures women take in comics even as they critique negative representations of women. The Web zine combines interviews with comics creators, retailers, and industry leaders, reviews of current publications, and critical essays about gender and comics. It showcases industry practices that attract or repel women, spotlights the work of smaller presses that often fell through the cracks, and promotes books that reflect their readers' tastes and interests. The Sequential Tarts are increasingly courted by publishers or individual artists who feel they have content that female readers might embrace and have helped to make the mainstream publishers more attentive to this often underserved market.

The Sequential Tarts represent a new kind of consumer advocacy group—one that seeks to diversify content and make mass media more responsive to its consumers. This is not to say that commercial media will ever truly operate according to democratic principles. Media companies don't need to share our ideals in order to change their practices. What will motivate the media companies is their own economic interests. What will motivate consumer-based politics will be our shared cultural and political interests. But we can't change much of anything if we are not on speaking terms with people inside the media industry. A politics of confrontation must give way to one focused on tactical collaboration. The old model, which many wisely dismissed, was that consumers vote with their pocketbooks. The new model is that we are collectively changing the nature of the marketplace, and in so doing we are pressuring companies to change the products they are creating and the ways they relate to their consumers.

We still do not have any models for what a mature, fully realized knowledge culture would look like. But popular culture may provide us with prototypes. A case in point is Warren Ellis's comic-book series, *Global Frequency*. Set in the near future, *Global Frequency* depicts a multiracial, multinational organization of ordinary people who contribute their services on an ad hoc basis. As Ellis explains, "You could be sitting there watching the news and suddenly hear an unusual cell phone tone, and within moments you might see your neighbor leaving the house in a hurry, wearing a jacket or a shirt with the distinctive Global Frequency symbol . . . or, hell, your girlfriend might answer the phone . . . and promise to explain later. . . . Anyone could be on the Global Frequency, and you'd never know until they got the call."[17] Ellis rejects the mighty demigods and elite groups of the superhero tradition and instead depicts the twenty-first-century equivalent of a volunteer fire department. Ellis conceived of the story in the wake of September 11 as an alternative to calls for increased state power and paternalistic constraints on communications: *Global Frequency* doesn't imagine the government saving its citizens from whatever Big Bad is out there. Rather, as Ellis explains, "*Global Frequency* is about us saving ourselves." Each issue focuses on a different set of characters in a different location, examining what it means for *Global Frequency* members personally and professionally to contribute their labor to a cause larger than themselves. The only recurring characters are those at the communications hub who contact the volunteers. Once *Frequency* participants are called into action, most of the key decisions get made on site as the volunteers are allowed to act on their localized knowledge. Most of the challenges come, appropriately enough, from the debris left behind by the collapse of the military-industrial complex and the end of the cold war—"The bad mad things in the dark that the public never found out about." In other words, the citizen soldiers use distributed knowledge to overcome the dangers of government secrecy.

Ellis's Global Frequency Network closely mirrors what journalist and digital activist Howard Rheingold has to say about smart mobs: "Smart mobs consist of people who are able to act in concert even if they don't know each other. The people who make up smart mobs co-operate in ways never before possible because they carry devices that possess both communication and computing capabilities. . . . Groups of people using these tools will gain new forms of social power."[18] In Manila and in Madrid, activists, using cell phones, were able to rally massive numbers of supporters in opposition to governments who might otherwise have controlled discourse on the mass media; these efforts resulted in transformations of power. In Boston, we are seeing home schoolers use these same technologies to organize field trips on the fly that deliver dozens of kids and their parents to a museum or historic site in a matter of a few hours.

Other writers, such as science fiction writer Cory Doctorow, describe such groups as "adhocracies." The polar opposite of a bureaucracy, an adhocracy is an organization characterized by a lack of hierarchy. In it, each person contributes to confronting a particular problem as needed based on his or her knowledge and abilities, and leadership roles shift as tasks change. An adhocracy, thus, is a knowledge culture that turns information into action. Doctorow's science fiction novel *Down and Out in the Magic Kingdom* depicts a future when the fans run Disney World, public support becomes the most important kind of currency, and debates about popular culture become the focus of politics.[19]

Ellis's vision of the Global Frequency Network and Doctorow's vision of a grassroots Disney World are far out there—well beyond anything we've seen in the real world yet. But fans put some of what they learned from *Global Frequency* into action: tapping a range of communications channels to push the networks and production company to try to get a television series on the air.[20] Consider this to be another example of what it would mean to "democratize television." Mark Burnett, *Survivor*'s executive producer, had taken an option on adopting the comic books for television; Warner Bros. had already announced plans to air *Global Frequency* as a midseason replacement, which then got postponed and later canceled. A copy of the series pilot was leaked on the Internet, circulating as an illegal download on BitTorrent, where it became the focus of a grassroots effort to get the series back into production. John Rogers, the show's head writer and producer, said that the massive response to the never-aired series was giving the producers leverage to push for the pilot's distribution on DVD and potentially to sell the series to another network. Studio and network executives predictably cited concerns about what the consumers were doing:

"Whether the pilot was picked up or not, it is still the property of Warner Bros. Entertainment and we take the protection of all of our intellectual property seriously. . . . While Warner Bros. Entertainment values
feedback from consumers, copyright infringement is not a productive
way to try to influence a corporate decision." Rogers wrote about his
encounters with the *Global Frequency* fans in his blog: "It changes the
way I'll do my next project. . . . I would put my pilot out on the internet
in a heartbeat. Want five more? Come buy the boxed set." Rogers's
comments invite us to imagine a time when small niches of consumers
who are willing to commit their money to a cause might ensure the
production of a minority-interest program. From a producer's perspective, such a scheme would be attractive since television series are made
at a loss for the first several seasons until the production company ac-
cumulates enough episodes to sell a syndication package. DVD lowers
that risk by allowing producers to sell the series one season at a time
and even to package and sell unaired episodes. Selling directly to the
consumer would allow producers to recoup their costs even earlier in
the production cycle.

People in the entertainment industry are talking a lot these days
about what *Wired* reporter Chris Anderson calls "The Long Tail."[21] Anderson argues that as distribution costs lower, as companies can keep
more and more backlist titles in circulation, and as niche communities
can use the Web to mobilize around titles that satisfy their particular
interests, then the greatest profit will be made by those companies that
generate the most diverse content and keep it available at the most reasonable prices. If Anderson is right, then niche-content stands a much
better chance of turning a profit than ever before. The Long Tail model
assumes an increasingly savvy media consumer, one who will actively
seek out content of interest and who will take pride in being able to rec-
ommend that content to friends.

Imagine a subscription-based model in which viewers commit to
pay a monthly fee to watch a season of episodes delivered into their
homes via broadband. A pilot could be produced to test the waters,
and if the response looked positive, subscriptions could be sold for a
show that had gotten enough subscribers to defer the company's initial
production costs. Early subscribers would get a package price, others
would pay more on a pay-per-view basis, which would cover the next
phase of production. Others could buy access to individual episodes.
Distribution could be on a DVD mailed directly to your home or via

streaming media (perhaps you could simply download it onto your iPod).

It was the announcement that ABC-Disney was going to be offering recent episodes of cult television series (such as *Lost* and *Desperate Housewives*) for purchase and download via the Apple Music Store that really took these discussions to the next level. Other networks quickly followed with their own download packages. Within the first twenty days, there were more than a million television episodes downloaded. The video iPod seems emblematic of the new convergence culture—not because everyone believes the small screen of the iPod is the ideal vehicle for watching broadcast content but because the ability to download reruns on demand represents a major shift in the relationship between consumers and media content.

Writing in *Slate*, media analyst Ivan Askwith described some of the implications of television downloads:

> As iTunes and its inevitable competitors offer more broadcast-television content, producers . . . won't have to compromise their programs to meet broadcast requirements. Episode lengths can vary as needed, content can be darker, more topical, and more explicit. . . . Audiences already expect director's cuts and deleted scenes on DVDs. It's not hard to imagine that the networks might one day air a "broadcast cut" of an episode, then encourage viewers to download the longer, racier director's cut the next afternoon. . . . While DVDs now give viewers the chance to catch up between seasons, on-demand television will allow anyone to catch up at any time, quickly and legally. Producers will no longer have to choose between alienating new viewers with a complex storyline or alienating the established audience by rehashing details from previous episodes. . . . Direct downloads will give fans of endangered shows the chance to vote with their wallets while a show is still on the air. And when a program *does* go off the air, direct payments from fans might provide enough revenue to keep it in production as an online-only venture.[22]

Almost immediately, fans of canceled series, such as *The West Wing* and *Arrested Development*, have begun to embrace such a model as a way to sustain the shows' production, pledging money to support shows they want to watch.[23] Cult-television producers have begun to talk openly about bypassing the networks and selling their series directly to their most loyal consumers. One can imagine independent media producers using downloads as a way of distributing content that would never make it onto commercial television. And, of course, once you distribute via the Web, television instantly becomes global, paving the way for international producers to sell their content directly to American consumers. Google and Yahoo! began cutting deals with media producers in the hope that they might be able to profit from this new economy in television downloads. All of this came too late for *Global Frequency,* and so far the producers of *The West Wing* and *Arrested Development* have not trusted their fates to such a subscription-based model. Yet, many feel that sooner or later some producer will test the waters, much as ABC-Disney did with its video iPod announcement. And once again, there are likely to be many others waiting in the wings to pounce on the proposition once they can measure public response to the deal. What was once a fan-boy fantasy now seems closer and closer to reality.

While producers, analysts, and fans have used the fate of *Global Frequency* to explore how we might rethink the distribution of television content, the series premise also offers us some tools for thinking about the new kinds of knowledge communities that this book has discussed. If one wants to see a real-world example of something like the Global Frequency Network, take a look at the Wikipedia—a grassroots, multinational effort to build a free encyclopedia on the Internet written collaboratively from an army of volunteers, working in roughly two hundred different languages. So far, adhocracy principles have been embraced by the open-source movement, where software engineers worldwide collaborate on projects for the common good. The Wikipedia project represents the application of these open-source principles to the production and management of knowledge. The Wikipedia contains more than 1.6 million articles and receives around 60 million hits per day.[24]

Perhaps the most interesting and controversial aspect of the Wikipedia project has been the ways it shifts what counts as knowledge (from the kinds of topics sanctioned by traditional encyclopedias to a much broader range of topics relevant to specialized interest groups and subcultures) and the ways it shifts what counts as expertise (from recognized academic authorities to something close to Lévy's concept of collective intelligence). Some worry that the encyclopedia will contain much inaccurate information, but the Wikipedia community, at its best, functions as a self-correcting adhocracy. Any knowledge that gets posted can and most likely will be revised and corrected by other readers.

For this process to work, all involved must try for inclusiveness and respect diversity. The Wikipedia project has found it necessary to develop both a politics and an ethics—a set of community norms—about knowledge sharing:

> Probably, as we grow, nearly every view on every subject will (eventually) be found among our authors and readership. . . . But since Wikipedia is a community-built, international resource, we surely cannot expect our collaborators to agree in all cases, or even in many cases, on what constitutes human knowledge in a strict sense. . . . We must make an effort to present these conflicting theories fairly, without advocating any one of them. . . . When it is clear to readers that we do not expect them to adopt any particular opinion, this is conducive to our readers' feeling free to make up their own minds for themselves, and thus to encourage in them *intellectual independence.* So totalitarian governments and dogmatic institutions everywhere have reason to be opposed to Wikipedia. . . . We, the creators of Wikipedia, trust readers' competence to form their own opinions themselves. Texts that present the merits of multiple viewpoints fairly, without demanding that the reader accept any one of them, are liberating.[25]

You probably won't believe in the Wikipedia unless you try it, but the process works. The process works because more and more people are taking seriously their obligations as participants to the community as a whole: not everyone does so yet; we can see various flame wars as people with very different politics and ethics interact within the same knowledge communities. Such disputes often foreground those conflicting assumptions, forcing people to reflect more deeply on their choices. What was once taken for granted must now be articulated. What emerges might be called a moral economy of information: that is, a sense of mutual obligations and shared expectations about what constitutes good citizenship within a knowledge community.

We might think of fan fiction communities as the literary equivalent of the Wikipedia: around any given media property, writers are constructing a range of different interpretations that get expressed through stories. Sharing of these stories opens up new possibilities in the text. Here, individual contributions do not have to be neutral; participants simply have to agree to disagree, and, indeed, many fans come to value the sheer diversity of versions of the same characters and situations.

On the other hand, mass media has tended to use its tight control over intellectual property to rein in competing interpretations, resulting in a world where there is one official version. Such tight controls increase the coherence of the franchise and protect the producers' economic interests, yet the culture is impoverished through such regulation. Fan fiction repairs the damage caused by an increasingly privatized culture. Consider, for example, this statement made by a fan:

> What I love about fandom is the freedom we have allowed ourselves to create and recreate our characters over and over again. Fanfic rarely sits still. It's like a living, evolving thing, taking on its own life, one story building on another, each writer's reality bouncing off another's and maybe even melding together to form a whole new creation. . . . I find that fandom can be extremely creative because we have the ability to keep changing our characters and giving them a new life over and over. We can kill and resurrect them as often as we like. We can change their personalities and how they react to situations. We can take a character and make him charming and sweet or cold-blooded and cruel. We can give them an infinite, always-changing life rather than the single life of their original creation.[26]

Fans reject the idea of a definitive version produced, authorized, and regulated by some media conglomerate. Instead, fans envision a world where all of us can participate in the creation and circulation of central cultural myths. Here, the right to participate in the culture is assumed to be "the freedom we have allowed ourselves," not a privilege granted by a benevolent company, not something they are prepared to barter away for better sound files or free Web hosting. Fans also reject the studio's assumption that intellectual property is a "limited good," to be tightly controlled lest it dilute its value. Instead, they embrace an understanding of intellectual property as "shareware," something that accrues value as it moves across different contexts, gets retold in various ways, attracts multiple audiences, and opens itself up to a proliferation of alternative meanings.

Nobody is anticipating a point where all bureaucracies will become adhocracies. Concentrated power is apt to remain concentrated. But we will see adhocracy principles applied to more and more different kinds of projects. Such experiments thrive within convergence culture, which creates a context where viewers—individually and collectively—can reshape and recontextualize massmedia content. Most of this activity will occur around the edges of commercial culture through grassroots or niche media industries such as comics or games. On that scale, small groups like the Sequential Tarts can make a material difference. On that scale, entrepreneurs have an incentive to give their consumers greater opportunities to shape the content and participate in its distribution. As we move closer to the older and more mass market media industries, corporate resistance to grassroots participation increases: the stakes are too high to experiment, and the economic impact of any given consumption community lessens. Yet, within these media companies, there are still potential allies who for their own reasons may want to appeal to audience support to strengthen their hands in their negotiations around the boardroom table. A media industry struggling to hold on to its core audience in the face of competition from other media may be forced to take greater risks to accommodate consumer interests.

As we have seen across the book, convergence culture is highly generative: some ideas spread top down, starting with commercial media and being adopted and appropriated by a range of different publics as they spread outward across the culture. Others emerge bottom up from various sites of participatory culture and getting pulled into the mainstream if the media industries see some way of profiting from it. The power of the grassroots media is that it diversifies; the power of broadcast media is that it amplifies. That's why we should be concerned with the flow between the two: expanding the potentials for participation represents the greatest opportunity for cultural diversity. Throw away the powers of broadcasting and one has only cultural fragmentation. The power of participation comes not from destroying commercial culture but from writing over it, modding it, amending it, expanding it, adding greater diversity of perspective, and then recirculating it, feeding it back into the mainstream media.

Read in those terms, participation becomes an important political right. In the American context, one could argue that First Amendment protections of the right to speech, press, belief, and assembly represent a more abstract right to participate in a democratic culture. After all, the First Amendment emerged in the context of a thriving folk culture, where it was assumed that songs and stories would get retold many different times for many different purposes. The country's founding documents were written by men who appropriated the names of classical orators or mythic heroes. Over time, freedom of the press increasingly came to rest with those who could afford to buy printing presses. The emergence of new media technologies supports a democratic urge to allow more people to create and circulate media. Sometimes the media are designed to respond to mass media content—positively or negatively —and sometimes grassroots creativity goes places no one in the media industry could have imagined. The challenge is to rethink our understanding of the First Amendment to recognize this expanded opportunity to participate. We should thus regard those things that block participation —whether commercial or governmental—as important obstacles to route around if we are going to "democratize television" or any other aspect of our culture. We have identified some of those obstacles in the book, most centrally the challenges surrounding corporate control over intellectual property and the need for a clearer definition of the kinds of fair-use rights held by amateur artists, writers, journalists, and critics, who want to share work inspired or incited by existing media content.

Another core obstacle might be described as the participation gap. So far, much of the discussion of the digital divide has emphasized problems of access, seeing the issue primarily in technical terms—but a medium is more than a technology. As activists have sought a variety of means to broaden access to digital media, they have created a hodgepodge of different opportunities for participation. Some have extended access to these resources through the home, and others have limited, filtered, regulated access through schools and public libraries. Now, we need to confront the cultural factors that diminish the likelihood that different groups will participate. Race, class, language differences amplify these inequalities in opportunities for participation. One reason we see early adopters is not only that some groups feel more confidence in engaging with new technologies but also that some groups seem more comfortable going public with their views about culture.

Historically, public education in the United States was a product of the need to distribute the skills and knowledge necessary to train informed citizens. The participation gap becomes much more important as we think about what it would mean to foster the skills and knowledge needed by monitorial citizens: here, the challenge is not simply being able to read and write, but being able to participate in the deliberations over what issues matter, what knowledge counts, and what ways of knowing command authority and respect. The ideal of the in-formed citizen is breaking down because there is simply too much for any individual to know. The ideal of monitorial citizenship depends on developing new skills in collaboration and a new ethic of knowledge sharing that will allow us to deliberate together.[27]

Right now, people are learning how to participate in such knowledge cultures outside of any formal educational setting. Much of this learning takes place in the affinity spaces that are emerging around popular culture. The emergence of these knowledge cultures partially reflects the demands these texts place on consumers (the complexity of transmedia entertainment, for example), but they also reflect the de-mands consumers place on media (the hunger for complexity, the need for community, the desire to rewrite core stories). Many schools remain openly hostile to these kinds of experiences, continuing to promote autonomous problem solvers and self-contained learners. Here, un-authorized collaboration is cheating. As I finish writing this book, my own focus is increasingly being drawn toward the importance of media literacy education. Many media literacy activists still act as if the role of mass media had remained unchanged by the introduction of new media technologies. Media are read primarily as threats rather than as resources. More focus is placed on the dangers of manipulation rather than the possibilities of participation, on restricting access—turning off the television, saying no to Nintendo—rather than in expanding skills at deploying media for one's own ends, rewriting the core stories our culture has given us. One of the ways we can shape the future of media culture is by resisting such disempowering approaches to media literacy education. We need to rethink the goals of media education so that young people can come to think of themselves as cultural producers and participants and not simply as consumers, critical or otherwise. To achieve this goal, we also need media education for adults. Parents, for example, receive plenty of advice on whether they should allow their kids to have a television set in their room or how many hours a week they should allow their kids to consume media. Yet, they receive almost no advice on how they can help their kids build a meaningful relationship with media.

Welcome to convergence culture, where old and new media collide, where grassroots and corporate media intersect, where the power of the media producer and the power of the media consumer interact in unpredictable ways. Convergence culture is the future, but it is taking shape now. Consumers will be more powerful within convergence culture—but only if they recognize and use that power as both consumers and citizens, as full participants in our culture.

Afterword

Reflections on Politics in the Age of YouTube

Newscaster Anderson Cooper opened the Democratic CNN/YouTube debate with a warning to expect the unexpected: "Tonight is really something of an experiment. This is something we've never done before. What you're about to see is, well, it's untried. We are not exactly sure how this is going to work. The candidates on this stage don't know how it is going to work. Neither do their campaigns. And frankly we think that's a good thing."[1] The eight candidates seeking the Democratic Party's nomination for the presidency would face questions selected from more than 3,000 videos "average" citizens had submitted via YouTube. Speaking on NPR's *Talk of the Nation* a few days before, CNN executive producer David Bohrman stressed that the new format would give the American public "a seat at the table," reflecting a world where "everyone is one degree of separation away from a video camera."[2]

"Welcome to my Home, Candidates," said Chris of Portland, before demanding that the presidential hopefuls provide straight answers. Many of the questions came in the confessional form many associated with YouTube—speaking directly into a handheld camera from their own living rooms and kitchens. There were some powerful moments— a relief camp worker asking about Darfur, a man holding a semiautomatic weapon asking about gun control, a lesbian couple wondering about the candidates' perspective on gay marriage—and some questions on topics like the government's unsatisfactory response to Katrina, the minimum wage, and reparations for slavery which hadn't surfaced in previous debates.

Afterwards, most people only wanted to talk about the Snowman.

One short segment featured a claymation snowman talking about global warming, "the single most important issue to the snowmen of this country." As the video showed Junior's frightened face, the Snowman

271

asked, "As president, what will you do to ensure that my son will live a full and happy life?" The candidates chuckled. Cooper explained, "It's a funny video. It's a serious question," before directing the query to Dennis Kucinich. The serious-minded Kucinich drew links between "global warming" and "global warring," explaining how the military defense of oil interests increased American reliance on fossil fuels and describing his own green-friendly policies: "We don't have to have our snowmen melting, and the planet shouldn't be melting either." Follow up questions pursued other environmental policy issues.

CNN ended the broadcast by announcing a future debate involving the GOP candidates, but the status of this debate was far from resolved. By the end of the week, most of the front-runners for the Republican nomination were refusing to participate. Former Massachusetts governor Mitt Romney put a face on their discomfort: "I think the presidency ought to be held at a higher level than having to answer questions from a snowman."[3] CNN's Bohrman deflected criticism of this particular selection: "I think running for president is serious business . . . but we do want to know that the president has a sense of humor."[4]

Many bloggers also argued that the Snowman demeaned citizens' participation in the debates: "By heavily moderating the questions, by deliberately choosing silly, fluffy, or offbeat videos to show the nation, CNN is reinforcing the old media idea that the Internet entertains, but does not offer real, serious discussion or insight."[5] There would be a CNN/YouTube GOP debate, but behind the scenes negotiations delayed it and substantially toned down the content.

In this afterword, I will use the Snowman controversy as a point of entry for a broader investigation into the role of Internet parody during the pre-primary season in the 2008 presidential campaign. This debate about debates raises questions about the redistribution of media power, the authenticity of grassroots media, and the appropriateness of parody as a mode of political rhetoric. Parody videos, produced both by the public and by the campaigns, played an unprecedented role in shaping public perceptions of this unusually crowded field of candidates. By studying YouTube as a site of civic discourse, I want to better understand how convergence, collective intelligence, and participatory culture are impacting the political process.

I will pick up where chapter 6, "Photoshop for Democracy," left off—with a call for us to rethink the cultural underpinnings of democracy in response to an era of profound and prolonged media change.[6] The rise of networking computing, and the social and cultural practices which have grown up around it, have expanded the ability of average citizens to express our ideas, circulate them before a larger public, and pool information in the hopes of transforming our society. To do so, however, we have to apply skills we have acquired through our play with popular culture and direct them towards the challenges of participatory democracy. Chapter 6 showed how Howard Dean's so-called cybercampaign actually unfolded across multiple media channels, new and old, commercial and grassroots. I argued that the public was seizing control over the campaign process—for better and for worse—and speculated about new forms of political rhetoric that blurred our roles as citizens, consumers, and fans. A closer look at the role parody videos played in American politics in 2007 may help us to understand how we are or are not realizing the potentials of this new communication environment. Such videos give us an alternative perspective on what democracy might look like, though we have a long way to go before we can achieve anything like a revitalized public sphere in the online world. As Anderson Cooper suggests, none of us knows where this will take us—and for the moment, at least, that's a good thing.

Turd Blossom vs. The Obamatar

Debates about digital democracy have long been shaped by the fantasy of a "digital revolution," with its assumptions that old media (or in this case, the old political establishment) would be displaced by the rise of new participants, whether new media startups confronting old media conglomerates, bloggers displacing journalists, or cybercandidates overcoming political machines. The same month that CNN was hosting the debates, *Mother Jones* ran a cover story on the "Politics 2.0 Smackdown," thus linking the upcoming campaign to larger conversation about how the participatory platforms and social networks of "web 2.0" were impacting culture and commerce. The *Mother Jones* cover juxtaposes Karl Rove, dressed like an old-style politico, with Barack Obama, represented as a video game avatar. The caption reads, "Turd Blossom vs. The Obamatar," while an asterisked comment tells us that "Turd Blossom" was George W. Bush's nickname for his longtime political adviser and "The Obamatar" was a phrase the magazine coined. *Mother Jones* summed up the stakes: "Forget party bosses in smoky backrooms—netroots evangelists and web consultants predict a wave of popular democracy as fundraisers meet on MySpace, YouTubers crank out attack ads, bloggers do oppo research, and cell-phone-activated flash mobs hold miniconventions in Second Life. The halls of power will belong to whoever can tap the passions of the online masses. That kid with a laptop has Karl Rove quaking in his boots. And if you believe that, we've got some leftover Pets.com stock to sell to you."[7] *Mother Jones* reproduced the logic of a "digital revolution," even as it expressed skepticism that the changes would be as dramatic as advocates predicted.

This depiction of media change as a zero-sum battle between old powerbrokers and insurgents distracts us from the real changes occurring in our media ecology. Rather than displacing old media, what I call convergence culture is shaped by increased contact and collaboration between established and emerging media institutions, expansion of the number of players producing and circulating media, and the flow of content across multiple platforms and networks. The collaboration between CNN (an icon of old media power) and YouTube (an icon of new media power) might be understood as one such attempt to work through the still unstable and "untried" relations between these different media systems. Promoters and pundits alike represented the CNN/YouTube debates as a decisive event, raising expectations that opening up a channel for public participation might broaden the political agenda, rewrite the campaign rhetoric, or reveal the candidates' authentic personalities. Yet, it also represented a temporary tactical alliance between old and new media players on the eve of an important political struggle.

YouTube has emerged as a key site for the production and distribution of grassroots media—ground zero, as it were, in the disruption in the operations of commercial mass media brought about by the emergence of new forms of participatory culture. Yet, we need to understand YouTube as part of a larger cultural economy. First, YouTube represents the meeting ground between a range of different grassroots communities, each of which has been producing indie media for some time, but are now brought together by this shared media portal. By providing a distribution channel for amateur and semiprofessional media content, YouTube incites new expressive activities—whether through formal events like the CNN/YouTube debates or on a day-to-day basis. Having a shared site means that these productions get much greater visibility than they would if distributed by separate and isolated portals. It also means that they are exposed to each other's activities, learn quickly from new developments, and often find themselves collaborating across communities in unpredictable ways. YouTube has become a simple signifier for these alternative sites of production, creating a context for us to talk about the changes taking place.

Second, YouTube functions as a media archive where amateur curators scan the media environment, searching for meaningful bits of content, and bringing them to a larger public (through legal and illegal means). They can do this in response to mass media content, as for example they focused much more attention on Stephen Colbert's appearance at the Washington Press Club dinner, or to amateur content, as in the case of a home video recording of candidate George Allen's racist dismissal of a South Asian cameraman which effectively foreclosed his entry into the 2008 presidential race. Collectors are sharing vintage materials; fans are remixing contemporary content; and everyone has the ability to freeze a moment out of the "flow" of mass media and try to focus greater attention on what just happened.

Third, YouTube functions in relation to a range of other social networks; its content gets spread via blogs and LiveJournal entries, via Facebook and MySpace, where it gets reframed for different publics and becomes the focal point for discussions. YouTube content might be described as spreadable media, a term which shares some of the connotations of "memes" or "viral video," both commonly used terms, but which carries with it a greater sense of agency on the part of the user. Metaphors from genetics or virology still carry with them notions of culture as self-replicating or infectious, whereas thinking of YouTube content as spreadable focuses attention on both properties of texts and the activities of participants. Talking about YouTube content as spreadable also enables us to talk about the importance of distribution in the creation of value and the reshaping of meaning within YouTube culture.

Participation occurs at three distinct levels here—those of production, selection, and distribution. Each of these functions and relationships plays a role in the following analysis. None of these activities is new, even in the context of digital media, but YouTube was the first to bring all three functions together into a single platform and direct so much attention on the role of everyday people in this changed media landscape. Skeptical readers of this book have argued that in focusing so much attention on fans, I remain in the borderlands of the culture. They miss two points: first, in the age of convergence culture, there may no longer be a strong mainstream but rather a range of different niche sites of media production and consumption; second, in the cultural context of YouTube, what might once have felt like fringe activities are increasingly normalized, with more and more people routinely checking out and discussing content produced by amateur media makers and with mass media institutions routinely reworking their practices to incorporate this alternative site of cultural activity. The CNN / YouTube debates might be seen as an illustration of the negotiations now occurring between these alternative models for how culture gets produced and distributed.

Romney framed his distaste for the Snowman in terms of issues of respect, asserting that there was a proper way to speak to someone who wants to be the next president of the United States. Senior newscaster Dan Rather, however, argued that behind-the-scenes negotiations reflected more generalized anxieties about questions from unexpected quarters: "Candidates do hate, genuinely hate, audience participation, because they like to control the environment."[8] For Romney, the Snowman was a haunting specter of all that worried him about the new digital culture. During his press conference, for example, he mistakenly linked YouTube to public concerns about sexual predators, confusing conservative criticisms against the multimedia portal with those concerning MySpace.[9] Yet, Romney's campaign had itself launched an effort to get his supporters to create and circulate their own political advertisements.[10] None of the candidates—Republican or Democratic—could afford to ignore any potential platform that might allow them to reach undecideds or mobilize supporters. Techniques that seemed radical when deployed by the Howard Dean campaign four years earlier were now taken for granted by the most mainstream candidates; even establishment figures were experimenting with web 2.0 tools to increase their visibility and lower costs. Candidates were adopting avatars and moving their message into Second Life and other virtual worlds; they were using social network sites like MySpace and Facebook to rally their supporters, giving them means to contact each other and organize "meetups" without having to go through the centralized campaigns; candidates were sending out regular podcasts and Webcast messages to their supporters. Romney and the other candidates might fear the disruptive impact of web 2.0, but none of them was willing to forgo its affordances, and some candidates—Ron Paul for example—thrived online even as they failed to generate any traction through traditional media channels.

Bloggers and netizens often distrusted the YouTube / CNN debates for the opposite reason: because CNN's role in selecting the final questions protected mainstream media's historical gatekeeping and agenda-setting functions. Writing in *The Huffington Post*, media reform leader Marty Kaplan dismissed what he called the "faux populism" of the "Rube-Tube" debate as an act of corporate ventriloquism: "The notion that the CNN/YouTube debate represents a grass-roots triumph of the Internet age is laughable. The 4,000+ videos are pawns; the questioners are involuntary shills, deployed by the network producers in no less deliberate, calculating and manipulative a fashion as the words and stories fed by teleprompters into anchors' mouths."[11]

The Power to Negate and the Power to Marginalize

Far from advocating digital revolution, CNN's Bohrman openly dismissed new media platforms as "immature" and questioned whether the user-moderated practices of YouTube would have been adequate to the task of determining what questions candidates should address, given how easily such processes could be "gamed." Bohrman often cited what he saw as the public's fascination with "inappropriate" questions: "If you would have taken the most-viewed questions last time, the top question would have been whether Arnold Schwarzenegger was a cyborg sent to save the planet Earth. The second-most-viewed video question was: Will you convene a national meeting on UFOs?"[12]

Here, the CNN producer showed limited understanding of the role which parody was going to play in the buildup to this presidential campaign. Tongue-in-check questions about cyborgs and aliens allowed many to thumb their noses at the official gatekeepers and their anticipated dismay at being "forced" to put such content onto the public airwaves. Such gestures reflect a growing public skepticism about old media power as well as uncertainty about how far to trust emerging (though still limited and often trivial) efforts to solicit our participation. We might link this phenomenon back to the discussion of the Vote for the Worst movement among *American Idol* fans, for example. Given a toe-hold into mass media, the public seems to take great pleasure in its ability to negate its normal operating procedures, forcing the networks to act against their own interests if they wish to preserve the credibility of these mechanisms for popular participation.

Some such material made it into the final broadcast but only as part of an opening segment in which a smirking Cooper lectured the public about videos that did not belong on national television: "Dressing up in costume was probably not the best way to get taken seriously." Here, participatory culture's power to negate ran up against old media's power to marginalize. Old media still defines which forms of cultural expression are mainstream through its ability to amplify the impact of some user-generated content while labeling other submissions out of bounds. On YouTube, there were thousands of submissions, each equally accessible; on CNN, a corporate selection process had narrowed the field to maybe thirty questions; and the news coverage of the debates might focus on only three or four (maybe only the Snowman video). At each step along the way, the field narrowed, but those messages which survived gain greater attention.

Because the public openly submitted their videos through a participatory media channel like YouTube, the selection process leaves traces. Even if we can't know what happened within the closed-door meetings of the CNN producers, we can see which submitted questions got left out, which issues did not get addressed, and which groups did not get represented. The thousands of posted videos drew significant traffic to YouTube prior to the debates, suggesting that the promise of greater participation did generate greater public interest than more traditional debates.

Afterwards, some who felt excluded or marginalized deployed YouTube as a platform to criticize the news network. anonymousAmerican, a rotund man in a Mexican wrestling mask who speaks with a working-class accent, posted a video labeled "Fuck You, CNN." He describes his anger over the fact that CNN deployed his masked face but not his words: "This could lead the public to imagine that my question was insulting or irrelevant. We all know that CNN would never air anything insulting such as a host asking the only Moslem member of Congress if he's a terrorist or irrelevant like a very old man spending his show interviewing people like Paris Hilton (That would be Larry King, wouldn't it?)." Links lead to the question he submitted (calling for the immediate withdrawal from Iraq) and other political videos concerning the Bush administration's crackdown on civil liberties. His mask allows him both to speak as an everyman figure and to represent visually the process of political repression; it also links his videos to the Luchador tradition, where Mexican wrestlers often used their masked personas to speak out against social injustice.[13] CNN may have taken away his voice, but YouTube offered him a way to speak back to that silencing power.

The Birth of a Snowman

Writing in *The Wealth of Networks*, Harvard law professor Yochai Benkler suggests, "What institutions and decisions are considered 'legitimate' and worthy of compliance or participation; what courses of action are attractive; what forms of interaction with others are considered appropriate—these are all understandings negotiated from within a set of shared frames of meaning."[14] All involved in contemporary media recognize that our future culture will be more participatory, but there is widespread disagreement about the terms of our participation. A range of public controversies are erupting around the terms of our participation—struggles over intellectual property and file sharing, legal battles between media producers and fans, conflicts between web 2.0 companies and the communities they serve, or disagreements over the nature of citizen participation in televised debates. As average citizens acquire the ability to meaningfully impact the flow of ideas, these new forms of participatory culture change how we see ourselves ("through new eyes—the eyes of someone who could actually interject a thought, a criticism, or a concern into the public debate") and how we see our society (as subject to change as a consequence of our deliberations).[15] What "pissed off" anonymousAmerican at CNN was the way the debates had raised expectations of greater citizen participation and then offered up a high-tech version of *America's Funniest Home Videos*. Such heightened expectations motivated thousands to grab their camcorders or cell phones and produce videos for submission. Some were making their first videos, but many more had acquired their skills as media producers through more mundane and everyday practices, through their production of home movies or their participation in various fan communities, or through media sharing sites.

The strange history of the Snowman illustrates this process at work. The Snowman video was produced by Nathan and Greg Hamel, two brothers from Minneapolis.[16] Their debate video repurposed animations from an earlier, less-politically-oriented video showing a samurai attacking Billiam the Snowman while his young child watched in horror. The name of the Snowman, his high-pitched voice, and the video's aggressive slapstick paid homage to the Mr. Bill videos originally produced by Walter Williams for *Saturday Night Live* in the 1970s. The Mr. Bill segments represented an earlier chapter in the history of the networks' relationship to user-generated content: Williams had submitted a Super-8 reel in response to *Saturday Night Live*'s request for home movies during its first season.[17] The impressed producers hired Williams as a full-time writer, resulting in more than twenty subsequent Mr. Bill segments, all maintaining the low-tech look and feel of his original amateur productions. Williams's subsequent career might have provided the Hamel brothers with a model for their next step—from broad slapstick towards political satire. Starting in 2004, Williams deployed Mr. Bill as a spokesperson in a series of public service announcements about environmental issues (specifically, the threat to Louisiana wetlands).[18]

The Hamel brothers were surely surprised that Billiam had become the focal point for responses to the debate. Empowered by the media attention, they produced a series of other videos confronting Romney, the man who refused to debate a snowman. While these subsequent videos were not incorporated into the GOP debate, they did attract other media attention. When interviewed by CNN about a video in which Billiam tells Romney to "lighten up slightly," the brothers used their explanation to direct attention at a growing controversy within the blogosphere. During a campaign appearance in New Hampshire, Romney had been photographed holding a supporter's sign, which read "No to Obama, Osama, and Chelsea's Mama" (part of a larger effort to play on xenophobic concerns about Barack's "foreign sounding" name).[19] Another amateur videomaker had captured a confrontation at an Iowa campaign appearance where Romney told a critic of the sign to "lighten up slightly," insisting that he has little control over what his supporters might bring to an event.[20] Bloggers were circulating the video of what they saw as a disingenuous response. This Romney video fits into a larger history of footage captured by amateur videomakers that reached greater public visibility via YouTube and sometimes found its way into mainstream coverage. For example, one popular video showed John McCain joking with supporters, singing "Bomb, Bomb, Bomb Iran" in imitation of a classic rock-and-roll tune. The Hamel brothers were using their five minutes of fame to direct the media's attention onto a brewing controversy that might further undermine Romney's credibility.

Over just a few weeks, the Hamel brothers progressed from sophomoric skit comedy to progressively more savvy interventions into media politics, demonstrating a growing understanding of how media travels through YouTube and how YouTube intersects broadcast media. As they did so, they formed an informal alliance with other "citizen journalists" and inspired a range of other amateur producers to create their own snowman videos, including those which included a man wearing a snowman mask, or which recycled footage from old Christmas specials, in hopes that they might get caught up in Billiam's media coverage.

CNN had urged the public to find "creative" new ways to express their concerns, yet the producers clearly saw many of the more colorful videos as the civic equivalent of *Let's Make a Deal*—as so many people in colorful costumes huckstering to get on television. Some certainly were hungry for personal fame, but others were using parody to dramatize legitimate policy concerns. In the case of the Snowman, his question about global warming was not outside the frames of the current political debate, but the use of the animated Snowman as a spokesperson broke with the rationalist discourse that typically characterizes Green politics. The Snowman parody spoofed two of American politics' most cherished rhetorical moves. Snowmen are represented here as one more identity politics group; snowmen are made to "embody" larger societal concerns. We might compare Billiam's attempt to speak about the environment on behalf of snowmen with the oft-cited image of Iron Eyes Cody weeping as a Native American over the littering of the American landscape during the Keep America Beautiful campaign produced for the 1971 Earth Day celebration, or for that matter the ways that Al Gore deployed drowning polar bears to dramatize the threat of global warming in *An Inconvenient Truth*. The video also spoofs the ways both conservative and progressive groups make policy appeals in the name of protecting innocent children from some perceived threat.[21] We might link Billiam's frightened offspring back to the famous LBJ spot depicting a little girl plucking the petals from a daisy over the soundtrack of a countdown to a nuclear bomb blast.

Presidential candidates have long deployed animations and dramatizations as part of the rhetoric of their advertising campaigns, so why should voters be prohibited from using such images in addressing candidates? What's different, perhaps, is the way such videos appropriate popular culture contents (Mr. Bill) as vehicles for their message. As Benkler notes, mass media has so dominated American culture for the past century that people are necessarily going to draw on it as a shared vocabulary as they learn how to use participatory media towards their own ends: "One cannot make new culture ex nihilo. We are, as we are today, as cultural beings, occupying a set of common symbols and stories that are heavily based on the outputs of the industrial period. If we are to make this culture our own, render it legible, and make it into a new platform for our needs and conversations today, we must find a way to cut, paste, and remix present culture."[22]

Parody represents one important mode for reworking mass media materials for alternative purposes. Television commercials, for example, often provide simple, easily recognized templates for representing ideological concerns. A group called SmallMediaXL produced a series of spoofs on the differences between Republicans and Democrats modeled on a popular Mac/PC campaign. While the Apple commercials represent the PC as a stuffed-shirt middle manager and the Mac as a free-thinking hipster, SmallMediaXL depicts Republicans as "very good at looking after the interests of big business" and the Democrats as "being better at the people stuff." Here, the Mac/PC template invites us to comparison shop for presidential candidates, creating new personas who dramatize the differences between the two major parties and the consequences of their policies. No doubt, the producers turned to advertising images and rhetoric to express their critiques, recognizing that the power of Madison Avenue had already ensured that this iconography bore deep cultural resonances and would be widely recognized by a range of potential viewers.

Parody in High Places

In "The Spectacularization of Everyday Life," Denise Mann discusses the ways that early television deployed parody to signal its uncomfortable relationship to Hollywood glamour, positioning its technology—and its own stars—as closer to the public than their cinema counterparts.[23] Early television often spoofed the gap between Hollywood and reality, making fun of its overdramatic style and cliché situations, depicting television characters (such as Lucy in *I Love Lucy*) as fans who want but are denied access to film stars. In the process, these programs helped to negotiate television's emerging social status, stressing the authenticity and everydayness of its own modes of representing the world. Something similar has occurred as digital media has negotiated its own position within the media landscape. As we saw in chapter 4, amateur media makers often signal their averageness through parody, openly acknowledging their limited economic resources or technical means compared to more polished commercial entertainment.

Hollywood stars often embraced self-parody when they appeared in early television, showing that they were also in on the joke and were able to make the adjustments needed to enter our homes on television's terms. Something similar occurs when presidential candidates embrace self-parody as a campaign tactic. In one famous example, the former president and first lady reenacted the final moments of *The Sopranos*. Here, "Hillary" and "Bill" seek to become more like average Americans, tapping a YouTube trend in the aftermath of the HBO series's wrap-up. Through this video's jokes about Hillary's attempts to control her husband's diet and Chelsea's difficulty with parallel parking, the Clintons hoped to shed some of the larger-than-life aura they gained during their years in the White House and to reenter the lifeworld of the voters. A candidate who was otherwise closely associated with a culture war campaign against media violence sought to signal her own fannishness; a candidate often seen as uptight sought to show that she could take a joke.

Or take the case of a Mike Huckabee campaign commercial, originally broadcast but also widely circulated via YouTube. The spot's opening promise of a major policy announcement sets up its punchline: action-film star Chuck Norris is unveiled as the Arkansas governor's policy for securing the U.S./Mexico border. The video thus seeks to establish Huckabee's credentials as a man's man, even as it makes fun of his need to do so. The video both publicizes—and spoofs—the role of celebrity endorsements in American politics. And the notoriously underfunded Huckabee campaign hoped its grassroots circulation would attract mainstream media attention.

Manufacturing Dissent

Traditional campaign rhetoric stresses the seriousness of the choices Americans face, rather than the pleasures of participating within the political process. Both progressives and conservatives have displayed discomfort with the tone and content of popular culture. Most attempts to mobilize popular culture towards political ends are read contemptuously as efforts to dumb down civic discourse.

In a recent book, *Dream: Re-imaging Progressive Politics in an Age of Fantasy*, Stephen Duncombe offers a different perspective, arguing that politicos need to move beyond a knee-jerk critique of popular entertainment as "weapons of mass distraction" and learn strategies for "appropriating, co-opting and most important, transforming the techniques of spectacular capitalism into tools for social change."[24] Playing on a Walter Lippman phrase brought back into public awareness through Noam Chomsky's critique of propaganda (*Manufacturing Consent*), Duncombe calls on progressives to learn new strategies for "manufacturing dissent": "Given the progressive ideals of egalitarianism and a politics that values the input of everyone, our dreamscapes will not be created by media-savvy experts of the left and then handed down to the rest of us to watch, consume, and believe. Instead, our spectacles will be participatory: dreams that the public can mold and shape themselves. They will be active: spectacles that work only if the people help create them. They will be open-ended: setting stages to ask questions and leaving silences to formulate answers. And they will be transparent: dreams that one knows are dreams but which still have power to attract and inspire. And, finally, the spectacles we create will not cover over or replace reality and truth but perform and amplify it."[25]

Duncombe cites Billionaires for Bush as a primary example of this new kind of political spectacle. Billionaires for Bush used street theater to call attention to issues, such as campaign finance reform, media concentration, and tax cuts for the wealthy. Seeking to dodge attempts by conservative critics to paint their efforts as "class warfare," the group adopted a more playful posture, dressing up like cartoon-character versions of the wealthy, showing up at campaign stops, and chanting along with other Bush supporters. These "Groucho Marxists" encouraged supporters and bystanders alike to enter into the joking process, not simply to make fun of Bush but to see political activism as a fun activity. As we described in chapter 6, similarly playful tactics were adopted by True Majority during the 2004 campaign—including their spoof of *The Apprentice* to imagine George W. Bush being fired for incompetency.

As YouTube's cultural visibility has increased, more activists have adopted True Majority's "serious fun" approach, making parody videos as a more playful and pleasurable mode of political discourse. Consider, for example, how the HP Alliance, discussed in chapter 5, formed a partnership with Wal-Mart Watch, a group backed by the Service Employees International Union as a focal point for criticism for the retail chain's employment practices. The HP Alliance and the Boston-based comedy troupe the Late Night Players translated the union's agenda into a series of campy, over-the-top videos depicting further adventures impacting Hogwarts and the wizarding world. Harry and Hermione (who is played in drag) discover that the traditional business in Diagon Alley has been closed by "you know which superstore." If they want to keep "magic" in their community, Harry and his friends must do battle with Lord Waldemarte (whose Smiley Face exterior masks his evil intentions, such as exploiting his house elves, driving out local competitors, and refusing to provide health care to his underlings). Andrew Slack of the alliance told a *Chicago Tribune* reporter, "We don't want anyone feeling that they're being lectured at. We want to break away from that to what they're interested in, and humans tend to be interested in laughing."[26] The circulation of these spoofs, in turn, drove traffic back to the Wal-Mart Watch Website, where one could find a more straightforward discussion of their protest against the company.

Barely Political?

Most writing about the CNN/YouTube debates gets framed in terms of amateur media makers and commercial network, overlooking how many videos were submitted by semiprofessionals or even by editorial cartoonists for various newspapers and magazines. We might better understand the videos produced for the debates as emerging from the mixed media economy Yochai Benkler describes in *The Wealth of Networks*. Media producers with different motives—governmental agencies, activist groups, educational institutions, nonprofit organizations, fan communities—operate side by side, using the same production tools and distribution networks. YouTube constitutes a shared portal through which these diverse groups come together to circulate media content and learn from each other's practices. In this shared distribution space, short-term tactical alliances between such groups are commonplace. On YouTube, it becomes increasingly difficult to distinguish between videos produced by fans as a playful tribute to a favorite media property like *Harry Potter*, those produced by average citizens seeking to shape the agenda of the campaigns, those produced by activist organizations to promote a specific political objective, and those produced by small-scale comedy groups seeking to break into the commercial mainstream. Such distinctions may not necessarily be productive, given the ways that a

range of grassroots intermediaries grab content of all kinds and recirculate it through a range of blogs, discussion boards, and social network
sites often without regard to the circumstances of its origin.

A case in point might be the series of Obama Girl videos. The initial
video, "I Got a Crush . . . on Obama," was produced by advertising executives Ben Relles and Rick Friedrick in collaboration with actress and
model Amber Lee Ettinger and singer/comedian Leah Kauffman. These
media professionals wanted to use their sexy and irreverent content to
generate a buzz that might draw attention to a newly launched online
comedy site. In the original video, the scantily clad Obama Girl
describes how she fell in love with Obama during his talk to the 2004
Democratic convention, signals her growing passion for the man and his
ideas through stroking his campaign posters and kissing his photograph
on a Web site, and has the candidate's name printed on her panties.
News commentators often reduce women's political interests to which
male candidate is most attractive, reading them less as concerned citizens and more as groupies for the campaigns. The Obama Girl videos
turn such representations around, transforming the candidates into
beefcake embodiments of these women's erotic fantasies. The rapid-
paced images and the multilayered wordplay reward careful decoding,
requiring consumers to learn more about the campaigns in order to
"get" the jokes. But like the other media "snacks" associated with
YouTube, they may also be consumed on a more casual level, and we
cannot easily account for the range of meanings which emerged as these
videos were spread within different online communities, passed
between friends and co-workers, or mobilized by activist groups and
campaign workers.[27]

The buzz pushed the giggling Obama Girl onto the cable news circuit,
where she became one more pundit commenting on the election season.
The producers announced a partnership with Voter Vision, a multimedia political campaign marketing program which wanted to demonstrate the political value of "viral video." Somewhere along the way, the
videos had moved from entertainment to activism, from a parody of the
campaign into something that was explicitly intended for activist purposes. The slippery nature of such distinctions is suggested by the company's name—"Barely Political."

This hybrid media environment and the active circulation of content
beyond its points of origin make it hard to tell where any given video is

coming from—in both the literal and the metaphoric sense. Increasingly, we are seeing fake grassroots media being produced by powerful institutions or economic interests—what has become known as "Astroturf."

Al Gore's Penguin Army is perhaps the best known example of an Astroturf Internet parody. This cut-up animation spoof of *An Inconvenient Truth* was first posted by a user named Toutsmith from Beverly Hills, but further investigation revealed that it was professionally produced by the DCI Group, a commercial advertising firm whose clients included General Motors and Exxon Mobil; the firm also had historically produced content for the Republican Party.[28]

One of the best known Internet parodies of the 2007 campaign season, a remix of Apple's "1984" commercial where Hillary Clinton stands in for Big Brother, has a similarly dubious history. The video turned out to be the work of Phil de Vellis, an employee of Blue State Digital, an Internet company that provided technology to both the Richardson and Obama presidential campaigns. As both the company and the campaigns sought to distance themselves from his activities, de Vellis was forced to resign his job. He told the readers of *The Huffington Post*:

> I made the "Vote Different" ad because I wanted to express my feelings about the Democratic primary, and because I wanted to show that an individual citizen can affect the process. There are thousands of other people who could have made this ad, and I guarantee that more ads like it—by people of all political persuasions—will follow. This shows that the future of American politics rests in the hands of ordinary citizens. The campaigns had no idea who made it—not the Obama campaign, not the Clinton campaign, nor any other campaign. I made the ad on a Sunday afternoon in my apartment using my personal equipment (a Mac and some software), uploaded it to YouTube, and sent links around to blogs. . . . This ad was not the first citizen ad, and it will not be the last. The game has changed.[29]

The game has indeed changed, but it isn't necessarily clear what game is being played here or by whom. Will we see other such videos circulated by groups or campaigns which hope to maintain a "plausible deniability" about their roles in generating their content? What parallels might be drawn between this material which circulates without an acknowledged source and the "swift boat" efforts four years earlier which similarly claimed independence from the Bush campaign?

Parody as Pedagogy

We cannot reduce the complexity of this hybrid media ecology to simple distinctions between top-down and bottom-up, professional and amateur, insider or outsider, old and new media, Astroturf and grassroots, or even "serious fun" and "barely political." In such a world, grassroots and mainstream media might pursue parallel interests, even as they act autonomously. Consider, for example, a video which TechPresident identifies as one of the top "voter-generated videos" of 2007. The video starts with a clip of Joseph Biden joking during one debate appearance that every sentence Rudolph Giuliani utters includes "a noun, a verb, and 9/11," and follows with a database of clips showing the former New York mayor referencing 9/11. The video was produced and distributed by Talking Points Memo, one of the most widely read progressive political blogs. In many ways, all the parody does is amplify Biden's own political message, supporting his claims that Giuliani was exploiting a national tragedy for his own political gains. The ready access of digital search tools and online archives makes it easy for small scale operators, like the bloggers, to scan through vast amounts of news footage and assemble clips to illustrate their ideas in a matter of a few days. Such rapid response practices emerged late in the 2004 presidential campaign, when both Democratic and Republican supporters used amateur videos to support their competing interpretations of the presidential debates (such as a series of videos disproving Dick Cheney's claim that he had never previously met John Edwards).

Often, these playful tactics get described in terms of the need to adopt new rhetorical practices to reach the so-called *digital natives,* a generation of young people who have grown up in a world where the affordances of participatory media technologies have been commonplace. Researchers debate whether these young people are, in fact, politically engaged since their civic lives take very different forms from those of previous generations. They are, for example, more likely to get information about the world through news comedy shows and blogs than through traditional journalism. There is conflicting evidence about their willingness to vote, but most research shows that they are very concerned about issues such as the war and the environment and willing to translate their concerns into community service. W. Lance Bennett contrasts two different framings of this data: under what he calls the "disengaged youth paradigm," forms of participatory culture are seen as "distracting" emerging citizens from more serious inquiry, seducing them with the freedoms offered by virtual worlds rather than encouraging them to transform real-world institutions. Under what he calls the "engaged youth" paradigm, there is no such rigid separation between the kinds of civic engagement these young people find through their involvement in game guilds or the expressive freedom they experienced through circulating their do-it-yourself videos on YouTube and other forms of citizenly discourse. Young people are finding their voice through their play with popular culture and then deploying it through their participation in public service projects or various political movements.[30]

The activist deployment of parody videos can be understood as an attempt to negotiate between these two perspectives. Young people have come to see YouTube as supporting individual and collective expression; they often feel excluded by the policy-wonk language of traditional politics and the inside-the-beltway focus of much campaign news coverage. Parody offers an alternative language through which policy debates and campaign pitches might be framed, one that, as Duncombe suggests, models itself on popular culture but responds to different ethical and political imperatives. The often "politically incorrect" style of Internet parody flies in the face of the language and assumptions by which previous generations debated public policy. Such videos may not look like "politics as usual," yet the people who produced and circulated these videos want to motivate young voters to participate in the electoral process. Such a model sees Internet parodies as springboards for larger conversations—whether through blogs and discussion forums online or face-to-face between people gathered around a water cooler.

These parody videos bring the issues down to a human scale, depicting Bush as an incompetent reality show contestant, Romney as someone who's afraid to go man-to-man with a snowman, Giuliani as obsessed with 9/11, or Edwards as a narcissist with fluffy hair. Duncombe has argued that news comedy shows, such as *The Daily Show* or *The Colbert Report*, foster a kind of civic literacy, teaching viewers to ask skeptical questions about core political values and the rhetorical process that embodies them: "In doing this they hold out the possibility of something else, that is, they create an opening for a discussion on what sort of a political process wouldn't be a joke. In doing this they're setting the stage for a very democratic sort of dialogue: one that asks questions rather than simply asserts the definitive truth."[31] We might connect Duncombe's argument back to Benkler's larger claim that living within a more participatory culture changes how we understand our place in the world, even if we never choose to actively participate. Yet, there is also the risk, as Duncombe points out, that such parody "can, just as easily, lead into a resigned acceptance that all politics are just a joke and the best we can hope for is to get a good laugh out of it all." Here, skepticism gives way to cynicism. Nothing ensures that a politics based in parody will foster one and not the other.

The Downsides of Digital Democracy

If this chapter can be read as a defense of the Snowman as a meaningful and valid participant in a debate about the future of American democracy, it is at best a qualified defense. I have tried to move us from an understanding of the CNN/YouTube debates through a lens of digital revolution in favor of a model based on the ever more complicated interplay of old and new media and on the hybrid media ecology that has emerged as groups with different motives and goals interact through shared media portals. I have tried to move beyond thinking of the Snowman as trivializing public policy debates towards seeing parody as a strategy which a range of different stakeholders (official and unofficial, commercial and grassroots, entertainers and activists) are deploying towards their own ends, each seeking to use YouTube as a distribution hub.

While I believe very firmly in the potential for participatory culture to serve as a catalyst for revitalizing civic life, we still fall short of the full realization of those ideals. As John McMurria has noted, the democratic promise of YouTube as a site open to everyone's participation is tempered by the reality that participation is unevenly distributed across the culture. An open platform does not necessarily ensure diversity.[32] The mechanisms of user-moderation work well when they help us to evaluate collectively the merits of individual contributions and thus push to the top the "best" content; they work badly when they preempt the expression of minority perspectives and hide unpopular and alternative content from view.

Chuck Tyron has argued that the speed with which such videos are produced and circulated can undercut the desired pedagogical and activist goals, sparking short-lived and superficial conversations among consumers who are always looking over their shoulders for the next new thing.[33] To put it mildly, the user comments posted on YouTube fall far short of Habermasian ideals of the public sphere, as was suggested by one blogger's parody of the CNN/YouTube debates. Here, the candidates interact in ways more commonly associated with the online responses to the posted videos:

> *Sen. Christopher Dodd:* omg that video was totaly gay
>
> *Sen. Barack Obama:* Shut up Dodd thats offensive when u say gay like that.
>
> *Former Sen. Mike Gravel:* Check out my vids at youtube.com/user/gravel2008.
>
> *Rep. Dennis Kucinich:* to answre your question bush is a facist who only wants more power. hes not even the president you knopw, cheny is. i would b different because i would have a vice presidant that doesnt just try and control everything from behind the seens/
>
> *Sen. Hillary Clinton:* CHENEY CANT BE PRESIDENT BECUZ THE CONSTITUTION SAYS THE VICE PRESIDENT IS NOT THE PRESIDENT WHY DON'T U TRY READING THE CONSTITUTION SOMETIME??????!!!![34]

In this parody, YouTube is associated more with mangled syntax, poor spelling, misinformation, and fractured logic than with any degree of political self-consciousness or citizenly discourse. Yet, YouTube cannot be understood in isolation from a range of other blogging and social network sites where the videos often get discussed in greater depth and substance.

The insulting tone of this depicted interaction captures something of the no-holds-barred nature of political dialogue on YouTube. In an election whose candidates include women, African Americans and Hispanics, Catholics and Mormons, groups which have historically been underrepresented in American political life, online parody often embraces racist, sexist, and xenophobic humor, which further discourages minority participation or conversations across ideological differences. One popular genre of Internet parodies depicts insult matches between Hillary Clinton and Barack Obama or their supporters (typically represented as women and minorities). One prototype of this style of humor was a MADtv sketch, which drew more than half a million

viewers when it was posted online. The sketch ends with a Giuliani supporter clapping as the two Democratic campaigns rip each other apart,
suggesting an interpretation focused on the dangers of party infighting.
But this frame figures little in the public response to the video, whether
in the form of comments posted on the site (such as one person who complained about being forced "to pick between a Nigger and a woman") or
videos generated by amateur media producers (which often push the
original's already over-the-line humor to even nastier extremes). Here,
"politically incorrect" comedy provides an opportunity for the public to
laugh at the unseemly spectacle of a struggle between women and
African Americans, or may offer a justification for trotting out ancient
but still hurtful slurs and allegations—women are inappropriate for
public office because of, haw, "that time of the month"; black men are
irresponsible because they are, haha, likely to desert their families, to go
to jail, or to experiment with drugs.

Another Web site posted a range of Photoshop collages about the campaign submitted by readers, including ones showing Hillary in a yellow
jump suit waving a samurai sword on a mocked-up poster for *Kill Bill*,
Obama depicted as Borat in a parody which plays upon his foreign
sounding name, and Obama depicted as a chauffeur driving around
Mrs. Clinton in an ad for a remake of *Driving Miss Daisy*.[35] Such parodies
use humor to put minority candidates and voters back in "their place,"
suggesting that women and blacks are inappropriate candidates for the
nation's highest office. This problem may originate from the interplay
between old and new media: racist and sexist assumptions structured
the original MADtv segment, self-consciously playing with racial and
gender stereotypes even as it reproduces them; these racist and sexist
assumptions may account for why Internet fans were drawn to it in the
first place; the subsequent reactions amplify its problematic aspects,
though the amateur responses stoop lower than network standards and
practices would allow.

In doing so, Internet parody producers fall far short of the "ethical
spectacles" Duncombe advocates: "A progressive ethical spectacle will
be one that is directly democratic, breaks down hierarchies, fosters community, allows for diversity, and engages with reality while asking what
new realities might be possible."[36] By contrast, too many of the parody
videos currently circulating on YouTube do the opposite—promoting
traditional authority, preserving gender and racial hierarchies, frag-
menting communities, discouraging diversity, and refusing to imagine

any kind of social order other than the one which has long dominated American government. Speaking to a *Mother Jones* reporter, Lawrence Lessig explained, "If you look at the top 100 things on YouTube or Google it's not like it's compelling art. There's going to be a lot of questions about whether it's compelling politics either. We can still play ugly in lots of ways, but the traditional ways of playing ugly are sort of over."[37] All of this is to suggest that Romney would have faced things far more frightening than snowmen if he had ventured into the uncharted and untamed space of YouTube rather than the filtered and protected space provided him by CNN.

The advent of new production tools and distribution channels have lowered barriers of entry into the marketplace of ideas. These shifts place resources for activism and social commentary into the hands of everyday citizens, resources which were once the exclusive domain of the candidates, the parties, and the mass media. These citizens have increasingly turned towards parody as a rhetorical practice which allows them to express their skepticism towards "politics as usual," to break out of the exclusionary language through which many discussions of public policy are conducted, and to find a shared language of borrowed images that mobilize what they know as consumers to reflect on the political process. Such practices blur the lines between producer and consumer, between consumers and citizens, between the commercial and the amateur, and between education, activism, and entertainment, as groups with competing and contradictory motives deploy parody to serve their own ends. These tactics are drawing many into the debates who would once have paid little or no attention to the campaign process. As they have done so, they have brought to the surface both inequalities in participation and deep-rooted hostilities between groups within American society. Democracy has always been a messy business: the politics of parody offers us no easy way out, yet it does offer us a chance to rewrite the rules and transform the language through which our civic life is conducted.

For better and for worse, this is what democracy looks like in the era of convergence culture. Those of us who care about the future of participatory culture as a mechanism for promoting diversity and enabling democracy do the world no favor if we ignore the ways that our current culture falls far short of these goals. Too often, there is a tendency to read all grassroots media as somehow "resistant" to dominant institutions rather than acknowledging that citizens sometimes deploy bottom-up means to keep others down. Too often, we have fallen into the trap of seeing democracy as an "inevitable" outcome of technological change rather than as something which we need to fight to achieve with every tool at our disposal. Too often, we have sought to deflect criticism of grassroots culture rather than trying to identify and resolve conflicts and contradictions which might prevent it from achieving its full potentials. Too often, we have celebrated those alternative voices which are being brought into the marketplace of ideas without considering which voices remain trapped outside. As this book has suggested, the current moment of media change is bringing about transformations in the way other core institutions operate. Every day we see new signs that old practices are subject to change. If we are to move towards what Pierre Lévy called an "achievable utopia," we must continue to ask hard questions about the practices and institutions which are taking their place. We need to be attentive to the ethical dimensions by which we are generating knowledge, producing culture, and engaging in politics together.

YouTubeOlogy

anonymousAmerican,"Fuck You, CNN"
http://www.youtube.com/watch?v=xJRGb2zlBT0

"Ask a Ninja Special Delivery 4 'Net Neutrality'"
http://www.youtube.com/watch?v=H69eCYcDcuQ

Billiam the Snowman "CNN/YouTube Debate: Global Warming"
http://www.youtube.com/watch?v=-0BPnnvI47Q

Billiam the Snowman, "The Original Video"
http://www.youtube.com/watch?v=BJpZD_pGCgk

Billiam the Snowman "Billiam the Snowman Responds to
Mitt Romney" http://www.youtube.com/watch?v=CtU9ReDhFiE

CNN, "Snowman vs. Romney"
http://www.youtube.com/watch?v=NmVIm_JRHH4

"Donald Trump Fires Bush"
http://www.youtube.com/watch?v=RrYXY_JYzX8

"Keep America Beautiful"
http://www.youtube.com/watch?v=87S0jmdYCWI

Lyndon Johnson, "Daisy"
http://www.youtube.com/watch?v=63h_v6uf0Ao

Bill Holt, "Mitt Romney Meets Jaguar"
http://www.youtube.com/watch?v=Swr4JruUTpU

Hillary Clinton "Sopranos Spoof"
http://www.youtube.com/watch?v=shKJk3Rph0E

"Jackie and Dunlap on the CNN YouTube Democratic Debate"
http://www.youtube.com/watch?v=ZrPnWoZTjlQ

John Edwards, "Hair"
http://www.youtube.com/watch?v=Y1qG6m9SnWI

MADtv, "Hillary vs. Obama"
http://www.youtube.com/watch?v=YqOHquOkpaU

Mike Huckabee, "Chuck Norris Approved"
http://www.youtube.com/watch?v=MDUQW8LUMs8

Mckathomas, "Bomb Bomb Bomb, Bomb Bomb Iran"
http://www.youtube.com/watch?v=o-zoPgv_nYg

Obama Girl, "I Got a Crush . . . On Obama"
http://www.youtube.com/watch?v=wKsoXHYICqU

ParkRidge47, "Vote Different"
http://www.youtube.com/watch?v=6h3G-lMZxjo

RCFriedman, "Snowman Challenges Mitt Romney to Debate"
http://www.youtube.com/watch?v=e9RnExM4lu4&feature=related

RogerRmJet, "John Edwards Feeling Pretty"
http://www.youtube.com/watch?v=2AE847UXu3Q

SmallMediaXL, "I'm a Democrat, I'm a Republican"
http://www.youtube.com/watch?v=ApNyDMj7zLI

This Spartan Life, "Net Neutrality"
http://www.youtube.com/watch?v=3S8q4FUY5fc

Toutsmith, "Al Gore's Penquin Army"
http://www.youtube.com/watch?v=IZSqXUSwHRI

TPMtv, "I'm Rudy Giuliani and I Approve This Message"
http://www.youtube.com/watch?v=qQ7-3M-YrdA

"YouTubers & Snowmen Unite AGAINST Romney!"
http://www.youtube.com/watch?v=8xvEH-6R16o&feature=related

Notes

Notes to the Introduction

1. Josh Grossberg, "The Bert–Bin Laden Connection?" E Online, October 10, 2001, http://www.eonline.com/News/Items/0,1,8950,00.html. For a different perspective on Bert and Bin Laden, see Roy Rosenzweig, "Scarcity or Abundance? Preserving the Past in a Digital Era," *American Historical Review* 108 (June 2003).

2. "RSTRL to Premier on Cell Phone," IndiaFM News Bureau, December 6, 2004, http://www.indiafm.com/scoop/04/dec/0612rstrlcell/index.shtml.

3. Nicholas Negroponte, *Being Digital* (New York: Alfred A. Knopf, 1995), p. 54.

4. Ibid., pp. 57–58.

5. George Gilder, "Afterword: The Computer Juggernaut: Life after *Life after Television*," added to the 1994 edition of *Life after Television: The Coming Transformation of Media and American Life* (New York: W. W. Norton), p. 189. The book was originally published in 1990.

6. Ithiel de Sola Pool, *Technologies of Freedom: On Free Speech in an Electronic Age* (Cambridge, Mass.: Harvard University Press, 1983), p. 23.

7. Ibid.

8. Ibid., p. 5.

9. Negroponte, *Being Digital*.

10. Pool, *Technologies of Freedom*, pp. 53–54.

11. For a fuller discussion of the concept of media in transition, see David Thorburn and Henry Jenkins, "Towards an Aesthetics of Transition," in David Thorburn and Henry Jenkins (eds.), *Rethinking Media Change: The Aesthetics of Transition* (Cambridge, Mass.: MIT Press, 2003).

12. Bruce Sterling, "The Dead Media Project: A Modest Proposal and a Public Appeal," http://www.deadmedia.org/modest-proposal.html.

13. Ibid.

14. Lisa Gitelman, "Introduction: Media as Historical Subjects," in *Always Already New: Media, History and the Data of Culture* (work in progress).

15. For a useful discussion of the recurring idea that new media kill off old media, see Priscilla Coit Murphy, "Books Are Dead, Long Live Books," in

David Thorburn and Henry Jenkins (eds.), *Rethinking Media Change: The Aesthetics of Transition* (Cambridge, Mass.: MIT Press, 2003).

16. Gitelman, "Introduction."

17. Cheskin Research, "Designing Digital Experiences for Youth," *Market Insights Series*, Fall 2002, pp. 8–9.

18. Mizuko Ito, "Mobile Phones, Japanese Youth and the Re-placement of the Social Contract," in Rich Ling and Per Petersen (eds.), *Mobile Communications: Re-Negotiation of the Social Sphere* (forthcoming). http://www.itofisher.com/mito/archives/mobileyouth.pdf.

19. For a useful illustration of this point, see Henry Jenkins, "Love Online," in Henry Jenkins (ed.), *Fans, Gamers, and Bloggers* (New York: New York University Press, 2005).

Notes to Chapter 1

1. Joanna Pearlstein, "The Finale as Rerun When Trumping 'Survivor,'" *New York Times*, March 27, 2003.

2. ChillOne has his own story about what happened, and he has self-published his own account of the incidents described here. See ChillOne, *The Spoiler: Revealing the Secrets of Survivor* (New York: IUniverse, 2003).

3. Pierre Lévy, *Collective Intelligence: Mankind's Emerging World in Cyberspace* (Cambridge, Mass.: Perseus Books, 1997), p. 20.

4. Ibid., p. 237.

5. Ibid., p. 217.

6. Ibid., pp. 214–215.

7. Mary Beth Haralovich and Michael W. Trosset, "'Expect the Unexpected': Narrative Pleasure and Uncertainty Due to Chance in *Survivor*," in Susan Murray and Laurie Ouellette (eds.), *Reality TV: Remaking Television Culture* (New York: New York University Press, 2004), pp. 83–84.

8. Unless otherwise cited, these and subsequent quotes from Sucksters come from "ChillOne's Amazon Vacation Spoilers" thread at http://p085 .ezboard.com/fsurvivorsucksfrm12.showMessageRange?topicID=204.topic& start=1&stop=20. Except for major participants in the story, I have withheld names of posters here to protect their privacy. Where names appear, it is because I have gotten explicit permission from participants to print their user name.

9. Quotations from Wezzie and Dan are taken from a personal interview with the author, conducted via e-mail, in June 2003.

10. Lévy, *Collective Intelligence*, p. 61.

11. Marshall Sella, "The Remote Controllers," *New York Times*, October 20, 2002.

12. Daniel Robert Epstein, "Interview: Jeff Probst of Survivor," Underground Online, http://www.ugo.com/channels/filmtv/features/jeffprobst/.

13. For a useful history of *Survivor* spoiling, see "Fear and Spoiling at Survivor Sucks," http://p085.ezboard.com/fsurvivorsucksfrm32.showMessageRange?start=1&stop+20&topicID=74.topic.

14. Personal interview with author, May 2003.

15. See TapeWatcherB65, "The REAL Episode 1 Spoiler—Follow the Sun," http://p085.ezboard.com/fsurvivorsucksfrm12.showMessageRange?topicID=101,topic&start+1&stop=20.

16. Peter Walsh, "That Withered Paradigm: The Web, the Expert and the Information Hegemony," in Henry Jenkins and David Thorburn (eds.), *Democracy and New Media* (Cambridge, Mass.: MIT Press, 2003).

17. Lévy, *Collective Intelligence*, p. 70.

18. Emily Nussbaum, "Television: The End of the Surprise Ending," *New York Times*, May 9, 2004.

19. The wingedmonkeys, "Conference Call with Mark Burnett," *Survivor News*, http://www.survivornews.net/news.php?id=317.

20. Steve Tilley, "Will Survivor Survive the Internet?" *Edmonton Sun*, January 16, 2004.

21. Wezzie, e-mail correspondence with author, August 29, 2004.

Notes to Chapter 2

1. Jefferson Graham, "Idol Voting Strained Nerves, Nation's Telephone Systems," *USA Today*, May 27, 2003, http:www.usatoday.com/life/television/news/2003-05-26-idol_x.htm.

2. Jeff Smith, "Getting the Mssg: U.S. Wireless Carriers Mining the Airwaves for Ways to Profit from Text Messaging," *Rocky Mountain News*, May 19, 2003.

3. Ibid.

4. "AT&T Wireless Text Messaging Takes Center Stage with Unprecedented Performance on Fox's American Idol," *PR Newswire*, April 16, 2003.

5. Scott Collins and Maria Elena Fernandez, "Unwanted Wrinkles for Idol," *Los Angeles Times*, May 25, 2004, p. 1.

6. Stuart Elliott, "The Media Business: Some Sponsors Are Backing Off to Fine-Tune the Art of Blending Their Products into Television Shows," *New York Times*, January 22, 2003.

7. Jennifer Pendleton, "Idol a Standard for Integration," *Advertising Age*, March 24, 2003.

8. Penelope Patsuris, "The Most Profitable Reality Series," *Forbes*, September 7, 2004, http://www.forbes.com/home_europe/business/2004/09/07/cx_pp_0907realitytv.html.

9. Gary Levin, "No Summer Vacation on TV: Networks Aggressively Chase Audiences with Reality, Original Series," *USA Today*, June 3, 2004, p. 1D.

10. Carla Hay, "Idol Ups Stakes for TV Talent," *Billboard*, April 26, 2003.

11. Karla Peterson, "False Idols: How to Face Down a Media Monster So We No Longer Worship Moments Like This," *San Diego Union-Tribune*, December 16, 2002.

12. Vance Packard, *The Hidden Persuaders* (New York: Bantam, 1957).

13. Applebox Productions, Inc., marketing postcard, circa 2000.

14. Personal correspondence with the author, December 31, 2004.

15. Anthony Bianco, "The Vanishing Mass Market," *Businessweek*, July 12, 2004, p. 62.

16. Ibid., p. 64.

17. Ibid., p. 62.

18. Susan Whiting, remarks at the MIT Communications Forum, April 17, 2003. Streaming audio of the session can be found at http://web.mit.edu/comm-forum/forums/nielsen.html#audiocast.

19. Stacey Koerner, remarks at Media in Transition 3 Conference: Television, MIT, Cambridge, Mass., on May 3, 2003. Streaming audio of this session can be found at http://cms.mit.edu/mit3/.

20. Scott Donaton, *Madison and Vine: Why the Entertainment and Advertising Industries Must Converge to Survive* (New York: McGraw-Hill, 2004), pp. 10–11.

21. Michael Schneider, "Fox Revs Ford for Blurb Free 24," *Variety*, July 21, 2002.

22. Donaton, *Madison and Vine*, p. 18.

23. Stacey Lynn Koerner, David Ernst, Henry Jenkins, and Alex Chisholm, "Pathways to Measuring Consumer Behavior in An Age of Media Convergence," presented at the Advertising Research Foundation/ESOMAR Conference, Cannes, France, June 2002.

24. Steven J. Heyer, keynote remarks delivered before Advertising Age's Hollywood + Vine Conference, Beverly Hills Hotel, Beverly Hills, California, February 5, 2003. For a transcript of the remarks, see http://www.egta.com/pages/Newsletter%20-%20Heyer.pdf. All subsequent references to Heyer refer to these remarks.

25. Kevin Roberts, *Lovemarks: The Future Beyond Brands* (New York: Power House Books, 2004), p. 43.

26. Joe D'Angelo, "Ruben Debuts at #1 but Can't Match Clay's First-Week Sales," VH1, December 17, 2003, http://www.vh1.com/artists/news/1482928/12172003/aiken_clay.jhtml.

27. Theresa Howard, "Real Winner of 'American Idol': Coke," *USA Today*, September 8, 2002; Wayne Friedman, "Negotiating the American Idol Product Placement Deal," *Advertising Age*, September 29, 2003, accessed at http://www.adage.com/news.cms?newsId=38800.

28. Sara Wilson, interview with Carol Kruse, IMedia Connection, October 2, 2003, http://www.imediaconnection.com/content/1309.asp.

29. Robert V. Kozinets, "E-Tribalized Marketing? The Strategic Implications

of Virtual Communities of Consumption," *European Management Journal*, 17 (3) (1999): 252–264.

30. Roberts, *Lovemarks*, p. 170.

31. Ibid., p. 172.

32. Marc Gobé, *Emotional Branding: The New Paradigm for Connecting Brands to People* (New York: Allworth Press, 2001); John Hagel III and Arthur G. Armstrong, *Net.Gain: Expanding Markets through Virtual Communities* (Cambridge, Mass.: Harvard University Press, 1997).

33. Don Peppers, "Introduction," in Seth Gordon, *Permission Marketing: Turning Strangers into Friends and Friends into Customers* (New York: Simon and Schuster, 1999), p. 12.

34. Phillip Swann, *TV.Com: How Television Is Shaping Our Future* (New York: TV Books, 2000), pp. 9–10.

35. Ibid., p. 31.

36. Albert M. Muniz Jr. and Thomas C. O'Guinn, "Brand Community," *Journal of Consumer Research*, March 2001, p. 427.

37. Kozinets, "E-Tribalized Marketing?" p. 10.

38. Ibid., p. 12.

39. Preliminary findings were reported in David Ernst, Stacey Lynn Koerner, Henry Jenkins, Sangita Shresthova, Brian Thiesen, and Alex Chisholm, "Walking the Path: Exploring the Drivers of Expression," presented at the Advertising Research Foundation/ESOMAR Conference, June 2003.

40. David Morley, *Family Television: Cultural Power and Domestic Leisure* (London: Routledge, 1996).

41. James H. McAlexander, John W. Schouten, and Harold F. Koenig, "Building Brand Community," *Journal of Marketing*, January 2002, pp. 38–54.

42. Deborah Starr Seibel, "*American Idol* Outrage: Your Vote Doesn't Count," *Broadcasting & Cable*, May 17, 2004, p. 1.

43. Deborah Jones, "Gossip: Note on Women's Oral Culture," *Women's Studies International Quarterly* 3 (1980): 194–195.

44. Cass Sunstein, *Republic.Com* (Princeton, N.J.: Princeton University Press, 2002).

45. Wade Paulsen, "Distorted *American Idol* Voting Due to an Overtaxed American Power Grid?" *Reality TV World*, http://www.realitytvworld.com/index/articles/story.php?s=2570.

46. Staff, "The Right Fix for Fox," *Broadcasting & Cable*, May 24, 2004, p. 36.

47. Joan Giglione, "What's Wrong with the *American Idol* Voting System," May 24, 2004, no longer on the Web.

48. Wade Paulson, "Elton John Calls *American Idol* Voting 'Incredibly Racist,'" *Reality TV World*, April 28, 2004, http://www.realitytvworld.com/index/articles/story.php?s=2526.

49. "About Us," Vote for the Worst, http://votefortheworst.com/about_us.

For more about the effort, see Henry Jenkins, "Democracy, Big Brother Style," Confessions of an Aca-Fan, July 4 2006, http://www.henryjenkins.org/2006/07/democracy_big_brother_style_1.html, and Henry Jenkins, "Sanjaya Malakar, Leroy Jenkins, and the Power to Negate," Confessions of an Aca-Fan, April 3, 2007, http://www.henryjenkins.org/2007/04/sanjaya_malakar_leroy_jenkins.html.

50. Chris Harris, "Does Sanjaya Owe His Success to Howard Stern?" MTV.Com, March 20, 2007, http://www.mtv.com/news/articles/1555113/20070320/index.jhtml.

Notes to Chapter 3

1. Peter Bagge, "Get It?" http://whatisthematrix.warnerbros.com, reproduced in Andy and Larry Wachowski (eds.), *The Matrix Comics* (New York: Burlyman Entertainment, 2003).

2. On the commercial success of the films, see "The Matrix Reloaded," *Entertainment Weekly*, May 10, 2001.

3. Pierre Lévy, *Collective Intelligence: Mankind's Emerging World in Cyberspace* (Cambridge, Mass.: Perseus Books, 1997).

4. Franz Lidz, "Rage against the Machines," *TV Guide*, October 25, 2003, http://www.reevesdrive.com/newsarchive/2003/tvg102503.htm.

5. Devin Gordon, "The Matrix Makers," *Newsweek*, January 6, 2003, accessed at http://msnbc.msn.com/id/3067730.

6. Umberto Eco, "*Casablanca*: Cult Movies and Intertextual Collage," in *Travels in Hyperreality* (New York: Harcourt Brace, 1986), p. 198.

7. Ibid.

8. Ibid.

9. Ibid., p. 200.

10. Ibid.

11. Ibid., p. 210.

12. Bruce Sterling, "Every Other Movie Is the Blue Pill," in Karen Haber (ed.), *Exploring the Matrix: Visions of the Cyber Present* (New York: St. Martin's Press, 2003), pp. 23–24.

13. This and subsequent quotations are taken from Matrix Virtual Theater, Wachowski Brothers Transcript, November 6, 1999, as seen at http://www.warnervideo.com/matrixevents/wachowski.html.

14. "Matrix Explained: What Is the Matrix?" http://www.matrix-explained.com/about_matrix.htm.

15. Joel Silver, as quoted in "Scrolls to Screen: A Brief History of Anime," *The Animatrix* DVD.

16. Ivan Askwith, "A *Matrix* in Every Medium," *Salon*, May 12, 2003, accessed at http://archive.salon.com/tech/feature/2003/05/12/matrix_universe/index_np.html.

17. For a useful discussion, see Kristin Thompson, *Storytelling in the New Hollywood: Understanding Classical Narrative Technique* (Cambridge, Mass.: Harvard University Press, 1999).

18. Fiona Morrow, "Matrix: The 'trix of the Trade," *London Independent*, March 28, 2003.

19. Mike Antonucci, "Matrix Story Spans Sequel Films, Video Game, Anime DVD," *San Jose Mercury*, May 5, 2003.

20. Jennifer Netherby, "The Neo-Classical Period at Warner: *Matrix* Marketing Mania for Films, DVDs, Anime, Videogame," *Looksmart*, January 31, 2003.

21. Danny Bilson, interview with author, May 2003. All subsequent quotations from Bilson come from that interview.

22. See Will Brooker, *Using the Force: Creativity, Community, and Star Wars Fans* (New York: Continuum, 2002).

23. Neil Young, interview with the author, May 2003. All subsequent quotations from Young come from this interview.

24. John Gaudiosi, "*The Matrix* Video Game Serves as a Parallel Story to Two Sequels on Screen," *Daily Yomiuri*, April 29, 2003.

25. "Three Minute Epics: A Look at *Star Wars: Clone Wars*," February 20, 2003, www.starwars.com/feature/20040220.

26. Interview, Yoshiaki Kawajiri, http://www.intothematrix.com/rl_cmp/rl_interview_kawajiri.html.

27. For a useful overview, see Walter Jon Williams, "Yuen Woo-Ping and the Art of Flying," in Karen Haber (ed.), *Exploring the Matrix: Visions of the Cyber Present* (New York: St. Martin's Press, 2003), pp. 122–125.

28. Mizuko Ito, "Technologies of the Childhood Imagination: *Yugioh*, Media Mixes and Everyday Cultural Production," in Joe Karaganis and Natalie Jeremijenko (eds.), *Network/Netplay: Structures of Participation in Digital Culture* (Durham, N.C.: Duke University Press, 2005).

29. Paul Chadwick, "The Miller's Tale," "Déjà Vu," and " Let It All Fall Down," http://whatisthematrix.warnerbros.com/rl_cmp/rl_middles3_paultframe.html. "The Miller's Tale" is reproduced in Andy and Larry Wachowski (eds.), *The Matrix Comics* (New York: Burlyman Entertainment, 2003).

30. Paul Chadwick, *Concrete: Think Like a Mountain* (Milwaukie, Or.: Dark Horse Comics, 1997).

31. This shared vision may be why Chadwick was asked to develop the plotlines for the Matrix multiplayer online game. For more on Chadwick's involvement, see "The Matrix Online: Interview with Paul Chadwick," Gamespot, http://www.gamespot.com/pc/rpg/matrixonlinetentatvetitle/preview_6108016.html.

32. For a useful discussion of the continuities and discontinuities in a media franchise, see William Uricchio and Roberta E. Pearson, "I'm Not Fooled by That Cheap Disguise," in Roberta E. Pearson and William Uricchio (eds.), *The*

Many Lives of the Batman: Critical Approaches to a Superhero and His Media (New York: Routledge, 1991).

33. The audience's role in fleshing out Boba Fett is a recurring reference in Will Brooker, *Using the Force: Creativity, Community and Star Wars Fans* (New York: Continuum, 2002).

34. Janet Murray, *Hamlet on the Holodeck: The Future of Narrative in Cyberspace* (Cambridge, Mass.: MIT Press, 1999), pp. 253–258.

35. Ibid.

36. Ibid.

37. Mahiro Maeda, interview, at http://www.intothematrix.com/rl_cmp/rl_interview_maeda2.html.

38. Geof Darrow, "Bits and Pieces of Information," accessed at http://whatisthematrix.warnerbros.com, reproduced in Andy and Larry Wachowski (eds.), *The Matrix Comics* (New York: Burlyman Entertainment, 2003).

39. Jeff Gordinier, "1999: The Year That Changed the Movies," *Entertainment Weekly*, October 10, 2004, http://www.ew.com/ew/report/0.6115.271806_7_0_.00.html.

40. Murray, *Hamlet*, p. 257.

41. Maeda, interview.

42. Betty Sue Flowers (ed.), *Joseph Campbell's The Power of Myth with Bill Moyers* (New York: Doubleday, 1988).

43. See, for example, M. M. Goldstein, "The Hero's Journey in Seven Sequences: A Screenplay Structure," NE Films, September 1998, http://www.newenglandfilm.com/news/archives/98september/sevensteps.htm; Troy Dunniway, "Using the Hero's Journey in Games," Gamasutra.com, http://www.gamasutra.com/features/2000127/dunniway_pfv.htm.

44. Roger Ebert, "The *Matrix Revolution*," *Chicago Sun Times*, November 5, 2003.

45. David Edelstein, "Neo Con," *Slate*, May 14, 2003, http://slate.msn.com/id/2082928.

46. Fans are not the only people seeking for meaning through *The Matrix*. See, for example, William Irwin (ed.), *The Matrix and Philosophy: Welcome to the Desert of the Real* (Chicago: Open Court, 2002).

47. Brian Takle, "The *Matrix* Explained," May 20, 2003, http://webpages.charter.net/btakle/matrix_reloaded.html.

48. Ebert, "*Matrix* Revolutions."

49. John Gaudiosi, "'*Matrix*' Vid Game Captures Film Feel," *Hollywood Reporter*, February 6, 2003, accessed at http://www.thelastfreecity.com/docs/7965.html.

50. Stephen Totilo, "*Matrix* Saga Continues On Line—Without Morpheus," MTV.Com, May 26, 2005, http://www.mtv.com/games/video_games/news/story.jhtml?id=1502973.

51. Richard Corliss, "Popular Metaphysics," *Time*, April 19, 1999.

52. See, for example, Suz, "The *Matrix* Concordance," at http://members .lycos.co.uk/needanexit/concor.html.

53. David Buckingham and Julian Sefton-Green, "Structure, Agency, and Pedagogy in Children's Media Culture," in Joseph Tobin (ed.), *Pikachu's Global Adventure: The Rise and Fall of Pokémon* (Durham, N.C.: Duke University Press, 2004), p. 12.

54. Ibid., p. 22.

55. Marsha Kinder identified similar trends as early as 1991, arguing that children's media could be read as a site of experimentation for these corporate strategies and as the place where new consumers are educated into the demands of what I am calling convergence culture. Cartoon series such as *Teenage Mutant Ninja Turtles* and games such as *Super Mario Bros.* were teaching kids to follow characters across media platforms, to adjust fluidly to a changing media environment, and to combine passive and interactive modes of engagement. Marsha Kinder, *Playing with Power in Movies, Television and Video Games: From Muppet Babies to Teenage Mutant Ninja Turtles* (Berkeley: University of California Press, 1991).

56. Manuel Castells, *The Internet Galaxy: Reflections on the Internet, Business, and Society* (Oxford: Oxford University Press, 2001), pp. 202–203.

Notes to Chapter 4

1. AtomFilms, "Internet Users are Makin' Wookiee!" press release, April 23, 1999.

2. Chris Albrecht, personal interview, July 2005.

3. For more discussion of fans and new media, see Henry Jenkins, "The Poachers and the Stormtroopers: Cultural Convergence in the Digital Age," in Phillipe Le Guern (ed.), *Les cultes mediatiques: Culture fan et oeuvres cultes* (Rennes: Presses Universitaires de Rennes, 2002).

4. Paul Clinton, "Filmmakers Score with *Lucas in Love*," CNN, June 24, 1999, http://www.cnn.com/SHOWBIZ/Movies/9906/24/movies.lucas.love.

5. Josh Wolk, "Troop Dreams," *Entertainment Weekly*, March 20, 1998, pp. 8–9.

6. Manuel Castells, on p. 201 of *The Internet Galaxy: Reflections on the Internet, Business, and Society* (Oxford: Oxford University Press, 2003), defines "interactivity" as "the ability of the user to manipulate and affect his experience of media directly and to communicate with others through media." I prefer to separate out the two parts of this definition—so that "interactivity" refers to the direct manipulation of media within the technology, and "participation" refers to the social and cultural interactions that occur around media.

7. Grant McCracken, "The Disney TM Danger," in *Plenitude* (self-published, 1998), p. 5.

8. Lawrence Lessig, "Keynote from OSCON 2002," accessed at http://www.oreillynet.com/pub/a/policy/2002/08/15/lessig.html.

9. Clinton, "Filmmakers Score with *Lucas in Love*."

10. http://evanmather.com. The site is described here as it existed in 2000, at the time this essay was first written. As of 2004, Mather continued to be productive and the site hosted more than forty-eight digital films. Much of his recent work has taken him far afield from *Star Wars*, showing how his early fan work has paved the way for a much more varied career.

11. "When Senators Attack IV" (Ryan Mannion, Daniel Hawley), http://theforce.net/theater/animation/wsa4/index.shtml.

12. Patricia R. Zimmermann, *Reel Families: A Social History of Amateur Film* (Bloomington: Indiana University Press, 1995), p. 157.

13. Clinton, "Filmmakers Score with *Lucas in Love*."

14. "A Word from Shane Felux," TheForce.Net, http://www.theforce.net/fanfilms/comingsoon/revelations/director.asp; Clive Thompson, "May the Force Be with You, and You, and You . . . : Why Fans Make Better *Star Wars* Movies than George Lucas," *Slate*, April 29, 2005, http://slate.msn.com/id/2117760/.

15. Kevin Kelly and Paula Parisi, "George Lucas Interview," accessed at http://www.delanohighschool.org/BillBaugher/stories/storyReader$1624.

16. Clay Kronke, Director's Note, *The New World*, http://theforce.net/theater/shortfilms/newworld/index.shtml.

17. *Duel* (Mark Thomas and Dave Macomber), no longer online.

18. Mark Magee, "Every Generation Has a Legend," Shift.com, http://www.shift.com/content/web/259/1.html.

19. Probot Productions, no longer on Web.

20. Coury Turczyn, "Ten Minutes with the *Robot Chicken* Guys," G4, February 17, 2005, http://www.g4tv.com/screensavers/features/51086/Ten_Minutes_with_the_Robot_Chicken_Guys.html. See also Henry Jenkins, "Ode to *Robot Chicken*," Confessions of an Aca-Fan, June 20, 2006, http://www.henryjenkins.org/2006/06/ode_to_robot_chicken.html.

21. Henry Jenkins, "So What Happened to *Star Wars Galaxies?*," Confessions of an Aca-Fan, July 21, 2006, http://www.henryjenkins.org/2006/07/so_what_happened_to_star_wars.html.

22. Chris Albrecht, personal interview, July 2005.

23. Amy Harmon, "*Star Wars* Fan Films Come Tumbling Back to Earth," *New York Times*, April 28, 2002.

24. Will Brooker, *Using the Force: Creativity, Community and Star Wars Fans* (New York: Continuum, 2002), pp. 164–171.

25. For a fuller discussion, see Henry Jenkins, *Textual Poachers: Television Fans and Participatory Culture* (New York: Routledge, 1992), pp. 30–32.

26. Fan Fiction on the Net, http://members.aol.com:80/ksnicholas/fanfic/index.html.

27. Janelle Brown, "Fan Fiction on the Line," Wired.com, August 11, 1997, http://www.wired.com/news/topstories/0,1287,5934,00.html.

28. Brooker, *Using the Force*, p. 167.

29. David R. Phillips, "The 500-Pound Wookiee," *Echo Station*, August 1, 1999, http://www.echostation.com/features/lfl_wookiee.htm.

30. Richard Jinman, "Star Wars," *Australian Magazine*, June 17, 1995, pp. 30–39.

31. Homestead statement, official *Star Wars* Home Page, as quoted by Elizabeth Durack, "fans.starwars.con," *Echo Station*, March 12, 2000, http://www.echostation.com/editorials/confans.htm.

32. Durack, "fans.starwars.con."

33. Atom Films, "The Official *Star Wars* Fan Film Awards," http://atomfilms.shockwave.com/af/spotlight/collections/starwars/submit.html.

34. McCracken, *Plenitude*, p. 84.

35. Ibid., p. 85.

36. For an interesting essay that contrasts Peter Jackson's efforts to court *Lord of the Rings* fans with the more commercially oriented approach to fandom surrounding *Star Wars*, see Elana Shefrin, "*Lord of the Rings, Star Wars*, and Participatory Fandom: Mapping New Congruencies between the Internet and Media Entertainment Culture," *Critical Studies in Media Communication*, September 2004, pp. 261–281.

37. Raph Koster, "The Rules of Online World Design," http://www.legendmud.org/raph/gaming/gdc.htm.

38. Unless otherwise noted, quotations from Raph Koster come from a personal interview with the author conducted in October 2004.

39. Kurt Squire, "Interview with Raph Koster," *Joystick101*, http://www.legendmud.org/raph/gaming/joystick101.html.

40. Koster, "The Rules of Online World Design."

41. Richard A. Bartle, *Designing Virtual Worlds* (Indianapolis: New Riders, 2004), p. 244.

42. Raph Koster, "Letter to the Community," http://starwarsgalaxies.station.sony.com/team_commnts_old.jsp?id=56266&page=Team%20Comments.

43. Kurt Squire and Constance Steinkuehler, "The Genesis of 'Cyberculture': The Case of *Star Wars Galaxies*," in *Cyberlines: Languages and Cultures of the Internet* (Albert Park, Australia: James Nicholas, forthcoming). See also Kurt Squire, "*Star Wars Galaxies*: A Case Study in Participatory Design," *Joystick101*, http://www.joystick101.org.

44. Squire and Steinkuehler, "Genesis of 'Cyberculture.'" For another interesting account of fan creativity within *Star Wars Galaxies*, see Douglas Thomas,

"Before the Jump to Lightspeed: Negotiating Permanence and Change in *Star Wars Galaxies*," presented at the Creative Gamers Conference, University of Tampiere, Tampiere, Finland, January 2005.

45. I am indebted to Doug Thomas for calling this phenomenon to my attention. Thomas writes about cantina musicals and other forms of grassroots creativity in "Before the Jump to Lightspeed."

46. "Revamped *Star Wars* Game Leaves Old Players Grieving," *New York Times* News Service, December 12, 2005, p. 12.

Notes to Chapter 5

1. The assumptions underlying this argument are developed more fully in Henry Jenkins, "Childhood Innocence and Other Myths," in Henry Jenkins (ed.), *The Children's Culture Reader* (New York: New York University Press, 1998).

2. Unless otherwise noted, all quotes from Heather Lawver taken from interview with author, August 2003.

3. Heather Lawver, "To the Adults," http://www.dprophet.com/hq/open letter.html.

4. Ibid.

5. For more on the ways younger children use stories to work through real-life concerns, see Henry Jenkins, "Going Bonkers! Children, Play, and Pee-Wee," in Constance Penley and Sharon Willis (eds.), *Male Trouble* (Minneapolis: University of Minnesota Press, 1993).

6. Anne Haas Dyson, *Writing Superheroes: Contemporary Childhood, Popular Culture, and Classroom Literacy* (New York: Teachers College Press, 1997).

7. See, for example, Christine Schoefer, "Harry Potter's Girl Trouble," *Salon*, January 13, 2000, http://dir.salon.com/books/feature/2000/01/13/potter/index.html?sid=566202. For a rebuttal, see Chris Gregory, "Hands Off Harry Potter! Have Critics of J. K. Rowling's Books Even Read Them?" *Salon*, March 1, 2000, http://www.salon.com/books/feature/2000/03/01/harrypotter.

8. Ellen Seiter, *Sold Separately: Children and Parents in Consumer Culture* (New Brunswick, N.J.: Rutgers University Press, 1993).

9. James Gee, *Language, Learning, and Gaming: A Critique of Traditional Schooling* (New York: Routledge, 2005), read in manuscript form.

10. Flourish, interview with author, August 2003.

11. See, for example, Shelby Anne Wolf and Shirley Brice Heath, *Braid of Literature: Children's World of Reading* (Cambridge, Mass.: Harvard University Press, 1992).

12. Zsenya, e-mail correspondence with author, July 2005.

13. Flourish, interview with author, August 2003.

14. Sugar Quill, http://www.sugarquill.net.

15. Sweeney Agonistes, interview with author, August 2003.

16. Elizabeth Durack, "Beta Reading!" Writers University, http://www
.writersu.com/WU//modules.php?name+News&file=article&sid=17.

17. R. W. Black, "Anime-Inspired Affiliation: An Ethnographic Inquiry into
the Literacy and Social Practices of English Language Learners Writing in the
Fanfiction Community," presented at 2004 meeting of American Educational
Research Association, San Diego, accessible at http://labweb.education.wisc
.edu/room130/PDFS/InRevision.pdf.

18. Interview with author, August 2003.

19. Gee, *Language, Learning, and Gaming.*

20. "The Leaky Cauldron," June 16, 2001, http://www.the-leaky-cauldron
.org/MTarchives/000767.html.

21. Tracy Mayor, "Taking Liberties with Harry Potter," *Boston Globe Magazine*, June 29, 2003.

22. Stephanie Grunier and John Lippman, "Warner Bros. Claim Harry Potter
Sites," *Wall Street Journal Online,* December 20, 2000, http://zdnet.com.com/
2102-11_2-503255.html; "Kids 1—Warner Bros. 0: When the Big Studio Set Its
Hounds on Some *Harry Potter* Fan Web Sites, It Didn't Bargain on the Potterhead
Rebellion," *Vancouver Sun*, November 17, 2001.

23. Claire Field, interview with author, August 2003.

24. "Defense Against the Dark Arts," http://www.dprophet.com/dada/.

25. Ryan Buell, "Fans Call for War; Warner Bros. Claim Misunderstanding!"
http://www.entertainment-rewired.com/fan_appology.htm.

26. See http://www.dprophet.com/dada/.

27. "Fan Fiction, Chilling Effects," http://www.chillingeffects.org/fanfic.

28. Brad Templeton, "10 Big Myths about Copyright Explained," http://
www.templetons.com/brad/copymyths.html.

29. See, for example, Rebecca Tushnet, "Legal Fictions: Copyright, Fan Fiction, and a New Common Law," *Loyola of Los Angeles Entertainment Law Journal,*
1977, accessed online at http://www.tushnet.com/law/fanficarticle.html; A. T.
Lee, "Copyright 101: A Brief Introduction to Copyright for Fan Fiction Authors," *Whoosh!*, October 1998, http://www.whoosh.org/issue25/leee1.html.

30. Katie Dean, "Copyright Crusaders Hit Schools," *Wired*, August 13, 2004,
http://www.wired.com/news/digiwood/0,1412,64543,00.html.

31. Rosemary Coombe and Andrew Herman, "Defending Toy Dolls and Maneuvering Toy Soldiers: Trademarks, Consumer Politics and Corporate Accountability on the World Wide Web," presented at MIT Communication Forum,
April 12, 2001, accessed at http://web.mit.edu/m-i-t/forums/trademark/index
_paper.html.

32. "Muggles for Harry Potter to Fight Censorship," *Ethical Spectacle*, April
2000, http://www.spectacle.org/0400/muggle.html. See also Judy Blume, "Is

Harry Potter Evil?" *New York Times*, October 22, 1999, as republished at http://www.ncac.org/cen_news/cn76harrypotter.html.

33. "The Leaky Cauldron," June 13, 2001, http://www.the-leaky-cauldron.org/MTarchives/000771.html.

34. "Satanic Harry Potter Books Burnt," *BBC News*, December 31, 2001, http://news.bbc.co.uk/1/hi/entertainmanet/arts/1735623.stm.

35. Chris Mooney, "Muddled Muggles: Conservatives Missing the Magic in Harry Potter," *American Prospect*, July 11, 2000, http://www.prospect.org/webfeatures/2000/07/mooney-c-07-11.html. See "TalkBack Live: Do the *Harry Potter* Books Cast an Evil Spell?" July 7, 2000, http://transcripts.cnn.com/TRANSCRIPTS/0007/07/tl.00.html.

36. Phil Arms, *Pokémon & Harry Potter: A Fatal Attraction* (Oklahoma City: Hearthstone, 2000), p. 84.

37. http://www.cuttingedge.org/news/n1390.cfm.

38. Kathy A. Smith, "*Harry Potter*: Seduction into the Dark World of the Occult," http://www.fillthevoid.org/Entertainment/Harry-Potter-1.html.

39. Berit Kjos, "*Harry Potter* Book Shares Pre-Sale Frenzy with D&D," accessed at http://www.crossroad.to/text/articles/D&D-text.htm.

40. Berit Kjos, "Twelve Reasons Not to See *Harry Potter* Movies," http://www.crossroad.to/articles2/HP-Movie.htm.

41. Michael O'Brien, "Some Thoughts on the *Harry Potter* Series," Catholic Educator's Resource Center, http://www.catholiceducation.org/articles/a10071.html.

42. Berit Kjos, "*Harry Potter & The Order of the Phoenix*: 'It's Only Fantasy' and Other Deceptions," http://www.crossroad.to/articles2/phoeniz.htm.

43. Mary Dana, interview with author, September 2003.

44. "Muggles for Harry Potter to Fight Censorship."

45. Christopher Finnan, personal interview, April 2003.

46. See http://www.kidspeakonline.org/kissaying.html.

47. "About Us," The HP Alliance, http://thehpalliance.org/aboutUs.html. For a podcast interview with the HP Alliance's Andrew Slack, see CMS Podcasts, www.podcastdirectory.com/podshows/1909127.

48. *Harry Potter* Phenomenon Sparks Global Youth Activism," http://thehpalliance.org/news/globelYouthActivism.html.

49. Suzanne Scott, "Harry Potter and The Lockhart Paradox: Redefining and Romanticizing Canon in our Participatory Culture" (PhD diss., University of Southern California, in progress); Suzanne Scott, "Voldemort Can't Stop the Rock: Hot Topic, Wizard Rock and *Harry Potter* Punk," paper presented at Phoenix Rising, New Orleans, May 17–21, 2007.

50. Jennifer Vineyard, "*Harry Potter* Fandom Reaches Magical New Level Thanks to Wizard-Rock Bands," MTV, June 6, 2007, http://www.mtv.com/news/articles/1561855/20070606/id_0.jhtml; Melissa, "Wizards and Muggles

Rock for Social Justice," The Leaky Cauldron, April 18, 2007, http://www.the-leaky-cauldron.org/2007/4/18/wizards-and-muggles-rock-for-social-justice.

51. Grant McCracken, *Plenitude* (self-published, 1998), p. 60.

52. O'Brien, "Some Thoughts."

53. Connie Neal, *What's a Christian to Do with Harry Potter?* (Colorado Springs: Waterbook, 2001), pp. 151–152.

54. Denis Haack, "Christian Discernment 101: An Explanation of Discernment," Ransom Fellowship, http://ransomfellowship.org/D_101.html.

55. Denis Haack, "Christian Discernment 202: Pop Culture: Why Bother?" Ransom Fellowship, http://ransomfellowship.org/D-202.html.

56. "The Purpose of Fans for Christ," Fans for Christ, http://www.fansfor christ.org/phpBB2/purpose.htm.

57. Denis Haack, "The Scandal of *Harry Potter*," Ransom Fellowship, http://www.ransomfellowship.org/R_Potter.html.

58. Neal, *What's a Christian to Do?* pp. 88–90.

Notes to Chapter 6

1. See http://www.trumpfiresbush.com.

2. http://www.truemajority.org.

3. Garrett LoPorto, personal interview, October 2004.

4. Joe Trippi, "The Perfect Storm," Joetrippi.com/book/view/23.

5. For more on the Dean campaign's use of the Internet, see Henry Jenkins, "Enter the Cybercandidates," *Technology Review*, October 8, 2003.

6. Joe Trippi, *The Revolution Will Not Be Televised: Democracy, the Internet, and the Overthrow of Everything* (New York: HarperCollins, 2004), p. 227.

7. Hans Magnus Enzensberger, "Constituents of a Theory of the Media," in Paul Marris and Sue Thornham (eds.), *Media Studies: A Reader* (New York: New York University Press, 2000), pp. 68–91.

8. Trippi, *The Revolution Will Not Be Televised*, p. 4.

9. Ibid., p. 107.

10. Ibid., p. 225.

11. Nancy Gibbs, "Blue Truth, Red Truth," *Time*, September 27, 2004, pp. 24–34.

12. Jesse Walker, "Old Media and New Media: Like It or Not, They're Partners," *Reason*, September 15, 2004, http://www.reason.com/links/links091504.shtml.

13. Mark Dery, "Culture Jamming: Hacking, Slashing and Sniping in the Empire of Signs," Open Magazine Pamphlet Series, 1993, http://web.nwe.ufi.edu/~mlafey/cultjam1.html.

14. Pierre Lévy, *Collective Intelligence: Mankind's Emerging World in Cyberspace* (Cambridge, Mass.: Perseus Books, 1997), p. 171.

15. See http://www.back-to-iraq.com/archives/000464.php for a database of coverage of the role of bloggers in covering the Iraq war.

16. Farhad Manjoo, "Horror Show," *Salon,* May 12, 2004, http://www.salon.com/tech/feature/2004/05/12/beheading_video/index_np.html.

17. "Blogs Blamed for Exit Poll Fiasco," *Wired,* November 3, 2004, http://www.wired.com/news/politics/0,1283,65589,00.html?tw+wn_tophead_6; Eric Engberg, "Blogging as Typing, Not Journalism," CBSnews.com, November 8, 2004, http://www.cbsnews.com/stories/2004/11/08/opinion/main654285.shtml; Mark Glaser, "Exit Polls Bring Traffic Deluge, Scrutiny to Blogs, Slate," *USC Annenberg Online Journalism Review,* November 5, 2004, http://ojr.org/ojr/glasser/1099616933.php.

18. Nicholas Confessore, "Bush's Secret Stash: Why the GOP War Chest Is Even Bigger than You Think," *Washington Monthly,* May 2004, accessed at http://www.washingtonmonthly.com/features/2004/0405.confessore.html.

19. Christopher Lydon, "The Master of Meet Up: Scott Heiferman," Christopher Lydon Interviews, http://blogs.law.harvard.edu/lydon/2003/10/21.

20. Trippi, *The Revolution Will Not Be Televised,* p. 91.

21. See http://www.bushin30seconds.org.

22. Corrie Pikul, "The Photoshopping of the President," *Salon,* July 1, 2004, http://archive.salon.com/ent/feature/2004/07/01/photoshop/.

23. On Photoshop as a medium for responding to September 11, see Dominic Pettman, "How the Web Became a Tool for Popular Propaganda after S11," Crikey.com.au, February 3, 2002, http://www.crikey.com.au/media/2002/02/02-Jihadfordummies.html.

24. Lauren Berlant, *The Queen of America Goes to Washington City: Essays on Sex and Citizenship* (Durham, N.C.: Duke University Press, 1997).

25. For another useful discussion of citizenship and consumption, see Sarah Banet-Weiser, "'We Pledge Allegiance to Kids': Nickelodeon and Citizenship," in Heather Hendershot (ed.), *Nickelodeon Nation: The History, Politics, and Economics of America's Only TV Channel for Kids* (New York: New York University Press, 2004).

26. http://www.ew.com/ew/report/0,6115,446852_4_0_,00.html.

27. The Center for Information and Research on Civic Learning and Engagement, "Turnout of Under-25 Voters Up Sharply," November 9, 2004, http://www.civicyouth.org/PopUps/Release_1824final.pdf.

28. Walter Benjamin, "The Work of Art in the Age of Mechanical Reproduction," accessed at http://bid.berkeley.edu/bidclass/readings/benjamin.html.

29. Pew Research Center for the People and the Press, "Cable and Internet Loom Large in Fragmented Political News Universe," January 11, 2004, http://people-press.org/reports/display.php3?ReportID=200.

30. Jon Katz, "The Media's War on Kids: From the Beatles to Beavis and Butthead," *Rolling Stone,* February 1994, pp. 31–33, 97.

31. Dannagal Goldthwaite Young, "*Daily Show* Viewers Knowledgeable about Presidential Campaign, National Annenberg Election Survey Shows," September 21, 2004, http://www.annenbergpublicpolicycenter.org/naes/2004 _03_late-night-knowledge-2_9-21_pr.pdf. See also Bryan Long, "'Daily Show' Viewers Ace Political Quiz," CNN, September 29, 2004, http://www.cnn.com/2004/SHOWBIZ/TV/09/28/comedy.politics/.

32. Quotations taken from the official transcript of the broadcast accessed at http://transcripts.cnn.com/TRANSCRIPTS/0410/15/cf.01.html.

33. Michael Schudson, "Click Here for Democracy: A History and Critique of an Information-Based Model of Citizenship," in Henry Jenkins and David Thorburn (eds.), *Democracy and New Media* (Cambridge, Mass.: MIT Press, 2003), p. 55.

34. Michael Schudson, "Changing Concepts of Democracy," MIT Communications Forum, http://web.mit.edu/comm-forum/papers/schudson.html.

35. Ibid.

36. Ibid.

37. See, for example, R. J. Bain, "Rethinking the Informed Citizen in an Age of Hybrid Media Genres: *Tanner '88*, *K-Street*, and the Fictionalization of the News," Master's thesis, Comparative Media Studies Program, MIT, 2004; and Cristobal Garcia, "A Framework for Political Entertainment," paper presented at Media in Transition 3 Conference, MIT, Cambridge, Mass., May 2003.

38. John Hartley, "Regimes of Truth and the Politics of Reading: A Blivit," in *Tele-Ology: Studies in Television* (New York: Routledge, 1992), pp. 45–63.

39. David Buckingham, *The Making of Citizens: Young People, News and Politics* (London: Routledge, 2000).

40. Will Wright, personal interview with author, June 2003.

41. Peter Ludlow, "My View of the Alphaville Elections," *Alphaville Herald*, April 20, 2004, http://www.alphavilleherald.com/archives/000191.html.

42. These and subsequent quotes in this paragraph taken from Jane McGonigal, "'This Is Not a Game': Immersive Aesthetics and Collective Play," http://www.seanstewart.org/beast/mcgonigal/notagame/paper.pdf.

43. http://cdd.stanford.edu.

44. Henry E. Brady, James S. Fishkin, and Robert C. Luskin, "Informed Public Opinion about Foreign Policy: The Uses of Deliberative Polling," *Brookings Review*, Summer 2003, http://cdd.stanford.edu/research/papers/2003/informed.pdf.

45. David Thorburn, "Television Melodrama," in Horace Newcomb (ed.), *Television: The Critical View* (Oxford: Oxford University Press, 1994).

46. Ithiel de Sola Pool, *Technology without Boundaries: On Telecommunications in a Global Age* (Cambridge, Mass.: Harvard University Press, 1990), pp. 261–262.

47. Andrew Leonard, "Trapped in the Echo Chamber," *Salon*, November 3, 2004, http://www.salon.com/tech/col/leon/2004/11/03/echo_chamber.

48. Cass Sunstein, "The Daily We," *Boston Review,* Summer 2001, http://www.bostonreview.net/BR26.3/Sunstein.html.

49. Gibbs, "Blue Truth, Red Truth."

50. Sharon Waxman and Randy Kennedy, "The Gurus of What's In Wonder If They're Out of Touch," *New York Times,* November 6, 2004, p. A12.

Notes to the Conclusion

1. Ari Berman, "Al Gets Down," *The Nation,* April 28, 2005, http://www.the nation.com/doc.mhtml?i=20050516&c=1&s=berman.

2. See Anita J. Chan, "Distributed Editing, Collective Action, and the Construction of Online News on Slashdot.org," Master's thesis, Comparative Media Studies Program, MIT, Cambridge, Mass., 2002. For more on participatory journalism, see Dan Gilmor, *We the Media: Grassroots Journalism By the People, For the People* (New York: O'Reilly, 2004); and Pablo J. Boczkowski, *Digitizing the News: Innovation in Online Newspapers* (Cambridge, Mass.: MIT Press, 2005).

3. Berman, "Al Gets Down." For more on the debates about Current, see Niall McCay, "The Vee Pee's New Tee Vee," *Wired News,* April 6, 2005, http://www.wired.com/news/digiwood/0,1412,67143,00.html; Farhad Manjoo, "The Television Will Be Revolutionized," *Salon,* July 7, 2005, http://www.salon.com/news/feature/2005/07/11/goretv/print.html; Tamara Straus, "I Want My Al TV," *San Francisco* magazine, July 2005, http://www.sanfran.com/home/view_story/625/?PHPSESSID=d8ef14a995fed84316b461491d16f667.

4. Manjoo, "The Television."

5. Berman, "Al Gets Down."

6. Ashley Highfield, "TV's Tipping Point: Why the Digital Revolution Is Only Just Beginning," October 7, 2003, Paidcontent.org, http://www.paidcontent.org/stories/ashleyrts.shtml.

7. "BBC Opens TV Listings for Remix," *BBC Online,* July 23, 2005, http://news.bbc.co.uk/1/hi/technology/4707187.stm.

8. W. Russell Neuman, *The Future of the Mass Audience* (Cambridge, U.K.: Cambridge University Press, 1991), p. 54.

9. Ibid., pp. 8–9.

10. Betsy Frank, "Changing Media, Changing Audiences," MIT Communications Forum, April 1, 2004, http://web.mit.edu/comm-forum/forums/changing_audiences.html.

11. George Gilder, *Life after Television: The Coming Transformation of Media and American Life* (New York: W. W. Norton, 1994), p. 66.

12. Ibid., p. 68.

13. Marshall Sella, "The Remote Controllers," *New York Times,* October 20, 2002.

14. Henry Jenkins, *Textual Poachers: Television Fans and Participatory Culture* (New York: Routledge, 1991).

15. Marcia Allas, e-mail interview with author, Fall 2003.

16. Kimberly M. De Vries, "A Tart Point of View: Building a Community of Resistance Online," presented at Media in Transition 2: Globalization and Convergence, MIT, Cambridge, Mass., May 10–12, 2002.

17. Quotations in this paragraph taken from Warren Ellis, "*Global Frequency: An Introduction*," http://www.warrenellis.com/gf.html.

18. Howard Rheingold, *Smart Mobs: The Next Social Revolution* (New York: Basic Books, 2003), p. xii.

19. Cory Doctorow, *Down and Out in the Magic Kingdom* (New York: Tor, 2003).

20. All information and quotes in this paragraph taken from Michael Gebb, "Rejected TV Pilot Thrives on P2P," *Wired News*, June 27, 2005, http://www.wired.com/news/digiwood/0,1412,67986,00.html.

21. Chris Anderson, "The Long Tail," *Wired*, October 2004, http://www.wired.com/wired/archive/12.10/tail.html?pg=3&topic=tail&topic_set.

22. Ivan Askwith, "TV You'll Want to Pay For: How $2 Downloads Can Revive Network Television," *Slate*, November 1, 2005, http://www.slateuk.com/id/2129003/.

23. Andy Bowers, "Reincarnating *The West Wing*: Could the Canceled NBC Drama Be Reborn on iTunes?" *Slate*, January 24, 2006, http://www.slateuk.com/id/2134803/.

24. Information taken from the Wikipedia entry at http://en.wikipedia.org/wiki/Wikipedia.

25. "Neutral Point of View," Wikipedia, http://www.infowrangler.com/phpwiki/wiki.phtml?title=Wikipedia:Neutral_point_of_view.

26. Shoshanna Green, Cynthia Jenkins, and Henry Jenkins, "'The Normal Female Interest in Men Bonking," in Cheryl Harris and Alison Alexander (eds.), *Theorizing Fandom* (New York: Hampton, 1998).

27. My ideas about the kinds of media literacies required for participation in the new convergence culture were developed into a white paper for the MacArthur Foundation. See Henry Jenkins, with Katherine Clinton, Ravi Purushatma, Alice Robison, and Margaret Weigel, *Confronting the Challenges of a Participatory Culture: Media Education for the 21st Century*, http://projectnml.org.

Notes to the Afterword

1. For a video archive of the debates, see http://www.youtube.com/democraticdebate and http://www.youtube.com/republicandebate. I am indebted to Colleen Kaman and Steve Schultz for their assistance in tracking down references and materials for this study.

2. *Talk of the Nation*, "Digital Democracy: YouTube's Presidential Debates," July 18, 2007, http://www.npr.org/templates/story/story.php?storyId=120 62554.

3. Jose Antonio Vargas, "The Trail: The GOP YouTube Debate Is Back On," *Washington Post*, August 12 2007, http://blog.washingtonpost.com/the-trail/2007/08/12/the_gop_youtube_debate_is_back_1.html.

4. Ibid.

5. Jason Rosenbaum, "It's a Trap!," The Seminal, November 29, 2007, http://www.theseminal.com/2007/11/28/its-a-trap/. See also Micah L. Sifry, "How CNN Demeans the Internet," TechPresident, November 29, 2007, http://www.techpresident.com/blog/entry/14238/how_cnn_demeans_the_internet.

6. See Henry Jenkins, *Convergence Culture: Where Old and New Media Collide* (New York: New York University Press, 2006).

7. "Fight Different," *Mother Jones*, August 2007, p. 27.

8. "The YouTube-ification of Politics: Candidates Losing Control," CNN.com, July 18, 2007, http://edition.cnn.com/2007/POLITICS/07/18/youtube.effect/index.html.

9. Ana Marie Cox, "Will the GOP Say No to YouTube?," Time.com, July 27, 2007, http://www.time.com/time/politics/article/0,8599,1647805,00.html.

10. "Team Mitt: Create Your Own Ad!," http://www.jumpcut.com/groups/detail?g_id= 5DD3300851A311D C8DA1000423CF381C.

11. Marty Kaplan, "The CNN/RubeTube Debate," *The Huffington Post*, November 25, 2007, http://www.huffingtonpost.com/marty-kaplan/the-cnnrubetube-debate_b_74003.html.

12. Sarah Lee Stirland, "CNN-YouTube Debate Producer Doubts the Wisdom of the Crowd," *Wired*, November 27, 2007, http://www.wired.com/politics/onlinerights/news/2007/11/cnn_debate#.

13. Heather Levi, "The Mask of the Luchador: Wrestling, Politics, and Identity in Mexico," in Nicholas Sammond (ed.), *Steel Chair to the Head: The Pleasures and Pain of Professional Wrestling* (Durham: Duke University Press, 2005), pp.96-131.

14. Yochai Benkler, *The Wealth of Networks: How Social Production Transforms Markets and Freedom* (New Haven, Conn.: Yale University Press, 2006), pp. 274–275.

15. Ibid.

16. See "Snowman vs. Romney—CNN Reports," http://www.youtube.com/watch?v=NmVIm_JRHH4.

17. "Walter Williams," http://www.mrbill.com/wwbio.html.

18. Cain Burdeau, "Mr. Bill Tapped to Help Save La. Swamps," Associated Press, as reprinted at http://www.mrbill.com/LASinks.html.

19. http://www.tmz.com/2007/07/21/mitt-catches-s-t-over-hillary-bashing-sign/.

20. http://www.tmz.com/2007/07/23/romney-on-osama-sign-lighten-up/; http://www.dailykos.com/story/2007/7/23/31656/4987.

21. For more discussion, see Henry Jenkins, "Childhood Innocence and Other Modern Myths," *The Children's Culture Reader* (New York: New York University Press, 1998), pp. 1–40.

22. Benkler, *The Wealth of Networks*, p. 200.

23. Denise Mann, "The Spectacularization of Everyday Life: Recycling Hollywood Stars and Fans in Early Television Variety Shows," in Lynn Spigel and Denise Mann (eds.), *Private Screenings: Television and the Female Consumer* (Minneapolis: University of Minnesota Press, 1992), pp. 41–70.

24. Stephen Duncombe, *Dream: Re-Imagining Progressive Politics in an Age of Fantasy* (New York: New Press, 2007), p. 16.

25. Ibid., p. 17.

26. Sandra M. Jones, "Wal-Mart Case as Dark Lord," *Chicago Tribune*, July 1 2007, p.xx.

27. *Wired* represented YouTube as central to a new culture of media snacks in "Snack Attack!," *Wired*, March 2007, http://www.wired.com/wired/archive/15.03/snack.html.

28. *Wall Street Journal*, August 3, 2006, http://online.wsj.com/public/article/SB115457177198425388-0TpYE6bU6EGvfSqtP8_hHjJJ77I_20060810.html?mod=blogs.

29. Phil de Vellis, aka Parkridge47, "I Made the 'Vote Different' Ad," *The Huffington Post*, March 21, 2007, http://www.huffingtonpost.com/phil-de-vellis-aka-parkridge/i-made-the-vote-differen_b_43989.html.

30. W. Lance Bennett, "Changing Citizenship in a Digital Age," in W. Lance Bennett (ed.), *Civic Life Online: Learning How Digital Media Can Engage Youth* (Cambridge, Mass.: MIT Press, 2008), pp. 2–3.

31. Henry Jenkins, "Manufacturing Dissent: An Interview with Stephen Duncombe," Confessions of an Aca-Fan, July 23, 2007, http://henryjenkins.org/2007/07/manufacturing_dissent_an_inter.html.

32. John McMurria, "The YouTube Community," FlowTV, October 20, 2006, http://flowtv.org/?p=48.

33. Chuck Tyron, "Is Internet Politics Better Off Than It Was Four Years Ago?," FlowTV, September 29, 2007, http://flowtv.org/?p=797.

34. "Transcript: CNN/YouTube Democratic Debate," Defective Yetii, http://www.defectiveyeti.com/archives/002172.html.

35. Each of these examples taken from images submitted to http://politicalhumor.about.com/.

36. Duncombe, *Dream*, p. 126.

37. "Interview with Lawrence Lessig, Stanford Law Professor, Creative Commons Chair," *Mother Jones,* June 29, 2007, http://www.motherjones.com/interview/2007/07/lawrence_lessig.html.

Glossary

Books about media and popular culture are often criticized for their use of academic jargon, yet the business, fan, and creative communities have their own specialized languages for talking about the issues this book addresses. In writing this book I have been highly conscious of minimizing the use of terms that will impede my ability to reach the broadest possible range of readers, preferring where possible the term already being used in and around the media industry to terms that are used primarily in academic circles. But because this book cuts across multiple communities, each with its own slang and jargon, I am providing this glossary of core terms. Many of these words or phrases have multiple meanings in different contexts; my focus is on the ways they are deployed in this book's discussions. One of my goals in writing this book is to push toward a common language that will allow greater collaboration and negotiation between those sectors where media change is taking place.

501s/527s: Political groups that emerged in response to the McCain-Feingold Act and that sponsor their own advertising efforts independently from the official campaigns.

Achievable utopia: A term coined by Pierre Lévy to refer to the ways that his ideals about collective intelligence might inform and motivate further steps toward realizing his goals.

Action figure cinema: Fan-made films that use stop-action animation to stage stories using action figures as stand-ins for the characters.

Additive comprehension: According to Neil Young, the expansion of interpretive possibility that occurs when fictional franchises are extended across multiple texts and media.

Affective economics: A new discourse in marketing and brand research that emphasizes the emotional commitments consumers make in brands as a central motivation for their purchasing decisions.

Affinity spaces: According to James Gee, spaces where informal learning takes place, characterized by, among other things, the sharing of knowledge and expertise based on voluntary affiliations.

Alternate reality games: According to Jane McGonigal, "an interactive drama played out online and in real-world spaces, taking place over several weeks or months, in which dozens, hundreds, thousands of players come together online, form collaborative social networks, and work together to solve a mystery or problem that would be absolutely impossible to solve alone."

Alternative points of view: A genre defined by The Sugar Quill in which familiar stories are retold from the perspectives of different characters, helping to fill in gaps in our understanding of their motivations.

Anime: Japanese-produced animation or animation inspired by Japanese styles of animation.

Appointment television: Programs that viewers make a conscious decision to watch as opposed to viewing when they happen across them while channel zapping. Sometimes called "Must See TV."

Assets: Any element created in the production process. Increasingly, assets are digitized so that they can be shared across all of the media platforms involved in a franchise.

Astroturf: Term deployed in politics to refer to "fake grassroots" content, which often circulates without any acknowledgment of its source.

Attractions: Sergei Eisenstein's term for short, highly emotionally charged units, applied in this book to talk about segments of a television program that can be watched in or out of sequence.

The Beast: The game created to help promote Steven Spielberg's movie *A.I.*, an important early example of an alternate reality game.

Beta reading: A peer-review process within fan fiction communities where more-experienced writers mentor newer participants, helping them refine their work for publication.

Black Box Fallacy: The attempt to reduce convergence to a purely technological model for identifying which black box will be the nexus through which all future media content will flow.

Blogging: Short for "Weblogging," the term initially referred to a technological platform that allowed for easy and rapid updating of Web content. Increasingly, it has come to refer to a mode of publication of grassroots origin that responds to information circulated either by other bloggers or by the mainstream media.

Boots: In *Survivor* fandom, the term used to refer to contestants who have been voted off the series.

Brain trusts: Elite groups of spoilers who work on a closed list and make their findings available to the larger community.

Brand communities: According to Robert Kozinets, social groups that share common bonds with particular brands or products.

Brand fests: Industry term for social events (either corporately sponsored or grassroots organized) that pull together large numbers of highly committed consumers of a particular brand or product and provide occasions for consumer education, social networking, and shared expertise.

Canon: The group of texts that the fan community accepts as legitimately part of the media franchise and thus "binding" on their speculations and elaborations.

Casuals: Industry term for viewers who maintain minimal loyalties to particular programs, watching them when they remember and sometimes wandering off if a particular episode doesn't hold their interest.

Cease-and-desist letter: A letter issued by a commercial rights holder threatening legal action against a person seen as infringing on its copyright, requiring for example instant removal of any pirated material.

Challenges: Efforts to have specific books removed from classroom use or library circulation.

Cheat codes: Passwords that allow levels to be skipped or that open up previously locked or hidden levels in a game.

Cloudmakers: The best known of the collective intelligence communities that worked to solve the Beast.

Co-creation: A system of production where companies representing different media platforms work together from the conceptualization of a property, ensuring greater collaboration and fuller integration of the related media texts.

Collaborative authorship: Term coined in this book to refer to situations in which the central author of a franchise opens it to participation from other artists to shape it in ways consistent with its overall coherence but allowing new themes to emerge or new elements to be introduced.

Collective intelligence: Pierre Lévy's term to refer to the ability of virtual communities to leverage the knowledge and expertise of their members, often through large-scale collaboration and deliberation.

Lévy sees collective intelligence as a new form of power that operates alongside the power of nomadic migrations, the nation-state, and commodity capitalism.

Collective knowledge: According to Pierre Lévy, the sum total of information held individually by the members of a knowledge community that can be accessed in response to a specific question.

Combination platter movies: Term coined by Ang Lee to refer to films that borrow from multiple cultural traditions, specifically to refer to works that combine Asian and Western influences in order to circulate in the global market.

Commercial culture: Culture that emerges in a context of industrialized production and commercial circulation.

Complexity: A term used by writers such as Stephen Johnson and Jason Mittel to describe the properties of new television shows which place greater demands on the individual and social cognition of their consumers.

Consensus culture: David Thorburn's term for the kind of cultural works that emerge from mainstream media channels as they seek to identify common ideas or sentiments among their consumers.

Convergence: A word that describes technological, industrial, cultural, and social changes in the ways media circulates within our culture. Some common ideas referenced by the term include the flow of content across multiple media platforms, the cooperation between multiple media industries, the search for new structures of media financing that fall at the interstices between old and new media, and the migratory behavior of media audiences who would go almost anywhere in search of the kind of entertainment experiences they want. Perhaps most broadly, media convergence refers to a situation in which multiple media systems coexist and where media content flows fluidly across them. Convergence is understood here as an ongoing process or series of intersections between different media systems, not a fixed relationship.

Corporate convergence: The commercially directed flow of media content.

Corporate hybridity: A process whereby powerful media companies absorb elements from other cultural traditions—for example, from other national traditions or from subcultural and avant-garde movements—to head off potential competition for their markets.

Cult films: According to Umberto Eco, films that provide opportunities for fan exploration and mastery.

Cultural activators: My term for texts that function as catalysts, setting into motion a process of shared meaning-making.

Cultural attractors: Pierre Lévy's term for the ways that fans and critics cluster around texts they see as rich occasions for meaning-making and evaluation.

Cultural convergence: A shift in the logic by which culture operates, emphasizing the flow of content across media channels.

Culture jamming: A term popularized by Mark Dery to refer to the efforts of grassroots organizations to insert "noise" into the communication process by challenging or disrupting the corporate flow of media.

Cybersquatters: People who buy up domain names associated with a celebrity or media property with the goal of selling them back for an inflated price.

Delivery technologies: Relatively transient technologies—such as the MP3 player or the 8-track cassette—that facilitate the distribution of media content.

Devotees: According to Robert Kozinets, one of four classes of participants in online brand communities, characterized by lifelong interests in the brand but limited commitment to the social community.

Digital cinema: A term that can refer to films produced using digital cameras, shown through digital projection, enhanced through digital effects, or distributed via the Web. In this book, we are primarily referring to films distributed via the Web.

Digital enclaves: Cass Sunstein's term for online communities that have achieved a high degree of consensus in their thinking and are resistant to outside arguments.

Digital revolution: The myth that new media technologies will displace older media systems.

Digitization: The process by which images, sounds, and information get transformed into bytes of information that can move fluidly across media platforms and be easily reconfigured in different contexts.

Discernment: A movement in contemporary Christianity that engages with popular culture through exercises in moral judgment, seeing it as a way into understanding "what nonbelievers believe."

Disengaged youth paradigm: coined by W. Lance Bennett to refer to the concern that young people are failing to exhibit traditional markers of civic engagement and are retreating into fantasy worlds which have little to do with solving real-world problems.

Dispersed knowledge: According to James Gee, knowledge that can be drawn upon by any member of an affinity space or knowledge community.

Distributed knowledge: According to James Gee, knowledge held within an affinity space but not necessarily known by an individual participant.

Dithering: A process designed to fill in the information between the pixels in a Pixelvision movie but resulting in unpredictable fluctuations in the image quality from frame to frame.

Divergence: The diversification of media channels and delivery mechanisms. According to Ithiel de Sola Pool, convergence and divergence are both part of the same process of media change.

Do-it-yourself spin: Political talking points distributed by campaigns with the goal of having them be taken up on a grassroots level by supporters.

Eco-tourism: Travel inspired by the desire to engage with unmediated or undeveloped natural environments.

Emotional capital: Term coined by Coca-Cola president Steven J. Heyer to refer to the ways that consumers' emotional investment in media content and brands increases the brand's worth.

Encyclopedic capacity: According to Janet Murray, the properties that contribute to the perception that a fictional world is expansive and all-encompassing and that motivate the reader's further exploration.

Engaged youth paradigm: Coined by W. Lance Bennett to refer to the argument that young people are developing greater civic engagement and social consciousness through their involvement in participatory culture.

Engagement: An elusive concept deployed within the entertainment industry to talk about a desired relationship with consumers. Depending on who you talk with, an engaged viewer has a high degree of loyalty to a particular program, is attentive during the broadcast, may talk about the program content with others, and preserves the relationship through consuming additional transmedia materials.

Entertainment supersystem: Marsha Kinder's term to refer to the systematic extensions of franchises across multiple media platforms.

Ethical spectacle: Term coined by Stephen Duncombe to refer to ways that activist groups might deploy aspects of popular culture for the purposes of transforming society.

Expert paradigm: According to Peter Walsh, a structure of knowledge dependent upon a bounded body of information that can be mastered by an individual and often dependent upon the authorization bestowed on individuals by institutions of higher learning.

Expression: An emerging measurement of audience participation and engagement with media content, proposed by Initiative Media based on research done by the MIT Comparative Media Studies Program.

Extension: Efforts to expand the potential markets by moving content or brands across different delivery systems.

Extensive knowledge: According to James Gee, the knowledge and goals shared among the members of an affinity space or knowledge community.

Fair use: In copyright law, a legal defense for certain forms of copying and quotation that recognizes the rights, for example, of journalists and academics to cite a work for the purposes of critical commentary.

Fan culture: Culture that is produced by fans and other amateurs for circulation through an underground economy and that draws much of its content from the commercial culture.

Fan fiction: Sometimes called "fanfic," a term originally referring to any prose retelling of stories and characters drawn from mass media content but deployed by LucasArts in its establishment of a policy for digital filmmakers that excludes works seeking to "expand" upon their fictional universe.

Fansubbing: The amateur translation and subtitling of Japanese animation.

Fatal attractions: According to Phil Armes, works that are seemingly innocent but that lure children into engagement with the occult.

Final four: The contestants in *Survivor* who make it to the final episode.

First-choice medium: According to George Gilder, the idea that newer media systems will be based on narrowcasting principles that allow a high degree of customization and a greater range of options, so that each consumer gets the media content he or she wants rather than choosing the least objectionable option.

Folk culture: Culture that emerges in a context where creativity occurs on a grassroots level, where skills are passed through informal education, where the exchange of goods is reciprocal based on barter or gifts, and where all creators can draw from shared traditions and image banks.

Foundational narrative: According to Brenda Laurel, "a myth or set of stories or history or chronology" that helps to define roles and goals for participants (whether commercially authorized artists or grassroots community members).

Franchising: The coordinated effort to brand and market fictional content within the context of media conglomeration.

Free labor: A term deployed by web 2.0 critics to point to the reliance of such companies on the uncompensated creative work of their communities.

Grassroots convergence: The informal and sometimes unauthorized flow of media content when it becomes easy for consumers to archive, annotate, appropriate, and recirculate media content.

Grassroots intermediaries: Participants—for example, bloggers or fan group leaders—who actively shape the flow of media content but who operate outside any corporate or governmental system.

High-concept films: Originally, films that could be described in a single sentence. According to Justin Wyatt, films that build on a logic of "the look, the hook, and the book," that is, films that create visual and narrative elements that can be exploited across multiple media platforms and that form the central thrust of the marketing and merchandizing campaigns.

Home movies: Amateur films produced primarily for private consumption, often documenting family and domestic life, and widely regarded as technically crude and uninteresting to a larger public.

Horizontal integration: An economic structure in which companies own interests across a range of different but related industries as opposed to controlling production, distribution, and retail within the same industry.

Hybridity: When one cultural space absorbs and transforms elements from another, most often a strategy by which indigenous cultures respond to the influx of Westernized media content by making it their own.

Hybrid media ecology: Inspired by Yochai Benkler's discussion of the "wealth of networks," this term refers to sites where commercial, governmental, educational, activist, nonprofit, and amateur media producers operate side by side, often resulting in unexpected collaborations.

Hyperserial: According to Janet Murray, a new narrative structure in which individual stories contribute to a larger fictional experience, similar in meaning to transmedia storytelling.

Hypersociability: According to Mizuko Ito, a principle in Japanese popular culture where story information and experiences are designed to be shared "peer-to-peer" by participants face-to-face or via the Internet.

Immersion: A strong fantasy identification or emotional connection with a fictional environment, often described in terms of "escapism" or a sense of "being there."

Imperfect cinema: A term originally used to refer to works produced in the third world, with impoverished resources and limited technical skill, where such challenges have been turned into opportunities to spoof or critique Hollywood cinema. In this book the word is being used to suggest the ways that fan filmmakers negotiate between a desire to see how closely they can duplicate Hollywood special effects and an impulse to mask their technical limitations through parody.

Impression: The traditional audience measurement in the entertainment industry, essentially a count of the number of "eyeballs" watching a particular media segment at a particular moment in time.

Informal education: Learning that takes place outside the formal classroom, including extracurricular and after-school programs, home schooling, and classes at museums and other public institutions, as well as the less structured learning that occurs as people encounter new ideas through their engagement with news and entertainment media or in their social interactions.

Informed citizen: According to Michael Schudson, the idea that citizens may be able to access all of the available information on a matter of public policy before reaching a decision.

Insiders: According to Robert Kozinets, one of four classes of participants in online brand communities, characterized by strong commitments both to the brand and to the social community that grows up around it.

Inspirational consumers: According to Kevin Roberts, the most hardcore and committed consumers of a particular brand, who are most active in publicly expressing their brand preferences but who also exert pressure on the producing company to ensure its fidelity to certain brand values.

Intensive knowledge: According to James Gee, the knowledge each individual brings into an affinity space or knowledge community.

Interactivity: The potential of a new media technology (or of texts produced within that medium) to respond to consumer feedback. The technological determinants of interactivity (which is most often prestructured or at least enabled by the designer) contrasts with the social and cultural determinants of participation (which is more open ended and more fully shaped by consumer choices).

Intertextual commodity: According to David Marshall, a new approach to media production that integrates marketing and entertainment content as the story moves from the screen onto the Web.

Intertextuality: The relations between texts that occur when one work refers to or borrows characters, phrases, situations, or ideas from an-other.

I Wonder Ifs: A genre defined by The Sugar Quill in which fans speculate about narrative possibilities hinted at but not explicitly depicted in the original work.

Knowledge culture: According to Pierre Lévy, a community that emerges around the sharing and evaluation of knowledge.

Least objectionable program paradigm: The idea, common in industry discourse, that viewers watch not programs they love but rather the best available option on television in a particular time slot.

Liberation: According to Paul Duguid, the idea that a new media technology frees its users from constraints imposed by previous media institutions and technologies.

Licensing: A system in which the central media company—most often, a film studio—sells other companies the rights to develop spinoff products associated with the franchise while often setting strict limits on what those companies can do with the property.

Loser Lodge: Fan slang for the place where *Survivor* contestants go to stay when they are voted off the series.

Lovemarks: Term coined by Kevin Roberts, CEO Worldwide of Saatchi & Saatchi, to refer to companies that have induced such a strong emotional investment from consumers that they command "loyalty beyond all reason."

Lowest common denominator: Common idea that television programs appeal to basic human drives and desires—most often erotic or aggressive—though the term can be expanded to include a range of other emotional needs that cut across demographic groups.

Loyals: According to common industry discourse, the most dedicated viewers of a particular series, often those for whom the program is a favorite. Loyals are more likely to return each week, more likely to watch the entire episode, more likely to seek out additional information through other media, and more likely to recall brands advertised during the series.

Machinima: A hybrid of "machine" and "cinema," the term refers to 3-D digital animation created in real time using game engines.

Madison + Vine: An industry term that refers to the potential collaboration between content producers and advertisers in shaping the total emotional experience of a media franchise with the goal of motivating consumer decisions.

Manga: Japanese-produced comics and graphic novels.

Manhua: A distinctive style of comics that emerged from Hong Kong.

Mass culture: A system in which cultural goods are mass produced and distributed.

McGuffin: A phrase coined by Alfred Hitchcock to refer to a relatively arbitrary device that sets the plot of a film into motion.

Media: According to Lisa Gitelman's definition, "socially realized structures of communication, where structures include both technological forms and their associated protocols, and where communication is a cultural practice."

Media in transition: A phase during which the social, cultural, economic, technological, legal, and political understandings of media readjust in the face of disruptive change.

Media mix: According to Mizuko Ito, an approach to storytelling pioneered in Japan in which information is dispersed across broadcast media, mobile technologies, collectibles, and location-based entertainment sites.

Micropayments: A new model of digital distribution in which Web-based content can be purchased with small payments by establishing a common unit of credit.

Minglers: According to Robert Kozinets, one of four classes of participants in online brand communities, characterized by a strong social bond with the group but limited interests in the brand.

Missing moments: A genre defined by The Sugar Quill in which fans fill in the gaps between depicted events.

MMORPGS: Massively multiplayer online role-playing games, an emerging genre that brings together thousands of people interacting through avatars in a graphically rich fantasy environment.

Modders: Amateur game designers, most often those who modify existing commercial games.

Mods: Amateur modifications of commercial games.

Monitorial citizen: According to Michael Schudson, the idea that citizens may collectively monitor developing situations, focusing greater attention on problem spots and accessing knowledge on an ad hoc or need-to-know basis.

Monoculture: A term used by a range of media critics to denounce what they see as the lack of diversity in the entertainment and news content generated by media conglomerates.

Monomyth: According to Joseph Campbell, a conceptual structure abstracted from the cross-cultural analysis of the world's great religions. Campbell's Monomyth has been adopted in the advice literature for screenwriters and game designers, becoming what is now called the "hero's journey," in an attempt to tap mythic structures for contemporary popular culture.

MUDs: Multiple user domains, an early prototype for online communities that allowed multiple users to interact primarily through text.

Muggles: Term created by J. K. Rowling to refer to people who do not possess magical abilities.

Multiplatform entertainment: According to Danny Bilson, a mode of storytelling that plays itself out across multiple entertainment channels, more or less synonymous with what this book calls transmedia storytelling.

Mundanes: Fan slang to refer to nonfans; it carries with it a sense of an impoverished imaginary life.

Opposition research: Research campaigns conducted on opponents with the goal of finding points of vulnerability, whether scandals, contradictory or extreme statements, or other factors that would make them less attractive to voters.

Organic convergence: An industry term for the kinds of mental connections consumers form between bits of information drawn from multiple media platforms.

Origami unicorn: Coined by Neil Young after the addition of a minor detail to the director's cut of *Blade Runner*, which encouraged speculation that the protagonist Deckard might be a replicant; the term refers to any element added to a text that potentially invites reconsideration of other works in the same franchise.

Parody: In copyright law, refers to works that appropriate and transform copyrighted content for the purposes of making critical commentary.

Participation: The forms of audience engagement that are shaped by cultural and social protocols rather than by the technology itself.

Participatory culture: Culture in which fans and other consumers are invited to actively participate in the creation and circulation of new content.

Perfect storm: A metaphor borrowed by Joe Trippi from the film of that title to refer to the coming together of shifts in technologies, campaign practices, grassroots organizing, and public sentiment.

Pixelvision: A low-cost toy video camera that was created by Fisher-Price to allow children to become filmmakers but that has become a technology of choice for a range of amateur and avant-garde filmmakers.

Plenitude: According to Grant McCracken, the cultural state that emerges in a period of proliferating media channels and consumer options coupled with the diminished influence of cultural and economic gatekeepers.

Popular culture: Cultural materials that have been appropriated and integrated into the everyday lives of their consumers.

Power to marginalize: The power exhibited by mass media networks when they incorporate and yet trivialize content generated from grassroots media producers.

Power to negate: The power exhibited when grassroots communities seek to deploy authorized opportunities to participate in order to disrupt the normal operating processes of mass media.

Protocols: According to Lisa Gitelman, the set of economic, legal, so-cial, and cultural practices that emerge surrounding a new communications medium.

Public movies: In contrast to home movies, amateur-produced films that are intended for circulation beyond the filmmaker's friends and family and that draw their content from shared mythologies often appropriated from the mass media.

Pull media: Media in which consumers must seek out information, such as the Internet.

Puppetmasters: The people who design and facilitate an alternate reality game.

Push media: Media in which content comes to the consumer, such as broadcasting.

Rabbit holes: Points of entry into an alternate reality game experience.

Recaps: Summaries, posted on the Internet and often barbed in tone, of television programs.

Regimes of truth: According to John Hartley, the norms and practices that shape they way a particular medium or media form will represent the real world and the way audiences will assess the informational value of those representations.

Saved: According to Christian fundamentalists, someone who has actively embraced Christ as his or her personal savior.

Searchers: According to Christian fundamentalists, someone who has not yet accepted Christ into his or her life.

Serious fun: Term coined by True Majority to refer to the fusion be-tween political activism and popular culture.

Shared knowledge: According to Pierre Lévy, information that is believed to be true and held in common by all of the members of a knowledge community.

Shippers: Fan term for readers and writers invested in a particular kind of relationship between characters.

Skins: A digital mask or persona designed to be inserted into a game environment, one of the simplest and most widespread of a range of different approaches for amateur modification of commercial games.

Slash: A genre of fan fiction—or of fan cultural production more generally—that imagines a homoerotic relationship between fictional characters taken from mass media texts.

Smart mobs: A term coined by Howard Rheingold to refer to the ability of people using mobile and networked communications devices to organize and respond in real time to developing situations.

Sock puppet: A secondary identity or pseudonym used by a longtime poster of a discussion list, often to float information or propose ideas that they do not want to damage their reputation.

Sole survivor: A common term for the winner of *Survivor*.

Song vids: Amateur music videos that combine images taken from films or television shows with popular songs.

Sourcing: Within the spoiling community, getting information from sources directly involved in the production who may or may not be cited by name.

Spaceshift: The act of dubbing entertainment content so that it can be consumed on a different media platform.

Spin: Efforts by campaigns and other political groups to shape the public's response to events or messages.

Spoiling: Initially this term referred to any revelation of material about a television series that might not be known to all of the participants of an Internet discussion list. Increasingly spoiling has come to refer to the active process of tracking down information that has not yet been aired on television.

Story arc: Structure of television narrative in which subplots are developed across multiple episodes, sometimes even across an entire season or, in more extreme cases, across the full run of a series.

Sucksters: Participants in the Survivor Sucks discussion list.

Summer after Fifth Year: A genre defined by The Sugar Quill in which *Harry Potter* fans write beyond the ending of the most recently published novel.

Synergy: The economic opportunities that emerge in a context of horizontal integration where one media conglomerate holds interests in multiple channels of distribution.

Tacit knowledge: According to James Gee, knowledge that is not explicitly expressed but rather gets embodied through the everyday activities of an affinity space or knowledge community.

Talking points: Arguments constructed by campaigns to be deployed by their supporters.

Technological convergence: The combination of functions within the same technological device.

Tele-tourism: Travel inspired by watching television, as in visits to the locations where series are set or shot.

Ticket to play: According to Anne Haas Dyson, the right to assume a fictional role within children's play based on resemblance to the characters represented in the book.

Timeshift: The act of recording entertainment content so that it can be watched at a later time.

Tipping point: A term referring to the moment when an emerging paradigm reaches critical mass and transforms existing practices and institutions.

Tourists: According to Robert Kozinets, one of four classes of participants in online brand communities, characterized by weak social bonds with the group and transient interests in the brand.

Transcreation: A term coined at Marvel Comics to talk about their *Spider-Man: India* project, referring to the process of reinventing and localizing an existing fictional franchise to make it more acceptable and attractive to a particular national market.

Transmedia storytelling: Stories that unfold across multiple media platforms, with each medium making distinctive contributions to our understanding of the world, a more integrated approach to franchise development than models based on urtexts and ancillary products.

Uncertainty due to chance: According to Mary Beth Haralovich and Michael W. Trossett, a situation whose outcome is not known because it is going to be determined at least in part by random factors.

Uncertainty due to ignorance: According to Mary Beth Haralovich and Michael W. Trossett, a situation whose outcome is not known because information is unknown or has been withheld.

User-generated content: An industry term used to refer to content submitted by consumers, often in a context where the company asserts ownership over and makes a profit upon content freely contributed by its "community."

Vernacular culture: My term for culture that is generated by amateurs, a term intended to suggest the parallels between folk culture and fan culture.

Vernacular theories: According to Thomas McLaughlin, theoretical formulations posed by nonacademics, such as those of expert practitioners, activists, fans, or visionaries as they seek to explain their discoveries and insights.

Vidcaps: Slang term for video captures, images grabbed digitally from the television broadcast so that they can be examined more closely by the members of the knowledge community or so that they simply can be enjoyed by fans of the series.

Viewing repertoire: According to David J. LeRoy and Stacey Lynn Koerner, the selection of programs that an individual viewer watches on a regular basis.

Viral marketing: Forms of promotion that depend on consumers passing information or materials on to their friends and families.

Web 2.0: Term coined by Tim O'Reilly to refer to new kinds of media companies which deploy social networks, user-generated content, or user-moderated content. O'Reilly sees such companies as creating new kinds of value through supporting participatory culture and tapping the collective intelligence of their consumers.

Withering of the witherers: According to Grant McCracken, the diminished influence of traditional gatekeepers who blocked certain forms of cultural expression from gaining mainstream circulation.

Wizard rock: A genre of fan-produced music focused around the characters and themes found in the *Harry Potter* books. Wizard rock is performed at conventions and distributed through social network sites such as MySpace.

World-making: The process of designing a fictional universe that will sustain franchise development, one that is sufficiently detailed to enable many different stories to emerge but coherent enough so that each story feels like it fits with the others.

Zappers: Industry term for viewers who move nomadically and restlessly across the television dial, rarely watching more than small segments of any given program.

Index

ABC, 60, 123, 210, 222, 235–236, 264
ABC-Disney, 265
absolutists, 44
Abu Ghraib, 226
access, 259
access gap, 23
achievable utopia, 245–246
ACLU, 197
action figures, 145–148, 150–151
Action for Children's Television, 161
Action League Now!!!, 151
activism, 12
adbusting, 138
additive comprehension, 127–134
adhocracies, 262, 264–266
Adventures in Odyssey, 210
advertising, 7, 12, 20, 22, 66
Advertising Age, 67–68
Aeon Flux, 103,
affective economics, 20, 61–64, 70, 125, 130
affinity spaces, 185–186, 192–194, 270
Ain't It Cool News, 55
Akira, 112
Albrecht, Chris, 142–143, 153, 159
Alexander, Jesse, 124
Al Gore's Penguin Army, 287
Alice in Wonderland, 101
Alien, 116
Al Jazeera, 78
Allas, Marcia, 260
Alliance Talent Agency, 70
Almereyda, Michael, 155–156

Alphaville, 239–242
Alphaville Herald, 239–242
alternate reality games, 123, 130, 243–244
Amazon.com, 136, 210
American Booksellers Foundation for Free Expression, 204
American Express, 69
American Idol, 19–20, 59–61, 63–64, 68, 70–71, 76–92, 277
American Idol (personalities):
Clay Aiken, 71, 84, 86, 89;
Fantasia Barrino, 91; Simon Cowell, 87–88, 90; Elton John, 91;
Kimberley Locke, 84;
Sanjaya Malakar, 91–92;
Ruben Studdard, 71, 84–86, 89, 91
America Online, 86, 240. *See also* AOL
America's Army, 74–79, 218
America's Funniest Home Videos, 146, 279
amusement parks, 98
Anderson, Chris, 263
Anime, 102–103, 160–165
Anime Angels, 211
Annenberg Public Policy Center, 236
anonymousAmerican, 278–279
Antonucci, Mike, 106
AOL. *See* America Online
Apple Box Productions, 64–65
Apple (general), 79, 282; (commercials) "1984," 287
Apple Music Store, 264

Appointment TV, 121
Apprentice, The, 69–72, 84, 217, 284
apprenticeship, 29, 190, 249
appropriation, 18, 152–153, 256
Arms, Phil, 201
Arrested Development, 264–265
Artificial Intelligence: A.I., 127, 131
Askwith, Ivan, 106, 264
assessment, 85
Associated Press, 224
astral projection, 201
Astroturf, 287, 288
AT&T Wireless, 59, 87–89, 92–93
AtomFilms, 135, 142, 153, 158–160

Babylon 5, 119
Bagge, Peter, 95–96, 99, 103
banner ads, 65
Barely Political, 286
Barnes & Noble, 112
Barney, Matthew, 134
Bartle, Richard, 165
Batman: Hong Kong, 113
Baudrillard, Jean, 100–101
Baynes, Arthur, 239
BBC, 252–254
Bear Stearns, 71
"Beast, The," 127–132, 243
Being Digital, 5
Ben & Jerry's Ice Cream, 217
Benedek, Peter, 250
Benjamin, Walter, 234
Benkler, Yochai, 279, 281, 285, 290
Bennett, W. Lance, 288
Benning, Sadie, 155
Berlant, Lauren, 233
Bert (*Sesame Street*), 1
Bertelsmann Media Worldwide, 110
"Bert is Evil," 1–3
beta reading, 188–190
Bible, 101, 121–122, 214
Big Brother, 51–53, 111

Billboard Hot 100, 61
Billiam the Snowman. *See* Snowman
Billionaires for Bush, 284
Bilson, Danny, 99, 107–108, 127
Bin Laden, Osama, 1, 232
Bioware, 166–168
BitTorrent, 262
Black Box Fallacy, 14–16, 24, 223
Black, Rebecca, 189
Blade Runner, 118, 127
Blair Witch Project, The, 99, 103–105,
    117
bloggers/blogging, blogs, 224–230,
    248, 251, 280
blue America, 246, 248, 249
BMW, 218
Bochco, Stephen, 118
Bohrman, David, 271–272, 277
Bollinger, Dan, 32–34, 51, 57
Bollywood, 4
Borders, 112
brain drain, 38
brain trusts, 38–40
brand advocates, 73
brand communities, 79–80, 83, 88, 227
brand extension, 69
brand fests, 79
branding, 20, 62–64, 68–72, 76, 92
brand loyalty, 72
brands, 22
Broadcasting & Cable, 89
Brock, Jack, 201
Brooker, Will, 155
Brothers Grimm, 111, 141
Bruce Almighty, 210
Buckingham, David, 132, 237–238
Buddha, 100
Burnett, Mark, 25, 32, 37, 42–43,
    46–48, 51, 56, 69, 90, 227, 262
Burton, Tim, 117
Bush, George W., 217–218, 222–223,
    227, 230, 234, 273, 284, 289

"Bush in 30 seconds" contest, 232–231
Business Week, 66, 178

cable television, 66
Campaign 2004, 22, 29, 217–250, 257
Campaign 2008, 271–281
Campbell, Joseph, 100, 123
Carey, Mariah, 61
Carlson, Tucker, 236, 238
Cartoon Network, 136, 152
Casablanca, 99–100, 103
Cassidy, Kyle, 153
Castells, Manuel, 133
casuals, 74, 76–77, 81
CBS, 25, 36–37, 45–46, 48, 54, 57, 60,
    222–224, 231, 236
cease-and-desist, 195, 197
Celebrity Deathmatch, 151
Center for Deliberative Democracy,
    246
Center for Information and Research
    on Civic Learning and Engagement,
    234
Chadwick, Paul, 103, 113–115, 129, 132
Chan Chen, 115
Chan, Evan, 128
Chan, Jackie, 111
Charlie's Angels, 111
cheating, 270
Cheney, Richard, 230, 241, 288
Cheskin Research, 15
Chicago Tribune, 285
Chick-fil-A, 210
Children's Television Workshop, 2
chillingeffects.org, 197
ChillOne, 26, 28, 31–32, 34–35, 37,
    39–40, 42–46, 48–51, 54–57
China, 112, 114–115
Chomsky, Noam, 258, 284
Chow Yun-Fat, 115
Christian Gamers Guild, 211
Christianity, 21–22, 177, 203–205, 209–214

Christopher Little Literary Agency, 194
Chung, Peter, 103
Ciao Bella, 70
Citizen, informed vs. monitorial, 219,
    236–238, 269–270
citizen journalists, 251, 280–281
Clarkson, Kelly, 60
"click through," 65
Clinton, Hillary, 283, 287, 291–292
Clinton, William J., 230, 283
Cloudmakers, 127–132, 243
CNN, 1–3, 128, 144, 201, 238, 271–274,
    276–281, 285, 290, 293
CNN/YouTube, 271–272, 274, 276,
    278–279, 285, 287, 290–291
Coca-Cola Company, 60, 68–69, 70, 73,
    87–88, 92–93, 218
co-creation, 107–109
code, 166–167
Cohen, Ben, 217
Cokemusic.com, 72
Colbert Report, 289
Colbert, Stephen, 275
Cold Mountain, 210
Cole, Jeanne, 155
collaborationism, 173, 177–183
collaborative authorship, 97–98,
    110–115
collaborative sourcing, 51
Collective Detective, 243–244
collective intelligence, 2, 4, 20, 22,
    26–27, 29, 50, 52–54, 63, 97–99, 129,
    131, 172–173, 256–259
Colson, Charles, 212–213
Columbine, 201
Comedy Central, 235–236
comics, 14, 96,103, 110–111, 260–263
commercial culture, 27, 136
commodity exploitation, 62–63
communal media, 256
Comparative Media Studies program,
    12, 68, 80, 85, 155

complexity, 96–97, 270
Concepcion, Bienvenido, 147
Concrete, 103, 113–114
consensus, 86
consensus culture, 247
convergence, 2–8, 10–12, 14–24, 26, 59, 64, 68, 83, 97, 106, 117, 215, 232, 269–270, 293–294
convergence, corporate, 18, 111–112, 161, 269–270
convergence culture, 15–16, 21, 23, 136, 138–141, 253–254, 256–257
convergence, grassroots, 18, 57, 111–112, 140–141, 161, 257, 269–270
Coombe, Rosemary J., 197
Cooper, Anderson, 271, 273, 277
Coors Brewing Company, 69,
copyright, 141–142, 155, 159–160, 198–199, 259, 263
Corliss, Richard, 131
"cosplay," 115–116
Counterstrike, 167
Cowboy Bebop, 103
Creative Artists Agency, 60, 67
Crest toothpaste, 70
critical pessimism, 258–260
critical utopianism, 258–260
Crossfire, 236
Crouching Tiger, Hidden Dragon, 112, 114–115
cult films, 99–100
cultural activator, 97
cultural attractor, 97
culture. *See* commercial culture; folk culture; mass culture; popular culture; public culture
culture jamming, 225–226, 259
Current (network), 251–253
cybercampaign, 273

Daily Prophet, The, 178–184, 195–196
Daily Show, The, 235–238, 289

Dana, Mary, 204, 206
Darfur, 271
Dark Ages of Camelot, 157
Darrow, Geof, 103, 111, 120
Dautel, Dennis, 211
Dawson's Creek, 117–120
Dawson's Desktop, 99, 117–120, 123
DC Comics, 113
Dead Media Project, 13
Dean, Howard, 220–221, 223–225, 239, 273, 276
decentralization, 10, 255
Decisive Battles, 157
delivery technologies, 13–14
democracy, 22, 29, 55
Democratic National Convention, 235–236
Democrats, 232, 250, 271
"de-odorizing," 163
Dery, Mark, 225
de Sola Pool, Ithiel, 10–12, 247–248
Desperate Housewives, 264
de Vellis, Phil, 287
De Vries, Kimberly M., 260
Diamond, Neil, 151
DiCaprio, Leo, 92
Dick, Philip K., 100,
digital cinema, 16, 21, 135–142, 143, 146–148, 151–153, 230–233, 271–272, 284–285, 286–287
Digital Millennium Copyright Act of 1998, 141
digital revolution, 5–6, 11, 219–220, 237–238, 258–259
digitization, 11
discernment, 177–178, 208, 209–210
disengaged youth paradigm, 288
Disney, 110, 141, 201, 212, 262
Disney World, 262
divergence, 11
Dixie Chicks, 234
DIY culture, 136

Dobson, James, 212
Doctorow, Cory, 262
Donation, Scott, 67
Doom, 156
Down and Out in the Magic Kingdom, 262
downloads, 264–265
Dream: Re-imaging Progressive Politics in An Age of Fantasy, 283
Driving Miss Daisy, 292
Duel Masters, 136
Duncombe, Stephen, 283–285, 289–290
Dungeons and Dragons, 202
Durack, Elizabeth, 157
DVD, 15–16, 61, 66, 103, 113–114, 121, 136, 145, 163, 201, 262–263
Dyson, Ann Haas, 182–183

Early Show, The, 38
Earth Day, 281
Earth First!, 114
eBay, 7
Ebert, Roger, 124, 126
Eco, Umberto, 99–100
Edelstein, David, 124
education, 12, 178–180, 186–191, 257, 269–270
Edwards, John, 228–229, 288
80/20 rule, 72
Electra: Assassin, 103
Electronic Arts, 99, 107, 109, 130, 240, 242
Electronic Frontier Foundation, 197
Ellipsis Brain Trust, 36
Ellis, Warren, 261–263
emotional capital, 68–69, 175
empowerment, 29
encyclopedic capacity, 118
Endemol, 51
Ender, Chris, 46
engaged youth paradigm, 289

Engagement, 119–122
engagement TV, 121
Entertainment Weekly, 55, 86, 121, 136, 144
Enzensberger, Hans, 222
epistemology, 44
ethical dramas, 84, 185
ethical spectacle, 284, 292
Ettinger, Amber Lee, 286
expertise, 26–27
expert paradigm, 50, 52–54
expressions, 63, 66–68
extension, 19

Facebook, 275–276
Fahrenheit 9/11, 234
fair use, 22, 198–207, 267–268
Faith Highway, 211
Faleux, Shane, 148
fan culture, 177
fan fiction, 16, 38–41, 159–160, 177, 191, 196, 199
fans, 22, 29, 31–34, 76
Fans for Christ, 212–213, 215
FanLib.com, 177–183
fansubbing, 162–163
fantasy (genre), 100–101
Fark.com, 232
favorite series, 76
feminism, 260
Field, Claire, 195
Final Fantasy, 113
Finan, Christopher, 204
first choice media, 256
Fisher-Price, 153, 155, 158
Fitz-Roy, Don, 147
501s/527s, 229
Flourish, 187, 193
flow, 2, 275
Focus on the Family, 210, 212
folk culture, 136, 139–141, 161–162, 268–269

Forbes, 60
Ford Motor Company, 87–88, 93
Forrester Research, 66
Fortitude Films, 214
4orty2wo Entertainment, 130
Fountainhead, 157
FOX Broadcasting Company, 59–60, 67, 78, 80, 89, 92, 110
fragmentation, 19, 68, 248–250, 254–255
franchise, 19, 98, 107, 115
Frank, Betsy, 255
FreakingNews.com, 232
Frederick, Rick, 286
Free Labor, 142–143, 147, 271–272, 279–281, 293
Friendster, 71
From Justin to Kelly, 61
fundraising, 220
F/X, 135

Gabler, Lee, 67
Gaiman, Neil, 103
games, 7–9, 15, 22, 66, 74–79, 97–98, 103, 106, 109–110, 113, 118, 123–124, 128–131, 137, 156–157, 163–164, 166, 169, 202, 209–211, 239–241, 244
Gee, James Paul, 186, 192, 208
Gervase X, 46
Ghost in the Shell, 112,
Gibbons, Dave, 103
Gibson, Mel, 210–211, 214
Gilder, George, 5–6, 255–256
Gitelman, Lisa, 13–14
Global Frequency, 261–263, 265
globalization, 3, 21, 30, 103, 110–117, 203, 215–216
Godel, Esher, and Bach, 128
GoldenEye: Rogue Agent, 108
Google, 142, 293
Google Maps, 255
Gore, Albert, 241, 252–253, 281

gossip, 83–87, 185
Graff's, 71
Grand Theft Auto III, 157
Grant, Amy, 210
grassroots intermediaries, 222
Green, Seth, 152
Greenaway, Peter, 134
Grudge, The, 250
Grushow, Sandy, 67
Guardian, The, 110
Gulf War, 247
Gypsies, The, 169

Haack, Denis, 210, 212
hacking, 225
Hakuhodo, 164
Halen, Aaron, 150
Half-Life, 167
Halo, 157
Halon, Aaron, 150
Hamel, Nathan and Greg, 279–280
Hancock, Hugh, 157
Hank the Angry Drunken Dwarf, 92
Haralovich, Mary Beth, 28
Hardball with Chris Matthews, 195, 223
Hard Boiled, 103
Harley-Davidson, 79
Harmon, Amy, 153
Harry Potter (characters/places/things): Albus Dumbledore, 199, 207; Cho Chang, 184; Diagon Alley, 285; Draco Malfoy, 184; Dursleys, The, 206; Gryffindor, 184; Harry, 285; Hermione Granger, 186, 199, 285; Hogwarts, 21, 178, 181, 185, 191; Lord Waldemarte, 285; Ron Weasley, 199
Harry Potter (general), 19, 21, 142, 175–216, 283–285

Harry Potter (fans): *Witchcraft Repackaged*, 213; *Wal-Mart Watch*, 284–285
Harry Potter (websites/organizations): Daily Prophet, 178; Defense Against Dark Arts, 195; FictionAlley, 188; HP Alliance, 206–207, 284; Leaky Cauldron, 207; Muggles for Harry Potter, 197, 200–201, 204–207, 215; Sugar Quill, 186, 188; Virtual Hogwarts, 193, 203; www.harrypotterguide.co.uk, 195
Harry Potter and the Order of the Phoenix, 207
Harry Potter and the Sorcerer's Stone, 178, 202, 214
Hartley, John, 238
Hate, 96, 103
Haxans, 104
HBO, 60, 283
Heiferman, Scott, 230
Hendershot, Heather, 209
Herman, Andrew, 197
Heroes, 123
Heron, Gil Scott, 221
hero's journey, 123
Hero with a Thousand Faces, 123
Heyer, Steven J., 68–69, 72, 87, 93
Hidden Persuaders, 64
Highfield, Ashley, 253
Hill Street Blues, 118
historical fiction, 133–144
History Channel, The, 158,
hoax, 45–50
Hollywood, 16, 105–106, 250
home movies, 145–146,
Homer, 121–123, 125
home schooling, 179
Home Shopping Network, 70
Hong Kong, 110
horizontal integration, 98
horror, 209
Huckabee, Mike, 283

Huffington Post, 277, 287
hybridity, 114–115
hybrid media ecology, 288
hypersociability, 112
hypertext, 133

Ignacio, Dino, 1–3
IKONOS, 33
ilovebees, 130
immersiveness, 201–202
impressions, 63–65
Inconvenient Truth, An, 281, 287
Indiana Jones (franchise): *Indiana Jones* (film), 108; *Young Indiana Jones Chronicles* (TV), 108, 148
"indy" media, 231
inevitability, 11
informal education/learning, 186–194, 208
Initiative Media, 65, 67, 76, 80–81, 84–86, 92–93
inspirational consumers, 73, 90–92, 257, 284, 292
intellectual property, 141–142, 160, 162, 164, 176, 194–200, 216, 218, 267–269
interactive television, 59
interactivity, 5, 136,
Internet Galaxy, The, 133
intertextuality, 201–203
iPods, 15–16, 121, 264–265
Iraqi War, 78, 226, 278
i to i research, 77
Ito, Mizuko, 17, 112
Iwabuchi, Koichi, 163

Jackson, Janet, 225, 231
Jackson, Peter, 109
Jackson, Samuel L., 151
James Bond franchise, 59, 108
Japan, 17, 103, 114–116, 160–165
J. C. Penny, 71

Jeremiah Films, 213
JibJab, 232
Joan of Arcadia, 210
Joe Millionaire, 84
Jones, Deborah, 84
Joseph, Barry, 131–132

Kang, Jeevan J., 113
Kaplan, Marty, 277
Kapur, Shekhar, 110–112
Katrina, 271
Katz, Jon, 235
Kauffman, Leah, 286
Kawajiri, Yoshiaki, 103, 111
Kerry, John, 220, 227–228, 241, 250
KidSPEAK!, 204–206
Kill Bill, 292
Kingdom Hearts, 113
Kjos Berit, 202–203
Klebold, Dylan, 201
Klein, Christina, 112–114
knowledge, 20, 26–29, 30, 38, 44, 50,
    52, 54–55, 57, 87, 132–134, 265–267,
    269–270
Koster, Ralph, 142, 164–167, 172
Kozinets, Robert, 65, 79–80, 88
Kroll, John, 231
Kronke, Clay, 148
Kruse, Carol, 72
Kucinich, Dennis, 272, 291

Lapham, David, 103
Lanza, Mario, 38–41
Lawrence of Arabia, 150
Lawver, Heather, 178–180, 182, 193,
    195–197, 215
Lear, Norman, 234
Lee, Ang, 114–115
Left Behind, 210
Legally Blonde, 87
LEGO, 151
Leno, Jay, 235

Leonard, Andrew, 248
Leonard, Sean, 162
Lessig, Lawrence, 141, 167, 293
Let's Make a Deal, 281
Letterman, David, 235
Levi, 71
Levy, Joseph, 143, 146–147
Lévy, Pierre, 4, 26–29, 32, 38–39, 52,
    54–55, 80, 97, 133, 192, 226, 256, 258
Lewis, C. S., 212
licensing, 106–107
limited goods, 267
Lionhead, 158
literacy, 186–190, 208–209, 215–216,
    218–219, 269–270
LiveJournal, 181, 275
Living Dead, 116
localization, 3
London Independent, 106
Long Tail, The, 263
LoPorto, Garrett, 217–218
Lord of the Rings (franchise), 109, 127,
    210, 230
Lost, 122–123
Lost in Translation, 210
lovemarks, 20, 68–70, 175
loyals, 63, 74,76, 78, 80–81, 90
LucasArts, 21, 153, 158, 164, 171
Lucasfilm, 108, 147, 149, 153–159
Lucas, George, 117, 157
Lucas Online, 156
Ludlow, Peter, 239–243
Luhrmann, Baz, 111, 160
Lynch, David, 32–34

Machinima, 153–158
Machinima films: *Anna*, 153; *Halo
    Boys*, 157; *My Trip to Liberty City*,
    157; *Ozymandias*, 157
Madison Avenue, 20, 63, 141, 282
Madison + Vine conference, 68–69
Mad Magazine, 232

MADtv, 291–292
Maeda, Mahiro, 118–119, 122
Maines, Natalie, 234
Majestic, 99, 127
Major Bowles' Original Amateur Hour, 78
Making of Citizens, The, 238
Mall of *The Sims*, The, 166–171
Mandel, Jon, 60
M&M candies, 70
manga, 110–117
Mangaverse, 110, 114
manipulation, 268–269
Mann, Dennis, 282
Manufacturing Consent, 284
Marvel Comics, 112–113
Massachusetts Institute of Technology, 12, 15, 68, 80, 155, 255
mass culture, 139–140
mastery, 107
Mather, Evan, 144–145, 151
Matrix, The, 19–21, 95–134, 157, 210, 259
Matrix, The (actors): Keanu Reeves, 97, 102; Jada Pinkett Smith, 110; Hugo Weaving, 102
Matrix, The (characters / places / things): Agent Smith, 102, 124; B116ER, 119–120; Cypher, 101; Ghost, 128; Jue, 104; The Kid, 104–105; Locke, 128; Merovingians, 101; Morpheus, 101, 112, 115, 124, 128; Nebuchadnezzar, 104; Neo, 115, 119, 124; Niobe, 105, 128–129; Oracle, The, 124, 210; Osiris, 104–105; Persephone, 101, 124; Trinity, 101, 115, 124; Zion, 112, 114, 120
Matrix, The (franchise): *The Animatrix*, 112, 115–117, 124; *"Bits and Pieces of Information,"* 120; *"Déjà Vu,"* 113; *Enter the Matrix*, 101, 103–105, 128; *Final Flight of the Osiris*, 104, 118; *The Kid's Story*, 104–105; "Let It All Fall Down," 113; *The Matrix Online*, 129, 133; *The Matrix Reloaded*, 96, 101–102, 104–105, 124, 126; *The Matrix Revolutions*, 96–97, 105, 115, 124, 129; "The Miller's Tale," 113–114; *Program*, 111; *The Second Renaissance*, 118–120
Mattel, 70–71
Maxim, 71
Mayard, Ghen, 46
McCain, John, 280
McCain-Feingold Act, 229
McCarty, Andrea, 155
McChesney, Robert, 258
McCleary, Brian, 70
McCracken, Grant, 137–138, 161–163, 171, 208
McDonald, Gordon, 157
McDonald's (in-store promotions), 107
McGonigal, Jane, 129–131, 243–244
McGregor, Ewan, 160
McKnight, Laura, 239
McLuhan, Marshall, 10
McMurria, John, 290
Mead, Syd, 117
media-actives, 255
media concentration, 2, 5, 11, 18–19, 68, 216, 259
media in transition, 11
media jammers, 52
media literacy, 22, 260–270
"media mix," 112, 133
Meetup.com, 221, 230
Mehra, Salil K., 164
Mertes, Cara, 252
Microsoft, 8, 127, 129
military, 74–75, 218
Milkshakey, 36
Miller, Mark Crispin, 258
MIT. *See* Massachusetts Institute of Technology
MIT Anime Club, 162

Mitsubishi, 69
MMORPG, 163–166
mobile phones, 4–5, 9, 14, 17, 112, 138
modders/modding, 141, 166–171
Moebius, 111
Mole, The, 47
Monde, Le, 144
monomyth, 123
Monty Python and the Holy Grail, 157
Morimoto, Koji, 103
Morrow, Fiona, 106
Mother Jones, 273, 293
Moulin Rouge!, 160
MoveOn.org, 230–231, 234
Movies, The, 158
MP3, 16, 135
Mr. Bill, 279–281
Mr. President (avatar), 239–241
MSNBC, 195
MTV, 78, 151–152, 233, 255
MTV Networks, 255
MTV 2, 158
Muggle mindset, 207
multiplatform entertainment, 107–108
Muniz, Albert M. Jr., 79
Murray, Bill, 211
Murray, Janet, 118, 121
Muzyka, Ray, 166
Myrick, Dan, 104
MySpace, 274, 276,
mystery (genre), 209
mythology, 160–162

Napster, 9, 138, 142,
narrowcasting, 5, 222
NASCAR, 71
National Research Council, 74
Native Son, 120
NBC, 60, 72, 218, 222
Neal, Connie, 209, 213
Negroponte, Nicholas, 5, 11
Nelson, Diane, 194–196, 199–200

Neuman, W. Russell, 254
Neverwinter Nights, 168
New England Patriots, 72
New Line Productions, 109
New Orleans Media Experience, 1,
    6–10, 15
Newsweek, 99, 179
New York Police Department, 70
New York Times, 144, 153, 171, 256
Nickelodeon, 151, 234
Nielsen Media Research, 66, 74–75
1984, 101, 287
Nintendo, 270
Norris, Chuck, 283
NPR, 144, 239, 271
Nussbaum, Emily, 55

Obama, Barack, 273, 291–292
Obama Girl, 286
O'Brien, Michael, 208
O'Brien, Sebastian, 150
Odyssey, The, 103–134
O'Guinn, Thomas C., 79
Old Navy, 88
Oni Press, 104
open source, 265
Orwell, George, 101
Osama Bin Laden, 1–2
ourmedia.org, 252

Packard, Vance, 64
paganism, 202–203, 206
Paramount, 197
parody, 281–290
participation, 20–23, 64, 81, 84,
    110–115, 137, 158, 159–161, 175,
    188–190, 204–207, 233–234, 250,
    251–254, 268
participation gap, 23, 269
participatory culture, 2–3, 11–12, 24,
    177, 206–207, 209, 254–258, 274
participatoryculture.org, 252

Passion of the Christ, The, 211, 214
Paul, Ron, 276
PBS, 252
peer-to-peer, 215–216
People Magazine, 92
PepsiCo., 71
Perry, David, 104, 109–112, 128
personalization, 68, 255
Peterson, Karla, 61
Petrossian's restaurant, 71
Pew Foundation, 71, 235
Photoshop, 1, 3, 37, 145, 217–250, 292
Pike, Chris, 99, 117–119
Pixelvision, 153–156
Planet of the Apes, 117
play, 23, 29, 242
plenitude, 10, 163
Plenitude, 208
Pokemon, 111–112, 132–133, 161, 185, 201
polarization, 246–247
political economy, 7
politics, 22
Pop Idol, 60
popular culture, 139
Potter wars, 175, 176, 177, 295, 214
POV, 252
Power to Marginalize, 277–278
Power to Negate, 277–278
Probot Productions, 150
Probst, Jeff, 42, 46, 51, 56, 226
Proctor & Gamble, 70
product placement, 69–72, 87–88
prohibitionism, 172
Project Greenlight, 230–231
propaganda, 258
protocols, 13–14, 23
public culture, 22
Puppetmasters, 127–129
PXL THIS festival, 155

"rabbit hole, the," 128
Raiders of the Lost Ark, 150

Ransom Fellowship, 210
ratings, 60, 62, 72
RCA, 61
reality television, 19–20, 58–60, 78, 84, 86
Reason, 96, 224
recaps, 31
reciprocity, 219
recording industry, 9
Redstone, Sumner, 66
redundancy, 96
Reebok, 69
Reel Families: A Social History of Amateur Film, 145
relativists, 44
religion, 178, 208–209
Relles, Ben, 285
Republica, La, 144
Republican National Convention, 235–236
Republicans, 220, 287–288
resistance, 259
Restaurant, The, 69
return on investment, 62
Revolution Will Not Be Televised, The, 221
Rheingold, Howard, 261
Richardson, Ashley (avatar), 239–241
Riddick Chronicles, The, 111
Ring, The, 111
Roberts, Kevin, 69, 73, 88, 92, 257
Robertson, Pat, 213
Robot Carnival, 103
Rogers, John, 262–263
role playing, 186–187, 211–214
Rolling Stone, 235
romance (genre), 209
Romero, George, 116
Rome: Total War, 158
Romney, Mitt, 272, 276, 280, 289, 293
Rove, Karl, 273–274
Rowling, J. K., 21, 175–176, 178, 181–185, 193–194

Rubio, Kevin, 136
Rumsfeld, Donald, 226

Saatchi & Saatchi, 69
Sacks, Eric, 155
Saksa, Mike, 106
Salla, Jeanine, 128
Salon.com, 52, 106, 248
Sanchez, Ed, 104–105
San Diego Union-Tribune, 61
Sandman, The, 103
San Jose Mercury, 106
Satanism, 200–203
Saturday Night Live, 235, 279–280
Saturn, 79
Save the Internet, 285
Saving Private Ryan, 157
SBC, 83
scaffolding, 187
Schamus, James, 115
Scheppers, Lori Jo, 201
Schneider, Andrew, 120
Scholastic, 194
Schudson, Michael, 236–238
Schwarzenegger, Arnold, 277
science fiction (genre), 102, 168, 209, 213
Sci Fi Channel, 104
secular humanism, 203
Sefton-Green, Julian, 132
Seiter, Ellen, 184
Sella, Marshall, 256
September 11, 1, 232, 243, 261, 288–289
Sequential Tarts, 260
serialization, 33, 78, 133
Sesame Street, 1–3
700 Club, The, 213
7th Heaven, 210
Shadowmancer, 213
Shakespeare in Love, 143
Shaking the World for Jesus, 209
shared knowledge, 51
shareware, 267

Shawn, 34–36, 46–47, 52
Shelley, Percy, 157
Shiny Entertainment, 101
Showtime, 60
Sienkiewicz, Bill, 103
Silver, Joel, 103
SimCity, 169–171
Simmons, Russell, 234
Sims, The, 19, 169–171
Sims 2, The, 158
Simulacra and Simulation, 101
situated context, 15
60 Minutes, 223–224
Slack, Andrew, 285
Slashdot, 251–253
Slate, 124, 264
smart mobs, 221, 261–262
Smith, Dana, 147
Smoking Gun, The, 86
Snewser, 51, 57
Snowman, 271–272, 279–281, 290
soap opera, 33
sock puppet, 35
song videos, 159
Sony, 110, 117
Sony Interactive, 99,
Soprano, J. C. (avatar), 241–242
Sopranos, The, 133, 283
sourcing, 51, 54
spectatorship, 3
speculation, 51
"Spectacularization of Everyday Life,
    The," 282
Spiderman, 111, 112–113, 211
Spiderman: India, 113–115
Spiderman 2, 113
Spielberg, Steven, 127–128, 148
spin, 228–229
Spin City, 228
spoiling, 19–20, 25–58, 226
SquareSoft, 113
Squire, Kurt, 167–169

SSX3, 158
Stanford Center for the Internet and
    Society, 197
Stanford University, 246
Starcom MediaVest Group, 67
Star Trek, 105, 156, 196
Star Trek (characters): James Kirk, 197;
    Spock, 197
Star Wars (characters, locations,
    things): Admiral Ackbar, 151;
    Anakin Skywalker, 167; Boba Fett,
    117, 135, 168; Darth Maul, 160;
    Darth Vader, 135, 151; Death Star,
    150; Han Solo, 150, 168, 171; Jar Jar,
    147, 167; Mace Windu, 151; Mille-
    nium Falcon, 147; Obi-Wan Kenobi,
    126, 160; Princess Leia, 135; Qui-
    Gon Jinn, 160
Star Wars (franchise): 19, 21, 108, 111,
    138–139, 135–174, 257; *Star Wars
    Episode 1: The Phantom Menace*, 136,
    149, 160; *Star War Episode IV: A New
    Hope*, 19, 150; *Star Wars Episode V:
    The Empire Strikes Back*, 150–151; *Star
    Wars Episode VI: Return of the Jedi*, 149
Star Wars (fan culture): mythology, 21,
    135, 142, 148, 157; fan cinema (gen-
    eral), 135–174, 185; *Anakin Dynamite*,
    158; *Boba Fett: Bounty Trail*, 147; *Can-
    tina Crawls*, 169; *Christmas Crawl*,
    169–170; *Duel*, 150; *George Lucas in
    Love*, 136, 143–144, 146–147; *Godzilla
    versus Disco Lando*, 151; *Intergalactic
    Idol*, 160; *The Jedi Who Loved Me*, 147;
    Kid Wars, 147; *Kung Fu Kenobi's Big
    Adventure*, 151; *Les Pantless Menace*,
    144; *Macbeth*, 147; *The New World*,
    148; *Quentin Tarantino's Star Wars*,
    151; *Sith Apprentice*, 158; *Star Wars or
    Bust*, 135; *Star Wars: Revelations*, 148,
    159; *Toy Wars*, 150; *Troops*, 136; *When
    Senators Attack IV*, 144–145

Star Wars (games): general, 96–98; *Star
    Wars Galaxies*, 21, 142, 164–165,
    167–169, 172
Star Wars (miscellaneous): Jedi
    Knights, 168; Mos Eisley, 108
Star Wars (print): *Tales from the Mos
    Eisley Cantina*, 108
Star Wars (songvids): *Come What May*,
    160
Steinkuehler, Constance, 167–169
Sterling, Bruce, 13, 100
Stern, Howard, 92
Stewart, Jon, 235
Stewart, Sean, 128–130
Stories, 120
Stray Bullets, 103
Subscription-based model, 263–264
sucksters (Survivor Sucks commu-
    nity), 34–36, 39–40, 48
Sunstein, Cass, 86, 248–249
Super Bowl, 87, 231
Super-8, 146, 148, 279
Survivor, 19–20, 25–59, 61, 69, 90, 111,
    185, 226, 257
Survivor (contestants): Alex Bell, 42;
    Deena Bennett, 49; Gabriel Cade,
    39–40; Robert Cesternino, 42, 48;
    Richard Hatch, 47; Brian Heidik,
    37; Jeanne Herbert, 42; Dave John-
    son, 42; Ghandia Johnson, 30; Janet
    Koth, 42; Jenna Morasca, 40, 45, 54;
    Diane Ogden, 40; Gervase Peter-
    son, 46; Mike Skupin, 37; Christy
    Smith, 41; Heidi Strobel, 37, 40;
    Matthew Von Ertfelda, 42, 45, 54;
    Joanna Ward, 42, Ethan Zohn, 47
Survivor (episodes): *Survivor: Africa*,
    33, 47; *Survivor: Amazon*, 26, 49, 55;
    Survivor: The Australian Outback,
    37, 45; *Survivor: Greece*, 40; *Sur-
    vivor: Thailand*, 30; *Survivor: Vanu-
    atu*, 56

Survivor (fans), 38
Survivor Sucks, 31, 38
Swann, Philip, 75
Sweeney Agonistes, 188, 191
Swift Boat Veterans for Truth, 229
syndication, 30
synergy, 19, 106, 110

Taiwan, 114
Talk of the Nation, 239, 241, 271
talk radio, 229
Talking Points Memo, 288
Tapewatcher, 47
Tartakovsky, Genndy, 111
Taylor, Doug, 205
Taylor, G. P., 213
Technologies of Freedom, 10–12
Technologies Without Boundaries, 247
technology/ies, 13–15, 23
TechPresident, 288
tele-cocooning, 17
television, 9
Templeton, Brad, 197
Texans for Truth, 229
text messaging, 59, 90–91
TheForce.net, 135, 144
Think Like a Mountain, 114
"This Land," 232
This Week with George Stephanopoulos, 235
Thorburn, David, 247
3 Foot 6 Productions, 109
Time, 248
TiVo, 20, 66, 68, 137
Tobaccowala, Rishad, 67
Tolkien, J. R. R., 109, 122, 213
Touched by an Angel, 210
touch points, 63, 69
Toy Soldiers, 153
Toys "R" Us, 70
trademark, 194
"transcreation," 113

transmedia storytelling, 8–9, 20–21, 93–134, 214
Trippi, Joe, 220–223, 230
Trosset, Michael W., 28
True Majority, 217–218, 284
Trump, Donald, 69–71, 84, 217, 245
"Turd Blossom," 273
TV.Com: How Television is Shaping Our Future, 75
TV Guide, 38, 97
Twentieth Century Fox Film Corporation, 149
24, 119
"20 Million Loud" campaign, 234
Twin Peaks, 32–33; Laura Palmer, 33
Tyron, Chuck, 290

Ultima Online, 164–165
Umbridge, Dolores, 207
uncertainty due to ignorance/chance, 28
Unilever, 71
United States Department of Defense, 76
USA Today, 38, 86, 223
user generated content, 165, 167–168, 169, 253, 271, 274–275
user moderated content, 251–252
user supported content, 263
utopia, 38, 256, 258

YouTube, 274, 278, 280, 283–285, 287, 289–293

VandenBerghe, Jason, 150
Vanilla Sky, 111
VCR, 20, 33, 147
VeggieTales, 210
Verizon, 83
vernacular culture, 136, 161–163
VH1, 78
Viacom, 66, 156

Victory at Hebron, 209
vidcaps, 42
Video Mods, 158
videos, campaign (2008), 271–272, 274–278, 279–281
viral marketing, 217–218, 275, 286
Vivendi Universal, 110
Vote for the Worst, 91–93, 277
Voter Vision, 286
voting, 85–86, 89–93, 217–218, 236–237, 239–243, 277

Wachowski brothers, 21, 95, 97, 99, 101–103, 109–113, 115, 120, 126, 130
Waco, 157
Walker, Jesse, 224
Wal-Mart, 210
Wal-Mart Watch, 284–285
Walsh, Peter, 52–54
Ward, Jim, 153
Wardynski, Colonel E. Casey, 75–76
Ware, Paula, 201, 204
Warner Bros., 16, 21, 106, 110, 141, 176, 194–196
Washida, Yuichi, 164
Washington, D.C., 243
Washington Post, 224
Watanabe, Schinichiro, 103
Watchmen, 103
Way, The Truth & The Dice, The, 211
Wealth of Networks, The, 279, 285
Web 2.0, 177–183, 273, 276, 179–180
Webby Awards, 244
Wellner, Damon, 150, 230
West Wing, The, 133, 228
Wezzie, 32–34, 51, 56–57
Whale Rider, 210
What's a Christian to Do with Harry Potter?, 209
Whiting, Susan, 66
Wiccan, 208

Wicked City, 103
Wikipedia, 265–267
Williams, Diane, 160
Williams, John, 149
Williams, Walter, 279
Wilson, Pam, 52–53
Wired, 10, 144, 148, 263
Wishnow, Jason, 135
witchcraft, 202
withering of the witherers, 208
Wizard of Oz, The, 203
Wizard rock, 207
Wong, Tony, 113
Work of Art in the Age of Mechanical Reproduction, The, 234
world building, 116
world making, 21, 114–116
World of Warcraft, 171
World Trade Organization, 231
Wright, Chris, 40
Wright, Richard, 120
Wright, Will, 169, 171
writersu.net, 188, 197
Writing Superheroes, 182
WWF, 151

X-Files, The, 119, 187, 230
X-Men, 116, 123

Yahoo!, 177
Yahoo! Hot Jobs, 71
Yellow Arrow, 18
Yeoh, Michelle, 112, 115
Young, Neil, 99, 109, 127, 130
Yuen, Woo-Ping, 110–111
Yu-Gi-Oh!, 112, 132–133, 161

zappers, 74–76, 81–82
Zennie, Nancy, 204
Zhang Ziyi, 115
Zimmerman, Patricia R., 145–146
Zsenya, 186

About the Author

The founder and director of MIT's Comparative Media Studies Program, Henry Jenkins is the author or editor of twelve books on various aspects of media and popular culture, including *Textual Poachers: Television Fans and Participatory Culture, From Barbie to Mortal Kombat: Gender and Computer Games, The Children's Culture Reader,* and *Hop on Pop: The Politics and Pleasures of Popular Culture.* His career so far has included testifying before the U.S. Senate Commerce Committee hearing into Marketing Violence for Youth following the Columbine shootings, promoting media literacy education before the Federal Communications Commission, speaking to the Governor's Board of the World Economic Forum about intellectual property and grassroots creativity, heading the Education Arcade, which promotes the educational uses of computer and video games, writing monthly columns for *Technology Review* and *Computer Games* magazines, and consulting with leading media companies about consumer relations. For further exploration of the issues raised in this book, visit henryjenkins.org.

Convergence Culture was the winner of the 2007 Society for Cinema and Media Studies Katherine Singer Kovács Book Award.
